Commerce with the Universe

Commerce with the Universe

AFRICA, INDIA, AND THE AFRASIAN IMAGINATION

Gaurav Desai

COLUMBIA UNIVERSITY PRESS

NEW YORK

Columbia University Press
Publishers Since 1893
New York   Chichester, West Sussex
cup.columbia.edu
Copyright © 2013 Columbia University Press
Paperback edition, 2016

Library of Congress Cataloging-in-Publication Data
Desai, Gaurav Gajanan.
Commerce with the universe: Africa, India, and the Afrasian imagination /
Gaurav Desai.
pages cm
Includes bibliographical references and index.
ISBN 978-0-231-16454-2 (cloth : acid-free paper)—ISBN 978-0-231-16455-9 (pbk. :
acid-free paper)—ISBN 978-0-231-53559-5 (e-book)
1. Indic literature—History and criticism.   2. National characteristics, East
Indian, in literature.   3. East African literature (English)—History and criticism.
4. East Indians—Africa, East. I. Title.

PK2905.D55 2013
891′.1—dc23

Columbia University Press books are printed on permanent and durable acid-free
paper.
Printed in the United States of America

Cover designer: Noah Arlow
Cover image: © Getty Images

For Supriya

We must treat the Indian Ocean as the link it can be,
not the barrier that others would like it to be!
—JULIUS NYERERE, *Freedom and Development*

Business never dies in Africa;
it is only interrupted.
—NAZRUDDIN, IN V. S. NAIPAUL, *A Bend in the River*

CONTENTS

ACKNOWLEDGMENTS

If *Subject to Colonialism: African Self-fashioning and the Colonial Library* was my tenure book, *Commerce with the Universe* has ended up being my ten-year one. I began thinking and writing it in earnest in the academic year 2001–2002 when I was fortunate to have a National Endowment for the Humanities fellowship at the National Humanities Center in Research Triangle Park, North Carolina. There, in the immediate aftermath of the 9/11 attacks, I took refuge in the comfort offered by the more tolerant and cosmopolitan world of the twelfth-century Levant, historically and imaginatively conjured by S. D. Goitein and Amitav Ghosh. I completed the bulk of the work on the manuscript as well at the National Humanities Center, this time in 2009–2010, under the auspices of a Frederick Burkhardt Fellowship awarded by the American Council of Learned Societies. Without those two years at the National Humanities Center, and without the tireless and cheerful help of everyone there, this book would still be in the making. In the intervening years I received support from a number of institutions, to all of which I am tremendously grateful. My home institution, Tulane University, provided support through a number of grants for research and travel, including the Center for Scholars Grant, the School of Liberal Arts George Lurcy Funds for Research, the School of Liberal Arts Publication Subvention Fund, the Tulane University Research Enhancement Grant, the Provost's International Travel Fund, the Newcomb Fellows Grant, the Duren Professorship Program, and the Department of English 4+1 Fund. In May 2003 the Rockefeller Foundation awarded me a residency at its magnificent villa in Bellagio, and, if memory serves me right, I did manage to do some writing in between the distractions of the surroundings and the delicious gelato. More recently, I spent a month at a similar residency in Mojarca, Spain at the Valparaiso Foundation, and this allowed me to take a broader look at the project. In 2004 I benefited from a Visiting Fellowship at Clare Hall, Cambridge University, which was seminal in allowing access to the collections of the Royal Commonwealth Society housed at the university's library. Finally, an unplanned stay in Austin while evacuating from Hurricane Katrina during the Fall of 2005 resulted in very generous hospitality on the part of the English Department at the University of Texas and from the Harry Ransom Research Center, which offered me a travel grant to the collection.

In addition to such direct support from funding bodies, I have also benefited from collaborative work with colleagues in dialogue with whom many of the ideas in this book have been shaped. Here I would note two particularly important seminars that I took part in both in the summer of 2003. The first was a Faculty Development Seminar on "Postcolonial Theory and the Globalization of Culture" that I was asked to direct by the National Humanities Center with sponsorship from the DuPont Foundation. The second was an NEH institute that I attended as a participant at the East-West Center in Honolulu, Hawaii entitled "Re-Imagining Indigenous Cultures: The Pacific Islands." In each case the vibrancy and energy of the discussions in those seminars have remained with me over the years and have informed not only this book, but other side projects. Likewise, the collaborative ethic between contributors and the intellectual to and fro associated with editorial projects means that it would be remiss of me not to acknowledge the mark made on my thinking by all of the contributors to collections and special issues of journals that I have edited. In the context of *Commerce with the Universe*, I particularly thank those who contributed to my MLA volume on *Teaching the African Novel* and the special issue of *Research in African Literatures* on Asian-African Literatures.

Colleagues at a number of institutions have generously commented on this book at different stages of its writing. In addition to audiences at the African Literature Association, the African Studies Association, and the Modern Language Association, I thank my hosts and audiences at the Universities of Louisville, Richmond, UCLA, Albany State, North Carolina State, Colorado (Boulder), Duke, Northwestern, Williams College, Louisiana State, Michigan, Stanford, Washington and Lee, Hawaii (Manoa), Old Dominion, St. Olaf College, Connecticut (Hartford), Yale, Quito (Catholic University), Rio de Janeiro, Bahia (Federal University), Zhejiang, Seoul National, Mumbai, Vidya Bharati Mahavidyala (Amravati), and SNDT College (Mumbai). The Bombay English Association, the U.S.-based South Asian Literary Association, the Forum on Contemporary Theory in Baroda, and the Economic and Social Research Foundation in Dar es Salaam also hosted me for presentations under their auspices. Earlier versions of portions of chapters 2, 3, and 5 have appeared in the journals *Representations*, *PMLA*, and *Research in African Literatures*, and I am grateful to the editors and publishers for allowing them to be published here in revised form. I also thank my editor Philip Leventhal and the entire team at Columbia University Press for making the publication process such a pleasant one.

In the ten or so years over which I have written this book, I have made so many friends and incurred so many intellectual and personal debts that to list them all would be unseemly. At Tulane it would mean reproducing almost verbatim the faculty rosters of not only the Department of English and the Program of African and African Diaspora Studies but also of many others across the School of Liberal Arts. Nonetheless, I'd like to especially thank Elisabeth McMahon and Adeline Masquelier not only for their feedback on the introductory chapter but also for Africa-related discussions in general. Outside of Tulane the numbers are also large, and so for the sake of brevity I note only a few such friends and colleagues with whom I have had conversations on an ongoing basis: Susan Andrade, Srinivas Aravamudan, Ian Baucom, Ali Behdad, Rey Chow, Eleni Coundouriotis, Elizabeth DeLoughrey, Simon Gikandi, Geoffrey Harpham, Wail Hassan, John Hawley, Kevin Hickey, Abiola Irele, Eileen Julien, Mohamed Kamara, Prafulla Kar, Kwaku Korang, Amitava Kumar, Francoise Lionnet, Emad Mirmotahari, Pramod Mishra, Renu Modi, David Chioni Moore, V. Y. Mudimbe, Tejumola Olaniyan, Mala Pandurang, Charles Piot, R. Radhakrishnan, Rajeswari Sunder Rajan, Pallavi Rastogi, Sangeeta Ray, Stephane Robolin, S. Shankar, Joseph Slaughter, Barbara Herrnstein Smith, Faith Smith, and Jennifer Wenzel. They should not, of course, be held accountable by association for any of the claims I make.

Perhaps my greatest intellectual debt, however, is to three scholars whose work preceded mine and without whose labor this project could not even have been conceived. I did not have the honor of meeting any of them in person and two of them are now deceased. The work of S. D. Goitein on the Mediterranean and Indian Ocean world between the ninth and the thirteenth centuries, the archival and historical work of Robert G. Gregory on Asian societies in East Africa, and the oral and transcribed histories along with other editorial projects assembled by Cynthia Salvadori were all germane to this book. Especially in the case of Gregory and Salvadori, working in a field whose intellectual time had not yet come, they did not, in my estimation, receive the credit that they deserved. This book is a small attempt on my part to recognize their work.

Commerce with the Universe has seen my son Sameer grow from being a toddler to a teenager. We are a family of travelers, and Sameer grew up never needing to ask "are we there yet?" since he always seemed to enjoy the journey. But he did often ask "is it done yet?" when it came to my writing this book, and I can finally say, yes, it is done. For me the journey of writing has been as pleasurable as the arrival. I only hope that, whatever profession and passions he ultimately finds in life, he derives from them similar pleasure. Supriya Nair has been my best friend and interlocutor for almost two decades and her love, wisdom, and companionship sustain me every day. It is to her that I dedicate this book.

Commerce with the Universe

1. OCEAN AND NARRATION

"Darasingh the famous wrestler, Dilip Kumar the affable thief, and Manga-la the Indian girl. Who has not at one time dreamed of going to India and marrying one of these actresses with the voice of a nightingale?"[1] Thus queries the narrator in the Cameroonian director Jean-Marie Téno's 1993 film *Afrique, je te plumerai*. The film is a sharp critique of the history of European colonialism, particularly in Cameroon but more generally in the African continent as a whole. Drawing on documentary footage produced by the former colonial powers—footage originally meant to justify the colonial project to European metropolitan audiences—Téno captures the colonial acts of exploitative resource appropriation and the creation of an economy that is made dependent on the metropole. This relation of dependence, Téno suggests, works as well on the ideological register. Cameroonians, both in colonial times as well as in the postindependence era, are fed on a diet of Euro-American culture, which often demeans black bodies and neglects acknowledgment of black minds. Indeed, in one of the film's most telling scenes, the narrator, recalling his childhood, is shown reading a Tarzan comic along with a young girl. The images of the black "native" are stereotypically negative, the African presented as barely being able to speak at all, while Tarzan and Jane are engaged in their romance. The young narrator's gentle touch of his reading companion's finger as they read the romance together is Téno's way of showing that such literature invites young Cameroonians to identify themselves not with the black African characters in the background but rather with the white protagonists Tarzan and Jane. Téno's aim is to expose the ideologically charged nature of literary and cultural consumption.

Yet there is a moment in the film when the critical edge gives way to a sense of nostalgia, a remembrance of a childhood past, as the narrator puts it, before the arrival of "independence and its companion violence." The young narrator, along with two friends, gazes at a billboard of an Indian film and they decide to go watch the movie. Interspersed in the clip from the 1958 Hindi movie *Yahudi* are the narrator's childhood dreams of India and of marrying a beautiful Indian actress. Unlike the clear sense of indignation that Téno exhibits toward imported artifacts such as the Tarzan comics from the West, here, in the case of the Hindi film, an allowance is made for an alternative culture of consumption, a culture that traces its origins not to the history of colonial appropriation and indoctrination but to a differently configured, longer history of exchange. Téno, I suggest, is calling attention to an African imaginative space that looks to the East as opposed to the West.[2]

Such a relation to India as an alternative imaginative space is carried further in Mugo Gatheru's autobiography *Child of Two Worlds*.[3] The narrative provides a rare glimpse of a Gikuyu man's experiences as a student in India two years after Indian independence. Having acquired in 1948 admission and funding for a college education at Roosevelt University in the United States, Gatheru was denied a "certificate of good conduct" by the Kenyan colonial state. Without such a certificate he was initially unable to receive a U.S. visa and he decided to pursue his higher education in India instead.[4] With the financial support of African and Arab friends and the promise of social support in India by the family of the then current Indian high commissioner in Kenya, Apa Pant, Gatheru traveled to India in 1949 to enroll at St. Joseph's college in Allahabad. As his narrative suggests, Gatheru's stay in India was not devoid of the aggravations of encounters with what he calls "pathologically colour conscious people" (128), but his overall experience in India was a far cry from the intense racism he had experienced in colonial Kenya. "Coming from a country like Kenya," writes Gatheru, "in which colonialism was very 'raw,' to a newly independent country like India was, to say the least, a tremendous experience for me emotionally and psychologically. There, for the first time in my life, I felt a free man—free from passes or being pushed here and there as if I were an undesirable animal"(130). India is by no means perfect, and Gatheru is quick to note that social taboos such as those associated with untouchability still retain much of their force despite the attempt of leaders like Gandhi to eradicate them. Gatheru's conscience is troubled when an untouchable man insists on calling him *sahib*, an appellation that reminds him of the Kiswahili word *bwana*, which structures the disgracefully unequal relationship between Africans and Europeans in a colonial world (131). Now, in this new context of India, being called *sahib* by an untouchable is, for, Gatheru "a very disturbing feeling" (132). Nevertheless, despite the challenges ahead, Gatheru is caught up in the euphoria of Indian independence, and it inspires him to dream of his own country's independence.

For the most part, however, apart from few instances such as Téno's and Gatheru's, and with the notable exception of the Kenyan writer Ngugi wa Thiongo, India and Indians have not received much representational space in the canon of colonial and postcolonial black African literature.[5] When (s) he appears, the Indian is inevitably cast as what E. M. Forster would call a "flat character."[6] Thus readers will remember the cameo appearance of the Indian *dukawallah* (shopkeeper) and trader in texts such as (and this list is not exhaustive), Bonnie Lubega's *Outcasts* (1971), Modikwe Dikobe's *The Marabi Dance* (1973), Legson Kayira's *The Detainee* (1974), Peter Palangyo's *Dying in the Sun* (1977), Mongane Serote's *To Every Birth Its Blood* (1983), Richard Rive's *Buckingham Palace: District Six* (1987), Shimmer Chinondoya's *Harvest of Thorns* (1990), Mia Couto's *Voices Made Night* (1990), and Tiyambe Zeleza's *Smouldering Charcoal* (1992). The representation of Indian women in black African literature has been even less prevalent and when thematized is often concerned with sexuality—David Rudabiri's *No Bride Price* (1967), Samuel Kahiga's *The Girl from Abroad* (1974), and David Maillu's *The Untouchable* (1987) remain the three most memorable depictions of the "unavailability" of the Indian woman to African men and the taboos surrounding interracial sexuality.[7]

Perhaps the best-known representation of the Indian shopkeeper in African literature is in Ngugi's early novel *Weep Not Child* (1964), which, incidentally, Ngugi dedicated to an Indian friend, Jasbir Kalsi. The novel is often read as casting Indians in a negative light, but, despite its investment in the stereotype of the cunning and exploitative Indian who, for instance, feigns fear and submissiveness in the company of the white settler only to beguile the settler into buying more goods from him (8) or the Indian who withholds the salary of an African employee so that the latter may be endlessly tied to him (32), there are also more ambivalent and perhaps even redeeming notes played in the novel.[8] The reference to Gandhi and his struggle against the British is a clear gesture of colonial affiliation—Indians too are ruled by "white men" in their country—and reports from Africans who have been to Burma suggest a different point of affinity; whereas among the highlands of Kenya the Indian traders all appear rich to the Gikuyu, in their own country many are poor (9). It is significant that Ngugi's reference to Indians is often through indirect reporting and rumors because it highlights the narrator's reluctance to pass a final judgment on them. So for instance, we are told that "it was rumoured that the white men in Kenya did not like [the Indians] because they had refused to go to war against Hitler" (9). On the one hand, this refusal to go to war is cast sympathetically by the young narrator who reads it as being in keeping with the nonviolence of Gandhi, the "strange prophet" who will lead the Indians to freedom (9). On the other, the white men around him say that Indians are cowards, and, notes the narrator not without some reservations, "the Africans were inclined to agree with this idea of Indian cowardice" (9).

The starkest instance of the novel's self-questioning about African-Indian relations is in a gesture of friendship offered to the young Njoroge by an Indian boy. Ngugi masterfully embeds the story in a conversation between Njoroge and his friend Mwihaki when they are discussing their fear of elders and whether or not parents are always right. The conversation triggers his memory of the time when he is surprised by the kindness of a young Indian boy who offers him a sweet. As he is about to eat the sweet, his mother rebukes him: "'Is it that you have not eaten anything for a whole year? Are you to be greedily taking anything you're given by anyone, even by a dirty little Indian?'" (40). Njoroge does as he is told, throwing the sweet away, but he is hurt at the offense he has caused the boy who has witnessed this exchange. He goes back to look for him in a few days so that he can "tell him something," but never finds the boy again (41). While the reconciliation remains incomplete, Njoroge does not share the memory with his friend Mwihaki either because he does "not want to criticize [his parents] in front of her" (40). In the larger narrative frame, however, the episode suggests that, even as it indulges in the stereotypes of the dukawallah, *Weep Not Child* opens up a more critical space for the representation of Indian-African relations.

Ngugi's more recent fictional engagement with India and Indians focuses not so much on the figure of the dukawallah in East Africa as on the experience of India by the African protagonist Kamiti in the novel *Wizard of the Crow.* Returning to the fictional country of Aburiria after receiving a BA in economics and an MBA from an Indian university, Kamiti is positioned to challenge some of the prevailing stereotypes he finds around him. Confronted by questions about the spicy food and presumably equally spicy sex life in India, as evidenced by the reference to the *Kama Sutra*, Kamiti is eager to provide a history lesson to a potential employer. He refers to Siddis—Indians of African descent—and speaks of the likes of Malik Ambar, an African general who ruled in India (55); he points to the role of Indians in African nationalist struggles against colonialism, particularly the legacy of Gandhi in inspiring nationalisms in Africa (56); he talks of Indians as masters of technology "producing some of the world's top computer scientists" (53) and of the significant presence of Indians in Silicon valley and in universities all over the world.[9] "An Indian is not all dukawallah and nothing else, just as the African is not all shoeshine and nothing else" (54). Kamiti wants greater ties between India and Aburiria since *"there are many things we could learn from India and other Asian countries, just as they have much to learn from us"* (55, my emphasis).

If *Weep Not Child* was a tentative opening to a critical self-questioning of African stereotypes of the Indian, *Wizard of the Crow* is Ngugi's most articulate rebuttal of such stereotypes. Ngugi's move is, I suggest, symptomatic of a larger trend in postcolonial African thought that is increasingly voicing critiques of the excesses of racially and ethnically based nationalisms in the interests of forging more plural ethnically and racially diverse nations. The most powerful critique is perhaps that offered by Achille Mbembe who writes that in the model of racial nationalism derived from Pan-Africanism, "blacks do not become citizens because they are human beings endowed with political rights, but because of two particularistic factors: their color and a privileged authochtony. Racial and territorial authenticity are conflated, and Africa becomes the land of black people. Since the racial interpretation is at the foundation of a restricted civic relatedness, everything that is not black is out of place, and thus cannot claim any sort of Africanity."[10] And yet, he continues, "the repertoires on the basis of which the imaginaires of race and symbolism of blood are constituted have always been characterized by their extreme variety. At a level beyond that of the simple black/white opposition, other racial cleavages have always set Africans against each other. And here may be enumerated not only the most visible—black Africans versus Africans of Arab, South Asian, Jewish, or Chinese ancestry—but also a range of others that can attest to the panoply of colors and their annexation to projects of domination: black Africans versus Creoles,

Lebanese-Syrians, metis, Berbers, Tuaregs, Afro-Brazilians and Fulanis; Amharas versus Oromos; and Tutsi versus Hutu."[11] What Mbembe urges is a more capacious understanding of Africa and Africanity than one that continues to draw on old colonial structures, which, as Mahmood Mamdani has shown, divided society into ethnicized natives (answerable to customary authorities) and a hierarchized order of racialized immigrants (answerable to civil law).[12] Mbembe calls for both new "practices of self" and "modes of self-writing" "imagined as a vast network of affinities."[13]

My book draws its inspiration from such new African imaginaries as Téno's, Gatheru's, Ngugi's, and Mbembe's. Urged by the compelling work of scholars who have increasingly focused on Indian Ocean histories and Africa's connections with them, it is invested in an expansive understanding of African territories and identities.[14] In particular, one of the projects of this book is to ask: What happens to our understanding of Africa — its history, its sense of identity, its engagement with modernity, and the possibilities of its future — if we read its long history as an encounter not only with the West, but also with the East?[15] The long history of trade and contact between Africa and India has meant not only the exchange of commodities such as cloth, ivory, gold, and slaves, or cultural practices such as cuisine, but also the exchange of linguistic elements, philosophical concepts, and political ideas. Such connections have existed ever since the time of the ancient civilizations of Egypt and Mohenjo-Daro. Indian silk has been found among the wrappings of Egyptian mummies. When the British explorer Speke was seeking the source of the Nile in the mid nineteenth century, he was aided by a map drawn from a Hindu Puranic source. Speke noted, "It is remarkable that the Hindus have christened the source of the Nile *Amara* which is the name of a country at the north-east corner of the Victoria N'yanza. This, I think, shows clearly that the ancient Hindus must have had some kind of communication with both the Northern and Southern ends of the Victoria N'yanza."[16] While there is evidence of trade between Egypt and India for several centuries prior to the advent of Christianity, the text *Periplus of the Erythraean Sea* from the first-century, Al-Masudi, the Arab historian and geographer (d. 956), and al-Idrisi, the twelfth-century Arab geographer, all refer to the maritime trade between the Indian and the East African coast in subsequent periods.

Much of this history is either lost to us or remains unknown. Some of it has seemed in the past distracting or even suspect in the immediate aftermath of European colonialism and the corollary rise of an Africa-centered paradigm that sought to restore African agency to a historical narrative that had for too long erased its legacy.[17] This is particularly the case when narratives of contact have risked being unidirectional, with Africa and Africans cast in a recipient role. How have African ideas and cultural practices traveled to the East not only through the travels of Indian and European traders and sailors but perhaps more importantly through the African diaspora itself? The work on this African diaspora in India, pioneered by scholars such as D. R. Banaji, Joseph E. Harris, and Shanti Sadiq Ali, has been recently supplemented by a range of scholars interested in Africa's diaspora in the East.[18] While the linguistic research of Léopold Sédar Senghor and his particular desire to engage in a comparative study of West African languages and Tamil has not had many recent takers, his desire to form an Indo-African studies center in Africa has finally come to fruition.[19] The establishment in 2007 of the Centre for Indian Studies in Africa at the University of Witswatersrand may not explicitly invoke the Senghorian dream, but its interest in "Comparisons," "Connections," "Cosmopolitanism," and "Collaborations" would have resonated with Senghor's interests.[20] The rapid growth of research groups and networks interested in the history and cultures of Indian Ocean exchanges are signs that an increasing number of scholars have begun to take an active interest in these exchanges across the Indian Ocean and ask what the long history of this contact may mean for our understanding of modernity, colonialism, and its postcolonial aftermath.[21]

While asking the question of what Africanists might gain from an eastward glance, I am also interested in what scholars of the Indian Ocean gain by placing Africa more centrally in their accounts. For just as some critics have argued that Paul Gilroy's compelling work on the Black Atlantic at times risks erasing Africa itself, the same is the case for much work that has taken place in the study of the Indian Ocean.[22] Consider here the classic statement in K. N. Chaudhuri's pioneering study of the Indian Ocean, *Asia Before Europe*: "The exclusion of East Africa from our civilizational identities needs a special word of explanation. In spite of its close connection with the Islamic world, the indigenous African communities appear to have been structured by a historical logic separate and independent from the rest of the Indian Ocean."[23] Work by scholars such as Michael Pearson has done much to disabuse us of the notion that East Africa and East Africans were untouched by the "historical logic" and the circuits of the Indian Ocean, but such erasure often enters even the most politically astute writings on the subject.[24] Thus, while I use Amitav Ghosh's seminal book *In an Antique Land* as both a historical as well as a theoretical anchor for my project, I also show that his enthusiasms for Indian Ocean cosmopolitanisms risk erasing the histories of sub-Saharan exchanges that were also simultaneously taking place.[25] Even as I focus my attention on texts authored by Asian writers in this book, I am centrally concerned with how African spaces, people, and ideas influence their social and textual lives.[26] And, while revising inherited nomenclatures is always a tenuous proposition (as is evident in my own invocation of the "Indian Ocean" in this book), I have nevertheless followed Michael Pearson's lead in subtitling the book *The Afrasian Imagination* as a form of protest against the ethnocentrisms that would label a shared ocean as only Indian.[27]

A transoceanic perspective also highlights the important role that Africa has played in the trajectory of the Indian independence struggle. I join scholars such as Sugata Bose, Isabel Hofmeyr, Thomas Metcalf, Tejaswini Niranjana, John Kelly, and many others who are increasingly arguing that the project of Indian nationalism cannot be understood without the role of the Indian diaspora in Africa, Fiji, the Caribbean, and beyond.[28] Studying the anxieties and political claims of the period extending from the last decade of the nineteenth century to the aftermath of British rule in India and Africa, one is insistently reminded not only of the importance of "Indians abroad" to the national awakening in India but also of the interconnectedness of various parts of the British Empire and the *experience* of that interconnectedness in the lives of colonial subjects.[29] Thus Indian activists in Bombay in the early decades of the twentieth century were equally watchful of the predicaments of their fellow Indians in South Africa and Kenya. Likewise, throughout their struggle against the discriminatory policies of white Kenyan settlers, Kenyan Indians drew inspiration from the Indian struggle in South Africa.[30] The first authoritative account of the *satyagraha* in South Africa written in Hindi, *Dakshin Afrika Ke Satyagraha Ka Itihas*, was penned by a South African-born Indian, Bhawani Dayal, who also participated extensively in the independence struggle in India.[31] Indians in East Africa monitored the independence struggle in India and often staged strikes in protest when leaders such as Mahatma Gandhi were jailed by the British colonial government. Heralds of the Indian cause such as the Rev. C. F. Andrews wrote comprehensively about the struggle of Indians throughout Africa as well as Fiji. Newspapers, such as Gandhi's *Indian Opinion* published in South Africa, had subscribers throughout the empire;[32] the *Times of India* regularly published articles about Indians in Africa and often reprinted articles from African newspapers.[33] And, if Indians were monitoring the struggles of their compatriots, so were the white settlers.[34] For instance, General Smuts, the prime minister of the Union of South Africa, was to note in 1923 that there was among the white settlers in South Africa "a profound sympathy" for white Kenyans.[35] For their part, white Kenyan settlers looked to the South African restrictions on Indian immigration as a model for preventing further Indian immigration into their own colony. As the Kenyan settler Captain Grogan was to famously put it, "The Union of South Africa has definitely closed the front door to Indians. We are the guardians of the back door."[36]

Indian women, in particular, played a central role in the forging of cross-regional and cross-racial alliances. That the position of Indian women in Africa was of keen interest to those back home in India is seen most spectacularly around the events surrounding the decision of Kasturba Gandhi and some of her female compatriots to join the *satyagraha* in South Africa. Protesting against the Marriage Ordinance of 1913 which rendered Indian marriages illegal, the women of both Tolstoy and Phoenix Farm engaged in a march designed to have them arrested. When they were sentenced to jail in Maritzburg, the plight of these women was immediately taken up by both men and women in India. At a "Ladies meeting" held in Bombay at the Hall of the Servants of India Society on November 20, 1913, Lady Petit, a Parsi woman of high social standing, proclaimed: "The particular grievance of our sisters in South Africa is, of course, the marriage difficulty, and touching as it does the honour of the whole Indian womanhood, it is perhaps the most serious of all. . . . It is our manifest duty here in India to hold meetings everywhere to support our brave sisters, and make a supreme effort at collecting funds which alone will enable them to carry on the struggle."[37] Her colleague, Lady Mehta, added, "All honour to these brave women for their self-sacrificing and suffering spirit! Who would have believed that Indian women were capable of such heroic conduct, standing shoulder to shoulder with their husbands, fathers and brothers! Really and truly our hearts bleed for them and go out to them in this their hour of harm, pain and suffering."[38]

It is by now commonly acknowledged that South Africa had a formative role in Gandhi's political growth, but Africa also played an important role in the political education of Sarojini Naidu, perhaps the most visible Indian woman of her time in the political arena in East and South Africa.[39] Naidu presided over the East African Indian Congress in Mombasa in 1924 and addressed Indians in South Africa that same year and again later in 1932 when she returned as part of an Indian delegation along with Srinivasa Sastri.[40] Her letters to Gandhi during her first visit demonstrate a newfound admiration on her part for Gandhi as a man who had touched the spirit of Indians in Africa: "I cannot sleep in South Africa," she writes, "and it is all your fault. You haunt the land and its soil is impregnated with the memory of your wonderful struggle, sacrifice and triumph. I am so deeply moved, so deeply aware all the time that here was the cradle of *satyagraha*."[41] Even as she is haunted by Gandhi's life in South Africa, Naidu finds her own political voice in the Transvaal, a voice that she would hone as the next president of the Indian National Congress back home. In the meantime, she remains aware of the incomplete project of achieving freedom in Africa. She wishes, she writes, that, given his failing health, she could transport Gandhi to recuperate in the highlands of Kenya, "but I was forgetting," she notes, "in spite of being the Greatest Man in the world you are a miserable Indian and may not have a sanctuary in the Highlands!"[42] It was to Sarojini Naidu that C. F. Andrews attributed the first genuine interracial alliance against settler politics in South Africa. In a letter to Gandhi after Naidu's visit to South Africa in 1924, Andrews wrote: "She has finally cemented the Native cause with that of the Indian as one cause. She made an impression both on the Native and on the Coloured people and everywhere I find that this unity has been strengthened by her visit. . . . She also left a healthy spirit behind among the Indian leaders themselves. They are not likely now to separate their cause from the Natives at all."[43] Such forging of political solidarity between Indians and black Africans, I will argue in the chapters that follow, was at times tenuous but also of great import in East Africa.

A MAP FOR READING

I begin the book with a close historical reading of Amitav Ghosh's *In an Antique Land*, a text that attempts to make connections between the cosmopolitan world of the twelfth-century Indian Ocean and the increasingly divisive world in which we live today. While I critique Ghosh's project in many ways, I find that it offers not only a rich history of connections between older worlds and ours but, moreover, a set of compelling theoretical propositions and new modes of writing about non-Western worlds and circuits of exchange. In other words, I am interested in this text not only for the resonances of its themes—such as Indian Ocean slavery or economic liberalism or the religious syncretisms of the past and their contemporary erasure—all of which reappear in the East African texts that I examine, but more importantly for what I take to be Ghosh's theoretical and methodological offerings to postcolonial critique. Here the question asked by one of Ghosh's interlocutors: "You're Indian—what connection could you have with the tomb of a Jewish man here in Egypt?" could be rephrased. My primary texts for the greater majority of this book are life narratives and a work of fiction by Indians in twentieth-century East Africa. What possible connection could there be to a text concerned with the lives of Muslims and Jews in the twelfth-century Levant? The answer, I suggest, is more than the obvious connections of Indian Ocean commerce, trade, and the possibilities of cosmopolitanism. It is also conceptual. Insisting on keeping Indian Ocean histories center stage, Ghosh's project tests the limits of the possibilities of engaging in a postcolonial form of critique that doesn't unduly prioritize the West or its inherited modes of academic disciplinary knowledge.[44] The (im)possibility of an exit from European conceptual thought, categories, and epistemological arrangements has been the subject of much postcolonial anguish, reminding us not only of Dipesh Chakrabarty's call for provincializing Europe but also of V. Y. Mudimbe's famous statement in *The Invention of Africa* that there is no possibility of an African gnosis that is not already framed in terms of its encounter with the West.[45] When V. S. Naipaul's narrator Salim in the novel *A Bend in the River* bemoans that "all that I know of our history and the history of the Indian Ocean I have got from books written by Europeans," he foreshadows a predicament faced by Ghosh.[46] While his own original textual sources are penned not by Europeans but by the traders and travelers of the Indian Ocean, Ghosh's project, despite his critique of the speculative acquisitions of European collectors in Egypt, is ultimately dependent on manuscripts now housed in the prestigious archival collections of the West. His extensive readings and footnotes to Western scholars, as well as his own training as an anthropologist at Oxford, are a testimony to the enabling scholarship of Western institutions. Nonetheless, by staging a history centered on the exchanges of the Indian Ocean and writing it in a way that defies the formal boundaries of both the discipline of anthropology and the conventions of historical writing, Ghosh's hybrid text invites us to experiment with styles and forms of thought and modes of address that exhibit disciplinary promiscuity.[47] How, Ghosh's book invites us to ask, can one write about communities that have seen their share of conflict in a way that both sheds light on what Mbembe has called their "vast network of affinities" and that at the same time does not sanitize the past?[48] In the book's own terms, how does one mediate between the writing of history as nostalgia and the inevitable encroachment of a postcolonial melancholia? Furthermore, what is the best way to bring together the fruits of historical research with the imaginative world of literature? If, as David Scott has compellingly argued, postcolonial critique is in need of a new horizon of possibilities, then, I suggest, despite its own strong critique of the intrusions of the West, Ghosh's work might provide one possible model for such an alternative critical project.[49]

I present a reading of Ghosh's text that endorses its larger political imagination of a world of tolerance and cosmopolitanism but at the same time cautions against the temptations of nostalgia. It is a reading that is interested as much in Ghosh's own positioning as an Indian anthropologist in Egypt in the 1980s as it is in Ghosh's search for a historical construction of a possible dialogue between the twelfth-century trader Ben Yiju and his Indian slaves, Ashu and Bomma. In staging a dialogue not only between various spaces in the Indian Ocean littoral but also between the eras of the medieval and the modern, *In an Antique Land* invites us to a richer and deeper sense of historicity than is possible in a study that is more limited in its temporal frame. How do concepts such as those of individual freedom and slavery travel across time? How do we make sense of the connections between market forces and human motivation and how are these connections structured by states as different as the Fatimid and the postcolonial? How do religious forms and experiences get hybridized and under what circumstances do they insist on a puritanical origin? What might connect the pirates of Aden in Ghosh's twelfth-century world with the contemporary Somali pirates that increasingly challenge the maritime routes of the Indian Ocean? And if, despite the many differences in their life stories, the twentieth-century Ghosh can find the story of the Indian slave Bomma empowering—can find that it gives him "a sense of entitlement" or a right to be there in Egypt and to tell this story—then what reservations and anxieties might the two fathers, Ben Yiju, a twelfth-century African Jew, and Jay, the twentieth-century Ugandan exile in Mira Nair's *Mississippi Masala*, share in common when they both, despite their own cosmopolitan pasts, find themselves resisting their daughters' desire to marry outside the fold?

To ask the question of what might connect the worlds and the worldviews of the Tunisian-Egyptian merchant Ben Yiju and the Ugandan exile Jay, or, for that matter, the Indian slave woman Ashu most likely abandoned by Ben Yiju on the Malabar Coast in the twelfth century and Bibi Taratibu, the African slave woman abandoned in the nineteenth century by the Indian Dhanji Govindji in M. G. Vassanji's *The Gunny Sack*, is to ask a series of questions that are at the heart of this book. What are the possibilities of cross-racial relationships in contexts of structurally unequal exchange?

What is the nature of cross-racial intimacy and how is it negotiated in times of crisis? What is the relationship between the state and the performance of identity? How do notions of citizenship and civic responsibility affect the ways in which individuals tell stories to themselves and to others about their lives? What is the role of ethnic identification in the fashioning of meaningful lives? How do market forces and economic status mediate interpersonal and interethnic relationships? How do societies that are in transition negotiate the demands of economic justice and human rights? What is the role of cultural and/or religious toleration in the making of social stability? What are the limits of cultural exchange, and how do we recognize the difference between relatively equal exchanges, on the one hand, and forced impositions, on the other? What are the ideal conditions for human solidarities—how do individuals with recognizably different filiations reach out to create productive affiliations? What are the most productive and meaningful ways in which societies incorporate strangers, outsiders, foreigners? How should we adjudicate between the rightful entitlements of indigeneity and the weighty politics of migration and diaspora?[50] How, and under what conditions, do settlers become natives?[51]

An important part of my project is to help generate a discussion of significant texts written by Asians about their experiences in East Africa that still remain under the scholarly radar. While I engage in a reading of M. G. Vassanji's canonical novel *The Gunny Sack* in chapter 7, I also devote a considerable amount of attention to lesser-known texts that are of great import to historians as well as literary critics. I begin my readings of Asians in East Africa by presenting a brief genealogy of Asian creative production in the twentieth century and by accounting for some of the silences and self-censorship undertaken by the community, particularly in the immediate aftermath of the Amin expulsions from Uganda. I then turn to a number of life narratives—travelogues, autobiographies, memoirs—that resonate with many of the themes of Ghosh's Indian Ocean tale. Among these are two texts, by turn, of the twentieth-century Indian travelers to the interior of East Africa, Ebrahimji Adamji, a young Bohra merchant, and Sorabji Darookhanawala, an elder Parsi traveler who was commissioned to write a book on business prospects in the interior. My reading of these two texts focuses on the performance of ethnic identity and the ways in which notions of social etiquette, hospitality, age hierarchies, as well as religious decorum differently affect the two travelers. I am interested in how each traveler engages with the Africans he meets in the interior and what this might say about Indian attitudes toward race in the early part of the twentieth century.

Unlike European travelers in East Africa who, for the most part, depended on Indians for the infrastructure and arrangements of their travels, but nevertheless found it unnecessary to devote much representational space to them in their narratives, both Adamji and Darookhanawala are astutely aware not only of black Africans but also of the Europeans who surround them. The differences in the ways in which they each approach Europeans in their narratives also shows the ways in which class, age, education, and the possibilities of racial passing inform cross-racial interactions. I present in this chapter an argument for a vernacular form of cosmopolitanism (the term is Homi Bhabha's) that I locate in the figure not of the more Westernized Darookhanawala, but of the seemingly more insular Adamji.

Darookhanawala's narrative is, among other things, a complaint against the incomplete project of modernity as fashioned by the British and a corollary plea for allowing Indians a greater role in the commercial development of East Africa. In the chapter that follows, I concentrate on the life narratives of three Indian men of commerce (Nanji Kalidas Mehta, Manubhai Madhvani, and Madatally Manji) who, by all measures, became some of the most successful entrepreneurs of their time. I read their narratives in light of the debates among historians of commerce on the relative role of ethnicity in commercial undertakings, but I am even more interested in the roles of literature, religion, travel, and nationalism on their commercial imagination. Contrary to the stereotype of the entrepreneur as a single-minded moneymaker, these narratives speak to the ways in which entrepreneurs were primarily responsible for the mythological charter that many Asians in East Africa later crafted for themselves. This mythological charter was based on the reading of commerce as romance.

In the next chapter, I read three autobiographies of two men and one woman who were recruited by President Julius Nyerere to partner with him in the project of forging a postcolonial socialist state in Tanzania. The predominant narrative of Asians in East Africa in the immediate aftermath of independence is that of economic and political disenfranchisement, and, in the case of Uganda and Kenya, this narrative is overwhelmingly true especially in terms of political office. But just as there are significant differences among Asians, there have always been differences between the three East African nation-states that we generally lump together as "East Africa." This chapter strives to chart out how Nyerere's leadership and vision of a socialist state, built on principles of equality and nonracialism, appealed to many Asians even as the economic policies associated with the Arusha Declaration jeopardized their economic interests. An admittedly small cadre of Asians, despite being economically injured by the nationalizations of their businesses and properties, chose to partner with Nyerere. I draw on the autobiographies of Sophia Mustafa, Al Noor Kassum, and J. K. Chande to highlight Asian insecurities and hopes, the charismatic qualities of Nyerere, the role of gender in the political sphere, and the fraught negotiations between the ideologies of managed economies and the demands of capital accumulation and growth.

Not all Asians, however, were enchanted with Nyerere and his socialist project, and a close reading of M. G. Vassanji's *The Gunny Sack* provides a glimpse at other views on the project of *Ujamaa*. *The Gunny Sack* has been read extensively and productively by scholars interested in issues such as immigration, diaspora, hybridity, and postmodernity, and many of these readings have influenced my own. Nonetheless, I argue that the novel is best read for its investments in the Tanzanian national frame and, as such, I read it as a form of dissident literature. The novel gives voice to a community for whom, I argue, independence is indeed "relatively painless," but socialism and the national service associated with it is emphatically not. Ultimately, the novel stages a postethnic nationalist critique—the narrator Salim leaves Tanzania not as an ethnic exile but as a political one—but before doing so it insists on establishing an itinerary of the Asian community in East Africa. Because it is the first novel to construct a genealogy for the community on both the mythological as well as historical registers, and because it does it in an epic fashion covering a number of generations, I suggest that *The Gunny Sack* occupies a similar inaugural role in the East African Asian literary tradition that Simon Gikandi has argued for Achebe's *Things Fall Apart* in the tradition of African fiction as a whole.[52] My reading of the novel seeks not only to elucidate the ways in which it challenges some of the prevalent black African stereotypes of Asians but equally importantly to explicate its handling of stereotypes of black Africans in the Asian community. If, borrowing a rhetorical structure from Clifford Geertz, Vassanji's project is one of anti anti-Asianism, it is also simultaneously the case that Vassanji wants to educate his Asian readers to remain alert to their own residual and often virulent racisms.

The chronotope of the ship, so productively deployed by Paul Gilroy in *The Black Atlantic*, also makes its way in many of the texts that I read in this book.[53] A model of a ship in the narrator's showcase becomes central to my reading of *The Gunny Sack*'s handling of ethnic stereotypes. The ship and sea voyages across the Indian Ocean are the primary loci of the imaginative figuration of Nanji Kalidas Mehta's travels and oceanic imagery lends itself to the title of Madhvani's book, *Tide of Fortune*. Even the earlier travelogues of Adamji and Darookhanawala into the East African interior are marked by the coastal and intercontinental concerns of their narrators. Likewise, Amitav Ghosh's text is centrally invested in the unmoorings offered by the multiple circuits of what Abdul Sheriff has labeled "Dhow Cultures."[54] If these oceanic concerns celebrate the hybridities, the syncretisms, and the cosmopolitanisms of a world past, they are counterpoised by a recurrent concern about more contemporary divisions. Here the Indian struggle for independence and the trauma of the Partition makes an insistent appearance. The Partition is a key aspect of Ghosh's *In an Antique Land*, where he finds himself unable to explain to his Egyptian friends his own childhood trauma in Dhaka witnessing Hindu-Muslim riots. It enters the fictional world of M. G. Vassanji when a fight erupts between the Hindu and Muslim cricket teams during a game that has a suitably neutral Christian Goan as the umpire. In the life narratives that I study, J. K. Chande, Al Noor Kassum, and Manubhai Madhvani, all students in India in the years leading up to independence, write about their interest in the freedom struggle and the ways in which it later affected their experience of East African independence. Sophia Mustafa found herself in the position of being a refugee in the midst of the Partition crisis, and, as I suggest in my reading of her narrative, this experience had a significant impact on her political partnership with the TANU party. Nanji Kalidas Mehta played an active role in the Indian struggle for independence, not only in the capacity of being a representative of East African Asians in the meetings of the Congress party but also in the more radical position of providing asylum to N. I. Patel, an Indian revolutionary who had escaped to East Africa under the threat of British imprisonment. Mehta's narrative suggests a keen interest in the project of Indian nationalism on both the material (financial) as well as symbolic planes. In addition to investing in projects commemorating the work of Mohandas Gandhi in Kenya as well as India, Mehta's growing frustrations with the Hindu-Muslim conflict and the resultant Indian Partition lead him from an earlier syncretic and tolerant religious disposition to a more muscular Hindu nationalism.

A second theme that resonates in many of the texts I study is a tendency toward an economic liberalism predicated on the workings of the marketplace. Its most explicit articulation is ironically in the anticolonial critique offered by *In an Antique Land*. I show that while Ghosh is critical of the forceful intrusion of the West in Indian Ocean commerce, his view of trade is in keeping with that of a liberal tradition that sees in commerce the

possibilities of racial, ethnic, and religious toleration. The same view is articulated in the autobiography of Nanji Kalidas Mehta, who presents a vision
of commerce as romance. Such economic liberalism also underwrites the
worldview of J. K. Chande and Manubhai Madhvani, and, while Madatally
Manji benefits considerably in contexts when the trade is in fact controlled
and not open, he nevertheless also bristles, like Sorabji Darookhanawala
many years before him, at the restrictions put on his business by the colonial
state. The dissident view of *The Gunny Sack* is, likewise, most explicit in its
critique not only of single-party government but also of the socialism of the
state. If, following the work of K. N. Chaudhuri, Andre Gunder Frank has
suggested in *ReOrient: Global Economy in the Asian Age* that the global
economy may well have flourished in the East before it came of age in
the West, and if, as Sugata Bose has argued, "there was no dearth of Asian
capitalists with supralocal, if not global, ambitions," then paying attention
to these more modern narratives allows for a small glimpse of the residues
of such a world.[55]

This book enters the world at a historical conjuncture that resonates
with some of the central issues that frame it. First, while the battle between
capitalism and socialism was felt by many to be definitively settled with the
collapse of the Berlin Wall and the end of the cold war, the dubious success of liberalization measures in many postcolonial African states along
with the more recent financial meltdowns in Europe and the United States
spurred by the excesses of speculative capitalism have given many analysts
reasons for pause. As Annar Cassam has suggested, this was something that
the socialist Julius Nyerere had predicted in 1991 when he said in an interview, "Yes, now we see the birth of a new god, one called capitalism which
supposedly has all the answers. . . . But the conditions being created on the
ground by this euphoria over capitalism give me reason to believe that, in
about ten years or so, the ideal of socialism will return — and more forcefully
than before."[56] Second, the economic rise of China has prompted even the
most vocal advocates of multiparty liberal democracy to question whether
it indeed marks the "end of history." Francis Fukuyama, for instance, has
recently admitted that while it may not offer the freedoms associated with
democratic nations, and while it may not be a model that others might
want to emulate, the Chinese model has shown the ability to "make large
complex decisions carefully, and to make them relatively well, at least in
terms of economic policy."[57] Thus the battle between multiparty liberal
democracy and a single-party state-controlled economy, a battle that many
thought had been definitively won, has, at least in this case, reappeared on

the stage. And, finally, China and India are rapidly and increasingly investing in Africa with the Indian Ocean claiming, once again, a "center stage" in the twenty-first century.[58] This last factor means that Africa's engagement with the East will increasingly preoccupy its leaders and its thinkers. In such a scenario, while remaining alert to and indeed critical of the inequities of any such exchanges, it would behoove us as Africanists (and especially as Africanists in the West) to be cautious of engaging in a rhetoric that echoes the tired claims of the "Asiatic Danger" in Africa much circulated in the first few decades of the twentieth century.[59]

This book offers no grand theory or political vision to address these new historical circumstances. Indeed, I share the skepticism of thinkers such as Richard Rorty and Kwame Anthony Appiah who both argue that political conundrums, and the challenges of forging human solidarities, may be better met by our common human capacity to imaginatively engage with narratives than with any recourse to theory or philosophy. Human solidarity, writes Rorty, is forged in the process of imagining "them" as "one of us," and this "is a task not for theory but for genres such as ethnography, the journalist's report, the comic book, the docudrama, and especially the novel."[60] Likewise, in *The Ethics of Identity*, a book that I often address silently throughout these chapters, Kwame Anthony Appiah notes, "What we find in the epic or novel . . . derives not from a theoretical understanding of us having a commonly understood common nature—not, then, from an understanding that we (we readers and writers) all share—but from an invitation to respond in imagination to narratively constructed situations. . . . And the basic human capacity to grasp stories, even strange stories, is also what links us, powerfully, to others, even strange others."[61]

The chapters that follow, and the books and lives that I read in them, may not offer definitive answers to contemporary predicaments in the Afrasian world. But by turning to a world that was also centered around Indian Ocean exchanges and African-Asian interactions, they alert us both to the possibilities of interracial and interethnic collaborations as well as the potential derailment of such alliances. They shed light on the circulation of people, ideas, and goods over the *longue durée* in conditions of relative conviviality and also those of gross injustices and inequalities. They offer insight into a range of issues that have become central to our contemporary understanding of world histories and have bearing on our collective attempts at creating fulfilling postcolonial futures. These include the pressing competing claims of indigeneity and diaspora, of secularism and religious belief, of hybridities and discourses of purity, of ethnic identities and political goals, and of (neo)liberal democracies and socialist aspirations. Differentiated by their immediate locus of address and historical circumstance, ultimately the books I read in the pages that follow each urge us "to keep alive a productive tension, between, on the one hand, a politics that aims to find ground for consensus, and on the other, an ethics that is suspicious of any normative foreclosing of the assertion of difference."[62]

2. OLD WORLD ORDERS

Amitav Ghosh and the Writing of Nostalgia

OF ANTIQUE LANDS AND FRIENDLY SEAS

If one were to think of a contemporary text that has appealed to a variety of critics for its vision of travel, migration, and the lived experience of cosmopolitanism, Amitav Ghosh's *In an Antique Land* would surely emerge as a contender.[1] On its first American appearance in 1993, Clifford Geertz celebrated its historical vision of a "multicultural *bazaar*," and his favorable reading was echoed with only minor caveats by numerous reviews in the *Times Literary Supplement*, the *New York Times Book Review*, the *American Scholar*, and similar brokers in the creation of metropolitan tastes.[2] Indeed, the book was much anticipated by its readership, excerpts of it having already been published in the literary journal *Granta*, with portions, in a more scholarly tone, appearing in an issue of *Subaltern Studies*, a journal on the radar of most scholars of postcolonial cultural studies.[3] One such early reader was James Clifford, whose much cited essay "Traveling Cultures" drew upon the excerpt in *Granta*. Clifford's reinvocation of *In an Antique Land* and its celebration of the "transit lounge" of culture in the opening pages of his collection of essays *Routes* has virtually sealed the already formidable canonical status of Ghosh's text in the domain of contemporary U.S. cultural theory.[4]

In an Antique Land is one of the few literary texts that is centrally concerned with the twelfth-century Indian Ocean trade between Egypt and India conducted by Jewish and Muslim traders and their slaves. Re-creating a history of this trade partly from documents discovered in the Cairo Geniza and partly through speculation, Ghosh's text traverses the conventional genres of fiction, nonfiction, life narrative, and travelogue, all of which will be genres of interest in the chapters to come. With its expansive spatial and temporal frame, Ghosh's text is a particularly appropriate point of departure for our readings of Indian Ocean exchanges. Its focus on a Jewish trader in twelfth-century Cairo and on contemporary Egyptians who are marked both by a continental African identity as well as a pan-Islamic consciousness speaks to Achille Mbembe's call for a wider and more capacious understanding of African identities than those that rely on an inherited discourse of race. Moreover, by focusing on a temporality that is, in part, prior to the advent of European colonialism in Africa, Ghosh's text invites us to ask broader questions about the nature of intercultural exchanges and specifically of the ways in which they are mediated by the political institutions in which they take place. The text's interest in the religious syncretisms of the past and their disruption with the advent of modernity will be echoed in our reading of Vassanji's *The Gunny Sack*, and, like Vassanji, Ghosh also grapples with issues of cross-racial romance and its vexed nature in the form of concubinage. Since commerce is at the heart of this Indian Ocean narrative, it resonates directly with the later experiences of the likes of Nanji Kalidas Mehta and Manubhai Madhvani. Yet, because the text also narrates Ghosh's own presence in Egypt in the 1980s as an Indian ethnographer, it enables us to thematize what for many observers is an unconventional role for an Indian in Africa—that of a scholar.[5] Finally, and perhaps most significantly, by introducing the Indian slaves Bomma and Ashu into the twelfth-century frame, Ghosh's text helps subvert the stereotypical image of the Indian in Africa as always having been in a position of privilege.

Written as a "history in the guise of a traveler's tale," *In an Antique Land* is at once a travelogue, a detective story, a romance with a lost world, and an anthropologist's attempt to write a dialogic ethnography.[6] It is not a text, I will argue, that is immune from some of the slippages of what we now commonly recognize as the Orientalist imaginary, but its participation in that discursive economy is calculated, ironic, or, as Ali Behdad might put it, self-consciously belated.[7] One way of describing the book is to suggest that the two main narratives interwoven here are those of anthropology and history. The anthropological narrative is that of Ghosh going to two villages in the Nile Delta in Egypt, the first time for almost a year in 1980–81 to conduct fieldwork related to his doctoral dissertation and then again briefly in 1988 and 1990. These later visits were arguably those of a writer less invested in the formal profession of academic anthropology and more those of someone seeking to reconnect with a community of friends left behind. They are also the visits of a writer who has, in the intervening years, found a renewed interest in the historical connections between the two lands of Egypt, the subject of his study, and India, which is, as immigration documents often say, his "country of origin." It is at this juncture, then, that the historical narrative enters the frame. For, in addition to being an ethnographic memoir, *In an Antique Land* is also the story of Abraham Ben Yiju, a Jewish merchant who was active in the India trade in the twelfth century. In its simplest form, it is the story of a man originally from Ifriqiya who went as a trader to Mangalore on the Malabar Coast sometime before A.D. 1132 and lived there for nearly two decades.[8] He seems to have had a female slave named Ashu whom he manumitted in 1132. It is likely that he married Ashu and had two children with her. As far as his business interests are concerned, he is known to have had a factory in the area that worked with bronze goods, and we also know that his overseas trade was primarily handled by a slave whose name and identity are subject to debate. There is evidence that in 1149 Ben Yiju went to Aden, a major gateway on the trade route between India and Egypt, and that at some point thereafter he moved to the city of Fustat, known today as Old Cairo.[9]

If the anthropological narrative is based on Ghosh's own fieldwork, the historical one is based on an extraordinary triumph of chance over will, of luck over intent. Medieval Jews believed that it was sacrilegious to destroy any piece of paper that might have the name of God inscribed upon it. Rather than allowing such papers to be destroyed naturally by the elements or by accidental fires, Jewish communities in a variety of places deposited such documents in a special chamber in the synagogue called the *geniza*. Soon, what was meant to be a practice related to documents of a religious nature was extended to almost all documents written in the Hebrew script, which came to be considered holy in itself.[10] Secular documents like trade records, everyday correspondence, deeds of manumission, and the like were all literally thrown into the geniza for proper, religiously sanctioned burial at a later date. Through what might have been an act of sheer negligence, one such geniza was never properly emptied, discarded documents collecting in it over a period of several centuries.[11] It is the discovery of this storehouse of documents—the Cairo Geniza—that enables the reconstruction of the story of Ben Yiju, since Ghosh's twelfth-century tale is based mainly on documents found in this, shall we say, dustbin of history.[12]

For much of our knowledge of the world of Ben Yiju and the Cairo Geniza we are indebted to the formidable work of S. D. Goitein. Born in April 1900 in a small village in Bavaria, Goitein pursued his studies at Frankfurt University where at the age of twenty-three he completed a dissertation entitled "Prayer in the Qur'an." Moving to Palestine thereafter, he became, in 1925, the first instructor of Islamic studies at the newly opened Hebrew University in Jerusalem. Research on the traditions of the Yemenite Jews that Goitein initiated at this post continued to resonate in his later work on the Cairo Geniza. In 1957 he moved to the United States to fill the chair in Arabic studies at the University of Pennsylvania and in 1971 was appointed as a long-term fellow at the Institute for Advanced Study at Princeton. It was in the United States that he concentrated on studying the materials from the Cairo Geniza and by the time of his death in 1985 he had completed numerous studies on the life and times of the people associated with it.[13] His crowning achievement was the six-volume study *A Mediterranean Society* (which, by my rough calculations, exceeds three thousand pages), but he also wrote a book entitled *Jews and Arabs: Their Contacts Through the Ages* (1955) and edited a volume, *Letters of Medieval Jewish Traders*, both of which are of immediate interest to readers of Ghosh.

After presenting a reading of the critical or "belated" Orientalism of the text, particularly of its representations of Islam in contemporary Egypt, I turn in the second half of the chapter to read Ghosh's book in the light of scholarship such as Goitein's. Unlike a typical travelogue, the last few pages of *In an Antique Land* are dedicated to an extensive documentation of sources, and, as such, I take them to be an invitation to readers on Ghosh's part to read the scholarly literature on this period. Goitein's work makes the most prominent appearance in these pages, but it is supplemented by the work of several other scholars. Through such a reading, I hope to draw attention to the political as well as aesthetic tensions in Ghosh's imaginative reconstruction of this older world and especially to his attempts to link it with our own contemporaneity. It should be clear by the end of this exercise that the point is not to decry Ghosh's fidelity to the historical record but rather to understand the dynamics of what might be called the production of history in a nostalgic mode.[14] I will suggest that the all-too-common structural affinity of such nostalgia with discourses of purity and authenticity is challenged in Ghosh's narrative, where cultural, racial, and economic hybridity, mixture, and exchange appear as privileged terms. A central part of my project is to track, in both the historical and the anthropological accounts, the political stakes involved in foregrounding these alleged mixings and to question what other processes they may elide.

WRITING CULTURE, WRITING HISTORY

One of the lasting legacies of the poststructural turn in the social sciences has been a detailed attention to the processes of writing. Representations, Paul Rabinow has noted, are "social facts," both in the sense that they enter the realm of the worldly, often affecting in no small measure the range of speakable "truths" about their referents, but also conversely in the sense that the only purchase we have on "social facts" themselves are through their representations.[15] It is this insight that has led a number of commentators to study the use of language, literary tropes, and narrative devices in ethnographic as well as historical texts. How is the "other"—cultural or historical—being constructed in the text? How is the author or the reader positioned in this scene of alterity? What is the relationship between the "author" and the bearer(s) of "authority" in this scenario? To what extent is an attempt being made to listen to the voice of the "other," and how is this voice made audible within the text? These questions have continued to resonate with different emphases in the disciplinary metacommentaries that have been provided for anthropology by the scholars associated with the seminal *Writing Culture* volume (particularly James Clifford, George Marcus, and Michael M. J. Fischer) and in history by scholars such as Hayden White and Michel de Certeau.[16]

What makes a text such as *In an Antique Land* so rich for such questioning is its insistently hybrid form, eschewing the generic demands of a classical ethnography or a realist historical treatise. Yet if there is here a reluctance to adopt the social scientist's discursive order, there is also a desire to hold on to some of the social scientist's authority. As a professional anthropologist turned author, Ghosh is clearly banking on the credibility of his disciplinary degree even when he knows that his greatest personal success is through his poetic vocation and his writing. Ironically, the stories he tells themselves speak to such career mobility. If the most depressing of these is that of the many university-educated Egyptian youth who, faced with severe unemployment in their own homeland, have to leave to seek unpleasant manual labor in Iraq, then perhaps the most personally meaningful to Ghosh is the story of Ben Yiju himself, who aspires to be a poet and continues to write poetry and practice calligraphy even while he is materially sustained by the Indian Ocean trade. For both Ben Yiju and Ghosh, and as I will later argue for Indian men of commerce such as Nanji Kalidas Mehta, it is the literary that ultimately sustains. A novelist with an already established record of literary success, Ghosh turns back in this hybrid text to reclaim the authority of the social scientist even as he seeks to demystify the fundamental methodological presuppositions of the social sciences.

The starkest example of such demystification of the methods of social science is the detective story involving the "Slave of MS H.6" and particularly its radically different presentation in two discursive contexts. In an article written for the scholarly journal *Subaltern Studies*, Ghosh presents the case for reading the slave mentioned in Ben Yiju's correspondence as an Indian man named Bomma who was most likely a member of the Magariva caste. The argument itself is intricate and not one that can be easily condensed, but it proceeds along the standard lines of interrogating the evidence according to established rules of historical argument. Beginning with a record of every available piece of writing in which he is invoked, proceeding to an account of the historical source (in this case the Cairo Geniza), moving on to potential disputes and alternative possibilities of identifying the ethnic identity of the slave, presenting both contextual as well as linguistic arguments for why the letters *B-M-A* in the original documents are most likely an inscription of the name Bomma, a common name among the lower castes of the region around Mangalore, Ghosh moves deftly from source to source, evaluating each on its own merits. Despite its acknowledgment of certain speculative moves necessitated by the lack of sufficient evidence, the distinctive tone of this longish article, with its 261 footnotes, is one of scholarly authority. Reframed in the larger narrative of *In an Antique Land*, however, the story of the slave becomes at once an important leitmotif, a vehicle for the author's own transhistorical travels, an allegory of the writing of history, and one, as well, that, by his own account, gives Ghosh "a sense of entitlement" (19), allowing him the right to be in the Egyptian "field."

"In the ten years that had passed since I first came across Goitein's brief reference to Abraham Ben Yiju and his Slave," writes Ghosh, "my path had crossed theirs again and again, sometimes by design and sometimes inadvertently, in North Africa, Egypt and the Malabar, until it became clear that I could no longer resist the logic of those coincidences" (99). Ghosh's travels are as much movements through a historical ethnoscape as they are attempts at doctoral ethnographic research. Presented as a travelogue, they foreground the fact that, in scholarly research as in everyday life, the processes of getting there are as exciting and important as "being there."[17] It is the processual nature of the undertaking, with an explicitly autobiographical narrator relating his search, his minidiscoveries, and his dead ends that help characterize *In an Antique Land* as a mystery or a detective narrative. Consider here the case of what we might as well label the "Scholar of Footnote 78." Footnote 78 of the *Subaltern Studies* article acknowledges the help of Dr. B. A. Viveka Rai in the author's understanding of Tulu religious history. "I am deeply grateful to Dr. Rai for this and innumerable other comments and suggestions, for his generosity with his time and his erudition, and for a great many kindnesses."[18] An otherwise unspectacular acknowledgment, read in the light of *In an Antique Land*, the footnote speaks volumes on the pursuit and framing of historical knowledge. For in this latter text two entire chapters are devoted to Ghosh's much anticipated meeting with Professor Rai in Mangalore, Ghosh having come up with a working hypothesis on the slave's identity and now eagerly awaiting a confirmation or a redirection from Professor Rai. We witness the exchange between the professor and the young researcher, we are taken through the professor's weighing of evidence hand in hand with Ghosh himself, and we are even party to the viewing of the film of Koti and Chennaya made several years ago by friends of Professor Rai. It is through this film that Ghosh himself begins to learn about the Tulu pantheon and its distance from high Sanskritic religion and works toward a new hypothesis surrounding Bomma's identity. The "Scholar of Footnote 78" thus becomes a major agent in the narrative unfolding of the text and allows Ghosh not only to demonstrate the lived experience of research but also to comment implicitly on the writing of history itself. Along with a critique of the conventions of writing history, the story of the search is stylistically rich, allowing Ghosh to weave an intricate narrative that moves between the historical and the contemporary. Thus the "dreams of Cairo" that Ghosh has in his earlier days in Lataifa allow him to shift between the modern and the medieval, just as the story of the forthcoming marriage between 'Eid and the Badawy girl segues into the story of Ben Yiju and Ashu.

While the mystery surrounding Bomma's identity drives the historical plot, the contemporary narrative is guided by the more everyday negotiations that ethnographers must undertake when they initiate their work in the field. In this light the passages about Abu Ali, Ghosh's landlord and self-appointed surrogate guardian, are some of the most memorable in the text. But even beyond the dramatic exchanges between Abu Ali and his houseguest involving such issues as the appropriate amount of rent, Ghosh finds that he must learn to live with the villager's doubts about his abilities: his young friends begin to doubt his knowledge of human sexuality, the women in the village question his abilities to bargain in the marketplace, and almost everyone challenges his religious beliefs.

During his stay in Egypt, Ghosh is repeatedly confronted by the villagers, who question him about Hindu customs, particularly the lack of circumcision among Hindu men, cremation, and the worship of cows—practices that seem shocking to them. As other critics have noted, the traditional roles of ethnographer and observed subject are reversed here, with the villagers doing the questioning and the ethnographer becoming the subject of scrutiny.[19] Much of the time, the incredulous questioning is narratively constructed as a site of humor, both on the part of the villagers, who, when not outraged by the beliefs themselves, use them to poke fun at the foreigner, but also on the part of the readers, for whom the villagers' scandalous horror itself provides a scene of amusement.[20] Yet, while Ghosh the narrator skillfully brings out the comedy of intercultural (mis)understanding, Ghosh the ethnographer is increasingly disturbed by it. At one point in the narrative, fed up over yet another round of questioning about cremation and circumcision, when Ghosh decides to walk out his friend Nabeel follows him. "They were only asking questions," he said, "just like you do; they didn't mean any harm. Why do you let this talk of cows and burning and circumcision worry you so much? These are just customs; it's natural that people should be curious. These are not things to be upset about" (204).

What Nabeel recognizes here is the fact that the villagers' questioning is, ironically, their way of embracing the young ethnographer and making him feel an accepted part of their world. So when the divorcee Busaina urges Ghosh to marry a good Muslim girl from the village and to settle down among them, this has more to do with a performative welcoming of Ghosh than any desire to assimilate him into a religious community.[21] Indeed, even the most explicit attempt at conversion, that of Ustaz Mustafa, is kept in check by Mustafa's own recognition that if Ghosh were to convert he would be going against the wishes of his father: "he had a son himself and it went against his deepest instincts to urge a man to turn against his father. And so, as the rival moralities of religion and kinship gradually played themselves

to a standstill within him, Ustaz Mustafa and I came to an understanding"
(52). Yet, though the connections of kinship and community ultimately
trump religion itself, Ghosh nevertheless remains uncomfortable with what
he experiences as the intrinsically religious framework of his reception in
the village. There is a residual Orientalism at work here insofar as Ghosh
approaches the community with a preconceived notion of the integral and
fundamental role of religion in it. At one point in the narrative, in what he
reads as a lapse in his own ethnographic duties, Ghosh declines to accompany Ustaz Mustafa on his visit to the mosque or to the family grave for the
reading of the Qur'an. "A part of me had wanted to go—" writes Ghosh,
"not merely that part which told me that it was, in a sense, my duty, part
of my job. But when the moment had come, I'd known that I wouldn't be
able to do it: I had been too afraid, and for the life of me I could not understand why" (49). Bothered by his own discomfort, Ghosh experiences here
the intrinsic tension between the twin demands of his chosen vocation—
seeking the native's point of view, but doing so without "going native."

Rather than editing out his own anxieties in the field, Ghosh leaves them
in for the reader's scrutiny, and it is this choice, I argue, that gives *In an
Antique Land* the character of a "belated" Orientalism. This is a text that
makes explicit its own Orientalist presuppositions even as it attempts to
overcome them. We will see this move again in Ghosh's handling of Islam
as well as his discussion of women, but we should first note that his construction of the community as fundamentally religious leads to a curious
forgetting on Ghosh's part: when the villagers repeatedly equate his "Indianness" with his "Hinduness," not once does he share with them the fact that
in India, too, there are Muslims, that it is indeed an error to conflate the
Indian nation with a particular religious ideology. Nor does Ghosh, despite
his attempts at bringing together the historical experiences of Egypt and
India, ever point out, either to the villagers or to his readers, the ironies
surrounding the discussions of cow worship. For cow worship, as scholars
of Ancient Egypt would tell us, was not only a part of the religion of the
ancient Egyptians, but bore a remarkable resemblance to the Hindu pantheon.[22] By allowing the villagers to persist in their reading of India as essentially Hindu, and of themselves as essentially the descendants of Arab Muslims with no ties to Pharaonic Egypt, Ghosh loses the opportunity to discuss
with them issues such as multireligious national communities and their own
hybridized histories.[23] To what might we attribute this silence? Is it simply
the result of the ethnographic tendency to be a gatherer rather than a dis-
seminator of information? Or is it, instead, something more particular to

Ghosh's estimations of the worldview of the *fellaheen*, as might be suggested from the various moments in the text when he almost wants to speak up, but doesn't? (For instance, his comment, "I sometimes wish I had told Nabeel a story" (204), or, later, referring to the investigating police officer at the tomb of Abu-Hasira, "He seemed so reasonable and intelligent, that for an instant I even thought of telling him the story of Bomma and Ben Yiju" [339]).

While Ghosh the ethnographer is reluctant to address such issues with the villagers, Ghosh the writer is much invested in both the issues of multi-religious communities as well as those of religious hybridities and syncretic practices. Indeed, the central thesis of the book is that there once was a community, in the very settings of Ghosh's contemporary travels in Egypt and the Malabar Coast, that was not only cosmopolitan and tolerant of religious differences but also marked by a significant degree of religious syncretism. The lifeblood of this community was the Indian Ocean trade which flourished unchecked and in harmony until the European arrival toward the end of the fifteenth century. Ben Yiju, for instance, while a member of a religious minority in the Fatimid Egypt of his time, was also alien among the ruling classes of the Malabar Coast. But, suggests Ghosh, despite this, and contrary to our own conceptions of the religious persecutions of the medieval world, Ben Yiju would have found himself, both in Egypt and in India, in societies that were relatively tolerant of religious minorities. Indeed, in Ghosh's portrayal of the medieval world a great majority of the religious persecutions are carried out by the Christian crusaders from Europe, with both Muslims and Jews being the victims of an aggressive religious ideology. While Ghosh does indeed refer to the Islamic Almohad persecutions of both Jews and Christians in 1145 and 1146 in Ifriqiya, Fez, and Marrakesh, they are framed in large part as a response to earlier attacks on Ifriqiya by the crusader King Roger II of Sicily. Ben Yiju's return to Aden and then to Egypt is likewise prompted by the disasters wrought upon his family by the continued conflicts of the Crusades. Similarly, Ben Yiju's stay in India is marked by a remarkably cosmopolitan aura, with Muslims, Jews, and Hindus interacting together in matters of trade and, in his own case, in matters of marriage as well.[24] Outside the orbit of Western Christendom, Ghosh's medieval world indeed comes across as the "multicultural bazaar" that Clifford Geertz celebrates.

The modern loss of this religiously plural world is impressed upon the ethnographer not only in the incessant questioning by the villagers about Hindu practices but also, and perhaps most significantly, in an unpleasant argument he has with the imam of Nashawy. The discussion begins, as often happens in the text, with a denunciation, this time by the imam, of the practices of Ghosh's Hindu community.[25] Having heard these rebukes in various contexts, and frustrated with his own efforts at getting the imam to share knowledge of traditional remedies and herbal medicines, Ghosh explodes at the imam's suggestion that he comes from a primitive, backward culture. The imam's measure of civilization and modernity is the West, and this to him is especially manifest in its technological superiority. "They're advanced," he says of the West, "they're educated, they have science, they have guns, they have bombs" (235). In the shouting match that ensues, Ghosh and the imam both assert the superiority of their own country's destructive weapons. The fact that this heated exchange is prefigured in the text by earlier friction between the men speaks as well to a certain link between conceptions of modernity and those of masculinity. Ghosh has, not too long before this episode, raised the imam's ire by asking his son Yasir, in the manner of small talk, whether he has any siblings other than a sister. The innocently posed question is felt, however, by the imam and his family, as a personal offense verging on an assault on the imam's vigor. Yasir responds, "It is all the same, my father has given me one sister and there is no reproach if he has not been blessed with any sons other than I" (195). If we remember that the imam has also suffered a public disgrace in that his first wife has walked out on him and set up her own separate household, we note that there are subtle undertones of the imam's emasculation, with their Freudian echoes in the rhetoric of guns, bombs, and injections. The borders drawn between "delegates from two superseded civilizations, vying with each other to establish a prior claim to the technology of modern violence" (236), are, at the same time, marked by male anxieties. And, furthermore, the imam's sense of emasculation and his hostility toward Ghosh find their parallel in Ghosh's sense of inadequacy and his simultaneous anger toward and envy of the West. In at least one version of the story, tellingly excised from the version that became *In an Antique Land*, but included in the earlier version in *Granta*, Ghosh counters with a distinct techno-envy: "For a moment then I was desperately envious. The Imam would not have said any of these things to me had I been a Westerner. He would not have dared. Whether I wanted to or not, I would have had around me the protective aura of an inherited expertise in the technology of violence."[26]

   I suggested earlier that *In an Antique Land* is a text that exposes its own Orientalist presuppositions even as it strives to correct them. A case in point is the representation of the Egyptian women whom Ghosh encounters in the villages. Ghosh enters the community with clichéd notions of the modesty of Muslim women and avoids any direct eye contact for fear of causing offense. He soon realizes that the women are amused by what they take to be his shyness, and the young teenage girls on occasion even tease him sexually. Increasingly embarrassed by such come-ons and yet drawn to the erotics of such events as the dances of the youth at the wedding of Nabeel's brother, the ethnographer polices his somewhat confused sexual feelings as though he is aware of being in the presence of a professional taboo. While he remains uneasy in his own dealings with the women, Ghosh nevertheless ends up presenting an image of the village women that is radically different from the modest and agency-less victim of patriarchy he has expected to find. Over and over again we meet women who take control of their lives, challenge their husband's infelicities, and walk out on them. Thus we remember the imam's first wife, who has set up her own household, Khamees's first wife, who walks out of her marriage proclaiming to the world that her husband is impotent, and Busiana, who chooses to leave her husband and fend for herself and her two children rather than stay in an unhappy marriage. Even the adolescent girls in town seem to have the upper hand in gender relations. In an amusing pastoral scene, two such girls tease and flirt with 'Eid, a young man who is tending to his family's livestock, only to trick him out of some of his fodder. Despite his own indirect access to it, the world of women is not quite as closed to him as Ghosh fears it might be. Remaining awkward in the company of women, Ghosh's ethnographic narrative nevertheless succeeds in subverting the gendered Orientalisms with which he approaches them.[27]

This same ability to present a complex social phenomenon in all its multidimensionality, while personally being uneasy with aspects of it, is evident in Ghosh's treatment of Islam. Distasteful as he finds the imam's pandering to the West, Ghosh also recognizes in it the falsity of prevalent stereotypes of traditionalist religious leaders. After all, while he is seen as old-fashioned by the youth of the village, the imam is not the repository of unchanging tradition, but rather one who seeks the power of medical science. He is, for instance, quick to discard the traditional herbal remedies for the more efficient injections that he has acquired from the West. Unlike the inventions of the anti-Western and "fundamentalist" imams by the secular and not-so-secular West, here we are in the presence of one who is in awe of Western-style modernity.

That this embrace of Western modernity by the imam has resulted in no great following among his constituency is an irony emphasized by Ghosh. The loss of the imam's credibility among the youth is dramatized by the rise to popularity of a young schoolteacher, Ustaz Sabry. Read with a certain amount of skepticism by the older generation, Sabry is admired by the younger villagers for his inspiring Friday sermons at the mosque and his learned, almost scholastic knowledge of Islam. University-educated, and with a greater sense of the global politics of modern Islam, Ustaz Sabry is the voice of a different kind of modernity—one that is self-consciously Islamist and not a mere copy of the West. This Islamist modernity is at once critical of any residual religious syncretisms of an older generation and, too, of any emulation of a secular one. Thus, for instance, in the various informal gatherings that take place at Sabry's home, there are extensive discussions of the need to stop believing in ghosts or worshipping at the shrines of saints—these practices being seen as vestiges of a pre-Islamic past. There are discussions of the moral corruption of Communism, which Ustaz Sabry, based on some prior conversations with a German Communist, often ironically tends to conflate with the West as a whole. The problem with Communism for Sabry and his followers is not its egalitarian, anticapitalist impulse, but rather its insistence on grounding it on a nonreligious foundation. Indeed, the setting up of a consumer's cooperative in Nashawy is meant to help avoid the greed of the capitalist. But such efforts, along with the increasing restrictions on religious syncretism, are meant to help the community "succeed in rooting out all exploitation and unbelief from the village" so that "people would see for themselves where the pure path of Islam lay" (147, 148).

An important aspect of the turn toward this university-generated Islam is a geopolitical critique of Western aggression. We hear a college student praising Sabry for the politically inspirational qualities of his sermons. Unlike those of the imam, who "doesn't seem to know about the things that are happening around us in Afghanistan, Lebanon and Israel" (141), Sabry's sermons make everyone feel that "they should do something about all that's happening in the world around us" (141). And in a passage that surely resonates with more meaning in a post-9/11 world than when Ghosh first wrote it, we learn that "it was Ustaz Sabry, for instance, who had first thought of raising money for the Afghans; in a speech at the mosque, he had talked of how Muslims were being slaughtered by Communists in Afghanistan, and the men of the village were so moved that they raised quite an impressive sum of money for the mujahideen" (146). By 1988, when Ghosh returns on his second visit, he is surprised to learn about the religious turn in his friend Jabir, who though still a young boy during the fieldwork year, has now returned from college. In his college years, Jabir tells him, he grew a beard in a distinctively Muslim style and spent many evenings with fellow students and teachers reading and discussing the Qur'an. "I was not involved in politics or anything," he said, "and I didn't join any groups or societies. But I learnt to recognize what is wrong and what is true" (308). Yet despite his avowed separation from political activism, his family, and particularly his mother, prevail upon him to shave his beard. "They were afraid," he said, "There's been trouble between the government and certain Islamic groups, and they were worried that something might happen to me" (309). If, at an earlier moment in his fieldwork, Ghosh has refrained from sharing with the villagers the story of his own childhood trauma of witnessing religious riots between Hindus and Muslims in Dhaka, claiming, with, some paternalism, that he "could not have expected them to understand an Indian's terror of symbols" (210), then surely in the years that have intervened it is a lesson that his interlocutors have learned.

Sympathetic to its critique of the West, the secularist Ghosh seems nevertheless disturbed by the rise of a religiously mantled modernity. But this unease does not blind him to the fact that its rise is rooted in the material conditions of the villagers, their despair over severe unemployment and the inability of the state bureaucracy to address their needs. At quite a remove from the racist images of a religion of fanatics who are unable to shed their so-called medieval lifestyles, this Islam attempts to find meaning and community in a global modernity gone awry.[28] Perhaps the most moving passages in *In an Antique Land* are those that portray this breakdown of hopes and aspirations, the quest for upward mobility accompanied by the reification of relations that can now only be gauged through the acquisition of commodities. On his return to Lataifa and Nashawy in 1988, Ghosh begins to see the signs of "new money." Young men who have left their families in search of jobs in Iraq send back money and commodities. New homes are being built in the villages, and the relatives left behind are rightfully proud of their new possessions. And yet this migrant labor has meant that families are separated, that the hostile working conditions and the negative treatment of these Egyptian migrants in Iraq are not talked about.[29] The young men still left behind are desperately trying to enter this "transit lounge of culture" and interpret the inability to enter it as a public announcement of failure. Relations between people have also altered, as Ghosh notices when his friend Jabir shuts the door of his room on his own family members. "I was astonished: in all the time I had spent in Lataifa and Nashawy, I had never seen anyone shut a door upon people in their own house" (305–6). As though to metaphorize the increasingly frozen nature of relations between people, Ghosh notes that, as refrigerators become commonly available in the villages, meat too is frozen, so that the traditional practices of sharing freshly slaughtered meat during the Eid festivities slowly disappear.

By 1988 things in the villages have changed so much that no more do the villagers feel the need to summon the Indian ethnographer to examine a diesel pump—the "Hinduki" machine—that, on his first visit, had unwittingly become a centerpiece for establishing his own authority. This technological advance is not without its own difficulties, however. In a telling symbol of the contradictions of modernity, Ghosh's night arrival on his return in 1988 is in the midst of an entirely dark village. The kerosene lamps that once lit Nashawy have been put away since the village has now been wired for electricity. Arriving in the middle of a power cut, the village seems to the ethnographer to be ominously suspended between a lost past and a future that is yet to be determined. Though reminiscent of the conventional anthropological mistrust of modernity, these observations are not in fact rooted in any dream or desire for the "unchanging native." Rather, they are, on Ghosh's part, the result of an acute awareness of and empathy with the indigenous desire to better their lot, while at the same time being subject to what he calls at another point the "tornados of grand designs and historical destinies" (15). What connects the contemporary narratives of the villagers to the historical narratives of Ben Yiju and his associates is precisely those negotiations that they must undertake in order to forge their own individual trajectories. The Crusades, on the one hand, and the Iranian revolution and the Gulf War, on the other, are the bookends within which global connectivity must be assessed.

There are at least two ways in which one can interpret the lives of commoners such as the villagers of Lataifa and Nashawy or the traders of Ben Yiju's times. One is to celebrate their will and determination, despite the odds, to make meaningful lives for themselves and their kin. The other is to bemoan their entrapment in the quagmires of history, which often work to limit their possibilities, to stall their will, to destroy their dreams. The former, we might say, is the domain of nostalgia, and the latter that of melancholia. The former remains optimistic about the possible future recovery of a fragile dream, while the latter is resigned to a mourning of its irretrievable loss. What makes *In an Antique Land* such a meaningful text for our own times is its insistence on a nostalgic optimism, even as it recognizes the encroachment of an inevitable melancholia. The writing of nostalgia, as Nicholas Dames has persuasively argued, is intricately tied to the pursuit of pleasure—"what is pleasurable to recall will be recalled, while the unworthy or the painful will erase itself."[30] Nostalgia is, in effect, a necessary forgetting of trauma and a celebration of recuperable memories that are oriented toward a desirable future. In this sense, the writing of history in the nostalgic mode is "always only the necessary prehistory of the present," promoting a vision of a future that is no longer burdened by the unpleasant aspects of the past and that allows the telling of "a life lived as a coherent tale, summarizable, pointed, and finally moralizable."[31]

Because of its insistence on dwelling on the pleasurable, nostalgic writing can recuperate even the most tragic situations into narratives of survival and determination. But, no matter how nostalgic, the melancholic always remains in the wings ready to make a sobering entry. Referring to Ben Yiju toward the end of his life, at one point Ghosh writes, "The letter he wrote on this occasion was a long one, like the last, but his mood and his circumstances were greatly changed and the *nostalgic exuberance* that had seized him upon his return to Aden had now yielded to a resigned and *broken-hearted melancholy*" (313, my emphasis). In the writing of Ben Yiju's life, Ghosh has himself created, up to this point in the narrative, a nostalgic vision. Despite the clear sense of alienation and loneliness that Ben Yiju feels on the Malabar Coast, Ghosh has nevertheless foregrounded the positive, the vibrant cosmopolitanism around him, the deep connections between members of different religious faiths, even the virtues of non-regulated interoceanic trade. But there is a strong awareness in the text that here, as elsewhere, there always remains the possibility that at some point the deferral of conflict might break down and with it might arrive not only a "broken-hearted melancholy" but also, significantly, a breakdown of the earlier order. A sure sign of such a breakdown is Ben Yiju's refusal to let his daughter marry a foreigner, which, in the light of his own marriage with the Indian Ashu, makes it seem "almost as though he were seeking to disown a part of his own past" (316). The great cosmopolitan connections that are drawn in the chronotopes of nostalgia are reversed in those of melancholia.[32] Melancholia cripples while nostalgia redeems, and, to underscore this lesson, the narrator approvingly notes about contemporary Mangalore, "But appropriately, Mangalore does not treat its lost history as a crippling melancholy: it has always been a busy, bustling kind of place, and today it is again a thriving, relatively prosperous city" (245).

In the remainder of this chapter I propose to investigate Ghosh's production of history in the nostalgic mode. Since the writing of nostalgia is as much about the forgetting as the remembrance of the past, I will attempt to foreground what it is that the text "forgets" in its desire to weave a nostalgic narrative. In the final analysis, like most commentators on Ghosh's text, and like the students in my classes who consistently enjoy studying it, I find the text's nostalgia not only appealing aesthetically but also inspiring politically. But, as a critic who has taken on Ghosh's challenge to read the historical scholarship on Ben Yiju's times, I find that the book deserves a more sustained scrutiny.

SYNCRETISM, ANTISYNCRETISM, AND THE "ENFORCERS OF HISTORY"

What is evident in *In an Antique Land* is that, despite its alleged mystery, Bomma's identity — as an Indian man and, moreover, one from a lower-caste, non-Sanskritic community — is a necessary and enabling fiction for Ghosh. Unlike the scholarly venue where Ghosh expresses no personal preference, his sense of delight in having finally discovered a subaltern presence who is in many ways the "other's other" — the lowest of the low — is not hidden from readers of the longer narrative. It is only such a subaltern who, outside the grasp of a majoritarian Sanskritic fold, would have shared with his master Ben Yiju an affinity for "the hidden and subversive counter-image of the orthodox religions" (263) of his time and invested in practices such as exorcism cults, magical rites, and the visitations to saints' tombs and shrines. Ghosh writes, "It was probably those inarticulate counter-beliefs, rather than the formal conversion that Bomma probably had to undergo while in Ben Yiju's service, that eventually became a small patch of level ground between them: the matrilineally-descended Tulu and the patriarchal Jew who would otherwise seem to stand on different sides of an unbridgeable chasm" (263).

The fact that the world of the Cairo Geniza exhibited a significant degree of religious syncretism is of great interest to Ghosh. The most literal form of this syncretism, he suggests, may well be seen in the language of the geniza documents themselves. Ben Yiju "and his friends were all orthodox, observant Jews, strongly aware of their distinctive religious identity," writes Ghosh. "But they were also part of the Arabic-speaking world, and the everyday language of their religious life was one they shared with the Muslims of that region: when they invoked the name of God in their writings it was usually as Allah, and more often than not their invocations were in Arabic forms, such as insha allah and al-hamdul-illah" (261). In addition, the close proximity of the religions meant that Judaism in Egypt would soon see the influence of Islamic Sufism and the practice of worshiping at the shrines of saints would become common to both the Jewish and the Islamic communities. Ghosh contends that such syncretic practices were, over time, policed, and with the advent of modernity their histories were erased. In such a context, any residual syncretism evident today is to Ghosh a privileged site of political resistance itself—and particularly of political resistance to the repressive state. For instance, Ghosh celebrates the folk narratives that he hears in Egypt about the saint Abu-Kanaka, whose grave is said to have resisted any efforts by the government to build a canal through it, and also the story of the Bhuta shrine in Mangalore, which has similarly put in check the construction of a road from the city of Mangalore to its new port. Ghosh sees in these narratives a popular critique of the ideologies and practices of state-sponsored "development."

Perhaps the most significant episode in the text in which the modern fate of syncretism is put to a test is the encounter Ghosh has in Egypt on his second visit in 1988. On his way back out of the country he decides to visit the tomb of the saint Sidi Abu-Hasira. Abu-Hasira, Ghosh has learned from the villagers, was a Jew from the Maghreb who came to Egypt and converted to Islam. He was recognized by the people as a man of extraordinary benevolent powers, a good man, endowed with the blessings of *baraka*. He developed a large following among the locals and he still had Jewish followers from Israel who attended the annual Mowlid in his honor in Damanhour. As it turns out, the Mowlid takes place during Ghosh's visit, but, although his friends in Nashawy and Lataifa persuade him to attend, he never quite makes it to the festival itself. Instead, he attempts a quick detour to the shrine on his way to the train station from which he plans to depart. What he sees there surprises him—the tomb itself is much bigger than similar tombs he has seen before. "It was," Ghosh notes, "a sleek, concrete structure of a kind that one might expect to see in the newer and more expensive parts of Alexandria and Cairo: in that poor quarter of Damanhour, it was not merely incongruous—its presence seemed almost an act of defiance" (333). While the sight of the tomb itself is dissonant, his expectations of a quick and quiet visit are shaken by the approach of armed police officers who quickly begin to interrogate him. Recognizing Ghosh as a foreigner, one of the officers demands an explanation for his visit to the tomb. The Mowlid is already over, the tourists are all gone, and therefore the presence of a foreigner at the tomb is, according to the officer, itself a cause for suspicion. But what baffles the officer most is the fact that Ghosh is neither an Israeli devotee on a pilgrimage nor a follower of any of the monotheistic religions with which he is familiar. "Neither Jewish, nor Muslim, nor Christian—there had to be something odd afoot" (334–35). The potentially dangerous visitor is escorted to the local police station for further interrogation. In this setting, to Ghosh reminiscent of the colonial buildings built by the British in India, and probably a testimony to the British occupation of Egypt—the two men face each other across what Ghosh sees as the resolutely modern, all too contemporary, colonially implicated divisions between peoples who once experienced a connected history. "You're Indian—what connection could you have with the tomb of a Jewish holy man, here in Egypt?" he is asked. He cannot find an immediate answer, but the book he eventually writes will attempt to provide one.

Finding himself at a narrative impasse at the moment of the officer's questioning, Ghosh nevertheless shares with the reader his own sense of excitement at the survival of a popular religious syncretism of the past: "It seemed uncanny that I had never known all those years that in defiance of the enforcers of History, a small remnant of Bomma's world had survived, not far from where I was living" (342). This is, in fact, an echo of an earlier moment in the text when Ghosh has visited, this time in the vicinity of Mangalore, a Hindu temple built by the Magariva community. He has arrived there in pursuit of a *bhuta* shrine of a spirit-diety called Bobbariya, legendarily named after a Muslim mariner and trader who died at sea. But just as Ghosh is surprised to find a modern concrete structure honoring Abu-Hasira, he is surprised to find that the bhuta shrine in this community has in fact been placed in a Hindu temple that is a testament to the high Sanskritic form of the religion. The main deity is Vishnu, a Brahmanical god, and the Bobbariya-bhuta is placed in a subordinate position. The bhuta itself has been stripped of its traditional iconography and is now represented as a Hindu god. Remarking on the ironies of such a representation, Ghosh writes, "The past had revenged itself on the present: it had slipped the spirit of an Arab Muslim trader past the watchful eyes of Hindu zealots and installed it within the Sanskritic tradition" (274).

It is the nostalgic impulse in Ghosh that chooses to read the survival of earlier religious syncretisms as potential spaces of modern "defiance" and "revenge." Such a reading, politically appealing as it is, nevertheless depends on a dismissal of the religious revisionism of the communities themselves. At one point during his visit to the temple, Ghosh notes, "It was not really a Bhuta-shrine any more, they explained proudly: it had become a real Hindu temple, and the main place in it was now reserved for Vishnu, the most Brahmanical of Gods" (273–74). The incorporation of the bhuta into the temple is experienced by the community, then, not as a gesture of religious syncretism but rather as an antisyncretic practice. The fact that this historically lower-caste community has appropriated for itself the symbols of high Brahmanical tradition in an attempt at upward mobility, and the fact that the temple prominently displays posters of a fundamentalist Hindu organization "notorious for its anti-Muslim rhetoric" (273), suggests that the Muslim trader here has been, contrary to Ghosh's enabling reading, disciplined, tamed, and co-opted into a resolutely Hindu cosmology. Likewise, in the case of the shrine of Abu-Hasira, Ghosh's representation of the police officers as ultimately blind to the richness of popular religion and its history may well betray a certain overzealousness on behalf of the political possibilities of religious syncretism. Let us remember that when the villagers in Lataifa and Nashawy encourage him to go to the Mowlid, they seemingly do so not out of any sense of religious conviction. "The Mowlid was a wonderful spectacle, I was told; there would be lights everywhere, stalls with pistols and airguns, swings and carousels; the streets would be lined with kebab-shops and vendor's carts and thronged with crowds of sightseers. The tourists alone were a good reason to go, they said, it was not often that one got to see foreigners in a place like Damanhour" (330). To the villagers the Mowlid is clearly a recreational activity, and perhaps also, as in the case of Moshin the taxi driver, an opportunity to make some money. To read the shrine as an act of defiance against "the enforcers of History" is to participate in the well-established and indeed often well-meaning anthropological discourse of "survivals" at the risk of erasing historically contingent and continually renegotiated cultural practices.[33]

The examples of the Magariva temple and the shrine of Abu-Hasira suggest at least two things about the nature of religious syncretism: one, that what at first appears to be religious syncretism may in fact be marked by antisyncretic tendencies and, two, that a practice that may seem to be syncretic, insofar as it engages the interests of more than one religious community, may in fact be experienced by the two communities in entirely different and possibly even nonreligious ways.[34] These insights into the limits of syncretism, it should be noted, are applicable not only to the modern world but also to the medieval context that Ghosh celebrates. To take just a couple of examples that Goitein's work provides for us, we can point to the religious reforms that Abraham Maimonides (son of the celebrated philosopher Moses Maimonides) attempted to introduce among Egyptian Jewry. Clearly influenced by Muslim practices around him, Maimonides, by virtue of his position as the *nagid* or the head of the Egyptian Jewry, insisted on introducing the practice of worship by prostration. But, rather than presenting this reform, along with the corollary emulation of the more solemn and intense character of Muslim worship, as matters of syncretism, he underlined instead their pure, authentic origins. These rites, Maimonides claimed, had originally been Jewish but had been forgotten through history. It was hoary, if buried, Jewish custom that he claimed to resuscitate and not any borrowing from Islam. Maimonides' followers were, however, unconvinced, and Goitein tells us that they even brought the case against what they saw as the clear Islamicization of Judaism before, ironically enough, the Islamic head of state.[35] Another dramatic example of the fissures between the syncretic and the antisyncretic is vividly presented in a letter that Goitein includes in one of the later volumes of his magnum opus.[36] The story in question is of Basir the bell maker, a Jewish family man who had taken of late to worshiping with the Sufis. Frustrated with his turn to asceticism, Basir's wife wrote a letter to the nagid, asking for an intervention on her behalf. I quote from the letter: "The maidservant, the wife of Basir, the bell maker, kisses the ground and submits that she has on her neck three children because her husband has become completely infatuated with [life on] the mountain with al-Kurani, *in vain and to no purpose, a place where there is no Torah, no prayer and no mention of God's name in truth.* He goes up the mountain and mingles with the mendicants, although these have only the semblance and not the essence of religion. The maidservant is afraid that there may be some *bad man who may induce her husband to forsake the Jewish faith, taking with him the three children.*"[37] In case the letter is not sufficiently self-explanatory, Goitein's gloss on it speaks eloquently to the limits of the syncretic in this world. Thus, he suggests, supererogatory worship is acceptable as long as it does not interfere with the core religious practices of one's faith.[38] The syncretic may be tolerated, but it must not be allowed to erode the power of the pure.[39]

To return, then, to the modern world and to the tomb of Abu-Hasira, we must ask: Who here is resisting whom? Just who are the so-called enforcers of History? In Ghosh's economy of popular syncretism, it is clear that the police officers are meant to represent the repressive apparatus of the modern nation-state. It is in defiance of these state actors, these "enforcers of History," that the shrine stands as a testimony to popular will. Notice that in this account it is the shrine itself that does the resisting. Much as in the case of the statue of the *bhuta* in the temple, it is the spirits of the past—whether those of Abu-Hasira or Bobbariya—that "revenge" themselves on the present. The nostalgia axiomatic of popular religiosity puts under erasure the agency of contemporary worshipers. In so doing it risks a misrecognition both of the role of the state and of the popular will, which, as the following news report from December 2000 suggests, actually ended up playing roles exactly opposite to those that Ghosh's *In an Antique Land* casts for them. I quote the report here in full:

> CAIRO—An Egyptian village has cancelled the festival of a Jewish saint attended annually by many Israelis, after protests by local people sympathetic to the Palestinian uprising. The Council of Demito village in the Delta province of Behira said it made the last-minute decision on Sunday after an outcry in the community. There have been calls to cancel the Moulid of Abu Hasira festival permanently. Local member of parliament Emad al-Sayyed had submitted a request to the People's assembly to have the festival called off because of public anger over Israeli "aggression" against Palestinians. Israeli-Palestinian violence in the last three months has killed at least 343 people, most of them Palestinian. The MP added that alcohol, dancing and singing at the festival offended the conservative mores of the mostly Muslim area. The Moulid of Abu Hasira, which had been due to begin on Tuesday, lasts eight days and celebrates the birth of a Moroccan Jew who lived and died in the village. There is no Jewish community in the area, and the festival has been organized by overseas Jewish groups with official Egyptian permission since Egypt signed a peace treaty with Israel in 1979. Jews from all over the world, particularly Israel, flock to the small village to visit his shrine.[40]

While the curt, almost clinical quality of this report as well as its reference to a conflict that has by now claimed many more lives (on both sides)—is foreboding, the fact worthy of note is that here the enforcers of History are allegedly the people themselves and not the state. Furthermore, this incorporation of the Mowlid of Abu-Hasira into a popular politics is quite explicit in articulating itself as resisting *both* the foreign pilgrims *and* the indigenous nation-state. That is why "protests" are necessary in the first place. The extra security at the tomb that Ghosh experienced about ten years before these later protests is better understood as both a response to, and a further provocation of, the struggle between an increasingly Islamicized populace and a decreasingly credible state. Those of us who have followed Ghosh's own presentation of Ustaz Sabry and his version of an Islamist modernity would be right to look for him and his friends among the protesters. It may not be a version of modernity that those of us who style ourselves as secular intellectuals may want to follow. But it seems necessary to be able to account for it and to recognize that the "popular" may not always generate forms of resistance that are palatable to a secular disposition, just as state repression, intolerable as it may be, in fact could end up upholding a multireligious, noncommunitarian society.

THE LIBERAL IMAGINARY

It is, I suggest, precisely at those moments when it relaxes its historicist rigor and begins to pursue a romance with a pre-Western world that Ghosh's narrative exhibits a preference for a poetic imagination over a historical one. I will ultimately defend this choice in my discussion of Ghosh's creative use of nostalgia, but it must also be noted here that for Ghosh's project to work, it must flatten out the micropolitics of the world before what he sees as the intrusive arrival of the Western powers. Much of my discussion of Ghosh's text in what follows will attempt to trouble this erasure, particularly with regard to the treatment of slavery, but at this point it must be acknowledged that Ghosh's metonymic use of tolerant, Fatimid Egypt belies other potential stories that are less tolerant but also set before the arrival of the dreaded West.[41] To recognize this is also to recognize that, despite its universalist—or at least anticommunitarian—appeal, Ghosh's vision of a multicultural Levant may be seen to participate—perhaps unwittingly—in a more contemporary polarizing politics.

In a seminal article, "Islam and the Jews: Myth, Counter-Myth, History," Mark Cohen suggests that discussions of the historical relationship between Jews and Muslims have become increasingly politically charged today.[42] The question "How have Jews fared in the Islamic world in medieval and modern times?" has sparked a great deal of debate, with some answers positing an interfaith utopia and others suggesting that Islamic treatment of Jews throughout history has been relentlessly persecutory. The "myth" of interfaith utopia, suggests Cohen, was first propagated by Jewish writers in the nineteenth century who, themselves frustrated by the anti-Semitism of the European world, turned to an alternative space of history in which Judaism was treated with respect and Jews were accepted as friends. This version of an interfaith utopia, suggests Cohen, was later appropriated by those who were sympathetic to the plight of modern Palestinians and critical of

Zionism and the State of Israel. In turn, there arose a "countermyth" that presented Jewish-Islamic history as one of continued conflict and emphasized the persecution of Jews by Muslims. This "countermyth" was explicitly rooted in a desire to argue for the legitimacy of the State of Israel and the cause of Zionism. Bemoaning the excesses of both myths, Cohen argues for a more balanced account that he calls history itself. Such a history would show that the fate of Jews in Islamic lands was contingent upon several factors, including the state of the economy at any given time, the personal disposition of the individual ruler in question, the vulnerability of the Islamic state in light of attacks from outside, and other factors that are of more material significance than religious doctrines and ideologies themselves.

To suggest this, then, is to suggest, along with Bernard Lewis, that the problem with a generalizable claim about Jews under Muslim rule is, in the absence of either historical, geographical, or what I will call performative specificity, that either version—both Cohen's "myth" and "countermyth"—can be persuasively argued.[43] It is always possible to compare the worst historical moments in one cultural frame with the best moments in another or to ignore the divergences between the doctrines and the actual practices of two religions so that one appears to be more favorable than the other. It makes more sense, therefore, to be nominalist in one's evaluation of the historical record, and it is such a nominalism that underwrites the scholarly work of Cohen, Lewis, and Goitein as well. Based on their work, much of what we know about the world of Ben Yiju does indeed suggest that Jewish traders in Cairo in the twelfth century experienced life under one of the most tolerant Islamic regimes. Goitein suggests that, while they were certainly not regarded as equals by their Muslim neighbors, Jews were allowed to practice their own faith, to live in religiously mixed neighborhoods (rather than ghettos), to pursue occupations of their own choosing, and to abide by a juridical code derived from and executed by their own religious authorities.[44] Practices that were prevalent at other times and places in Islamic and Christian history—such as the requirement that Jews wear specially marked clothes—were, according to Goitein, much more relaxed or nonexistent during Ben Yiju's times, and interfaith business relations were the norm rather than the exception. While none of this tolerance prevented occasional suspicion of those who were not believers of one's own religion, such suspicion seems to have affected both Jews and Muslims. Jews did, however, have to pay a special poll tax in exchange for their protected status as a religious minority, but, ironically, it may have been precisely this tax and its economic importance to Muslim rulers that underwrote the religious tolerance of the state. Indeed, economic calculations were also at work when later, in 1198, an overzealous ruler established himself in Yemen and forced the mass conversion of local Jews. We learn, however, from a letter in the Cairo Geniza that, when foreign Jewish traders called at the port of Aden, the ruler declared, "'No foreigner should be molested.' He ordered that everyone should pay a third of the poll tax. We disbursed this and he dismissed us graciously, thank God."[45] In his annotations to the letter, Goitein points out that the imposition of the one-third poll tax was itself unlawful, since non-Muslims were supposed to be taxed only in their domicile. But the incident shows not only that the traders were content to buy their freedom for this amount, but, more significantly, that the ruler recognized the economic importance of the traders and that no amount of religious conviction would let him forgo the material benefits they provided. Persecuting the traders would have been tantamount to eating the goose that laid the golden eggs, and thus the traders were perhaps economically exploited but otherwise left alone.[46]

Religious tolerance is seen as intimately related to the economic interests of the state, and this vision deeply informs the work of both Goitein and Ghosh. The most explicit admission of this orientation occurs in the preface to the second volume of Goitein's *A Mediterranean Society*. Here, in an autobiographical aside on his ongoing research on the geniza documents, Goitein writes,

> I believe I would have missed many aspects of the Geniza documents had I not been granted the opportunity of observing the American scene for many years. Authoritarian Germany, where I spent my childhood and youth, and the Jewish society in Palestine and later Israel, with its socialist, welfare and protectionist tendencies, which I saw most of my working life, were utterly different from the Geniza society, which was loosely organized and competitive in every respect. This vigorous free-enterprise society of the United States, which is not without petty jealousies and cheap public honors, its endless fund-raising campaigns and all that goes with them, its general involvement in public affairs and deep concern (or lip-service as the case may be) for the underdog—all proved to be extremely instructive. *We do not wear turbans here; but, while reading many a Geniza document one feels quite at home.*[47]

In Goitein's construction what binds contemporary American society with the world of the Cairo Geniza is precisely the importance of the free market and a minimalist state.[48] Germany and Palestine/Israel fail because the state is too authoritarian in one case and too socialist and welfare-oriented in the other.

This romance with free-market economics and the minimalist state is an undercurrent throughout much of Goitein's work.[49] He writes at one point that, "in many respects, the area resembled a free-trade community. The treatment of foreigners, as a rule, was remarkably liberal." And again, "the machinery of the state was relatively loose in those days, that is, the technique of making life unbearable was not yet as perfected as it is in our own days." But to talk of a minimalist state is by no means to talk of a weak one. The power of the state is still necessary to ensure the smooth functioning of the free-market economy. The state as protector of private property, including of course its own interests, is not to be undermined. "Officially appointed spies and the secret police saw to it that visitors from foreign countries did not evade their customs duties and did not engage in any activity detrimental to the state. Quarrels between individuals and community strife often invoked the intervention of the governments or their local officials. Thus, it was not so much the looseness of the machinery of the state as positive factors that contributed to the amazing degree of the freedom of movement and to the comparatively close unity of the Mediterranean world."[50]

Despite Ghosh's own critique of the West, particularly its imperialist history, *In an Antique Land* shares with Goitein's work an uncanny disposition in favor of free-market economics and the market-oriented state. Its overwhelming acceptance of the proposition that multiculturalism would follow if only the market were left to work on its own draws ultimately on a liberal imagination. As I will argue in the chapters that follow, such an imagination, with its preference for unhindered commerce and limited state intervention, is also central to many of the twentieth-century Indian travelers and traders in East Africa. So, for instance, one of the key complaints of the Parsi traveler Sorabji Darookhanawala is that the colonial state in Kenya, rather than fostering economic growth and trade, suppresses it in the interests of protecting the highlands as a whites-only area. Darookhanawala argues for more trade and suggests that, because of their long commercial presence in East Africa, Indians might be better positioned to complete what he sees as the incomplete project of modernity undertaken by the British colonial state. Nanji Kalidas Mehta, likewise, turns in his autobiography to figuring commerce between Indians and Africans as a romance, an allegedly noncoercive exchange that is distinct from the political coercion of the colonial state. For their part, J. K. Chande and Al Noor Kassum, both Tanzanian Asians who were recruited by President Nyerere to help in the project of nation building after independence, have to balance their allegiance to the political liberalism and idealism of their leader, on the one hand, and the realities of a socialist state economic policy that is set to curtail private ownership and free trade, on the other. This unease with state socialism and corollary sympathies not only for commerce but also for more democratic forms of governance is also a fundamental marker of M. G. Vassanji's *The Gunny Sack.*

In the liberal imagination the critical role of the state in guarding the interests of market flows ensures, as did the commerce clause in the early jurisprudence of the United States, that tolerance itself becomes an interest of the state.[51] Yet it goes without saying that nothing can be tolerated that might threaten the economic interests of the state. The episode in Ghosh's narrative that best speaks to this is the account of the raid on Aden by pirates from the island of Kish (Qais).[52] The heroes of this event are the Adenese soldiers who protect not only their own territory from the incursions of the attackers but also, and more importantly in Ghosh's reckoning, the incoming ships of the wealthy merchant Ramishr of Siraf. Order is restored, trade and private property protected, and the "villains of the piece" (257), the pirates from Qais, are soundly defeated and forced to retreat. This version of the story is entirely consistent with the sympathies of the trader Madmun, whose letter to his business friend and partner Ben Yiju provides Ghosh with much of the eyewitness flavor of the event. But Ghosh makes use of poetic license to go further, imagining a drunken Bomma (who, we have been told by Madmun, has just demanded more money than the allowance allocated to him by Ben Yiju) cheering the Adenese soldiers into battle. To imagine someone who was legally a slave, rebelling against what he perceived to be an inadequate allowance from his master, as nevertheless simultaneously being in complete sympathy with the interests of his master is to make a strong statement indeed about the role of affective relations within the institution of slavery.

There is a second aspect to this episode that is no less significant. Despite his acknowledgment that the raid was carried out by sailors who were allied to the king of Qais, Ghosh chooses to downplay the political significance of the attack. Foregrounding its piratical nature rather than its interstate political attributes allows Ghosh to read it as continuous with the numerous activities of pirates throughout the Indian Ocean. Such activities, writes Ghosh, were, even at their worst, "a nuisance rather than a serious threat to commerce, and neither (the rulers of Qais) nor any of the powers of the Indian Ocean, no matter how large or well-armed, ever tried to gain control of the seas or to take over the trade routes by force" (257). It is important for Ghosh to establish piracy as a nuisance rather than a serious threat since one of the central claims he wants to make is that it is only with the arrival of the Portuguese in 1498 that violence enters the Indian Ocean trade. It was then that the peaceful traditions of commerce were disrupted by a player who introduced armed navies to take control of the trade. "Unable to compete in the Indian Ocean trade by purely commercial means, the Europeans were bent on taking control of it by aggression, pure and distilled, by unleashing violence on a scale unprecedented on those shores. . . . As always, the determination of a small united band of soldiers triumphed easily over the rich confusions that accompany a culture of accommodation and compromise" (288). Yet Ghosh's contention that intrusion by force of arms arrived only with Europeans seems somewhat questionable given the little we do know about the Indian Ocean trade in this period. For instance, we know there was a significant decrease in trade in the Persian Gulf after the Fatimid ascendancy in Egypt and the decline of the Abbasid powers in Baghdad in the early eleventh century. The Indian Ocean spice trade was now centered on Egypt and the Red Sea, resulting in the rise of Aden as a competing and increasingly prosperous center of trade.[53] Nestled in the Persian Gulf, the rulers of the island of Qais, who Goitein tells us were described by the geographer Yakut as the "*overlord(s)* of that whole sea and as ruler(s) of Oman," were understandably disturbed by their loss of commercial power to the newly prosperous port city in the Red Sea.[54] The raid on Aden is properly understood in the context of this history not as the opportunistic thievery of a group of pirates but rather as an alliance of political and economic forces of resistance.[55]

While Ghosh's anticolonial narrative bears emotional freight, a more layered understanding of the history of the Indian Ocean trade suggests that the balance of tolerance and intolerance is not so easily established. In addition to the ties between the state and commerce that we find between the rulers of Qais and the pirates of Aden, we note that from time to time rulers with an interest in the trade would do what they could to retain control of it. Thus, writes K. N. Chaudhuri, under the Ayyubid as well as the Mamluk rulers of Egypt (1170–1517), care was taken to prevent the excessive entry of Frankish merchants into the trade, and "it seems that the Egyptian government exercised its sovereignty and control over the Red Sea and the Indian Ocean commerce, not by constructing strong naval fleets, but by instituting a system of safe-conduct passes."[56] These safe conduct passes may well be the precursors of the *cartazes* later issued by the Portuguese as a form of toll for uninterrupted commerce.[57] And, although European arms played an important role in raising cross-cultural barriers in Indian Ocean commerce, cultural factors were always historically at play. "Anti-Jewish propaganda grew under the Fatimids' successors, the Ayyubids and the Almohids," writes Andre Wink, "reaching a climax in the thirteenth century, when Mediterranean unity had been lost entirely, and the Mamluks of Egypt imposed discriminatory laws which caused a further deterioration of the position of the Jews. Egypt, after the fall of Constantinople in 1204, virtually monopolized the Indian transit trade but the Jews were expelled from this trade and an association of Arab traders known as the *karimi* took over."[58] It may be true, as Ghosh suggests, that before the arrival of the Europeans no political power in the Indian Ocean ultimately succeeded in dictating the terms of trade through sheer force, but it was not for lack of trying.[59]

If Ghosh downplays the internal rivalries between various rulers on the Indian Ocean stage, it is no less interesting to note a similar dismissal on his part of any real tensions and conflict within the African frame. I refer in particular to the brief appearance in the book of the "tribes" around the port city of Aidhab in present-day Sudan. Ghosh tells us in his notes that the people in question were members of "one of the Beja tribes of Sudan and southern Egypt who are referred to frequently by medieval Arab geographers and travelers" (371). To the Arab travelers and the merchants of whom Ghosh writes these seminomadic desert peoples, characterized by their public nudity, were a "breed of no regard" (quoting Ibn Jubair, 371). The Beja's attitude toward these travelers was one of "suspicion bordering on hostility," and this too, Ghosh's tone suggests, is to be seen as a nuisance rather like that posed by the Indian Ocean pirates. Once again, a closer look at history might indicate that this hostility was not necessarily the simple response of a closed primitive society, but rather the result of a longer period of contact. For instance, we learn from A. Paul's *A History of the Beja Tribes of the Sudan* that contact between Arabs from the north and the indigenous Beja had, by the time of Ben Yiju's travels, already been taking place for several centuries, with the Beja providing the northerners with slaves and camels, two important commodities in the growth of their empires and economies.[60] In addition, writes Paul, the Beja resistance to the northerners increased in the tenth and eleventh centuries in reaction to the exploitative conditions by which their labor and natural resources were acquired. "The mines were worked entirely by slave labor, by methods no better than those employed by the Pharaohs and the Ptolemies, and if anything the exploitation was harsher and more thorough. Emeralds appear to have been valued more highly than gold, and the output must have been considerable since, although the caliphs attempted repeatedly to increase their direct control of the mines but had to be content with a tithe of a third, or even as little as a fifth of the output, yet the wealth of the Fatimids and of their successors was prodigious."[61] Beja suspicion, bordering on hostility, would make sense in this context.

If, in the interests of portraying a harmonious twelfth-century Indian Ocean world, Beja slavery is left out of the narrative, a similar silence surrounds the more contemporary references to Zar rituals in the text. In the interests of a purer practice of Islam, Ustad Sabry and other teachers, we are told, have united villagers against a man "who was known to perform exorcism rituals for women, secret Ethiopian rites called the Zar" (146). This brief reference is supplemented by no additional commentary on Ghosh's part in the notes. What Ghosh fails to note is that this process of purifying Islam is also, in this case, a process of de-Africanizing it. Research on the Zar suggests that it came to Egypt sometime in the eighteenth century (although this date is speculative), carried there by black slaves from Ethiopia. The ritual itself is a form of spirit possession that is common across the continent. Once again, as in the case of connections with pre-Islamic Egypt, Ghosh does not adequately foreground connections, in this case, with more contemporary black Africa. While privileging cross-oceanic syncretisms and connections, Ghosh's text risks erasing the cross-continental ones.[62]

CAPITALISM AND SLAVERY

The importance of slave labor in the commercial rise of the Middle East is underscored by Goitein in his discussion of what he calls the bourgeois revolution of the eighth and ninth centuries. The Arab conquests in North Africa resulted not only in the general movement of people across wider territories but, argues Goitein, also in the creation of large reserves of cheap and free labor. The new towns being built by the conquerors increased demand for consumer goods, thus stimulating trade. Military service was increasingly being performed by a corps of slaves, and, with government bureaucratic service being treated with some skepticism by the pious, commercial activity began to resonate with religious approval and sanction. Both Muslims and Jews in Fatimid Egypt, hence, participated in the trade that resulted from this socioeconomic upheaval.[63]

If the institution of slavery was one of the conditions of possibility for this "bourgeois revolution," its status as a lived "structure of feeling" is somewhat open to debate.[64] Eager to distance slavery in the Arab world from the plantation slavery of the Americas, scholars have repeatedly noted religious edicts in both Islam and Judaism on the humane treatment of slaves. Thus, for instance, both religions considered the manumission of a slave virtuous and an honorable deed on the part of the owner. Likewise, there were restrictions on the degree to which slaves could be worked, with specific proscriptions against their ill-treatment. The fact that some slaves were recruited into military service and indeed could rise considerably in rank has led scholars to emphasize the radical distinctions between slavery in the Middle East and that across the Atlantic.[65] Ghosh himself is alert to the distinctions and warns the reader that "the terms under which Bomma entered Ben Yiju's service were probably entirely different from those suggested by the word 'slavery' today: their arrangement was probably more that of patron and client than master and slave, as that relationship is now understood" (259).[66] Ghosh goes on to note that slaves in this context could find themselves in positions with greater privilege than the poor free folk and could "generally be sure of obtaining manumission" (260).

While the cautionary note distinguishing transatlantic slavery from Arab forms is essential, it risks coming across as an apology. Ghosh's own nostalgic narrative risks such a sanitized view of slavery, and it does so especially when it seeks to link the ideology of servitude to a religious foundation. Slavery in the world of Ben Yiju and Bomma, suggests Ghosh, is a "spiritual metaphor" (260), a man's enslavement to God finding itself a worldly manifestation in a slave's devotion to his master. This Sufi-inspired vision was articulated through poetry in which "it was slavery that was the paradoxical embodiment of personal freedom; the image that represented the very notion of relationship, of human bonds, as well as the possibility of their transcendence" (261). The implication here is that if we fail to see this paradox, we do so because we approach it with a post-Enlightenment, Eurocentric understanding of freedom. To authorize his claims, Ghosh refers the reader to Franz Rosenthal's much cited book *The Muslim Concept of Freedom Prior to the Nineteenth Century*, but a close reading of this source suggests that, despite the philosophical and poetic links between enslavement to God and enslavement to man, human bondage remained, nevertheless,

a shameful prospect. Thus, writes Rosenthal, "the idea of slavery, in meta-
phorical usage, stood for the most loathsome condition of mankind, to be
avoided at all costs." Furthermore, he notes, in refutation of the "privileged
status" argument, that "regardless of their position and the social advantages
derived from it, the unfree status of individuals was always considered a
personal disgrace. And it should be noted that it is often the point of stories
showing slaves in a good light that good things could be found even in the
persons of lowly slaves."[67]

Orlando Patterson has persuasively argued that what characterizes slavery in almost all contexts is the "social death" of the slave and the denial of
the slave's honor. In this sense, whether or not slaves could look forward
to their manumission and whether or not they occupied positions of considerable power, it is still the case that they were acting not as free agents
but always on behalf of their masters.[68] We might ultimately never know
exactly how slaves in the Arab world incorporated the ideologies of their
times, but we do know that there were slave rebellions, the most famous
one occurring in Iraq in the ninth century.[69] Slaves sought their freedom
and often escaped from their masters. And, while Ghosh portrays an ami-
cable relationship between Bomma and Ben Yiju, even a quick look at the
strictures on the treatment of "heathen" slaves that Abraham Maimonides
laid down for his coreligionists raises an ugly side. I quote only two: "8. If
the master smites the eye of the slave and diminishes its vision, or his tooth
and it becomes loose, then we hold as follows: if the slave can still use them
he does not become free; if not, he becomes free; 9. If his eye is dim and its
vision poor, or if his tooth is loose and the master smites him and knocks out
his loose tooth or blinds his dim eye, then we hold as follows: if he could use
it even to the smallest degree heretofore he goes out free; if not, he does not
go out free."[70] That such strictures were necessary speaks volumes about the
harsher aspects of human bondage.

Even if such violence was the exception, the systemic inequities between
masters and slaves suggest that exploitation was not entirely absent from
either the twelfth-century commercial world that Ghosh depicts or, despite
the mythological charters later drawn up, in the Indian Ocean commerce
centuries thereafter. At one point Ghosh notes that the amount of money
Bomma spent shopping for his master on one of his trips to Aden would
have "paid the wages of a mason or builder for more than two and a half
years" (255–56). The amount of money circulating in the Indian Ocean
trade was enormous compared to the costs of labor. Without involving ourselves in debates over whether or not this society could be characterized as

engaging in a "slave mode of production," we can easily establish that surplus value was being generated not only through trade but also through the
manufacture of commodities. Thus, for instance, we remember that in addition to Bomma and Ashu, Ben Yiju also had a number of other Indian slaves
who worked in his bronze factory on the Malabar Coast. Since the Indian
Ocean slave trade was characterized by multidirectional movements, just as
Africans would be captured and sold in foreign lands, Indians would also be
brought over as slaves to the African continent. As we will see in later chapters, other Indians in Africa, notably in nineteenth-century Zanzibar, would
themselves become slave owners and financiers of the slave trade. If we may
characterize these relationships as economic exploitation, for female slaves
the possibility of sexual exploitation was never far behind. Like Zanzibar
and the East African coast in later centuries, India, in Ben Yiju's time, suggests Ghosh, "bore a reputation as a place notable for the ease of its sexual
relations" (228) where concubinage was thought to be the norm rather than
the exception.

Perhaps the greatest insight into the problematic of slavery in the medieval world, and of Ghosh's creative handling of it, comes not from what
Ghosh writes but from what he leaves out. Since he was a meticulous student of Goitein's oeuvre, the story I refer to could not have escaped Ghosh's
notice. Its absence from *In an Antique Land* supports the basic lesson of
deconstructive critique—that a text's silences may often say more than its
utterances. The story is that of the Indian slave Safi and his protestations
about the fate of a young Indian slave girl who was abandoned by her master on the coast of Somalia. Safi, Goitein tells us, was the business agent
and legal slave of the head of the Jewish high council in Egypt. As such
he would have commanded a certain amount of authority by virtue of his
connection with the master. Yet his fate in this particular episode is of some
interest to us in understanding the precarious nature of a slave's social status. I quote in full Goitein's telling of the story:

> In December, 1144, there arrived among the Jewish merchants of Egypt and the
> Maghreb returning from India, Safi, "the pure, sincere," the slave and agent of
> the head of the Jewish academy in Old Cairo, and one Ibn Jamahir, a notable,
> well known to us as a troublemaker from other papers relevant to the India trade.
> Safi insulted the notable in the presence of Muslim fellow merchants, accusing
> him of having disposed of a slave girl, after having had a child by her, in Berbera
> on the African coast. Ibn Jumahir filed a complaint of slander against him with
> the governor of the town. The governor, well aware of the special status of Safi,

tried to consult the Jewish merchants staying in town, most of whom, however, disregarded his invitation. After Ibn Jumahir's Muslim friends had given witness, the governor ordered Safi to be flogged. "What!" exclaimed Safi, "I, the ghulam of the Head of the Academy, should be flogged?" His protest was of no avail, for he was flogged and jailed. One of the Jewish merchants from the Maghreb intervened, and Safi was set free—"not without loss of money," whether for himself or his liberator, is not stated.[71]

This story is also about two Indian slaves—one male and the other female. But it is one that speaks not to the romance of intercultural bonding but to the unjust nature of human bondage. No matter how privileged a slave might seem, this story tells us, he was always susceptible to "social death."[72] And no matter how romantic an alliance between the Jewish traveler Ben Yiju and the Nair woman Ashu (or, looking forward to Vassanji's text, between the Indian Dhanji Govindji and the Swahili Taratibu) might appear to the modern imagination, these relationships were simultaneously stories of sexual exploitation and abandonment.[73] While the records give no clear indication of what happened to Ashu, Ghosh notes, "There are many conceivable endings to Ben Yiju's story and if the most pleasing amongst them is one which has him returning to Ashu, in the Malabar, the most likely, on the other hand, is a version in which he dies in Egypt, soon after his daughter's wedding, and is buried somewhere in the vicinity of Fustat" (328).

I suggested earlier that Bomma's status as the lowest of the low is an enabling fiction for Ghosh. Bomma, Ghosh told us in his prologue, is not one of those for whom we can imagine "properly human, individual, existences" (17). He is not one of the "literate and the consequential, the wazirs and the sultans, the chroniclers and the priests—the people who had the power to inscribe themselves physically upon time" (17). If, as sympathetic readers, we can celebrate Ghosh's nostalgic reconstruction of the character of Bomma, we must do so with the knowledge that here too the melancholic is under erasure. The abandoned concubine, defended in her time by her fellow traveler Safi, has yet to find a modern spokesperson.[74]

Notwithstanding such silences, and despite its nostalgic renditioning of a pre-European past, *In an Antique Land* challenges us to think beyond both the generic conventions of academic disciplines and the limitations of narrowly nation-centered histories. The contrapuntal treatment of twelfth-century travelers and Ghosh's own interlocutors allows for consideration of the continuities and disjunctures in the experiences of those earlier travelers and the more recent ones who have to cope with the demands of nation-states that attempt to maintain a nonaligned politics yet get pulled into the politics of the cold war. While Ghosh's narrative itself risks erasing the linkages between Egypt and the rest of sub-Saharan Africa, its attempt to write a cross-regional history opens the possibility of articulating shared experiences not only across the ocean but also across the larger region of North and East Africa. In the chapters that follow I draw inspiration from Ghosh's text and move to a consideration of some aspects of the Asian experience in East Africa. My interest is in drawing attention to texts and lives that have hitherto been relatively understudied, but yield significant insight into the nature of cross-ethnic alliances and their potential failures.

3. POST-MANICHAEAN AESTHETICS

Asian Texts and Lives

A Banian is a very prominent and, I may add, a very picturesque person wherever found upon the east coast. He is a wonderfully sharp, shrewd, clever fellow, ever keeping an eye open for the main chance and grasping at whatever he sees, or fancies he sees it. He grasps at shadows often enough, but he had rather do this a thousand times than miss one real chance. See him at his books, and you see a man lost to all the world. Tailor-fashion he sits upon his low couch—a mattress spread upon the ground—and surrounded by a row of cash and other boxes; his only garments a thin cloth about his loins and a red peaked cap upon his head; a heavy moustache, twisted into points in a Napoleonic fashion, and coloured green, upon his lip; spectacles upon his nose; a paper in one hand and a reed-pen in another; his head bent forward, his eyes peering through his glasses at the paper below, he looks the personification of abstraction; he might be an alchemist on the verge of discovering the philosopher's stone, or a divine about to seize upon the origin of moral evil. This man is one of the great powers in Eastern Africa.
    —*Charles New*, Life, Wanderings and Labours in Eastern Africa

This image of the Indian (and more particularly the *banian*) as a crafty and shrewd opportunist in the passage from Charles New's *Life, Wanderings and Labours in Eastern Africa* is in keeping with a long tradition of English discourse on that figure. Recall the famous speech in 1788 by Edmund Burke in the impeachment of Warren Hastings, in which Burke declares not the

Englishman but "the black *banian*, that is the master."[1] Burke suggests that the *banian* outsmarts the newly arrived young and inexperienced English officer in India, secures his employment, and then proceeds to use this position to tyrannize both his fellow subjects as well as the young officer. The Englishman, in Burke's scenario, is left to be no more than a "melancholy spectator" witnessing the corruption but unable to stop it. Almost a century later, traveling to East Africa, Charles New expresses a similar note. In the chapter from which the epigraph to this chapter is taken, New sounds a note of helplessness: echoing David Livingstone's claim that Indians along with Arabs were participants in the East African slave trade, New regretfully notes that no matter how much the British intervene, the slave trade is not easily curtailed. To this particular "melancholic spectator" in East Africa, the *banian* appears "picturesque," that is, neither sublime nor beautiful but rather something naturalized into the larger canvas of the East African landscape. Much like a predatory animal, the *banian* is alert to any shadow that may be cast by potential prey and he will strike a hunt at every opportunity. But, if he is instinctual like a beast of prey, New's *banian* is also speculative, "a personification of abstraction." Here, the mystical elements of magic and divinity long associated with an Oriental metaphysics intervene to further enhance the *banian*'s mastery over his environment.

The figure of the Indian in East Africa in New's 1874 account is at once one of awe and one of danger. Such an ambivalent reading of the Indian was also registered by Sir Bartle Frere who, sent to Zanzibar in 1873 to investigate and help curtail the slave trade, was surprised to find the economic prowess of the Indian traders and noted that "throughout the Zanzibar coastline . . . all banking and mortgage business passes through Indian hands. Hardly a loan can be negotiated, a mortgage effected, or a bill cashed without Indian agency."[2] A year before Frere's visit, Richard Burton, in 1872, had published his two-volume work *Zanzibar: City, Island and Coast*, where he mentioned not only the long-standing presence of Indians in Zanzibar but also their trading reach in areas such as Mozambique, Madagascar, and the Comoro Islands.[3] Burton portrayed the Indian community as a tightly knit group of individuals who were protected by the Arab sultan, and he described at some length the habits and lifestyles of the various Indian communities, such as the Parsees; the Hindu Bhattias, Brahmins, Wanis, Lohars, and Khattris; and the Muslim Bohras, Menons, Khojas, and Ismailis.[4] In 1869, three years before the publication of Burton's majestic volumes, Cope Devereux, an English naval officer, noted the presence of about six thousand "natives of India, the wealthiest, the most persevering, energetic and trustworthy of the whole population."[5] Devereux suggested that "if it were not for these people, the trade of Zanzibar would entirely fail. Their system of credit and faith in one another is extraordinary; distance and time being little thought of. They take bills on their countrymen living at Bagdad and other distant places. They trade principally in ivory, gum copal and cloves, the former being brought from the interior of Africa in exchange for American cotton, Venetian beads and brass wire."[6]

Noting such Indian initiative and enterprise in East Africa, some late nineteenth-century British administrators like Sir Harry Johnston and Frederick Lugard enthusiastically called for further Indian immigration to East Africa. Citing the long history of what he called "The Asiatic Colonization of East Africa" Johnston advocated for the establishment of an Indian agricultural colony, an "America for the Hindu" that would become, as he put it in a speech delivered to the Royal Society of the Arts in London on January 25, 1889, "the granary, the market for the manufactures and the home for the overflow populations of British India."[7] Echoing this sentiment, Frederick Lugard wrote, "It is not as imported Coolie labour that I advocate the introduction of the Indian, but as a colonist and settler."[8] Lugard's claim was based, interestingly, on the as-yet-unnamed idea of the dual mandate — the idea that British colonialism was based on both economic gain and on the civilizing mission.[9] Thus, wrote Lugard, the Indian in East Africa would serve a role beneficial to the African. "The African, too, is extremely imitative. The presence in his midst of a fully clothed people would be to him an example of decency which he would speedily imitate. His wants would become identical with theirs, and thus, while his status was improved, and a new encouragement given to trade, he would be compelled to exert himself and to labour in order to supply those wants. Moreover, the methods of agriculture, the simple instruments of the Indian ryot, the use of the bullock, the sinking of wells, the system of irrigation and the manuring of soil &c. &c. would soon be imitated by the African and the produce of his land would thus be vastly multiplied."[10] The Indian in Lugard's scenario would serve not only as a role model for the "uplifting" of the African but would furthermore encourage the African to enter the labor force. Having developed suitable agricultural methods in India, the Indian would emerge as a "teacher" for the African agriculturalist.

The Indian colony proposed by Johnston and Lugard was not to materialize in the near future, even though such proposals were to reappear toward the end of the First World War when officials such as Theodore Morison and some Indians such as the Aga Khan were to advocate for an Indian

colony in the territories formerly occupied by Germany.[11] The positive tone
in which Winston Churchill described the Indian presence in East Africa
in his book of 1908, *My African Journey*, was in keeping with the larger narrative of British Indians as it was then articulated by British colonial officers,
many of whom, like Lugard, had had extensive experience with Indians in
British colonial India. But what Churchill witnessed in the "Highlands of
East Africa" was not appreciation of Indian enterprise but rather growing
resistance bordering on hostility toward Indians on the part of the white
settlers. Indeed, Churchill noted that, at the turn of the century, settler
colonialism in Kenya exhibited less concern with the resistance of the local
African and more with that of the fellow Indian settler. "For observe it is not
against the black aboriginal that the prejudices and interests of the white settler or trader are arrayed. . . . It is the brown man who is the rival."[12]

Weighing the competing claims of the white settlers and the Indian
migrants, Churchill suggests that there is room for both.[13] "The mighty continent of tropical Africa," writes Churchill, "lies open to the colonizing and
organizing capacities of the East."[14] The white settler, the Indian, and the
African all have their part to play in the development of the colony, as long
as certain policies, or, as Churchill puts it, "matters of practical administration" are followed.[15] Thus, while the Indian is to be rewarded for his past
and continued contribution to the British Empire by a relatively nonrestric-
tive immigration policy to parts of the empire such as East Africa where
there are no lower-class European populations, Indian migration to those
colonies that are populated by Europeans of a wider class range is to be curtailed. Furthermore, even when the Indian is to be received in East African
territories, he is to be encouraged to settle not in the highland areas, "which
promise the white man a home and a career," but rather in the "enormous
regions of tropical fertility to which he is naturally adapted."[16]

In retrospect, Churchill's position may be read as a careful compromise
between Indian demands for recognition and white settler demands for
exclusive landholding in the highland areas. But its reception among the
settlers and their allies was far from welcoming. Perhaps the most acerbic
attack came in the form of an article published in the *Empire Review* in
1910 by an author only identified as "Traveller." Arguing that the presence
of the Indian in Kenya had resulted in cities that are full of dirt and squalor,
the author further castigated the Indian as someone who is "exploiting the
native but doing him no good, teaching him, no doubt, how to trade and barter, but also the vices and trickery of the East, without making any attempt
to educate or elevate him."[17] Because of his willingness to live in meager

surroundings and have an austere lifestyle, the presence of the Indian in any capacity other than that of unskilled laborer will result in a competition with the white settler in which the latter will be squeezed out. Thus, wrote Traveller, "We can draw a line beyond which no Asiatic can come into a white colony, by allowing him no political or commercial rights; grant him no licenses for any trade or profession, no title to land nor lease of land or house except to live in, and demand proof that he is employed as a labourer, and so on. With these restrictions he will do no harm, and occasionally he may be of much use."[18]

If Traveller's tone here seems to border on paranoia and hate, such anti-Asian rhetoric was not uncommon at the time. Indeed, even Sir Harry Johnston's early endorsement of the Indian presence in Africa in 1889 had been met with a challenge. One member of the audience had remarked that Johnston had not paid sufficient attention to the encroachment of Indian shopkeepers in Natal and the threat they posed to white settlers. Not convinced by the laissez-faire "let the best man win" position offered by Johnston in response, the interlocutor felt compelled to write in his position to the journal editor. In an echo of Thomas Macaulay's 1835 "Minute on Indian Education," Traveller retorted, "Ten Englishmen, members of the English speaking community, are of more value for the civilisation and advancement of Africa than one thousand Indians, speaking Cutchi or Guzarati [*sic*]."[19] Johnston's interlocutor was raising here not only the issue of a competition between brown and white traders but also, as was to be later articulated by General Smuts at the Imperial Conference in London in 1923, the specter of a competition between two civilizations—one of the East and the other of the West.[20] This notion of a civilizational competition was to recur not only in many of the debates and arguments of the first three decades of the twentieth century, but, as we saw in the encounter between the Imam and Amitav Ghosh, it continues to underwrite contemporary anxieties.

Increasingly agitated over the denial of rights that they, as British subjects, felt they ought to irrevocably have, Indians countered with a critique of their own. For instance, in an April 1921 letter written by Mangal Dass addressed to the acting chief native commissioner, O. F. Watkins, the Indian Association in Nairobi responded to allegations of Indian traders "cheating" Africans by challenging the very premises of the notion of "cheating." For one, they argued that it was historically not the Indian who cheated the African, but rather the European who "drank Eno's Fruit Salt with the object of impressing the natives with his ability to swallow boiling water, or tried to convince them of his supernatural powers with the aid of a gramophone."[21] But more importantly, it was not the Indianness of the Indian that was at issue, but rather something that was intrinsic to the nature of trade: "It is the essence of all trade to take advantage of the other man's needs or ignorance and where biased people call it cheating, the more reasonably inclined would term it the profits from the trader's enterprise." While the Indian Association would not condone any acts of deliberate fraud and cheating, the letter noted, it was not blind to the fact that such accusations came from a racially antagonistic settler community.[22] In another letter that was critical of the missionaries' collaboration with the settlers, the political leader M. A. Desai admonished the missionaries to "practice what you preach: is it too much to expect of you to preach and practice the 'Fatherhood of God and Brotherhood of human beings'?"[23] The letter, which referred to Jesus as an Asian, was published by the Indian newspaper *East African Chronicle* because its original recipient, the settler-run *East African Standard*, refused to publish it as blasphemous.

The responses of Mangal Dass and M. A. Desai encapsulate the two major foci of the debate between the white settlers and the Indians—the economic arguments and the cultural/religious/civilizational ones. Alert to both these aspects, C. F. Andrews, Mohandas Gandhi's trusted friend and collaborator, also turned the table on white settler accusations of the Indian exploitation of the African.[24] Reading the statements of the Economic Commission and the Petition of the Convention of Associations as the "most sinister sign of the times" (71), Andrews was scandalized after his visit to East Africa in 1919–20 by what he saw as the unholy alliance between settlers and missionaries. Pointing to the history of religious toleration on the part of the British Empire in colonies such as India, Andrews wrote that the insistence of the white settlers on an exclusively *Christian* civilization was "the strangest travesty on the part of the British Commonwealth that I have ever met in any part of the world, not even excluding that strange phenomenon which I found in the Boer States. For in the Transvaal, the issue was kept strictly on political lines, however harsh and crude. Here, religion has entered politics, and a combination of forces has resulted which lends itself all too readily to cant and hypocrisy" (53).

Having criticized the missionary complicity with settlers, Andrews turned next to the settlers, who, he alleged, had been the greatest exploiters of the African, taking away lands and compelling the "African to work on those lands for his master's profit" (72). By creating a system whereby the African laborer has been separated from his rural household, the European settler has been responsible for the disintegration of the African social order, and he has done so, wrote Andrews, with impunity.[25] The Indian, noted Andrews, has certainly not been beyond reproach for trading practices that may be unscrupulous and opportunistic, but he has not reduced the African into servitude as has the European settler. On the contrary, the Indian has taken on the African as an apprentice and "trained more African workmen than all the industrial and technical schools put together" (78). This sense of the Indian contribution, wrote Andrews, he had gathered, during his trips to East Africa, not from Indians, but from European employers. Unlike the landed settlers, most "practical men" in Kenya, suggested Andrews, welcome the Indian immigrants for their contribution to the workforce. There was no question of competition between the Indian and African in this expansive stage of colonial development: "The Indian artisan, who would do steady and regular work, and had the intelligence to train the native under him, was in great demand and could always earn money" (80). Andrews noted that the Indian was welcomed not only by those responsible for projects such as public works but also by the Africans he had met. "Before I left Uganda, Sir Apollo Kagwa and the Baganda Chief Justice handed me a document signed by themselves, on behalf of the 'Lukiko' stating that the Baganda desired the Indians to remain because they did good to the country. They also wished more Indians to come out" (82). This sentiment of the elders, wrote Andrews, was echoed by the young Baganda leaders: "One of the young Bagandas said to me at the end of my visit, 'We shall look more and more to India, in the future, to help us'" (82). Thus, Andrews concluded, the claim that the Indian has been more detrimental to the African than the European could not be persuasively made.[26]

Such potential collaboration between Africans and Indians was the cause of much concern among the settlers. In their memo on the case against the Indians, Lord Delamere and Kenneth Archer accused Indians of "stirring up disaffection amongst the native tribes."[27] They were referring in particular to the relationship between the Gikuyu leader Harry Thuku and his friends in the Indian community, particularly the secretary of the Indian Association, M. A. Desai. Of great concern to the settlers were the series of resolutions passed both by Indian leaders and by the East Africa Association led by Thuku in separate meetings on July 10, 1921. Indians proclaimed the convergence of African and Indian interests: "The Indians have never expressed their desire, or ambition to rule the Native or to gain supremacy over them and further the British Indians fully endorse and support the policy of the rights and privileges asked by them being extended alike to all subjects of the British Government including the indigenous Natives of the Colony."[28] For its part, Thuku's organization put forth a well-publicized statement of support for Indians. The E.A.A. put on record "that in its opinion the presence of Indians in the Colony and Protectorate of Kenya is not prejudicial to the advancement of the Natives, as has often been alleged by the Convention of Associations and some of the writers in the press, and is of further opinion that next to missionaries the Indians are their best friends."[29] Furthermore, when, three days later, the Indian delegation went to represent Indian claims in London, Thuku authorized them to speak also on behalf of Africans. A telegram in support of the Indian delegation was sent by Thuku to several London officials as well.[30]

The political solidarity between Thuku and Desai has been described by several historians, including Keith Kyle in an important early essay, and so most of that history does not warrant repetition here.[31] What is important to note, however, is that Harry Thuku's autobiography, published since Kyle's article appeared, gives further evidence that, contrary to the settler claims that Thuku was used as a mere "tool" by Indians, there was in fact a genuine pact of mutual respect and trust between Thuku and his Indian friends and, moreover, that settler racism was something both constituencies experientially shared.[32] Thus, for instance, in the autobiography we learn not only of the beginnings of a friendship between Thuku and Desai, who often socialized after work in the latter's room, but also of the later supportive visits of Desai and his friend Acharyar to Thuku's mother while he was imprisoned and of the colonial government's failed attempts to get Thuku to indict his Indian supporters.[33]

African opinion on the Indian presence was not, however, monolithic. The *East African Standard* published two letters, both in February 1923, by Africans who were critical of the Indian presence. The first, by Kip Rotich Bin Mabuwi, worried that if Indians gained control of the colony they would ruin the country by not providing free medicines as did the British, and this would lead to tremendous suffering. The second, by Jaluo Obner Oweyo, echoed the sense that the country would be ruined by Indians and that the Indian would not take care of a sick African as well as could a European.[34] We do not know much about the authors of these letters, so it is difficult to fully contextualize them, but we do know more about Z. K. Sentogo, a leader of the Young Baganda Association, who, in *Sekanyolya*, a newspaper published in Luganda (with a translated version in Kiswahili and a special supplement published in English), chastised the Indian community. Referring to the same Indian delegation to London that Thuku's organization supported, Sentogo wrote, "In the excitement caused by this situation, we the natives of this country are rendered inarticulate and our interests likely to be ignored. . . . The Indians have done nothing in the way of native education and, though the members of the delegation can be called educated, the mass of Indians are illiterate and inferior in education to the natives. What our fate would be under Indian rule we dare not contemplate. . . . Our education and training has been carried out on western lines as being best for our advancement. . . . Can this be possible under two opposing civilizations, one Eastern and the other Western leading to a confusion of ideas on conduct, morals, etc.?"[35]

It is tempting to read Sentogo's rhetoric of the clash of civilizations, and particularly the moral dangers of Eastern civilization, as continuous with the settler and missionary discourse of the time. But to see it merely as such is to make the same mistake the settlers did: erasing African agency, if only for an opposite political purpose. In other words, just as it was inaccurate (not to say insulting) for the settlers to read Thuku as a mere tool in Indian hands, it is equally problematic for us to see Sentogo as no more than a pawn in the struggle among immigrants. Rather, Sentogo's rhetoric is best read, as Michael Twaddle has persuasively done, as a complex set of negotiations between the interests of a younger expatriate Baganda community in Nairobi and an older established Buganda kingdom back home. This negotiation, Twaddle shows, was further complicated by the Young Baganda Associations' sense of the competing demands of loyalty to traditional authorities in Buganda on the one hand and the British colonial system on the other. When, as we noted earlier, Sir Apollo Kagwa welcomed the Indian representative C. F. Andrews with open arms, this, along with the feared rumors that Indians wished to establish an East African colony of their own, further disturbed the young Sentogo. Thus, Twaddle points out, if Sentogo's anti-Indian rhetoric derived from an already available missionary discourse about the East, it was also rooted in the interests of an upwardly mobile educated class of Africans who sought security in the colonial civil service and was legitimately alarmed by the prospect of increasing Indian competition.[36]

The different positions on Indians taken by Thuku and Sentogo remind us that one of the greatest challenges of any historical sketch is that of striking a balance between individual positions held by members of a given society and the aggregate or general position that encapsulates what might be considered the rhetorical norm of that society. Thus an account of the tensions between Europeans, Asians, and Africans in a racially divided colonial world risks eliding the internal divisions within these communities — divisions not only of class and gender but also of other hierarchical and nonhierarchical kinds. Factors such as religion, age, caste, the relative degree of incorporation into family networks and neighborhood communities, and inherited traditions and societal norms (to name only a few) have a profound effect on the ways in which individuals imagine themselves and their relations with others. Nonetheless, despite these various contingencies, what is clear is that the presence of Asians in East Africa since long before the beginning of formal European colonialism meant that, at least in British East Africa, colonialism was necessarily structured not through the simple binary division between the "settler" and the "native" proposed by Frantz Fanon, but through a rather more complex struggle between a variety of actors — the colonial authorities in England, the white settlers in East Africa (particularly Kenya), the "Asians" of East Africa, the colonial Indian government in India, and the so-called "natives" in the Fanonian framework, the black Africans of East Africa.[37] Rather than insisting on a reading of colonialism as purely binary, it is more useful in this context to read it as a process that was more ideologically disjunctive and dispersed.[38] To be sure, the tropes of self and other that Fanon employed in his reading of the cultures of colonialism are overwhelmingly present in this expanded colonial archive, but the particular valences of good and evil, superiority and inferiority, civilization and savagery, intelligence and emotion, rationality and sensuality, are not so easily mapped onto a white/black racial dichotomy. And yet, because Fanon's work was to have a profound impact on a whole generation of anticolonial and postcolonial thinkers in Africa, we must pause now to revisit one of his most cited claims.

MANICHAEAN AESTHETICS
AND THE COLONIAL LEGACY

In his account of the workings of colonialism, Frantz Fanon writes, "The colonial world is a Manichean world. It is not enough for the settler to delimit physically, that is to say with the help of the army and the police force, the place of the native. As if to show the totalitarian character of colonial exploitation the settler paints the native as a sort of quintessence of evil. Native society is not simply described as a society lacking in values. It is not enough for the colonist to affirm that those values have disappeared from, or still better never existed in the colonial world. The native is declared inaccessible to ethics; he represents not only the absence of values, but also the negation of values."[39] Fanon elaborates his thesis by focusing on the various mechanisms—military, judicial as well as ideological—that are mobilized by the settler in his continual effort to retain colonial privilege. Thus, writes Fanon, "the settler's work is to make even dreams of liberty impossible for the native. The native's work is to imagine all possible means for destroying the settler. On the logical plane, the Manicheism of the settler produces a Manicheism of the native. To the theory of the "absolute evil of the native" the theory of the "absolute evil of the settler" replies (93).

Fanon's vision of a starkly Manichaean colonial world was to resonate with the experiences of a number of colonized intellectuals and writers who, in the Africa of the fifties and early sixties, fought against the oppressive restrictions of colonial society in the hopes of creating a socially just, independent future. While this battle against colonialism was fought, as I outlined earlier, on several fronts, an important terrain of the struggle was that of ideology and culture. It is in this latter domain that literary texts became crucial carriers of the ideologies of liberation, not only in their representational aspirations but also in their very act of entry into the "worldliness" of national politics. As a result, an integral aspect of the literary criticism that emerged in the postcolonial African context was an ideological analysis of the nature of literary "commitment" to anticolonialism, independence, and, particularly in the eyes of Marxist critics, to a classless future.

Of the many literary critics of this generation who were inspired by Fanon, perhaps the most influential was Abdul JanMohamed, who published his study *Manichean Aesthetics: The Politics of Literature in Colonial Africa* in 1983. *Manichean Aesthetics* sought to articulate a sociopolitical theory of literary production that took into account the binary divisions of the colonial world that Fanon had previously laid out. The European colonial writer, wrote JanMohamed "sought to rationalize the whole imperial endeavour" (2) and produced an ideology justifying colonialism. In response, the African writer sought to demystify that ideology and spoke instead of the traumas of colonialism. What was of interest to JanMohamed was not only the form in which colonial ideology took fictional shape but also its "negative influence" on African writing. "The dialectic of negative influence," wrote JanMohamed "is in fact a literary manifestation of the Manichean sociopolitical relation between the colonizer and the colonized" (8).

This Manichaeism, JanMohamed was to insist (thereby distancing himself from a more orthodox Marxism), was a matter primarily of race rather than class. In colonial society, he writes, "the function of class is replaced by race" (7). "The major distinction in such a society is *experienced* in terms of race, which unlike the horizontal division that defines class relations, can function both horizontally and vertically: regardless of the native's relation to modes of production or the amount of wealth he may accumulate, he will always be considered inferior by the colonialist" (7). In the colonial African contexts that interested him, JanMohamed would select for his study "three Europeans" and "three Africans" from three different parts of the continent. Such a choice would enable the presentation of the typology of the Manichaean aesthetic through a set of contrasts between white writers and black ones.

And yet there is perhaps some truth to the claim that JanMohamed's choice of writers and regions was itself somewhat overdetermined by his theoretical presuppositions. Ironically, despite the fact that his intellectual mentor Frantz Fanon had experienced his most substantial engagement with Africa in the northern part of the continent, JanMohamed's interests lay mainly in sub-Saharan Africa, the black Africa of the popular imagination. To include Africa north of the Sahara would have had important repercussions on a model that rigorously sought to read colonial politics in stark contrasts of black and white. But additionally, there was also the uncomfortable position of Nadine Gordimer in this neat schematic. By virtue of race, she was European. But by virtue of birth she was African. *Manichean Aesthetics* displays a valiant but ultimately compromised effort to understand the liberal ethic of a writer such as Nadine Gordimer. To be fair, JanMohamed seems acutely aware of the difficulties of labeling her "European" in an unproblematic manner. Yet it is a choice that he feels we ultimately must make in the context of what was then apartheid South Africa. Writing on Gordimer's novel *The Conservationist*, JanMohamed suggests that the ambiguous subjectivity in the novel is a stylistic correlative of Gordimer's

> practical dilemma as a white South African writer. The bifurcation inculcated by apartheid has so antagonized the population of South Africa along purely *racial* lines that a radical white person, sympathetic to the black plight, is faced with the quandary of how to define herself as an "African." Because blanket repression has oversimplified the political situation in South Africa—in a *racial* war people will be killed because of their *skin color*, not because of their political and social beliefs and practice—it becomes difficult for anyone to imagine the detailed social and cultural ramifications of the "Africanization" of a white person.
>
> (125)

There is reason to believe that, even as his book was being published, JanMohamed was already thinking ahead to a more complex account of colonialist literature and its Manichaean legacy. No less than two years later he published in *Critical Inquiry* a now canonical essay, "The Economy of Manichean Allegory: The Function of Racial Difference in Colonialist Literature." In this essay JanMohamed sharpened his focus on white colonial literature by differentiating it further between that which worked on an "imaginary" as opposed to a "symbolic" plane. Drawing on the framework of Lacanian psychoanalysis, JanMohamed posited that "imaginary" texts are structured by "objectification and aggression" (84), while "symbolic" texts are "more aware of the inevitable necessity of using the native as a mediator of European desires" (85). If Joyce Cary represented the former, Gordimer, along with Conrad, wrote in the latter register. While discreetly reticent on revisiting the issue of the "Africanity" of Gordimer, this new reading at least suggested that by "becoming reflexive of its context, by confining itself to a rigorous examination of the 'imaginary' mechanism of colonialist mentality," Gordimer's writing managed to "free itself from the Manichean allegory" (85).

There is a second shift in this essay that is so subtle and unannounced it has not received much attention in the critical commentary surrounding it: the shift in terminology from "settler" to "conquerer." Just as the Lacanian symbolic order allowed for an escape route for the liberal white South African writer, I want to suggest that specifying the binary in terms of "conqueror/native" as opposed to "settler/native" allowed for the possibility of some settlers in Africa being differentiated from other settlers who were decidedly "conquerors." In other words, just as Gordimer could be a white South African and yet ultimately be seen to side with the oppressed natives, this alternative formulation also allowed for the possibility of some settlers to be aligned with the natives rather than the conquerors. This move from settler to conqueror was never explicitly theorized by JanMohamed, and it may well have been an unconscious one. But its resonances in his new framework and beyond are nevertheless of significance to the central concerns of my project.

My interest in JanMohamed's positioning of Gordimer and his subtle shift in this essay on reading colonial societies as starkly divided along the "conqueror/native" binary as opposed to the "settler/native" binary (79) is not unrelated to the curious biographical fact that JanMohamed himself is a Kenyan-born descendant of "Asian" heritage. His shift from the category of settler to that of conquerer was in keeping, then, with a larger narrative in which Asians in East Africa had resolutely cast themselves as immigrants, and perhaps even as "settlers," but insistently differentiated themselves from the European "conquerors" of Africa. For all its emphasis on race and racial politics, *Manichean Aesthetics* maintained a curious silence on the non-black, nonwhite subjects of Africa. Indeed their only presence, in the introduction, is an afterthought: "Gordimer's depiction of the effects of apartheid on the conscience of liberal white South Africans must be read in conjunction with La Guma's representation of the more drastic consequences of apartheid for the blacks (*as well as 'Coloureds' and Indians*)" (10, my emphasis). JanMohamed's bracketing is, I suggest, not accidental but rather symptomatic of a generation of East African Asians who came of age in a newly postcolonial context. Many Asians in East Africa, for right or wrong, felt uncertain about their political and economic futures in the newly independent states. A few left with the arrival of independence. Some held on to their British passports to hedge their bets. Others promptly took up (or attempted to take up) citizenship within the African countries of their residence. This array of individual and family choices about future residence was also accompanied by more personal ideological tendencies manifest on the political register. Liberal Asians, among them many Asian intellectuals, chose to identify with the newly independent nations and with their fellow black citizens. Hence the trauma associated with an uncertain future was accompanied by the performative insistence on shared histories and political alliances. It is in this context that a book that was explicitly about the racialized structure of the colonial encounter could retain a remarkable silence on the racial heritage of its author. The Manichaean framework of the settler/native lent itself to a liberal hope that Asians and black Africans could both see themselves as "native." But the same Manichaeism on the streets often resulted in a reverse judgment. The question was too divisive to pose in a still developing academic analytic of colonial society.

Nonetheless, just a few years before *Manichean Aesthetics* was published, a fictional representation of the Asian African predicament was memorably offered by the Indo-Trinidadian writer V. S. Naipaul in his novel *A Bend in the River*. The novel deserves a considerably more detailed reading than I can offer here, but readers will remember that one of the greatest sources of anguish in the text is the character Salim's sense that his Indian African heritage has no discursive space in the ongoing postcolonial discussions of African hopes and futures. In his conversations about Africa with his fellow Asian friend Indar, Salim notes, "I felt that between us lay some dishonesty,

or just an omission, some blank, around which we both had to walk carefully. That omission was our own past, the smashed life of our community."[40]
Indar, who has tried willfully to "trample on the past" to accommodate to
a world "in movement" (141), finds that he cannot forget the pain associated not only with the loss of his family's assets on the East African coast
but also of its sense of security there. He is enraged with his community,
which he says has given energy "but in every other way left us at the mercy
of others" (142). His rage is shared by Salim, who claims that everything he
knows about the history of the Indian Ocean he has learned from the book
of Europeans. Indians in East Africa "were buried so deep in their lives that
they were not able to stand back and consider the nature of their lives. They
did what they had to do" (16) and, in the process, suggests the biting opening
sentence of the novel, they "allowed themselves to become nothing" and
found that they had no place in the world.

Naipaul's rendering of the Asian predicament is arguably too acerbic in
tone, but the central anxieties of his text resonate in a number of reflections
by East African Asians in postcolonial times. In her 1999 book *Nomadic
Identities*, May Joseph, a Tanzanian Asian who now resides in the United
States, presents a moving account of being jarred by Mira Nair's *Mississippi
Masala*, which was released in 1991. The film set in the context of Amin's
Uganda brought back to her long-repressed memories of her own family's
anxieties about the anti-Asian sentiments in Dar es Salaam in the 1970s.
Meditating on the performance of citizenship, Joseph recalls her desper-
ate attempts to expressively stage her citizenship through renewed efforts at
getting the *ngoma* dances just right, by deemphasizing the Asian accent in
her Swahili, by making sure that her school assignment of maintaining the
shamba (vegetable garden) would make the mark. "Despite the anti-Asian
graffiti present in the streets on the route home," she writes, "I was determined to prove that I had assimilated. But being defined inauthentic proved
a more potent force than my expressive stances. Clearly, more was needed
than speaking perfect Swahili—most important, a sense of historicity in
relation to this transitioning place of Tanzanian socialist citizenship."[41]

Joseph's account of the postcolonial trauma of a community no longer at
ease, of a community that over time recognized the need to investigate its
own historicity, is one that resonates throughout a three-volume collection
of interviews, essays, and published writings by Kenyan Asians compiled
by Cynthia Salvadori. Published in 1996, the three volumes of *We Came
in Dhows* provide a remarkable view both of the Asian presence in Kenya
in colonial times as well as the more recent self-conscious attempts on the

part of the different Asian communities to revitalize the memories of their multiple legacies. Salvadori's editorial juxtaposition of Asian accounts with photographs and commentaries from private family collections, colonial newspapers, and British travel narratives not only enhances the aesthetic texture of the record, but, more importantly, records the unevenness of the political and economic status of the Asian presence. The various vignettes themselves are engaging and range from the hilarious to the depressing, from the poetic to the prosaic, from the triumphant to the defeatist. They are stories of intercultural connections and disappointments, of the possibilities of a world blind to racial animosities and one in which racism seems inescapable.

There are of course various tributes to the likes of Allidina Visram and A. M. Jevanjee, the former a Khoja trader who came to East Africa in 1863, eventually opening over 170 branches of his store all over British East Africa, and the latter a Bohra who also became a very successful trader, a political advocate on behalf of the Indian community and the founding publisher in 1901 of the newspaper *African Standard*. But, in addition to these stories of high achievers, there are also stories about persons of more modest habitation. Among them is that of Jose Antao, a Goan who worked as a cook, first for various British colonial officers, including the governor of Kenya, and eventually for the prestigious hotels in Nairobi. But, recalls his son, "he remained a Goan at heart" and never ate any of the English food that he himself cooked. He always came home to eat his "rice curry, fish, good spicy Goan dishes" (2:2). There is the story of the grandmother who "cured the DC's earache." It so happened that once the district commissioner in Lamu developed what seemed an incurable earache, and, with no European doctor on hand, decided to turn to the Indian community. "So Great-grandmother asked for a small bottle and filled it with a child's urine and told her son to take it to the DC and put a few drops in his ear, but under no circumstances to tell him what it was, and once the necessary drops had been taken to throw the rest of the bottle away" (1:27) The DC's letter of thanks seems to indicate that the medicine had worked!

As though to remind us that not all Asians in colonial Kenya were traders or indentured laborers working on the railway, we read the tale of Shamsu Din, an Indian who came to Kenya as a young boy and found work on a white man's ranch taming wild animals for eventual shipment to various animal parks and zoos worldwide. And the internal diversity of the Asian community is also seen in narratives of those who found themselves marginalized for reason of caste and class. One Cutchi Muslim has this to say about an alternative nonsegregated school his father set up in 1925. "Alaya's School was very important to us because we Cutchis were very uneducated. We had come over, long, long ago, as artisans. We were suppressed by our Indian brothers here, for they treated us as labourers, without any respect. When the British came in they associated only with the prominent wealthy Indians, people who were of the Ismaili and Bohra and Ithnaseri communities, and some Hindus" (1:79).

There are, as well, stories of encounters with European racism. "The Europeans were generally happy to accept our hospitality," remembers Madan Aggarwal. They would "sit in our shops and drink tea or even have meals with us in our rooms behind the shop. But they never reciprocated" (3;65). Racial difference often erupted into outright conflict. One such instance is demonstrated in the vignette of "the Indian who thrashed a European" who tried to prevent him from getting on a railway platform (2:50). Another is the story of Captain McStead, the British military staff officer at Tsavo. Lalchand Sharma writes, "Out of his hatred for us there emerged a treason trial. Several of us fuel contractors, who supplied wood for the railway engines, were framed by McStead for allegedly aiding and harbouring the German enemy during World War I" (3:142).

Memories of relations with Africans vary in the volume from friendly to removed. Haroun Vangawalla, a Bohra, remembers life as a child in Vanga: "We used to play with the local boys, going out on the dhows, or fishing. Sometimes we would go with them to pluck mangoes illegally. . . . We'd sometimes go to their houses and eat their food, fish and rice. But they didn't come to eat at our house. I think they were afraid of going into Indian homes just as we were afraid of going into European homes. We studied together, too, for we were all Muslims" (1:46–47). In contrast, narrating his childhood in Kisii, Gulab Gudka of Kisumu says, "We children didn't have anything to do with the African children. The Africans were illiterate in those days" (2:172). On African responses to Indians, the volumes in general have less to say, but at least one stray comment suggests the colonial hierarchies in place: "Now, the Africans had been taught to salute and/or doff their hats when Europeans drove past. They'd see our car coming in the distance and do likewise, but as soon as we got close they'd straighten up and put their hats back on, saying in a disappointed way, 'Aaah, muhindi tuu'—'it's only Indians'" (3:47).

Salvadori's volumes are also tremendously useful for the light they shed on the lives of Indian women and on interracial marriages between Indians and Africans. There are sketches of Indian women who stand out as exceptional for their times. One such is the story of an elderly woman who had arrived in Mombasa in 1866 by dhow and walked all the way to her husband's shop in Takaungu (1:44). Another is of the Goan Ezalda Zuzarte (better known as Nana), married to J. Dias, an owner of a timber mill in Eldama Ravine: "Nana took an active part in the wood-logging in the abundant forest there. She was a rather wild sort and the life suited her. They used a tractor for dragging logs, and Nana was one of the first women in Kenya to drive a tractor, certainly the first Asian woman to do so. Nana was also an excellent horsewoman, for the only way to get around in the forest was on foot or on horseback. Horses remained one of her main passions right to the end of her long life. She was a crack shot, too, and certainly killed at least one lion" (2:134). And, if the likes of Nana were exceptional, the volumes remind us of the many Indian women who were the primary managers and salespersons in their family dukas while their husbands were traveling to trade. These women, who have been, for the most part, completely written out of history, get their few moments in these communal life histories. So, for instance, Fidahussein Adamali says of his mother, "While [father] was off at Mungushu my mother looked after the shop in Kiu, as she did when he went up to Nairobi to buy goods. She was a very thrifty woman, a good businesswoman herself. She too understood Kikamba and also a bit of Maasai, although she was too shy to speak" (3:5).

The asymmetry of Indian men marrying African women, but Indian women marrying within the community is confirmed by Shabberali Esmail of Lamu, who notes, "Our Bohra girls always married other Bohras, but sometimes Bohra men would marry local women such as Swahilis. The children of my grandfather's brother Amiji, for instance, intermarried locally. Usually when the husband died the woman would return to her own people and take the children with her, so that the half-caste children did not become part of the Bohra community" (1:18). But, while the notion that mixed-race children were not assimilated into Indian communities is also confirmed by Govindji Sutaria, a Hindu Bhatia man from Mombasa (1:31), Mohammedali Karimjee of Takaungu writes that his father's second marriage (after the death of his first Indian wife) was with a Swahili woman. Mohammedali was a product of that second union and was brought up as a Bohra, going to the Bohra school and praying at the Bohra mosque in Takaungu (1:44–45).

In her "Notes on the Compilation," Cynthia Salvadori makes clear that her aim in putting together the volumes was primarily to enable the efforts of a community that was only now (in the 1990s) beginning to publicly come to terms with its African history.[42] As she puts it, "Europeans were writing their stories about Kenya as they saw it for over seventy years, the Africans have been at it for thirty years. This book is giving the Indians an opportunity to record their histories as they wish to" (3:193). While such a recording inevitably risks a nostalgic and perhaps triumphalist take on a community's history, the effort, Salvadori suggests, is worth the risk.[43] What is most striking to Salvadori is not so much the nostalgia and the creation of a heroic past, but rather the deletions that she was asked to make by her interviewees. "A person from Lamu recalled how 'the [colonial] DC used to walk all around town in the early morning making sure it was kept clean' but later asked me to delete that in case the authorities took it as a criticism that the town is filthy today. . . . Another person told me proudly that Kenyatta and Koinange had spent three nights as guests at his father's home, and then asked me to delete it because 'the relatives of the said gentlemen might not like it'"(3:193). Such deletions, suggests Salvadori, "indicate the paranoia the Indians feel in Kenya's present political atmosphere" (3:193).

Such paranoia and its corollary self-censorship is evident in a letter written to the Ugandan journal *Transition* in an early issue from 1968. Signed as the "Under Dog," the letter is penned by a self-identified "third generation Asian in Kenya" who is bitter about the fact that "Kenyan" has become a "bankrupt nationality for an Asian."[44] The letter itself is in response to a much debated and controversial piece by Paul Theroux published in a previous issue of the journal.[45] Claiming that hatred toward Asians had become a fashion among both whites and blacks in East Africa, Theroux wrote, "I believe the Asians to be the most lied-about race in Africa" (47). While his most immediate locus of analysis were recent statements made by Kenya's president, Kenyatta, and by other members of the KANU political party, Theroux suggested that such sentiments, which were an "infringement of individual rights, a thinly veiled threat of actual harm, and a gross neglect of . . . libertarian principles" (48), were part of a larger ideology of Asian disenfranchisement. Not wanting to associate himself with the few Indophiles who assert the "innate nobility of the Indian," Theroux notes, "I am frankly as worried by the person who says the Asian is saintly as by the person who says the Asian is a bloodsucker. There is a remarkable similarity in the sentimental attachment the Indians and Africans have for *place*: both Asians and Africans speak with nostalgia and affection for the mangoes in Tabora, the meadows and gardens in Entebbe, the beaches in Dar es Salaam, and so forth. But this is probably not so remarkable when one considers that often the Asian in Africa is in the land of his birth. We all like to be home; in most circumstances it is the safest place to be" (51).

Theroux's observation that anti-Asian sentiment is pervasive not only in the black citizenry but also in the white settler community is taken one step further by Shiva Naipaul in his travelogue *North of South*. For Naipaul, the racial predicament of East Africa's Asians can only be explained by what is popularly known as the "divide and rule" strategy of colonial politics. "The African was taught—and eventually came to believe—that his destiny was inextricably linked with the destiny of the white man. Marginality was thrust upon the Asian. Both black and white could regard him as an outsider intruding into *their* special relationship."[46] In this scenario the promise of a European-styled modernity and the possibilities of assimilation into its core values meant a greater identification on the part of the African with European culture. Not desirous of advocating for an alternative, Eastern form of modernity and thereby having no purchase on the African imagination, the Asian became an anomaly.

"The settler's work is to make even dreams of liberty impossible for the native. The native's work is to imagine all possible means for destroying the settler," Fanon had written. But in this scheme at least, colonial ideology functioned to hold out the promise of modernity and eventual liberty to the African, while cathecting the source of African anger and resentment toward a clearly visible alien community. Thus, rather than following the Manichaean logic that Fanon had outlined, in which the theory of the "absolute evil of the native" was to be answered by the theory of the "absolute evil of the settler" (93), a triangulated process emerged in which both the white "settler" and the "native" could point to the intruding Asian as the source of that absolute evil.[47] Like the characters Salim and Indar in his brother's novel, Shiva Naipaul suggests that the blame lay in great part with the Asians themselves. Not ones to assimilate with Africans in their new surroundings, and insistent on retaining old world communal affinities ("In East Africa as in India, a Patel is a Patel before he is anything else" writes Naipaul [118]), the East African Asian "did not evolve a picture of himself in keeping with his changed circumstances" (118). The failure, in other words, was not so much a failure of acts of commission as of a critical act of omission. It was, to Shiva Naipaul, the failure of the imagination. "Few people are more prosaic than the East African *bania* (merchant) and have so fractional a perception of the world. Other men—and they have been few and far between—have had to sing on their behalf. But the European knew—and still knows—how to sing his own songs. More importantly, he knows what kind of songs he must sing. This near total absence of imagination has played no small part in the downfall of the East African Asian" (119).[48]

"ASIAN-AFRICAN" LITERATURES: GENEALOGIES IN THE MAKING

Shiva Naipaul's 1978 assessment of the "near total absence of imagination" on the part of East African Asians is, in retrospect, inaccurate, but it registers a still commonly held view that Asian literary production in Africa really only begins in the 1960s. As is widely known, well before Naipaul, the Ugandan writer Taban Lo Liyong had already made a plea in 1965 urging his fellow East Africans to help overcome what he felt was the literary barrenness of East Africa. What is less well remembered is that in his manifesto Liyong specifically took up the issue of Asian literary creativity: "Our citizens of Asian origin have been taking more care of family businesses than engaging in literary works."[49] Liyong urged religious and community leaders such as the Aga Khan to play a role in fostering a cultural renaissance in East Africa. While his call indeed had its intended effect, provoking a whole generation of creative writers and artists into a flurry of activity, in retrospect, as Simon Gikandi has suggested with regard to East African literatures in indigenous languages, and as Robert Gregory has outlined with regard to Asian cultural production, Liyong's critique seems to have missed out on a whole range of existing literary activity.[50] In the Asian context much of this activity was focused on theater, and, while some of the plays written and produced in English were subsequently published and are available to us today, many of the performances were in Indian languages such as Gujarati and Punjabi, and transcripts of those performances are not part of our scholarly records.

Gregory dates the serious organization of Asian dramatists, poets, and artists to 1948 with the inauguration of the Oriental Art Circle in Nairobi. This group, formed by the Indian high commissioner Apa Pant and his wife Dr. Nalini Devi, encouraged the fostering of cultural links between the various Asian communities as well as with Africans. Based at the Kenya Cultural Center, the group presented monthly plays, poetry readings, as well as music and dance performances. The plays often had multiracial casts, with Europeans and Africans playing roles that called for non-Indian characters.

The Oriental Art Circle also extended itself into the realm of radio with a weekly program of music and poetry. Gregory notes that, while this group was the most active, a number of cultural organizations were established around this time in the various cities and towns of East Africa. Some of the more ambitious organizations relied on the patronage of the more success-ful members of the Asian community. Three years before Liyong's plea to the Aga Khan, for instance, the religious leader, along with entrepreneurs like Nanji Kalidas Mehta (who will make a longer appearance in chapter 5), had contributed money to establish a National Cultural Center in Kampala that would hold "a national theatre, a language hall, and many offices for promotion of a variety of arts including film production."[51]

The British Council's annual drama competition, the Kenya Drama Festival, and the East Africa Drama Festival, which was inaugurated as an annual event in Kampala in 1950, all played an enormous role in fostering theatrical creativity in the Asian community. Kuldip Sondhi's *Undesignated* won first prize at the Kenya Drama Festival in 1963; his 1965 play, *With Strings*, won as best original play of the year. Jagjit Singh's *Sweet Scum of Freedom* won the third prize in 1971 in the BBC African Service Competi-tion for radio plays. But, in addition to these award-winning titles, a number of plays both in English and in Indian languages were written and produced onstage as well as on radio in the late fifties through the early seventies. At the same time, authors such as Jagjit Singh, Amin Kassam, and Bahadur Tejani also wrote poems, and this period saw the publication of Bahadur Tejani's novel *Day After Tomorrow* and Peter Nazareth's *In a Brown Man-tle*. While these plays and poems are rarely read or taught as a vital part of the African literary canon today, editors of the earliest anthologies tellingly considered them as an integral part of a developing multiracial African lit-erary culture. Thus, for instance, Sondhi's *Sunil's Dilemma* was included by Gwyneth Henderson and Cosmo Pieterse in their collection *Nine Afri-can Plays for Radio*, and Pieterse's *Ten One-Act Plays* included three scripts authored by Asian writers. Likewise, some of the most circulated poetry written by Asians in this period is available to us through editions such as David Cook and David Rudabiri's *Poems from East Africa* and Wole Soy-inka's *Poems of Black Africa*.[52] The point of noting such anthologizing is to recognize that, despite the then ongoing debates about who was or was not an "African" writer—anxieties that, as we have already noted, continued to haunt projects like JanMohamed's well into the eighties—the incorporation of Asian writing within the larger category of "African literature" seems, at least in these cases, not to have posed any dilemmas. While white settler literature was clearly seen to be a part of the colonial other, Asian writers were read as being part of the African canon.

These developments in the fifties and sixties were departures in magnitude but not in kind from previous investments by East African Asians in the institutions of literature and culture. As early as 1912, a notice appeared in the *Indian Voice* stating that the Goan Institute of Nairobi had voted to embark on a literary magazine whose primary objective would be "to excite and stimulate [literary] composition amongst members."[53] On July 22, 1915, the Nairobi Municipal Council entertained a petition from a Goan named A. R. Nazareth for the building of an Indian theater. It is unclear whether the theater as proposed was subsequently built, but Mr. Nazareth left the meeting equipped with the necessary building codes, including "the provision of satisfactory exits" that formed part of the licensing agreement.[54]

Poetry and theater were, in those early decades of the twentieth century, central institutions in the cultural lives of the community. Newspaper accounts from the period provide details on a number of performances. A note in the *East African Standard* of January 18, 1918, mentions European attendance at a "Hindustani" play, *The Serpent*, performed at the Nairobi Indian Theatre. The moral of the play allegedly was that "no man should covet the wife of his neighbour unless under penalty of dire happenings."[55] Such didacticism is also suggested in an *East African Standard* reporting of March 7, 1914, on a play performed at the Nairobi Indian Theatre with four hundred Indians in attendance. "The subject really took the form of a lecture on drink, and was staged as a drama."[56] Theater was also used by the community as a fund-raiser. Multiple performances of the Urdu play *The Silver King* were staged in December 1914 at the Auctioneer's Hall in Nairobi. Raising money for the Indian troops engaged in the war, it played to sold-out audiences.[57]

An article in the June 6, 1914, issue of the *East African Standard* provides a rare glimpse of early twentieth-century Indian theater in Mombasa. A European critic, invited to a play to be performed by the New Indian Opera and Theatrical Company, showed up instead (because he couldn't read the Gujarati language on the ticket) at a play put on the same night by a rival Indian group, the New Rising Star Company. The European's assessment of the play is not uncharacteristic of the time, so that he notes, for instance, that "to the European ear these interminable Indian melodies become almost as monotonous as an African *n'goma*, though of course, it must be classed as music—music of an arrested development." The Gujarati play performed that evening was *The Binding Promise, or, Out of Evil Comes*

Good, a morality play about the sacrifices that a king must make in the interests of his subjects. By admission of his Indian interlocutors, this play, written by an unknown playwright, was not as well regarded as the upcoming performance the next Saturday, to which the reviewer was invited. That play, *Khubsurat Bala* (1910), was penned by the writer Agha Hashr Kashmiri, who had previously made his literary reputation on Urdu adaptations of plays by Sheridan and Shakespeare. The critic, having attended this performance as well, finds it a "travesty" and a "strange medley manufactured to give the comics a show." But despite the reviewer's biases, his recording of the performances is among the very few written documents available that give us a sense of Asian theatrical activity of the time. For instance, we learn that these performances were attended by an exclusively male audience (we don't know whether special shows were staged for women, as later became common with film screenings) and that the crowd included both Indians as well as Swahilis. The women's roles were played by boys. The performances were long—with the first evening's show beginning at 9 P.M. and ending at nearly 3 A.M. The atmosphere was raucous, with much audience applause and engagement. Most importantly, the brief write-up in the newspaper underscores that, at least among the Indians in Mombasa of the time, theater performances were prevalent and not infrequent and isolated events.[58]

Literature, particularly poetry, was also recognized as a privileged site of recording the highest achievements of individuals, and it is thus no accident that the earliest Asian literary text on record in East Africa is a poem written by Roshan, a railway worker, in honor of Lt. Colonel J. H. Patterson, who is credited with having killed the man-eating lions at Tsavo. Dated January 29, 1899, around the time of Patterson's resignation from the service and his departure, the Urdu poem sings his praises and bemoans the departure.[59] Commemorative poems such as these played a significant role in the Indian community in East Africa.[60] For instance, the visit of Prince Gaikwad, the brother of the maharaja of Baroda, who came to Kenya on a hunting expedition in September 1912, called for such composition. The Indian community made much of this royal visit, the press reporting on the prince's itinerary with extended coverage of the various social receptions held in his honor. A poem authored by "J.M.G." appeared in a *Supplement to the Indian Voice,* and it gives some insight at the very least into the author's if not the community's take on the significance of the royal visit for East Africa. Billed as the first visit of Indian royalty to East Africa, the poet insists that the visit will promote interest in the region among other Indians and will result in more such visitations. Addressing East Africa, the poet writes, "Thus will thy fame be surely made, / The foundation of thy celebrity truly laid; / Rajahs and Princes from the Eastern clime, / Will honour thy shores from time to time." For this to happen successfully, however, in a problematic trope that was to become familiar in subsequent Asian writing in East Africa, a slumbering Africa must wake up and play the role of seductress: "Awake, East Africa, now is thy time, / Bewitch thy tourists from the Eastern clime, / Gird up thy loins, stir up thy charms, / Provide amusement to the Prince's arms" ("Advance East Africa"). Such African hospitality is taken to further sacrificial extremes in a verse drama, "Message from the Prince," composed by the same author and published a few weeks later in another *Supplement to the Indian Voice*. Here the setting is Mombasa, and the occasion is the anxious wait for the prince's return from the hunting expedition on which he had embarked over a month earlier. A messenger finally arrives from the interior with news that the prince and his party are alive and well and that their hunting has been bountiful. In no small part this success is because, the poem tells us, the Elephant King has declared to his subjects: "Throw open the gates of our Kingdom wide, / Not a single specie [*sic*] of our wealth thou shall hide, / It shall never be said that our Royal Guest, / Was treated by us as we treat all the rest." In both these poems the vision of Africa as the ultimate playground for Indian male fantasies is left entirely unchecked, and it is perhaps in recognition of this that the newspaper's editor, in publishing the verses, also warily notes, "For this ebullition the Editor is not responsible."[61]

But, if poetry was the vehicle for exalted expressions, it was also the means to express pent-up anger and frustration on the part of Indians who felt that they had been cheated or exploited by the system of labor that had recruited them. A poem appearing in the *Indian Voice* on April 19, 1911, entitled "To Africa" and signed "by a disgusted Indian clerk on retiring from the service of the Railway," is written either by or in the voice of someone who clearly had had a rough time in Africa. The harsh tone speaks to the labor conditions of Indians on the railways, ending on a parting note: "But I must surely leave and see thee no more, / As soon as my three years penance is o'er, / In my native home I would rather be, / a beggar, than here a Monarchy."[62] The poem seems to have generated at least passing interest among readers, since the following week a column, "An Appreciation," on the poem appeared in the *Indian Voice* speaking to its merits. Unconcerned with the negative portrayal of Africa, the commentator noted that the "short piece of poetry is full of plays of irony, humour, wit, beauty and other merits that come under the head of versification." Linking the poet to the long tradition of British poetry (Browning, Byron, Milton, Spencer, and Dryden are all cited), the major concern of the commentator was not the thematic particularities of the poem, but rather what he considered to be its stylistic excellence. And such literary excellence on the part of an Indian, suggested the commentator, deserves to be noticed in a world in which "ability beneath the dark skin is regarded as the height of presumption."[63] In retrospect it seems clear that, at least among the readership of the *Indian Voice*, claims not only to literacy but, moreover, to literary ability were integral in making an argument for political recognition in a racially hierarchized colonial setting.

Even this brief glance at literary and theatrical activities in East Africa suggests that contrary to popular conceptions, Asians were not uninterested in the imaginative life in the first half of the twentieth century. What is true, however, is that most of the literary work was inward looking, oriented toward its own community, and not, as Naipaul would have it, a song sung for the attention of other communities in order to advocate for its pressing issues. Indeed, it was precisely such a shift in focus that the South African Indian author P. S. Joshi appealed for in a similar literary context, when, as conference chair of the first annual conference of the South African Non-European Arts Congress held in Johannesburg in 1945, he remarked: "What we really need at present is a literature by Non-Europeans endowed with a feeling for the sufferings of their people, we need authors to write about Indian, Cape Coloured, Malay, and Bantu life. We need artists who could faithfully and vividly depict the life of the suffering humanity in South Africa. We need intellectuals who could create an impression on the world by their literary achievements. We need a Booker T. Washington or a Rabindranath Tagore to focus world attention on our sufferings, aspirations and ideals."[64]

Such a focus on the sufferings, aspirations, and ideals of the newly emerging postcolonial African nations was central to mission of the Ugandan journal *Transition*. Founded by Rajat Neogy, a young Ugandan of Bengali origin in 1961, *Transition* by all accounts soon became one of the most vibrant cultural journals in Anglophone Africa. The journal staged some of the liveliest debates between authors who were often prodded by Neogy to be provocative and the all-too-often scandalized but nevertheless devoted readership. Including contributors of all races, writing from within Africa but also from Asia, Europe, and the Americas, *Transition* flirted with controversy until it fell victim to its own political risk taking. On October 18, 1968, Neogy was arrested and charged with sedition for publishing in his journal an article by M.P. Abu Mayanja and an anonymous letter by a university student, both of which were critical of Uganda's ongoing constitutional reforms. Acquitted by the court but continuing to be detained under emergency powers, Neogy was later stripped of his Ugandan citizenship, which the authorities claimed was found to be "irregular." If Neogy's statelessness was symptomatic of what would later happen to a number of other Asians under Idi Amin's regime, he was unwittingly caught in a different global struggle between the superpowers. Without his own knowledge, *Transition* was financed for a number of years by the Congress for Cultural Freedom, an organization that was later found to be a front for the CIA. Despite his protests that he had no knowledge of this linkage, and despite the fact that there was no evidence that the CIA had any role in the editorial decisions or content of the journal, Neogy and *Transition* never fully recovered from these revelations. Rendered stateless and vulnerable to further arrests and detentions, Neogy left Uganda a broken man, and, after reestablishing *Transition* in Accra, he eventually handed over the editorship of the journal to Wole Soyinka.[65]

There have been many developments on the East African literary landscape since the early years of *Transition*, but, in our conceptions of the growth of Asian literary traditions in particular, we should remain alert to some of the gaps that exist even as we relate the post-1960s narrative.[66] For instance, while increasing scholarly attention has been paid to East African Asian fiction written in the English language, the literary production of Asians in both Swahili and Indian languages has received less scrutiny. It is worth remembering that the first published Swahili-Gujarati dictionary, Alidina Somjee Lilani's 1890 *A Guide to the Swahili Language in Gujarati Characters*, was, as the subtitle suggested, "chiefly for the use of Indians having relations with Zanzibar," but, the author hoped, would also be of value to the occasional "Englishman who cares to master the sounds of the Gujarati characters."[67] The educational inspector in Kutch, Dalpatram Khakar, endorsed the publication as a sign of the growing commercial interest of Indians in East Africa, calling for further books on "the trade of Africa, and the way in which it can be carried on successfully by our people" (12). Explicitly utilitarian in its interests, the invocation of the image of the Englishman learning Gujarati through the mediation of this Swahili dictionary nevertheless suggests that Lilani harbored a more fertile communicative desire than sheer mechanical interest in a mercantile process.

Some East African Asians have also on occasion taken up the Swahili language for literary purposes. Sadru Kassam's play *Bones*, for instance, appeared in an edited collection entitled *Short East African Plays in English*, but was in fact originally written in Swahili and translated for the collection by the playwright.[68] Again, in his overview of Indian contributions to Swahili literature, Abdulaziz Lodhi notes that *Poems from Kenya* by Ahmed Nassir was originally composed in Swahili. Other Asians who have published in Swahili include Farouk Topan, who, in addition to editing two collections of Swahili poetry, wrote two satirical plays, *Mfalme Juha* in 1971 and *Aliyeonja Pepo* in 1973. Lodhi himself published a book of Kiswahili poems in 1986 entitled *Tafkira*.[69]

Writing and performance in Indian languages has also, for the most part, remained under the radar. Vanoo Jivraj Somia's *A History of the Indians in East Africa* is a work of an organic intellectual writing a communal history that at times risks overt flattery. Nevertheless, Somia's position as an active member of the community allows him to share details of the literary accomplishments of some of his peers that have been completely overlooked by literary historians. For instance, he writes of Tulsidas Purushottam Suchak, who wrote a well-received Gujarati play, *Somnathne Khole* ("On the lap of Somnath"), first published in 1967 and reprinted in 1999; Jagdish Dave, "an expert in Gujarati language and literature," who published a number of books and poems; Vinay Jivanlal Brahmabhatt, the son of the Gujarati section editor of the *Kenya Daily Mail*, who wrote award-winning short stories in Gujarati; Shantshila Keshubhai Gajjar, author of a number of short stories, who, after moving to Britain, was "the first Indian woman to edit and publish a women's quarterly in Gujarati under the title of 'Sangna' (meaning companion or female friend), in the Western world." Among the other women writers mentioned by Somia are Kamala Chunilal Nathwani, Kusumben Ishwarlal Popat, Nirmalaben Bhatt, and Gulsham Ahmed.[70]

Furthermore, even as Asian writers have taken up the genre of fiction and autobiography and embraced what were traditionally considered Western genres such as the novel, popular cultural forms and performances have continued to develop alongside these genres, even though they may not have received their share of critical commentary. Citing groups such as the Nairobi-based Wednesday Arts Circle and the Panjabi Kavi Sabha (Punjabi Poetry Society), formed in 1967, Cynthia Salvadori notes in her 1989 book, *Through Open Doors: A View of Asian Cultures in Kenya*, that the tradition of poetry recitals and theater has continued over the years. The Punjabi group held three major programs each year, and a similar Mombasa-based Urdu Poets Group continued to stage annual poetry readings at the time of her writing. In 1980, Salvadori writes, a group of writers from the Kokan region in India formed the Kokan Urdu Writers Guild, publishing over a dozen books of poetry, criticism, short stories, and biographical sketches in

Urdu.[71] Likewise, in *From Jhelum to Tana*, Neera Kapur-Dromson recreates the centrality of theatrical performances in the social life of the Indian community in Nairobi. She writes of the Hindus and Muslims who crossed religious affiliations to put on productions together in an effort to collect money for soldiers during the Second World War and later describes the extensive stagings of the *Ramlila* over a nine-day period during the Hindu festival of Dassera.[72] Kapur-Dromson relates her own involvement in a theater group named Natak in the 1970s and of the Hindi plays they staged over the years. *Aashiana* (Nest), she writes, scripted in March 1983 after the military coup attempt was "a plea of the mostly lower middle class working class Asians" for multiracial tolerance. Performed at the Kenya National Theatre, it played for four nights to a packed audience of four hundred (397).

Scholars have yet to fully account for the ways in which literature and the poetic imagination played a role in the political and cultural self-fashioning of Indians in Africa over the century. An excellent model for such research has recently been presented by Zarina Patel in her biography of Makhan Singh, one of the founding fathers of trade unionism in Kenya. Patel provides a compelling account of the central role of poetry in Singh's development as a political activist. Singh, writes Patel, was a dedicated poet, composing and reciting poetry at various public venues throughout his career. The earliest poem attributed to him, "Makhan Singh Gharjakia" is a tribute written in Punjabi to Guru Nanak dated November 27, 1928. The poems that followed over the years were all written in Punjabi and were centrally concerned with issues of social justice, anticolonialism, antiracism, nationalism, and workers' rights. Patel's book provides excerpted translations of some of these poems, and she also highlights the performative role of poems such as Singh's in the public culture among Kenyan Indians at the time. So, for instance, the poetry group Kaviya Phulwari (Garden of Poetry) was formed in 1928, primarily composed of Sikh men, among whom Makhan Singh was the youngest. "The poets would meet regularly and recite their compositions at various public places and especially at festivals such as Vaisakhi, Basant, Eid and Diwali."[73] In sharp contrast to the image of the Indian disinterested in literary culture, Patel shows how poetry was valued as a moral and political voice of conscience. Writing of Singh's activities in 1937, Patel notes, "In April the Shri Santana Dharma invited him, as on previous occasions, together with other Hindu, Muslim and Sikh poets to a *Kavi Darbar* (Poetry Gathering). In August he attended a *Kavi Sammalam* (Poetry Session) organized by the Arya Samaj. The invitation stipulated that the poems must be moral and social in character and could be written in Hindi, Urdu or Punjabi. The following year he participated in a *Bazm-I-Adab* (Poetry Session) held at the Railway Indian Institute, in which English, Hindi and Punjabi were added to the traditional Urdu languages of expression" (85). In addition to such public performances, as owners and operators of the Khalsa Press, printing in "Gurumukhi, Gujarati, Urdu, Hindi, English and various African languages," Makhan Singh and his father Sudh Singh also played a pivotal role in the dissemination of literary and religious texts in print (34).

Having provided this brief overview of the texts and lives of Asians in late-nineteenth- and twentieth-century East Africa, in the chapters that follow I turn to a number of life narratives as well as one work of fiction to highlight the role of the imagination in East African Asian life. In so doing I hope to show that Asians in East Africa have always, in fact, sung the songs that Shiva Naipaul could not hear and that their melodies, despite the prejudices of the European critic in Mombasa in 1914, have never been those of an "arrested development."

4. THROUGH INDIAN EYES

Travel and the Performance of Ethnicity

This chapter and the two that follow are interested in individual narratives and the local knowledges that they produce. Reading lives at this scale considerably muddies the general categories within which we think and narrate histories. It also muddies the political and ethical stakes that often, implicitly if not explicitly, frame our historical narratives—the closer we examine individual lives, the harder it often gets to sort out those that might seem to us to be ethically exemplary from those that seem less so. In the texts I examine, we will encounter individuals who were allied with the British colonial enterprise but were also, at the same time, social activists; we will meet individuals who became fabulously rich, but who also engaged in social welfare and philanthropy; and, finally, we will meet individuals whose personal economic interests were jeopardized by the nationalization of their enterprises, but who nevertheless lent support to the socialist ideals of their time.

My concern with these narratives is twofold. I am interested, of course, in what light they may shed on the diversity of the Indian experience in twentieth-century East Africa, but I am also keen on reading these texts as *narratives*, as stories that the authors have told not only to their potential readers but also to themselves. In his magisterial study *Sources of the Self*, Charles

Taylor has reminded us that "one is a self only among other selves. A self can never be described without reference to those who surround it."[1] If so, I am interested in examining the nature and extent to which Indians enacted "relational selves" in East African contexts.[2] How did they imagine themselves vis-à-vis the others that surrounded them? How do relational identities emerge in these texts, and what are the moral and ethical stakes attached to them? How do individuals negotiate the multiple layers of possible identification in any given context—when, for example, does one identify as a Parsi as opposed to an Indian, as an Indian as opposed to a British subject, as a Brahmin as opposed to a Hindu, as a younger brother as opposed to a sibling, as an Indian migrant in East Africa as opposed to a settled Kenyan?

In this chapter I focus on two early twentieth-century travelers, Ebrahimji Adamji and Sorabji Darookhanawala, who both undertook journeys into the East African interior. My reading of their narratives attempts to foreground the ways in which ethnicity is configured through a performance of identity that is structured both through social norms as well as through willful personal determination.[3] Adamji's narrative mediates between the ethical imperatives of a Muslim upbringing and the learned environment of a Christian schooling. It also negotiates between the relatively less empowered position of a young adult in the Bohra community and the aspirational desires of a businessman whose family is at risk of losing social standing. Social and family etiquette demands from Adamji a certain respect for his elder brothers, but his own impatience with their incompetence surfaces at several points in the narrative and ultimately, I suggest, results in it remaining unpublished in his lifetime. Adamji's text provides a glimpse of the Indian community's expectations of hospitality in early twentieth-century East Africa and it also showcases the widening circles of ethnic affiliations that sometimes inform the ways in which people decide on the company they keep. In the context of later accusations of exclusivity that were made against the community, Adamji's text allows for a more intimate understanding of how early travelers to the interior negotiated a sense of belonging in spaces that were alien to them. The text is of significance as well because it is written by a *failed* merchant. While the dominant trope associated with Asian enterprise is indeed one of commerce as romance, here, in Adamji's case, commerce is the distinct site of depression and potential failure.

Sorabji Darookhanawala's text is noteworthy for the ways in which it performs an exceptionalist ethnic identity, presenting the Parsi community as "not-quite" Indian even though it is commonly read as such. The text anticipates by several decades Homi Bhabha's late-twentieth-century reflection on the colonized subject "as almost the same but not quite," while engaging in acts of racial passing meant at once to impress darker subjects (both Indian and African) incapable of such passing *and* to point to the ultimate futility of the political possibilities of such passing.[4] At the same time that it cultivates an assimilationist space in the project of British colonialism, the text also registers an Indian exceptionalism—modernity in Africa, Darookhanawala argues, might best be delivered not by the British colonizers but by Indian commercial men. As we will see in the chapters that follow, this protectionism of the British state and its reluctance to allow the economy to be run on the principles of the free market was echoed in many ways by the postcolonial states as well—in the case of Kenya, for instance, through import restrictions and in Tanzania through a managed economy. While a few entrepreneurs found themselves benefiting from such an economy (because they worked in industries that were protected from import competition), many found the restrictions of the market a challenge.

TWO INDIAN TRAVELLERS, EAST AFRICA, 1902–1905

In 1997 the Friends of Fort Jesus Museum in Mombasa published an important volume entitled *Two Indian Travellers, East Africa, 1902–1905,* edited by Cynthia Salvadori and Judy Aldrick. The volume included two narratives by Indian men, one traveling from Mombasa to Uganda in 1902 and the other making five journeys to the East African interior between 1902 and 1905. As such, they are the earliest known travel accounts by Indians into the interior and an invaluable lens for our reimagining of the Indian encounter with Africa and Africans. Remarkably though, despite their narrative interest, the accounts have received little to no commentary by critics, save the rich editorial documentation by Salvadori and Aldrick that accompanied their publication.[5] A comparative reading of these two texts allows for a closer look at the ways in which religious orientation, class standing, age, and ethnic identification can influence the experience of travel, so that two individuals who may otherwise seem to share a common national identity ("Indian" or "Hindustani") may nevertheless experience their journeys in remarkably different ways.

The journeys undertaken by the two travelers followed the same route on the train and similar routes from the Kisumu terminal. To the best of our knowledge, their accounts were written almost contemporaneously. *Africa in Darkness* by Sorabji M. Darookhanawala, was published in Bombay in Gujarati in 1905. By the time the text was published, Darookhanawala, who was in his late fifties, had already died. While Darookhanawala actively edited his text for publication before his death, what efforts the author of the second text, Ebrahimji Noorbhai Adamji, made to publish his account remain unclear. Adamji's *My Journeys to the Interior* saw its first publication as an English translation (from Gujarati) in the collection edited by Salvadori and Aldrick. In the meantime, from the period during which it was penned—most likely around 1905—until it was published in translation, it lay among the family papers of Adamji's son Abdulhussein in its original manuscript form, written in a ledger. The single surviving copies of each of these texts are in the private possession of family heirs, thus they are only available to us mediated by translation. Furthermore, in the case of Darookhanawala's text in particular, we are told the editors took the liberty of reorganizing its contents, making it into "a more cohesive account" (106). Fortunately, the editors were meticulous in reprinting the table of contents from the original version, enabling us to reconstruct the narrative as the author first presented it.

Let us begin with the preliminaries. Who were these individuals—Adamji and Darookhanawala? Ebrahimji Adamji was the youngest of four brothers of a prominent Muslim Bohra merchant family in Mombasa. Having made their fortune by supplying British troops with rations during their war against the Nandi in 1897–98, Adamji's family had begun trading in ivory and financing the transportation of goods to and from the interior.[6] Following the general practice of Indian merchants at the time, the family partnered with two Baluchi men to conduct the actual trade into the interior, financing their travels and equipping them with trade goods to be later remunerated in the form of ivory.[7] The immediate context of Adamji's travel to the interior was the family's fear that the two Baluchis had absconded with their assets, leaving them with a significant financial loss of around forty-five thousand rupees. As the narrative indicates, while his first visit was in search of the potentially lost family assets, Adamji's return trips to the interior were engendered by a newly acquired desire for travel itself. Adamji, it is important to note, was a young man of about eighteen when he undertook his first expedition to the interior, and by the time he writes his narrative, after four more trips to the interior, he is no more than twenty-one years old. Clearly immersed in the everyday prayers and rituals of his Muslim upbringing, as one of the first generation of Indian schoolboys in Mombasa to attend the secondary school set up for Arab and Indian boys by the Church Missionary Society in 1894, at key junctures in his narrative Adamji inserts moral codes that he has picked up from his Christian teachers. Thus, for instance, he notes at the outset of his narrative the "saying in English" that "Occupation brings enjoyments" (13), a conception of self that pervades the entire trajectory of his narrative. Adamji, a fully incorporated member of his Bohra community, is also marked, then, by his Christian education. According to the editors, he is most likely the only member of his immediate family to be fluent in English (5). While he is of Indian heritage, we must remember that he is Mombasa born, and at the time he writes this narrative he has never been to India. When he refers to "home," then, it most resolutely means the coastal city of Mombasa and not any place in India.

In contrast, Sorabji Darookhanawala was almost fifty-five when he undertook his journey to the interior; unlike Adamji, he was by then a well-traveled man. References to the English Channel suggest that he may have taken at least one trip to Europe, but he most certainly has his feet in both Africa and the Indian subcontinent. Born in India and trained as an engineer, Darookhanawala appears to have moved to Zanzibar in the 1870s to work on one of the sultan's steamers. He was later promoted to become the first Health Department officer in the sultanate and was responsible for monitoring the sanitation conditions in Zanzibar (185–186). Darookhanawala was a member of the Parsi community, and, as his narrative suggests, this was an identity that was dear to him. Followers of Zoroastrianism, and originally a diasporic community from Persia, the Parsi community had settled in western India in the tenth century. Presenting themselves as cosmopolitan subjects of empire, Parsis embraced a Western sense of modernity during the British Raj and were often regarded by both the British and other Indians as more Westernized.[8] In Zanzibar Darookhanawala (hereafter referred to as Sorabji) rose to become a community leader, involving himself in religious affairs and social welfare.[9] He soon managed to secure the patronage of the legendary Ismaili entrepreneur Allidina Visram, who was then establishing his empire of trading stores all over the interior. It was Visram who sponsored Sorabji's 1902 visit, securing help and accommodation for him at various stores along the journey and subscribing in advance to purchase 150 copies of the book that Sorabji pledged to write about his expedition. Thus, unlike Adamji's narrative, we note that Sorabji's text comes with an audience already inscribed even before it is written—the audience consists not only of Visram, the main sponsor, but also seventy-five other subscribers in Zanzibar and forty more in Mombasa, all members of an already established or aspiring merchant or professional class. An important aim of Sorabji's narrative, then, is to report on the conditions of the interior and their conduciveness to further enterprise and trade.

Ebrahimji Adamji writes that his first journey to the interior was made not to "admire nature's beauty" (13), but rather one borne out of desperation. His elder brother Mohammedali's failure to recover the family's assets from the two Baluchi men means that they are faced with a serious financial crisis. Despite his best efforts at persuading his elder brothers to let him undertake the journey into the interior, he is unable to gain their sanction. Adamji is "deeply depressed" by his brothers' intransigence (15). After Mohammedali undertakes a second trip that is aborted midway because of an outbreak of bubonic plague in Nairobi, Adamji decides to take matters in his own hands and leaves for the interior without telling his family. The narrative of his five trips is certainly one of discovery of new places and experiences, but most importantly it is, as is so often the case with texts about travel, a journey of self-discovery. "Travelling," writes Adamji in the very first sentence of his narrative, "is like a school and the traveller is like a student" (13). Furthermore, traveling is therapeutic: "During his travels on this earth he learns so much and it brings him so much happiness that he forgets his sorrows during this time. In this happy state he wants to proceed farther and farther and is eager to learn more and more about new and wonderful things" (13).

The relationship that Adamji draws between travel and happiness is a curious one since the tone of the text is overwhelmingly melancholic. Adamji is often prone to depression. At the opening of his narrative his depression is as much rooted in what he perceives as his elder brothers' lack of confidence in him as it is rooted in his family's distress over financial matters. An important narratorial imperative, then, is to tell the story of how the author Ebrahimji, the youngest of four brothers, managed to secure the respect and admiration of his elder brothers as well as of his larger community.[10] It is, in this sense, a story of coming to maturity and of gaining family and societal respect. Returning to Mombasa after having secured the ivory that earlier eluded the family in the interior, Adamji writes of his brothers, "Their attitude towards me changed. From that day onwards my brothers respected me" (30). Likewise, in the larger community, "my name was spoken with respect. . . . They regarded me as definitely clever and courageous to have undertaken such a dangerous journey on my own" (30). But, if there is a sense of accomplishment at this moment in the text, Adamji remains till the end of his narrative insecure about the leverage he has with his brothers and continues to remain sensitive to the larger community's reading of his family enterprise. He cannot, for instance, persuade his brothers to stop engaging in the ivory trade, and his many warnings that the trade was becoming increasingly risky land on deaf ears. We know from both textual as well as extratextual sources that the Adamji ivory trading enterprise did indeed fail and that the family had to find other means of livelihood. In the text the scene of failure is present but understated. Returning to Mombasa from one of his trips to Kisumu, Ebrahimji is accompanied by his brother Mohammedali to the offices of Messrs. Hansing and Co. where he is instructed by his brother to sign any documents that he is given without bothering to read them. The dutiful younger brother does as instructed and notes, "As we were returning home, my brother Mohammedali told me that they were the official documents of all our property. I felt very sad about it but nothing could be done"(58). The family firm is here being liquidated and Ebrahimji Adamji will, we know from extratextual sources, use his knowledge of English to go on to become the Mombasa representative for the British firm Whiteaways, the John White Shoe Company, and other English firms (77).

From the beginning of the narrative to its end, the family's financial woes have a profound effect on Adamji. At one point he claims that he "can't write any more about this subject because I find it painful" (16). He claims that "there is no disease as bad as depression" (13) and adds that when he contemplates the vicissitudes of life he feels so bitter that "even my pen stops writing" (13). It is through travel that Adamji seeks a cure, a more hopeful take on life, and, if the various triumphs in securing ivory bring cheer and light to his otherwise anxious persona, it is the company he keeps on his various journeys that sustains him. The narrative presents a fascinating array of both personal choices on the part of Adamji as well as socially accepted codes of association and obligation that are worth noting. In Adamji's view, for travel to be pleasurable it must be conducted with fellow travelers, preferably those with whom one already shares a set of beliefs, dispositions, and tastes or those whose lives and careers one aspires to emulate. On his first journey, the one he has embarked on without telling his family, he is relieved to find two fellow Bohra men in the same train compartment and pleased that at least one of them will make the journey up to Kiu, a station almost three-quarters of the way to Nairobi. On the second journey he sets out with the Baluchi man Shambe bin Abdulla, who will act as his trading agent in the interior and who has been equipped for this role with a number of items for trade purchased by the Adamji family. They have each bought tickets for third-class travel, but, by the middle of the journey, Ebrahimji manages to secure for himself an "upgrade" to second class thanks to the invitation of an elderly Bohra man who, along with three other men, has a reserved a second-class compartment. The interpersonal performances of etiquette involved here, and the manner in which they evolve from station to station as the men journey onward, is a particularly engaging (and socially instructive) experience for the reader. Adamji, who has met the four gentlemen at the original point of departure at Mombasa, prearranges for some mangoes and tender coconuts to be delivered to Mazeras station. He is approached by one of the younger men in the party to see if the latter can purchase some coconuts. Adamji says that they are not for sale, but after keeping a couple for himself, he sends the rest with the young man for the "Seths" (a term of respect for elderly, usually wealthy, gentlemen). A few stations later, Adamji is summoned by one of the gentlemen, who invites him to sit with them in their compartment. When the train reaches Voi around dinnertime, a crucial decision must be made—should Adamji return to his compartment for his meal or should he stay? As the narrative suggests, this is no small matter given the symbolic role of communal meals in the society and the performative role they play in enacting social hierarchies. "These Seths," writes Adamji, "urged me to eat with them, so I accepted and sat down to have my meal with them. The reason I did not make a fuss was that although I was young and alone, I was the son of a businessman too. I did not demur further out of courtesy, for had I protested further, they would have said 'this Bohra boy is being arrogant.' So I respectfully accepted their invitation to dinner" (34). Notice here the societal expectation that a young man such as Ebrahimji should demur from sharing a meal with such important men as the Seths. Notice, too, how by not refusing, Ebrahimji is enacting his privileged position of being the "son of a businessman," a position unavailable to his Baluchi companion, who, we must remember, has been left behind in the third-class compartment (giving the lie, incidentally, to Adamji's statement that he [Adamji] is "alone"). The saga of invitations and demure acceptance continues into the journey; Adamji returns to his third-class compartment after dinner and spends the night "sitting up, dozing on the hard bench" (34). However, once the train reaches Nairobi and one of the four travelers disembarks, Adamji is acutely aware of the potential of securing a spot in the second-class compartment: "So instead of four there were three in their compartment. So it was possible for them, if they wanted, to invite a fourth passenger into their compartment" (34). Will they or won't they? The invitation does not come forth immediately, undoubtedly to Adamji's disappointment, but after a suitable interval at the Kikuyu station he is summoned by Seth Mohammedali, who says: " 'My son, stay here with us.' So, again, without demurring, I accepted his invitation and thanked him for looking after my well being" (34).

I have dwelt on this story at some length because it demonstrates the notions of hospitality and patronage that Indians in East Africa, and indeed elsewhere, had assimilated as part of their social upbringing, especially when Adamji lived, but also, in many cases, for generations after. Throughout the narrative there are instances where the obligations of hospitality come as foremost priorities, even when the guest (such as Adamji) may have come for the purpose of securing an outstanding debt from the host. Oftentimes, while business and trade are clearly on everyone's mind, no mention is made of such matters until the guest has been served food (often on a communal plate to be shared with the host) and tea (preferably with a milk base rather than water) and has had a chance to bathe and rest. Business propositions and discussions can only take place afterward, and in Adamji's narrative they often take place in the context of a walk to the local bazaar that is both social as well as trade related. Over and over again we are told of the number of shops in the area, the exact ownership details, and the current state of the business. Greetings from friends and news of other places and people is often the primary glue of conversations, but the stores also serve as protobanks, where advances of money can be sought on a credit note written to a branch of the store in Mombasa, or money can be handed over for safekeeping, which may be collected later from a store branch on the coast. In lieu of credit notes, immediate partnerships can also be made, as Adamji does on one occasion with the agent of Allidina Visram in Kisumu. Here Adamji invites the agent to purchase half a consignment of ivory that has arrived on a caravan led by Adamji's Baluchi debtor, thus making available the cash needed to pay for the transportation permits and the porters (28–29).

Ethnic identifications are central to the orbit of hospitality and often (though not always) to the choice of companionship. The narrative demonstrates this quite well in the concentric circles of ethnic identification that Adamji and his fellow travelers inhabit. Thus, for instance, note this passage about a train journey from Mombasa to Kisumu: "There was a Lohana in my Compartment who had also boarded the train at Mombasa and was going to Kisumu. I did not know anyone so I went and sat with him at the station" (21). Or again, "Because there were no Bohras in Machakos, I went to stay at Khoja Dhalla Esmail's place" (68). In both instances, the suggestion is that in the absence of the immediately proximate identity marker—in this case

"Bohra"—the traveler will choose to associate with the next available order of ethnic identification. While the choice of traveling companionship may well be a matter of Adamji's personal dispositions, the narrative suggests that the codes of hospitality that were expected of Indians wherever they found themselves in the East African landscape were socially structured. When a stranger came into town, he could expect to receive hospitality from either a close business associate or a member of his own immediate community (say a Bohra or a Lohana). If no such person could be found, then he would seek hospitality from the next order of identification—in most cases, religion. We see this in the case of Adamji's first unannounced visit to Kisumu in the middle of the night when he runs into Khoja Ladha, an accountant working for the firm of Allidina Visram. Adamji writes that as soon as Ladha learns that he has no place to stay, "he at once ordered, in their Cutchi language, another Khoja young man to take this Bohra, that is me, to the shop" (22). In the context of a newly founded town such as Nairobi where the railhead had reached barely four years earlier, the narrative gives us a glimpse of a prototypical hotel on the premises of A. M. Jivanji's godown and bungalow. There is no direct reference to a monetary transaction involved in such stays, but the language invites us to speculate on this possibility: "These rooms were a great convenience to travellers. There were always anywhere from five to eleven lodgers there from different places such as Kiu, Kitui, Muranga and Mombasa," observes Adamji. "They took special pains to try to satisfy the needs of various types of travellers staying in their guest rooms" (41–42).

And what of travels to areas where there might be no Indians at all? Here we see Adamji taking refuge in "native" huts and trading with Africans for perishables such as "milk, carrots, maize and chickens" (38). At times he prefers staying in the African homes to putting up the canvas tent that he carries. Unlike the hospitality offered by business partners and fellow Indians in the more remote areas for which no money is directly exchanged, the use of the African homes often accompanies a trade transaction between Adamji and the host in question. With the exception of one incident with a man from Kavirondo who is suspicious and hostile toward him (his suspicion most likely rooted in the fact that Adamji and his party have approached him after dark in search of a caravan—nightfall being often associated in East African societies with nefarious activities), all the other exchanges that Adamji reports with Africans come across as relatively benign and friendly ones. This should not suggest that the exchanges are in any way unproblematic or that we can't discern traces of Adamji's relative position of privilege in them. After all, one need only point to the many porters that Adamji employs over his travels and remember the harsh conditions of labor this entailed.[11] Nor is the conversation that Adamji reports between himself and one of his African hosts on the matter of clothing and nakedness devoid of a certain ethnocentrism on Adamji's part (37). Nevertheless, remembering Mary Louise Pratt's reading of European travel narratives in Africa as arising in the context of the "reconception of Africans as a market rather than as a commodity,"[12] one might argue that the tenor of the conversation and Adamji's own advocacy of clothing comes across more as a matter between a trader and a potential customer—of Adamji trying to create a new market for cloth among uninterested Africans, than it does of missionary zeal.[13] Then again, it is entirely possible that, despite his conversation with his host, the single young Bohra man, arriving from a coastal society that has a very conservative dress code, is not too disturbed by the healthy nudity that surrounds him. The following narration certainly suggests so: "Many native men and women were bathing completely naked in this river which is called the Aswadera. One young healthy Kavirondo woman came and stood next to us. Alibhai Dalal asked her politely, 'Maber?' which means how are you? She replied, 'Maber kende,' which means, 'very well' and then she said he was very clever" (45).[14]

Adamji's relations with most of the Africans he meets are cordial if not friendly, and his relations with Europeans are of a similar order. As we see in his meeting with Dr. MacDonald on the banks of the Wadera River, most of the conversation, which incidentally is conducted in Kiswahili, after the British doctor has offered him and his companion some milk, amounts to small talk. On one of his later train journeys, having repeatedly turned down an invitation from a couple of Bohra acquaintances to join them in their compartment so as not to be a burden on them, Adamji eventually gives in to his ethnic associational sensibilities: "In my compartment there were some Greeks and Europeans so I preferred to sleep in Ebrahimji's compartment" (67). Adamji's choice to sleep in the compartment with the Bohras rather than the Europeans is of note here, especially in the context of his prior exposure to Europeans—unlike many members of his community, Adamji, we recall, has had a European missionary schooling, and, as the liberal use of the English language in the text suggests, language itself would not have been a barrier. Nevertheless, unlike Sorabji Darookhanawala, who we will soon see, enjoys the company of Europeans, Adamji tends to be most comfortable in the midst of those he finds most familiar. Such familiarity of experience is most often religiously based, but not always so.

The Swahili language offers an important point of commonality, and it is a language that we hear used in the narrative among traders of Indian origin who may or may not share a common Indian language. While his ethnicity is never specified, at one point in the narrative Adamji writes of securing as a travel companion a man born in Mombasa who can speak fluent Kiswahili. Adamji bonds with him immediately: "He was like a *brother* to me"(54), claims Adamji, suggesting that for him social identities are based not only on national or racial identities but on culturally shared codes of experience.

We cannot be certain as to why Ebrahimji Adamji's narrative was never published, and whether or not this had to do with the author's own sense of social propriety. One plausible reason may lie in Adamji's conflicted feelings toward his elder brothers. Social propriety and accepted age hierarchies mean that the author remains a dutiful younger brother. Nevertheless, throughout the narrative Adamji's displeasure and sometimes even contempt for his brothers does not escape the reader's attention. For instance, referring to the Baluchi Hasham who has safeguarded some ivory belonging to the Adamji family, ivory that the elder brother Mohammedali had failed to secure, Adamji writes, "As he was talking he must have realized that I was not like my brother [Mohammedali]. There was no doubt that I was clever, generous and courageous" (24). Earlier, referring to the same failure on Mohammedali's part, the author notes of his brother and his Baluchi companion, "They were so scared that neither of them even made any inquiries, they just ran away like children. They did not try to accomplish even a little of what they had been told to do"(15). At yet another point in the narrative, when his own path crosses his brother Abdulhussein's during a trip, the tone is one of mild irritation. Here one can see the truth of the claim often made about the motivations for travel—even in the context of a socially needy individual such as Adamji—travel is at one level about getting away from family and all the strictures that family relations entail.[15] In many ways the writing of the narrative is for Adamji a "working out" of his feelings toward his brothers, and, while he continues to follow the proper codes of respect toward his elder brothers, his narrative comes across as an "I told you so" statement to the brothers who have refused to follow his business advice. One can only speculate that the author, recognizing this tension, may have ultimately chosen to keep the account private.

That the book was not in fact published during the author's lifetime does not mean that it wasn't intended to be published or otherwise circulated when it was first written. There is sufficient textual evidence to make this claim. For instance, at one point in the narrative when Adamji discloses that he had regretted his purchase of unsatisfactory merchandise from a fellow Bohra merchant who had pushed a hard sell, he is careful not to name the merchant (31). In other instances, Adamji's text often reads like a public acknowledgment and note of thanks to all the individuals who have lent him support on his travels. Here, too, the narrative is self-conscious about its framing—on the one hand Adamji wants to register his gratitude, on the other he is careful not to seem to indulge in flattery : "I am not flattering or praising anyone unduly when I say that Seth A. M. Jivanjee and Co. went out of their way to look after the best interests and comforts of all Bohra travellers" (41). If flattery of others is unbecoming in such a narrative, so is self-praise. Adamji's text betrays a deep anxiety about seeming to be boastful even when the form and structure of the narrative—that of a triumphant return with a prize that others have sought and failed to obtain—are predicated on precisely such boastfulness. Thus, when on his first journey Adamji is accompanied by a gentleman who likes to talk about his own accomplishments, Adamji comes up with what we might consider to be a vernacular theory of autobiography. Reminding his readers that great men never boast about themselves, just as diamonds do not proclaim their value, Adamji notes that "it is wrong to boast and praise yourself all the time" (19).

Yet, the narrative is all about self-praise. Adamji's way of mediating this tension is in keeping with the larger community's assessment of the relationship between human agency and God's will. In a telling discussion of the phenomenal success of a fellow businessman, a discussion one imagines must have been held with at least a twinge of envy, Adamji writes, "We started talking about Alibhai Mulji Jivanji Karachiwala who was known as A. M. *Jivanji & Co.* God had helped him make millions in a short time. It is not surprising because God has the power to do whatever he wishes to do. He made Alibhai a millionaire and there is nothing unbelievable or surprising about it because God's powers belong to God" (17). Jivanji is the passive receptacle of divine benevolence here—he has little to no agency. How are we to read this?—if God was good to Jivanji, he may also decide to be good to us? Or, if Jivanji is so successful, don't think that it is because he is smarter or better than us but rather because it is God's will? Or, instead, if we ourselves don't make it big, it isn't because there is anything inherently wrong with us but because it is God's will? Whatever the formulation, the undercurrents of each of them percolate at various points in Adamji's narrative. In terms of his own successes from time to time, Adamji can at once point liberally to them and insist that they are really the will of God. "I thanked God again and again. You need God's blessing in everything you do. . . . All that I have written about myself is nothing but the truth. I have not written this to praise myself. I have written truthfully, describing what actually happened. I know it is bad taste to praise oneself. I have written this [account] because it is the truth, not to boast about myself" (31). This then, is in keeping with the larger moral that Adamji's narrative wants to make, a moral that welds together the work ethic that Adamji associates with his missionary schooling (with its emphasis on occupation and the dangers of idleness) and the emphasis on God's will that he inherits from his Islamic background. Thus, "if things still go wrong after careful thinking and hard work, then you can blame fate. You can't blame fate if you don't work. It is true that you cannot fight fate but it is wrong to fold your arms and do nothing and then blame your destiny" (32).

In contrast to Adamji's more personal and family-driven narrative, Sorabji Darookhanawala's text reads as a manifesto for modernity. As such, it draws on the preexisting figuration of Africa that pervaded both the European as well as the Indian imagination of the time. Africa is seen as primitive, in need of civilization and light, and the text is an early instantiation of the struggle between European and Indian claims of modernity. In translating the original title *Andarama Rahelo Africa* as *Africa in Darkness*, the editors risk evacuating a significant rhetorical claim being made here—a more accurate translation would be *In Darkness Remains Africa*, a title that clearly points to what Sorabji Darookhanawala sees as the hitherto incomplete project of modernity engaged in by the British, a project that he claims may better be completed by his fellow Indians. While he remains a loyal subject of the British empire, gifting, for instance, new clothes to young Gikuyu children at the Roman Catholic Mission in celebration of King Edward VII's coronation day (127), or approving the imperial project of Britain in the Transvaal and elsewhere (162), he is critical of what he sees as the inadequate development of East Africa on the part of the British. Everywhere he goes—from the small town of Jomvu near Mombasa where he finds high-quality clay that can be made into roof tiles and utensils, to the river banks in Nairobi where the land yields potatoes, vegetables, and barley, which could be further developed to cultivate wheat and cotton, to the highlands of Kenya where he finds the soil to be unmatched in its fertility—Sorabji sees missed opportunities and fortunes waiting to be made. He wants the colonial government to reduce the tariffs on the railway so more people can use it for commercial gain (129) and he insists that developing agricultural production and mining in Kenya could rocket the country to an enviable economic state. "This country," writes Sorabji, "could supply enough cotton for England, and by so doing would give a great blow to the American cotton trade, and this place would prosper" (127). The greatest hurdles to such prosperity, Sorabji notes, are the "strict" and "backwards" rules that the state enforces. "The Government is to be blamed for that. Until a liberal attitude is adopted and experienced officials come to run the Government, the country will suffer. Brave people who want to be adventurous cannot do so until the Government becomes more liberal" (126). Hearkening back to a world of unfettered commerce, much as that outlined in Ghosh's depiction of the early Indian Ocean trade, Sorabji reads colonialism as a distinct barrier to economic growth and prosperity.

In 1902 Sorabji would have counted himself among such "brave" people whose dreams of prosperity were being thwarted by the state. While, as Robert Gregory has suggested, the white settler claims for exclusivity in the highlands had not yet been fully realized, with Indians being permitted to purchase land as late as 1905, Sorabji nevertheless meets with resistance.[16] His efforts at purchasing land near the highland property of a French missionary are frustrated by the commissioner who "was not willing to give that permission as he wished to keep that area reserved for the Europeans. I did not press for my claims. If I had forced him, I could have bought the land but at great expense" (129). Sorabji writes that he is "very much against this treatment of the Indians" (163), but, in keeping with his general disposition of wanting to maintain good relations with Europeans, he feels that it is a pill that for now he must swallow. Interestingly, what irks him more than the ill treatment is the lack of business sense—it is in the government's interest, he claims, to open up the country for development. It is in the government's interest to lower the tariff on the railway to a point where it yields a maximum gain: "The English have first right to profit from the railway but the Railway will be useless if there is no way of making a profit" (163), rues Sorabji, recognizing the racist policies that are in direct conflict with a liberal economy. Commenting on the underdevelopment of infrastructure and industry in Uganda, Sorabji angrily notes, "The English have not made any development in the area. They have not improved trade and they have not been able to provide tools for improved farming. The improvements and development depend on the Government which has hardly done its duty. The reason for that may be that the Government wants to improve the area for Europeans only" (149).

The major culprit in this scenario, writes Sorabji, is not British imperial will but rather the bureaucratic "narrow-minded old-fashioned officials" (149) who are sent to govern. In a revealing comment that combines class as well as gender prejudices, Sorabji refers to these officials as "effeminate" and goes on to note that "if the officials are from noble families they rule nobly and the development is greater." (149) But, claims Sorabji, East Africa has received only commoners as officials, people who engage in petty discriminations based on race. "Their treatment of the natives because they are black and have a different lifestyle is unfair," he complains, "The able natives are not given a chance to prove themselves because of their colour" (149).

As will become clear a little later, despite his claim on behalf of Africans here, Sorabji is not himself immune to racial prejudice. What I want to observe for the moment, however, is that, despite his resentment of European racism (and his critique of it in a book written in Gujarati and never meant to be translated), Sorabji chooses *not* to challenge white privilege while he is in East Africa. On the contrary, he often seeks the company of Europeans, and the role they play in his narrative is central to his sense of self. Before setting out on his journey, Sorabji equips himself with letters of introduction to "the Traffic Manager, the Sub-Commissioner, a Dr. French and the French Missionaries Reverend Father" (119), all Europeans who provide him with hospitality and assistance on his travels. Waiting for his luggage to arrive at Voi, he strikes up a conversation with a couple of Greeks and a German trader and arranges to travel with the German to Kilimanjaro. While the trip has to be abandoned because of a luggage delay, Sorabji takes the opportunity to inform his readers about his earlier friendship with a German civil engineer who, he writes, "became so friendly with me that he didn't like any other companions, he liked my company" (124). This German, Sorabji tells us, believing the latter to be a prosperous man, had been so keen on entering into a business partnership with him that he resigned from his job only to find in Sorabji an uninterested player.[17] Sorabji's trips to the highlands near Kikuyu station are peppered by visits to the French priest Hemery who offers to sell him the land that the commissioner prevents him from buying. Later, when the marine superintendent in Kisumu does not allow Sorabji to travel first class on the government steamer since first-class travel is restricted to government officials, the deputy commissioner of Uganda sends him a message that he can travel the following day on a different government charter. On this voyage across Lake Victoria, Sorabji has the opportunity to befriend the European captain, who, we are told, "came to know that I was a skillful boatman" and thus "became very friendly with me and asked my advice now and then" (141).

Unlike Adamji, then, who, we remember, slips away from his train compartment rather than spend the night with European travelers, Sorabji actively solicits the companionship of Europeans who, for the most part, reciprocate. Situated in a colonially structured world when power was associated with Europe, the depiction of friendly relations with Europeans is meant in this narrative to render Sorabji with a higher authority and status than his less Westernized readers. And, if European companionship accords status, the possibility of passing as European gives the author further cultural capital. There are two spectacular instances in the text where the site of dining presents Sorabji with the opportunity for a European rather than an Indian affiliation. The first is at the train station of Kibos where Sorabji arrives in time for dinner. Tired by now of eating the English food served on the train, he approaches the Hindu stationmaster and asks if he could have some Indian food, for which he is willing to pay any price. "When he saw me in English clothes and speaking perfect English," writes Sorabji, "he was completely flabbergasted. He did not know what to say. I told him I was a Parsi and would be very happy to eat whatever food he was cooking. After my explanation, he was relieved of his anxiety and gladly set about preparing a meal for me" (131). The element of passing as European in the eyes of the Hindu stationmaster is noteworthy here, but what is even more interesting is what follows. After three hours of cooking, the Hindu returns with "two thalis full of puris with one dollop of chutney on the side," a meal that Sorabji finds too sweet for his palate. "How could I possibly swallow the stuff! I picked up just one puri, to please him, and then pushed the thali away with my other hand. I could see the distress on his face so I made some lame excuse" (131). If this moment speaks to class privilege (Sorabji the "passibly" European first-class passenger does not really have to be too concerned about offending the stationmaster), it also performs an ethnic distancing in the moment of culinary longing—Sorabji is tired of English food and wants an Indian meal. The Indian meal he is offered is nevertheless one that he finds alien. Sorabji has to take comfort in English food—tea and biscuits and later sardines, jam, and butter (131). What is being dramatized here is the Parsi's distance from a normative Indianness, and at one point in the narrative Sorabji is quite explicit in articulating it: "The Parsis," he writes "should not be considered as native Indians but because the Parsis have lived in India for hundreds of years they are taken as natives of India" (165).

A second scene of dining in the text replicates such distancing, except in this new context the immediate "other" is not Indian but African.[18] In a description of a visit to an island in Lake Victoria, a description that indulges in the most primitivist stereotypes of "untouched" Africans, Sorabji describes the islanders showing great curiosity over the cooking of the rice and chicken that is being prepared for his meal. He proceeds to describe the scene: "When my food was ready my cook arranged my plate, glass, knife and fork, a bottle of sauce and salt on a mat. They watched all this carefully and were talking amongst themselves. I could not understand what they were saying but I guessed that they were wondering about all the things laid out for eating. When everything was ready, my food was brought to me on a plate. They were fascinated to see me eat with a knife and fork and spoon. About a hundred people assembled to watch me eat" (154). While Sorabji's "civilized" dining is a spectacle for the islanders on the lake, it is no less a show that he puts on for his Indian readers. The use of a knife, fork, and spoon, not to mention the bottle of sauce on the side, is as alienating an experience for his non-fork-wielding Indian readership as it is for the Africans. Sorabji is calculatingly fashioning himself here in the image of a European rather than an Indian traveler.[19]

Sorabji's embrace of Europeans and a Europeanized identity is not disconnected from his own sense of Parsi identity as an exceptional one. Suggesting a typology of ethnicity Sorabji often refers to an individual as a "true" or "typical" Parsi. We learn of the Parsi businessman Kamani who has died in shock and humiliation after his Zanzibar-based enterprise goes bankrupt. Sorabji is quick to assert that even in the midst of his great loss Kamani paid back his investors since, "like a true Parsi," "he was an honest and admirable businessman who died because of his principles" (173). At another point we are told of a "typical" Parsi man in Nairobi who has come upon some hard financial times because he has been unable to save. "Because a Parsi lives in such a grand style even when he is not earning much, there is no possibility of his saving any money for lean days" (126). What might appear to be a censure here is, in fact, not such at all—for, in accord with the popular imagination of the time, the Parsi is seen here to approximate the European. Unlike the frugal Indian who will make do with less, the Parsi is a consummate spender. Lest there be any doubt about this valence, Sorabji spells it out in another discussion. Referring to the European prejudice against Indians, the author notes, "They have never met a true Parsi, who is always neat and tidy in his habits, who knows how and when to spend money. Some Parsis even surpass the English in the open-handed way they spend their money" (165). Such a manner is in direct contrast to the thrifty habits of even the richest non-Parsi Indian who, writes Sorabji, "is not at all conscious of his physical cleanliness and his clothes are such that if he stands for a short while near you, you do not need to take any medicine to induce vomiting because your stomach heaves with bile" (164–65). Culture, Sorabji suggests, rather than class, separates the Parsi from other Indians since "the life style and way of dressing are the same for the rich and poor Indians" (165). When he goes on to write that "Memons, Bhatias, Khojas and Banias are all alike in their unclean manners" (166), he clearly risks offending the sensibilities of some of his readers and sponsors. Nevertheless, the reformist agenda that drives his text overrides such concerns of patronage. He is unequivocal in his critique and goes to the point of arguing that Indians who do not change their "disgusting habits" (165) should not seek to travel by first- or second-class train compartments, for by doing so "they make life miserable for their [more polished and well groomed] companions" (166).

We do not know, regrettably, how Sorabji's Gujarati readers took such reformist critique, but we do have some sense from the text as to how at least one African responded to a related reformist attempt on Sorabji's part. Spending a period of twelve days on the shores of Lake Victoria, Sorabji engaged through interpreters with some local Kavirondo men:

> When I was preaching about not going naked I felt that I was doing a very noble thing but as my interpreter was explaining to them what I was saying, one of the elderly men started shaking with rage. He told me that I was a very wicked man to have only seen the nakedness of sex. He said that God had created them naked and they remained naked to please God. He said that he hated people who looked at them with ignorant eyes. He said they were living in family groups and felt perfectly happy being naked, and it was because I was full of lust I covered myself. When the interpreter told me all this, I became pale with shock and shame. I was very embarrassed so I changed the subject. I asked them questions about their customs but they started walking away in anger.
>
> (133)

Unlike Adamji's casual discussions with Africans about clothing, Sorabji's self-described "preaching" clearly works on an explicitly articulated and patronizing moral register. The elderly man's angry response suggests that such conversations are not new to him but rather very familiar. Indeed, the hatred that the elder registers against people who look at his culture with "ignorant eyes" can only be read in the context of the increasing missionary presence and the demands of Western-styled modernity that were already making their mark on the cultures of the area. Despite his own tendency to read the Africans he encounters as living in relatively isolated and "untouched" societies, Sorabji's engagement with the Kavirondo and other Africans in the interior should be more accurately read as part of a longer history of contact, trade, and cultural interaction.

The Africans we meet in Sorabji's narrative can be divided into two broad categories—there are those he employs either as porters or as a boat captain and there are those he visits or otherwise attempts to describe in an ethnographic fashion. His relations with the former are often tense, with Sorabji often exceeding the bounds of humane treatment and his laborers responding with subtle or not so subtle resistance. So, for example, he writes at one point of poking the porters who carry him with the end of a stick and threatening to beat them (144). The porters, in turn seem to have a difficult time balancing him—"When they changed sides we were afraid of being toppled so we shouted, but they could not understand our language" (143). The result is that Sorabji—who has specially equipped himself with a bentwood rocking chair that would be perched high above the porters so as to enable him "to observe and enjoy the countryside" as he traveled— is reduced to walking much of the distance alongside the porters. Again, when he charters a dhow on his return trip from Uganda, he and his fellow passengers observe structures that look like minarets on a distant island. Despite the Swahili captain's assurance that no such minarets exist, Sorabji commands the unwilling captain to sail the dhow to the island. After sailing for a good part of the day and reaching the island, the captain's position is confirmed since no minarets are to be found. At a later point in the journey, when the captain wants to stay the night on an island rather than moving forward, Sorabji, aware of the fact that the crew may be "tired of rowing and of raising and lowering the sail of the boat" (152), nevertheless commands him to set forth. The tension that continues to develop between Sorabji and the captain and the ways in which the captain tries to outsmart his employer comprise, along with the story of the porters, a textbook case of what James Scott has memorably described as the "Weapons of the Weak."[20]

If Sorabji's relations with the Africans he employs are fraught with tension, his narrative framing of other Africans is in keeping with the split discourse on Africans that he inherits from the European colonial archive. Dorothy Hammond and Alta Jablow identify this split in British writings on Africans as follows: "There are two sets of projections. In one, Africans represent the pejorative negation of all good traits of the British. In this set of images, the African is lewd, savage, instinctual, thoughtless, in short the 'beastly savage,' which is by far the most common projection. The other depicts a nostalgic view in which Africans represent the former, now lost, values of the British. Here, the African is the 'noble savage,' an image restricted to particular tribes or individuals. As ever, the 'noble savage' serves the writer as a critique of his or her own society."[21] Both of these representations make their way into Sorabji's text.

Salvadori rightly suggests that Sorabji's narrative is usefully read in the context of the existing European tradition of travel writing as "his writing seems to be loosely based on his familiarity with the books of famous African explorers such as Burton, Speke, Livingstone, and Stanley who had made Zanzibar their base" (101). Indeed, the very first European mentioned in the text is not a personal acquaintance but a colonial statesman and writer. In the preface the author acknowledges his debt to "Mr. Johnston, the Commissioner of Central Africa," whose book he claims has provided him with useful information about East African wild animals (117–18).[22] From Johnston Sorabji derives a classificatory system for distinguishing between various African ethnicities that is based on the racial (and racist) typologies of the day. Sorabji recognizes that the act of classification and distinction renders an authority to the text similar to the authority he claims for himself when he shows that he can appreciate the differences between various kinds of coffee.[23]

Readers of *Africa in Darkness* need to exercise some caution in interpreting the text since the valences Sorabji puts on his different depictions of Africans are unfortunately made more difficult by the editorial reordering of his original text when it was translated and published in English. Consider, for instance, his description of the "Manyema" as "man-eating demons" (179). An obsession with alleged cannibalism among the Manyema was a central component of European travel writing and was in keeping with the increasingly prevalent and sensational tales that Hammond and Jablow suggest began to circulate in the mid to late nineteenth century.[24] Sorabji's text clearly drew on this sensationalist archive and presented the Manyema to his readers even though his own travels brought him nowhere near Manyema territory. Why, we might ask, would a travel narrative that purports to tell of the author's personal encounters include a description of people whose territory the author has never visited? Here, the placement of the discussion of the Manyema in the original text offers a clue since it differs quite significantly from that in the translated text. Whereas the translation groups the discussion along with other "General Impressions" at the end of the book, in the original, the Manyema are the opening salvo—they are our first glimpse of Africa—"There are many incredible and unbelievable events described in old books. Many of them have been exaggerated like stories in the 'Arabian Nights' but some of them I can verify from things I have seen with my own eyes in East Africa" (179). Thus begins the original Gujarati text, drawing the reader in, establishing the sense of both mystery and discovery, and soon, in the discussion of the Manyema—of danger. One cannot, as Hammond and Jablow point out, underestimate the "commercial value of literary sensationalism" especially in a travel book that is meant to titillate and seduce its audience. "So valuable an adjunct to the literary tradition was the theme of cannibalism," write Hammond and Jablow, "that it remained one of the most persistent conventions."[25]

Salvadori admits that "at first reading" the discussion of the Manyema "sounds bizarre" but then goes on to explain cannibalism as a product of the devastating violence of the slave trade which Sorabji's text exposes. Sorabji does not himself make this causal connection, the only explicit connection made in the text between slavery and cannibalism being the story of a Manyema slave woman on the coast who has allegedly "cannibalized her master's children" (180). Once again, it is important to note that in the original text, this discussion immediately proceeds from the book's sensationalist opening and is, in fact, far removed from the later discussion of the horrors of slavery. The Gujarati text opens with Manyema cannibalism and closes with Arab brutality. As rendered in the English translation, however, the discussion of Manyema cannibalism (with its specter of the African as primitive and savage), placed toward the end of the narrative, seems at odds with the surrounding text that is concerned with depicting the plight of helpless (and innocent) African slaves brought from the interior.

Thus, just by virtue of their placement in the text, the Manyema end up playing different roles in the Gujarati original and the English translation. The same case may be made about the Masai and the Nandi, who are seen to be "dishonest," and the Gikuyu whose assessment varies from page to page. But whatever we may make of the specific nature of the ethnic representations, the larger narrative trajectory is, I argue, a movement from what Hammond and Jablow label the "pejorative" projection of Africans to the "nostalgic," "noble savage" one. Thus, while the Manyema are projected in the pejorative frame, the Kavirondo, despite their anger with him, are presented by Sorabji as "truthful, honest, and God-fearing" (133) Africans who have the utmost "integrity" (132) and a code of ethics that matches the highest principles of "Good Thoughts, Good Words and Good Deeds" (133) of his own Zoroastrian religion. In perhaps the first published commentary on Indian-African marriages in East Africa that is available to us, Sorabji relates a tale intended to showcase the superior virtues of the Kavirondo relative to the Punjabi. The section "A Punjabi's Marriage with a Kavirondo girl and how it ended" narrates the story of a Punjabi settler who fell in love with a Kavirondo girl and secured permission from her father to marry her. But the Punjabi community finds the marriage unacceptable and threatens to excommunicate him. "Thoroughly intimidated" by his community, the Punjabi returns the young bride to her father who is angered by the Punjabi's "heartlessness" and "low morals." Despite the pleas of the Punjabi, who asks his father-in-law to retain the bride price of eight cows, he finds the cows returned outside his shop. Sorabji's tale here is primarily intended to display the honor of the Kavirondo and, as he puts it, the "goodness of such a tribe" (136), but it also serves in retrospect as a symbolic marker of what was to become one of the major points of contention in the Indian-African cultural encounter—the endurance of endogamy among East African Indians.

If the text positions us to admire the Kavirondo despite their nakedness, by the end of the narrative it is the abject condition of African slaves that most captivates our attention. Here the narrative seeks to foreground the humanity of the slaves and draw attention to the inhumane treatment they have received in the hands of Zanzibari Arabs. The ideological work being done here should come as no surprise. While the author's feelings toward the horrors of slavery are arguably genuine, they are not untouched by the imperial context that surrounds them. Thus, writes Sorabji of the slaves, "the late Queen Victoria saved them from their miserable life of slavery by making them free with the help of other European countries. The Queen should be blessed for abolishing slavery from this world" (171). The author's own loyalist position may have interfered here with his ability to question whether factors other than the abolition of slavery may also have motivated British intervention, but what is even more striking in the discussion is the lack of any mention of Indian involvement. While the nature and extent of such involvement in the actual trade has been the subject of some debate, there is no question that Indians were, at the very least, slave owners.[26] Even though slavery as an institution was not abolished in Zanzibar until 1897, the active sale of slaves was prohibited by law in 1873. Sorabji's first arrival in Zanzibar around the late 1870s would have come in the wake of the closure of the Zanzibar Slave Market in 1873, the same year that the British began to enforce criminal charges against any Indians engaging in the trade. Earlier, in 1860, about six thousand slaves belonging to British-protected Zanzibari Indians had been emancipated by C. P. Rigby, the British consul in Zanzibar. In order to hold on to their slaves or to purchase new ones, some

Indians gave up their British affiliation and became the sultan's subjects. As subjects of the sultan, Indians continued to engage in slavery until 1870, when the British decided that under the treaties made by them with the sultan no Indians in Zanzibar could own slaves. But, as Robert Gregory suggests, despite their earlier involvement in financing the Arab slavers as well as being slaveholders themselves, many Indians helped with the abolition of slavery. The Khoja merchant Tharia Topan, for instance, was knighted in 1890 for his role in the abolition of slavery. Topan, himself a former slave owner, is said not only to have freed his slaves but to have given them land to farm at a nominal rent.[27] One of the most prominent members of the Indian community, and likely the first Indian in Africa to have been knighted by the queen, it is inconceivable that Sorabji would not have known of his abolitionist activities. The fact that Topan gets no mention in Sorabji's text is a curious one.

Two possibilities present themselves as reasons for this silence. The first is that Sorabji, while recognizing the horrors of slavery, is uncertain and ambivalent about the postabolitionist transition. In a book intended to attract more Indian businessmen and traders to East Africa, Sorabji has to admit to the labor shortage caused by emancipation. The economy of Zanzibar, he writes, has suffered of late because of colonial intervention and "the abolition of slavery. It is difficult to get labourers to work on the land which used to be tilled by the slaves. This has led to grass growing wild on the fertile land, turning it into jungle" (169). The solution he proposes is to induce Africans from the interior to come to Zanzibar as wage laborers. In keeping with the ethnocentric rhetoric of the time, Sorabji argues that such labor would be good not only for the economy of Zanzibar but also for the laborer who would be exposed to civilization and "a little culture" (170). By the time his book is published, the future of the labor supply is still uncertain, but while this uncertainty can be signaled in the text, it cannot be allowed to derail the primary interest of the narrative—to encourage prospective Indian entrepreneurs to look to East Africa as both a site of opportunity and a mission to complete the project of modernity that the British have hitherto promised but not delivered.

That Tharia Topan and his role in the curtailment of slavery receives no mention may also be due to a second reason, more personal, having to do with patronage. The book is dedicated to Seth Allidina Visram Lalji, who, we are told, "was the Leader of Zanzibar, Uganda and Mombasa; An Adventurous Trader" and "clever, generous, modern in his ideas" (112). At one point in the preface, Sorabji suggests that the book that follows will be as much about Visram as about his own travels (117). This turns out not to be the case, with Sorabji's narrative centering more on his own journey and less on Visram, but nonetheless it seems that the book cannot, in this context of patronage, allow for a shadow to be cast on Visram by a competing and successful businessman. I will return to Allidina Visram in the next chapter, since he is indeed an important figure in the history of Indian commercial presence in East Africa, but, before doing so, I want to conclude my discussion of the two texts under consideration here with one final observation.

In my reading of these early twentieth-century travel narratives by Adamji and Sorabji, I have shown how the two authors, separated by age, prior travel history, ethnic/religious identity, and family position experienced and narrated their journeys in different ways. Despite the relative similarity of the infrastructure they depended on for their travels—they both took the newly built railway, employed porters to carry them and their supplies through difficult terrain, traveled on the steamers and smaller boats on Lake Victoria, and had recourse to varying degrees of Indian as well as African hospitality in the interior—they nevertheless framed their narratives, and indeed themselves, as narrators in ways that were marked by their own sense as ethical selves engaging with others. For Adamji, the primary sources of both identity and anxiety were his standing as a trader in the larger Bohra community as well as his conflicted feelings toward his elder brothers. For Sorabji, it was the project of modernity—styled most resolutely in the image of the British, but, significantly, being undertaken not by the British but by Indians—that most interested him. His impatience with settler racism, which he personally experienced in relation to the "white" highlands reservations, but also observed in the context of barriers to commerce, is spelled out in the text meant for Gujarati readers but not acted upon or made evident to any of his European companions. Rather, Sorabji reserves his most acerbic critique for the unclean habits of his fellow Indians who he thinks demean the image of the Indian in the eyes of fellow European travelers.

While, on first impression, the young Adamji who prefers the company of his Bohra community to Europeans may come across as more parochial in his dispositions than the well-traveled, Anglicized Sorabji, such an assumption, I suggest, must be made with caution. Both Adamji and Sorabji are cosmopolitan subjects in their own right, if by cosmopolitanism we mean an attitude that embraces the world of difference, cultural or otherwise.[28] Indeed, by some measures, such as those of cultural tolerance, a healthy respect for the identities of others, an ability to easily and almost unself-consciously move between one or more cultural registers, Adamji's text may be seen to be marked by a cosmopolitan ease that is, in fact, less evident in Sorabji's narrative. Consider, for example, the actual linguistic heteroglossia of Adamji's text—this is evident not only in the interspersing of English and Swahili words in a primarily Gujarati text but more significantly in Adamji's transcription of an English or Swahili word in Gujarati script.[29] The ease of the transitions between the languages and the randomness of the linguistic shifts suggest that Adamji is equally at ease in all three languages and that he does not necessarily associate one or the other with a particular aspect of his identity or activities. The same is true with the ease with which Adamji moves between the English time system and the Arabic-Swahili system of time in which the twelve-hour day starts with 1 (7 A.M. in English time). The editors err, I think, in trying to suggest that Adamji's choice of time system depends on whether or not he means to record accuracy. Thus they suggest that when Adamji "wrote that the train left the station at 11:30, he means on the dot, whereas when he wrote the train arrived at Kisumu at Arbi 4, he implies about that time (10 o'clock)" (7). However, the text does not bear out this analysis, since there are several occasions when just the opposite is the case. Rather than attempting to make sense of Adamji's choice of recording time in terms of precision versus approximation (with its unfortunate connotations of English time being seen as precise and Arabic-Swahili being approximate), it may be more useful to read it, along with his linguistic fluency, as a register of his multiple intimacies with the world of the Swahili and the English. Such a reading, along with other clues, both textual—such as his excitement when he meets a trader from Karachi who speaks Urdu and with whom, therefore, he can get "a good opportunity to speak that language" (23)—and extratextual—such as his eagerness to embrace the symbols of modernity (he was one of the first Indians in Mombasa to own a bicycle [77])—suggest that cosmopolitanism must not be judged solely by the company one keeps.

In other words, I am arguing that, even as he appears to favor the company of his own kind (however narrowly or broadly circumscribed), Adamji's multiple intimacies with the world of the Gujarati Bohra, the Swahili, and the Europeans are to be read as continuous with the cosmopolitanisms long associated with the Indian Ocean.[30] He is, to put it metaphorically, a direct descendant of the trader Ben Yiju and his Indian slave. Ironically, by these lights, the more extensively traveled Sorabji, despite his embrace of Europeans and European-styled modernity, or rather because he privileges them so much, seems to have lost out on the more vernacular forms of cosmopolitanism that mark Adamji's text. To put it in the more contemporary lingo of postcolonial studies, Sorabji has yet to provincialize Europe.[31] Secure in the long legacy of Indian Ocean cosmopolitanism, Adamji, on the other hand, has never felt the need for such provincializing.

5. COMMERCE AS ROMANCE

Mehta, Madhvani, Manji

In February 1968, J. S. Mangat, then a lecturer in history at the University College in Nairobi published a provocatively titled article in the *East Africa Journal*: "Was Allidina Visram a Robber Baron, or a Skillful and Benevolent Commercial Pioneer?"[1] The question, as posed, signaled the prevalent postindependence distrust of Asian traders as exploiters, and Mangat's aim was to argue that early traders such as Visram may have contributed to the economic infrastructure of East Africa more than they had been given credit for. Born in Kutch, India, Visram arrived in Zanzibar at a very young age.[2] He found employment with the merchant Sewa Haji Paroo, who was then involved with financing the caravan trade. After the death of his employer in 1897, Visram took over the business, expanding the reach of the trade to include further territories in Uganda, Kenya, the Congo, and Southern Sudan. While he operated independently as a trader with no partners, Visram relied, like many others who were to follow him, on a number of new arrivals both from within his Ismaili community as well as from other Indian communities to help set up *dukas* (shops) first along the traditional trade routes into the interior and then along the projected route of the Uganda railway. In 1898, well before the Uganda railway had reached the interior,

Visram had set up a store in Kampala from which he proceeded to expand further into such rural outposts as Jinja, Masaka, Mbarara, Toro, Hoima, Nimule, and Gondokoro. At these various stores, Visram and his agents would sell products as varied as tables and chairs, rice, salt, beads, and textiles and would purchase local produce from African farmers. By 1909, Visram was reported to have "17 agents operating in the Congo with about Rs. 400,000 worth of trade goods advanced by him," and he had already begun to diversify his commercial activities by opening "soda making factories and furniture-making shops in Kampala and Entebbe; oil mills at Kisumu and the Coast, obtaining oil from sesame and copra; a soap making factory at Mombasa in 1907; two small cotton ginning establishments in Mombasa and Entebbe; and saw mills in Uganda near Nyeri" (34). Visram also engaged in the transportation business, both cart based over land and the operation of boats and a steamer on Lake Victoria.

While Visram clearly did well for himself, in assessing his contribution, Mangat quotes from a report by the chief secretary in Entebbe, who noted: "'He [Visram] was always ready to help the encouragement of local industries by buying native crops which no one else would touch, at prices which meant a loss for him. I remember myself that when natives on Elgon were encouraged in 1909 to make beeswax, and made it in large quantities, no buyer could be found except Allidina, who paid locally a higher price per lb. than the product would fetch delivered at Liverpool. The same thing happened in the early days of the cotton industry in the Eastern Province'" (34). Drawing on such colonial reports, Mangat claims that the activities of early Asian traders such as Visram "stimulated greater local production in various parts of East Africa and subsequently contributed to the transition from a barter to a money-based economy" (34). Their activities, writes Mangat, "had greater significance for economic development in the early years than the mere exploitation of the commercial potential of the interior for personal profit would suggest" (34). Furthermore, he notes, in addition to heralding agricultural and economic growth, entrepreneurs such as Visram often engaged in socially conscious philanthropy. The Namirembe Cathedral, local hospitals, the Red Cross in Kampala, and the local Indian school, built in Mombasa by his son Abdul Rasul in the name of his father, were only some of the beneficiaries of the estimated nine million rupees that the Visram family donated.[3]

I introduce this sketch of Allidina Visram, popularly known as the "uncrowned King of Uganda," for a number of reasons. First, I hope it helps further contextualize Sorabji Darookhanawala's narrative and his tribute to his patron. As we will soon see, Visram is a personal link not only back to Darookhanawala but also to two men who were to become, by all accounts, the two most successful Asian entrepreneurs in colonial Uganda, Nanji Kalidas Mehta, the founder of the multinational Mehta Group, which today controls assets of over 350 million dollars with over 15,000 employees worldwide, and Muljibhai Madhvani, the founder of the Madhvani Group, which reports its Uganda assets alone at over 200 million dollars with over 10,000 employees.[4] By noting the connection between Visram, Mehta, and Madhvani, I underline the significance of information and business networks that have been much discussed by economic historians as important elements in the growth of capital and trade. At the same time, however, we must pay heed to the fact that networks alone cannot guarantee business success — Visram's own family enterprise dissipated soon after his death, and by 1924 mismanagement by his successors led to a liquidation of the enterprise.[5] In this chapter I present a reading of the autobiographies of Mehta, Madhvani, as well as the Kenyan entrepreneur Madatally Manji to show how commercial success is contingent upon a whole array of factors — structural, informational, economic, technical, managerial, and, often, just sheer luck. In so doing I hope to complement the already formidable scholarly literature in East African economic theory and history by providing a more personal, flesh-and-blood account of commercial behavior than is often called for by the more abstract and quantitative demands of the disciplines of economics and commercial history. However, as a student of literature and culture, my aim in this chapter is not merely to share with my colleagues in economics the power and insights of life narratives in understanding commercial behavior. Rather my interest is in debunking the all-too-common assumption, which we encountered earlier in Taban Lo Liyong's plea to fellow East Africans, that men of commerce, being too devoted to the pursuit of economic gain, are disconnected from the life of the imagination. On the contrary, this chapter will highlight the role of the imagination — literary, religious, national, philanthropic, and cosmopolitan — in the making of commercial men. To be sure, some of the particular ways in which these authors imagine their relation to commerce, to the nation, to religious difference, to family, and in particular to gender relations will not appeal to many of us as readers, but the task of the cultural critic, it seems to me, is to draw attention to these conundrums rather than to ignore them.

Before turning to the autobiographies of Mehta, Madhvani, and Manji, it is important to sound some of the warnings that scholars who have spent

considerable attention to such matters in other contexts have raised. There
are three levels at work here. The first involves the reading of the individual entrepreneur as either a heroic figure or as an exploiter instead. (Or, in
Mangat's terms, "Skillful and Benevolent Commercial Pioneer" or "Robber Baron"). The second is in the reading of the "ethnic" character of the
capitalist enterprise, a reading, it is well to recall, that harks back at least to
Max Weber's discussion of the relationship between Protestant values and
capitalism.[6] Finally, the third issue is the debate between the virtues of free
markets and capitalist development, on the one hand, and those of managed economies, nationalized industries, and socialist development, on the
other. Each of these issues has a long history of debate among historians of
commerce, a history that is far too complex for me to reproduce here. Nevertheless, it may be useful to briefly signal the relevance of these issues to
the life narratives under study.

On the first issue of hagiographical readings of successful entrepreneurs,
Sanjay Subrahmanyam has righty cautioned that "there is a real danger . . .
in entrepreneurial history: that of falling into the celebration of the great
Captain of Industry."[7] Writing entrepreneurial history in a political context
where that history has been ethnicized or racialized, as is the case with Asian
entrepreneurship in East Africa, one is particularly susceptible to this danger. Situated within that context, the narratives of the Indian "pioneers,"
whether those who ended up fairly successful and rich or those who had
more modest ventures, often bear a family resemblance to each other. The
plot commonly involves a relatively young boy (it is always only boys) arriving alone on the shores of Zanzibar or Mombasa, often driven there by pov-
erty at home. The boy finds employment with an established trader and is
seen to work long hours under demanding conditions. In a year or two, either
at his own initiative or otherwise encouraged by his employer, the young
man branches out on his own, setting up a similar store either in the same
town or further in the interior, sometimes turning to his former employer for
goods on credit. Having accumulated some capital on his own, the budding
merchant sends off for a younger brother or cousin or some other relative or
else forms a partnership with a newly made friend in the region of his current abode. With such help he is better positioned to expand his business,
either by setting up more shops or diversifying his interests. He may become
involved in transportation and distribution in addition to primary trade. If he
is particularly adventurous, he may consider getting involved in small-scale
processing such as, for example, the ginning of cotton in Uganda.

The fact that this mythical narrative resembles the story of Allidina Visram is not entirely accidental. Much like Mohandas Gandhi was to propel the nationalist imagination of Indians home and abroad, the story of Allidina Visram, emptied, of course, of the posthumous liquidation of the enterprise, was to stoke the interest of many an Indian entrepreneur and social historian.[8] And as we will soon see, this particular form of the narrative—the rags to riches tale—structures each of the narratives that I turn to in this chapter. The task of our critique will be to be mindful of the seduction of this narrative even as we pay attention to its innermost logic. A significant part of the seduction, it bears remembering, is the erasure of business failure, which, as Gijsbert Oonk has recently pointed out in an important article, provides a corrective to the univocal myth of Asian commercial success.[9]

Closely related to such a mythical narrative, then, is the emphasis put on the ethnic aspect of such entrepreneurship, and it is here that we arrive at Subrahmanyam's second caution—that against the "classic trap" of seeking "Oriental essences" in the nature of merchant-state relations or of cultural traits that seem to underwrite entrepreneurial success (viii). The keywords here are well circulated—hardworking, industrious, thrifty, trustworthy (and thereby, in economic terms, creditworthy), family based, honorable, generous, risk taking. Many of these values or traits will be invoked in the entrepreneurial narratives we will read, and many may well be intimately tied to entrepreneurial success. But to note these qualities among a group of entrepreneurs in East Africa is not to suggest that such qualities are either the exclusive attributes of a particular ethnic community or that they are in some ways essential qualities of those ethnicities. Rather they are to be understood as traits that are invoked, nurtured, and indeed developed historically through the actual performance of the commercial exchanges.[10] Further, these are attributes that cannot properly be used to "explain" the relative success of ethnic communities—some of them may be necessary conditions for success, but, as many examples of failed entrepreneurs would show, they are hardly sufficient conditions for success. This cautionary point is even more significant when comparative claims are made in the evaluation of two or more ethnic groups. The "culturalist" position that would emphasize certain traits can all too easily be mobilized to "explain" the failure of a given group without sufficient attention to some of the other structural or institutional constraints that may in fact be more determinative of their relative failure.[11]

In the context of East African discourses on development, perhaps the most heated debate on the role of ethnicity in the growth of capitalism was generated with the publication of David Himbara's 1994 book, *Kenyan Capitalists, the State and Development.* Studying commercial and industrial development in Kenya from colonial times to the early nineties, Himbara argued that "commercial and industrial development was largely pioneered by local capitalists of Indian descent since the founding, in the modern sense, of the countries of the region" and that, contrary to the expectations of projects of Africanization, black Kenyan capitalists had not been well served by the independent state (4–5). Further, Himbara argued that most scholars who had studied the Kenyan economy had, under the influence of dependency theory, misread local Asian capital as "foreign" capital, as opposed to seeing it as a homegrown development. This meant that they had paid insufficient attention to the ways in which local entrepreneurs of Indian ancestry had drawn upon their long history of commercial success in the area to further expand their enterprises after the Second World War (8). Himbara's attention to local Indian enterprise was not in itself objectionable, but what bothered some readers was a tendency in his account to present the history of Indian commercial growth in what seemed to be a triumphalist tone while presenting what he saw as the relative commercial failure of black Kenyans in a disparaging manner. So, for instance, Himbara argued that the most prevalent reason attributed to the "poor performance" of black entrepreneurs—the "discriminatory barriers erected by the colonial state" did not take into account the fact that "the most successful commercial and industrial entrepreneurs did not emerge from within the white settler community—which was state protected—but from the Indian commercial community. . . . The success of the Indians had little to do with the favorable treatment by the state, and everything to do with their experience, accumulated over a number of centuries, in East African coastal merchant activity" (75). As opposed to such long-standing experience, Himbara posed the problems of the new companies established by black Kenyans in the mid forties as resulting from "a lack of basic understanding of business goals, lack of experience in management, and lack of control of company finances" (76).

The most incisive critique of Himbara's position was made by Michael Chege in two important essays.[12] Chege first faulted Himbara on methodological grounds, showing that the small sample of enterprises studied by Himbara skewed his analysis in favor of urban enterprises and the industrial sector. The most glaring absence was the contribution made by African agriculturalists, argued Chege, noting that "from 1964 to the mid-1980's the engine of growth by all professional accounts lay not in immigrant groups but in African-run smallholder agriculture" amounting to 30–40 percent of the GDP as opposed to 10–13 percent of the GDP attributed to the multinational and Asian-controlled industrial sector ("Paradigms of Doom," 560). On the particular matter of the discriminatory barriers of the colonial state as a factor in black African entrepreneurial achievement, Chege held that Himbara's revisionist account dismissed the difficulties too easily: "In the eyes of the new revisionist history . . . obstruction of African business under colonial rule is portrayed as a carefully cultivated 'myth,' citing as evidence the limited credit and training opportunities open to Africans since the Mitchell years, and wholly oblivious to the impact of the systemic injustices of the era and the rebellion they provoked in Mau Mau" ("Introducing Race," 223). Furthermore, Chege found Himbara's account to be overly enamored by Asian success so that his analysis downplayed the successes of African-owned firms if they had Asian managers, but did not downplay the successes of Asian-owned firms that relied on African management and labour ("Introducing Race," 225). Such a tendency also meant Himbara could not adequately account for those Asian enterprises that had failed, failure only being emphasized by Himbara on the African side. Thus, concluded Chege, "Asian capital has indeed played a key role in Kenya's industrial growth, not to mention the outstanding professional and philanthropic work associated with Kenyans of Asian origin. . . . But if Himbara is to be believed the faults are all on one side. There have been no bankruptcies (or 'total failures') among Kenyan Asian entrepreneurs worth recalling or documenting. Unless propped up by political handouts, however, African businesses seem perennially prone to bankruptcy" ("Paradigms of Doom," 564).

Noting sardonically that "ethnic adulation . . . is not a recognized method of explaining sources of high economic growth" ("Introducing Race," 220), Chege reminded economic historians that "in the search for a new paradigm of capitalism in Africa especially, it should never be forgotten that this is not the first time that cultural stereotype has been called upon to explain the continent's relative backwardness" (229). Chege's concern was not only with the representations of the past but more urgently with the ways in which academic theories can fuel ongoing racial and ethnic antagonisms. With regard to the case of Himbara's book, Chege noted, "In the acrimonious Kenyan race debates of 1996, Asian activists waived copies of it as proof that 'the economy' was fully dependent on their efforts not on the Africans . . . these are the exact words of Himbara. African racists in turn used it to demonstrate Asian chicanery, Asian trade 'domination' and 'exploitation'; a vicious circle of two nonarguments was thus closed" ("Paradigms of Doom," 563).

Chege's critique of Himbara is not to be read, I think, as an endorse-ment of the Kenyan state or even of the commercial and economic cli-mate for black African enterprises in postcolonial times. If he seemed to rise to the defense of black enterprises, it is because he believed them to be unduly slighted in Himbara's account. Chege recognized that further com-mercial and economic growth for Kenya is vital to its future, and for this he proposed two solutions. First, an "'enabling' law-driven governance frame-work, deregulation and a stable macro-economic environment." Second, a more robust form of 'social capital' and civic engagement across communi-ties. "Social capital" argued Chege, "varies with community not ethnicity. Because it is premised on the intensity of voluntary civic engagement by private citizens, it is therefore a malleable human artifact; it makes for a rapid 'supply response' to new opportunities, and like physical capital it is subject to depreciation if not kept in good repair. The interface between a liberal economic environment and civic action may explain better the com-mercial differences between the various 'Asian' groups in Kenya as well as the variations in entrepreneurship within African communities" (Introduc-ing Race, 230).

We will have occasion to get a closer look at the workings of "social capital" and the role of civil society in the lives of Asian entrepreneurs in East Africa, but before turning to them let us note that Chege's advocacy of deregulation points to the third significant point of contention that has informed the debates on commerce and industry in East Africa—that of the relative role of the state in regulating and monitoring commerce. Here the two extremes are the ideologies of the free market, on the one hand, and the nationalization of industries, on the other—capitalist development or socialist development, in other words.[13] Since the end of the cold war and the collapse of the Soviet states, urged (some would say forced) by the structural adjustment programs of the IMF and the World Bank, African countries have today greatly liberalized their economies, moving increas-ingly toward a free market–oriented capitalist economy. But this was not always the case in the immediate context of independent Africa, and, to varying degrees, both politicians and academics in the early years displayed an ideological leaning toward socialism, nationalization, and planned econ-omies.[14] In the following chapter I will turn to three narratives by Asians in Tanzania who worked with President Julius Nyerere—one of the most articulate proponents of African socialism or *Ujamaa*. For now, however, what is of immediate interest is the fact that while entrepreneurs such as Mehta, Madhvani, and Manji were, for the most part, firm advocates of capitalist development, they were also alert to the ways in which controlled economies could benefit those commercial enterprises that were based on import substitution. This, as we will see, was particularly the case with the enterprise of Madatally Manji, who benefited greatly from the disruptions to foreign trade brought about first by the Second World War and later, in newly independent times, by import controls. The autobiographies I examine in this chapter provide an excellent lens for understanding how these entrepreneurs and others like them negotiated through the policies of the colonial state and the newly independent state in ensuring their own economic success.

The tensions between nationalist intellectuals, capitalist entrepreneurs, and the economic policies of newly independent states was eloquently captured by the political economist Yash Tandon in his remembrance of Jayant Madhvani after the latter passed away in 1971. "Jayant and I had known each other for many years, although we were not friends in the ordinary sense of the word. I am naturally allergic to capitalists, particularly the tycoonic ones; and Jayant was similarly allergic to intellectuals, particularly of the leftist brand."[15] Tandon goes on to note that Madhvani and he were moving in

> opposite streams of our national life. One stream was flowing from the colonial days. The powerful undercurrent of this stream was private enterprise. . . . Jayant as the foremost capitalist industrialist of Uganda, was rowing fast along this stream. The other was an upstream current destined to lead the country to a socialist port. It derived its force from the ship's chief navigator at the time Milton Obote. If Madhvani was a tycoon, Obote could be likened to a typhoon. Obote had begun to destroy feudal ramparts, colonial chains and emerging capitalist tendencies with typhoonic gusto, especially after 1966.
>
> (10)

There has been much water under the bridge (to continue Tandon's acquatic metaphor) since those early days of nationalism, and Uganda since the 1990s has actively embraced, not without societal tensions and conflict, the ship of free enterprise. But while African states and many Africanist economists have moved to a position that is more sympathetic to capitalism and neoliberalism, this is not yet the case for the greater majority of Africanist historians and cultural critics. Thus the third and final caution (made as much to myself as to my readers): while there is, for some, as Subrahmanyam suggested, a danger in being seduced by the victorious narratives of the "Captains of Industry," there is also, for others, the reverse danger of prejudging entrepreneurs and capitalists as intrinsically and solely exploitative. As we sail through these narratives, we must remain alert to both these undercurrents in our thoughts, since neither extreme seems to account fully for the complex ways in which we all inevitably commerce with our universe.

NATIONALISM, RELIGION, AND PHILANTHROPY: NANJI KALIDAS MEHTA'S *DREAM HALF-EXPRESSED*

Born in 1888 in the village of Gorana, Gujarat, Nanji Kalidas Mehta was raised in a family that ran a grocery shop, engaged in money lending, and bought, ginned, and sold cotton in the nearby town of Porbander (6).[16] Schooled until the age of eleven, completing the fourth-form education that was the highest available to him in the village, Nanji apprenticed in his father's shop—measuring cloth, weighing articles for sale, and delivering them to customers. Mehta's uncle Gokaldas had already established himself as a trader in Zanzibar and, having returned to India after his five-year sojourn, later sailed to Madagascar, first to work under a Bohra trader and then to start his own business. Taking his sons with him to Madagascar, Gokaldas later summoned Mehta's elder brother Gorkhandas and some of the other cousins in the household (17). Impatient with being left behind, "something invincible in me heard the call of the sea and I was mentally ready to go abroad," writes Mehta, marking the onset of a long-lasting love of the sea and travel in general: "The sea had a great hold upon my imagination and I watched it with peculiar emotion that never got stale with the passing of years" (17). Like the twelfth-century trader Ben Yiju, and so many traders like him, the sea becomes for Mehta a symbol of "freedom and enterprise" (35). Over the years, Mehta would traverse this particular sea separating India from the East African coast at least forty-five times, and his travels would take him further on to South Africa, Europe, Japan, and many ports and cities in between.

Mehta's *Dream Half-Expressed* is a remarkable account of the life and travels of a man who came of age in the era of colonially mediated mercantile expansion. The autobiography was dictated by Mehta in Gujarati and published in the original in 1955.[17] Intent upon making it available to a wider audience, Mehta's family and friends translated it into English, updated it to take into account events since its original publication, and put it in circulation in 1966, three years before the author's demise.[18] The tone of the narrative is reflective, at times nostalgic, and often explicitly didactic.

In reading Mehta's account here, I want to signal a number of inter-related issues that may enhance our understanding of the advent of Indian merchant capital in East Africa. Most significantly, the narrative articulates the mythological charter that often accompanies Indian claims about the community's contributions to East African modernity. The charter insists on reading commerce as romance rather than conflict, the latter a feature associated not with Indians but with the form of bureaucratic modernity introduced by the colonial state. Indeed, Mehta's narrative echoes Sorabji's earlier claim that the colonial state is a hindrance to Africa's modernity, a modernity that they both suggest Indian commercial enterprise is only too eager to foster. Such commerce-driven modernity must, however, be tempered with a calibration of social responsibility and philanthropy. Thus one of the central concerns of *Dream Half-Expressed* is the responsibility of the rich toward the poor.[19] Even though the narrative does not dwell upon the many monetary contributions that Mehta made toward charitable causes in both East Africa and India, it does foreground the establishment of a residential school for girls in Gujarat, and, as my reading will show, this school serves as an important axis that connects Mehta's philanthropy with his developing sense of a gendered nationalism.

Mehta's relationship to the Indian struggle for independence is yet another important aspect of his tale. The narrative proceeds from Mehta being a restless young boy interested in making a decent living to becoming a wealthy industrialist whose greatest passions are religion and Indian nationalism. Along the way, as my reading will show, he moves from a position of celebrating religious syncretism and tolerance to one that is more circumspect and skeptical about the possibilities of interreligious understanding between Hindus and Muslims in India. Whether or not this is in keeping with a general tendency toward a more conservative position associated with the acquisition of wealth and increasing age, it is clearly marked as well by his visits to, and fascination with, imperial Japan. The militarism of the Japanese, both in the actual theater of war as well as in the industrial workplace, makes, I suggest, an impact on Mehta that reverberates with his own sense of the appropriate development of a disciplined Hindu India. Mehta's fascination with Japan as a counterpoint to Western colonialism and a Western-styled modernity is worth noting, since such non-Western, global affiliations have often escaped the attention of scholars, who, for the most part, characterize Indian nationalism as a binary opposition between the British colonizers and their Indian colonized subjects. Mehta's narrative points urgently to the need to locate some of seeds of Indian nationalism in its diaspora, both in Africa as well as, in this case, Japan and the Far East. Indeed, the flows of peoples and ideas between these different regions of the world is a central thematic of the work, Mehta finding, for instance, long-lost Japanese friends whom he had first known in East Africa during his later travels to Burma (239).

Finally, just as travel is an important catalyst for Mehta's financial and spiritual growth, the role of mythology, folklore, and literature in general is equally significant in his self-fashioning. In an important study of law, culture, and market governance in late-colonial India, Ritu Birla writes that the figure of the colonial subject "most often evokes a Shakespeare-quoting member of the English-educated native elite, as in Macaulay's famous 'Minute on Education.'" Birla suggests that, rather than focusing solely on such a figure, it may be of some interest to focus on "the colonial subject as an economic actor subject to new market disciplines" (6). Birla proposes in her book to pay attention to vernacular capitalists who are engaged in "key contests with colonial governance." She suggests that addressing "the indigenous capitalist in this way, as a complicit figure 'folded into' new discourses of modernity, opens new ways of narrating the history of colonial capitalism" (6).[20] While in my reading of Mehta's *Dream Half-Expressed* he appears as one instance of such a figure of the vernacular capitalist negotiating with new discourses of modernity, I want to suggest, at the same time, that this particular economic actor also has a whole array of literary and mythological texts at his disposal. In other words, sharing Birla's aim of decentering the Shakespeare-quoting elite from the center stage of colonial subjectivity, I want nevertheless to retain here a sense of a "vernacular" literacy that not only accompanies but also significantly informs the capitalist as economic man.[21] Indeed, Mehta's narrative insists on presenting Mehta as a man of literature: "Ever since childhood," he writes, "I have been fond of reading. I used to buy books from three to four annas that I got as pocket expenses. I carried books with me during my travels. I owe my mental development to travels in India and foreign lands and to reading books" (316). Tending to an elderly father who suffers from weak eyesight, Mehta as a young boy reads religious narratives of Vaishnava saints aloud to him (24), and he continues to read religious texts such as the *Shrimad Bhagavata* (199) as he gets older. In Mombasa, Mehta's introduction to the principles of the Arya Samaj are primarily through his reading of the

Satyartha Prakash, a religious treatise written by the founder, Dayanand Saraswati, who, Mehta notes, was also an eager advocate of the Hindi language. At many points in the narrative, religious and other vernacular texts are the subject of recitation and performance. On his first voyage to Africa, for instance, his fellow passenger Vallabhdas Moola recites verses from the Ramayana and Mahabharata around mealtime, and the Maher youths on board recite *dohas* from folk literature. In Madagascar, Mehta notes that during the main festivities "young and old, met together, sang country ballads and devotional songs and acted different scenes from Indian plays" (52), and he mentions at least one occasion in Lugazi when he has arranged for a "Hari Katha" recital of religious stories to the accompaniment of music and songs (170). Similarly, on his trips to India Mehta is drawn to theatrical performances, and the most memorable ones for him are the productions of Kalidas's plays *Shakuntala* and *Kumara Sambhava* performed at Shantiniketan under the auspices of Rabindranath Tagore (161). Even as *Dream Half-Expressed* foregrounds the centrality of vernacular literary traditions in the formation of modern colonial subjects, Mehta is also alert to the literariness of his own narrative project. Referring at times to his "imaginative self" (17), Mehta often reflects on the difficulties of autobiographical representation. "As I pen these words," he writes, "the half-forgotten dreams of youth play hide and seek upon the canvas of my mind and produce indescribable emotions" (24). By the end of his narrative, his life is still a "dream half-expressed," or to put it more prosaically, an imaginative project that is yet incomplete.[22] While the commercial plot is of course central to Mehta's narrative, the text invites us to pay attention to the author not as the narrowly circumscribed figure of *homo economicus* (as Ian Watt makes of Robinson Crusoe) but rather the more expansive one of a man of commerce who is also a nationalist, a traveler, a religious believer, and a reader of literature.

Since *Dream Half-Expressed* is the only available autobiographical account of the establishment of Indian trade and commerce in East Africa in the first half of the twentieth century, and since it remains, for the most part, unknown and unread by scholars, it may be of some use here to outline the highlights of Mehta's commercial narrative.[23] It begins with the young Mehta leaving for Majunga, Madagascar, in December 1900 (30). Working in his brother's shop, he remains in his employ until an outbreak of the plague and returns to India as part of the mass exodus of Indians affected by the epidemic. By 1904, with one uncle in Jinja, Uganda, a brother in South Africa, and a cousin in Lourenço Marques (now Maputo), Mozambique, Mehta steals some gold from the household and runs away in the hopes of returning to Africa. Planning to join his brother in South Africa, he is instead offered a job on the way in Zanzibar, which he accepts. Soon he is summoned to Uganda by his uncle in Jinja. His uncle sets him up as an assistant to a devout Muslim Baluchi man in the neighboring town of Kamuli, and Mehta forms a good working relationship with his employer. After conducting trade on behalf of the Baluchi for a couple of years, Mehta, with the former's blessings, sets up a shop of his own. Soon he decides to expand his business and employs an assistant to take care of the shop while he goes on trading expeditions. He experiments with cotton growing and ginning, opens more shops, and informs his father in India that he will not "be sending back more than Rs 200/- every year for his personal use" because he has decided that "profits made from the business should be ploughed back in the country [Uganda] in new ventures" (98). He begins touring the country, purchasing cotton, and asks for his younger brother and, later, a cousin to join him (100). By 1913 the Ugandan colonial government had put restrictions on the purchase of cotton by middlemen, enacting a law that cotton could only be purchased by the ginners themselves (113). Mehta describes the formation of the "Association of Colonial Merchants" and their agitation in London with the secretary of state for the colonies. He soon acquires a license to work as a purchasing agent for the ginnery Hansing and Co., for which he earns a 5 percent commission. Mehta finds himself in India at the outset of the First World War in 1914 and surmises that, given the scarcity of goods caused by the war, if goods could be safely transported they would provide handsome dividends. Having accumulated some capital through such trade, by 1916 Mehta is well positioned to diversify his interests from being a trader of commodities and purchasing agent for cotton to becoming a cotton ginner himself. He sets up two ginneries, acquiring steam engines from Kenya and ginning machines from India, the latter of which he manages to import into Uganda after much resistance and bureaucratic wrangling on the part of the British agricultural commissioner (137). Mehta reports that in 1917 the two factories, along with his cloth trading business, had brought in a profit of 550,000 rupees. Adding more ginneries in 1918 and thereafter, Mehta also brings in more family members from India, offering them one-eighth shares of the business (138).

As the ginning business grows, so do Mehta's ambitions. He finds, however, that the colonial bureaucracy in Uganda is set up to limit Indian entrepreneurial ambition and he overcomes this hurdle by entering into a partnership with the Bombay-based textile mill of Mathurdas Nanji and Co., which allows for a loan of ten million rupees (143). With this newfound

Indian capital, Mehta purchases greater amounts of cotton for ginning and invests in land both in Uganda as well as in Tanganyika, where, after the First World War, the allied forces had acquired formerly German-controlled lands.[24] In the Tanganyikan auction alone, Mehta acquires "twenty thousand acres of land with factories" at a cost of ten lakhs of rupees (154). Reflecting on his yearly visits to these sisal plantations between 1921 and 1934, the older Mehta writes of his emotional attachment to the land. When his nephew later sells off the land, Mehta writes, "my heart grew very restless and was overpowered with emotions which could only be said to be indescribable" (155). While one need not detract from Mehta's nostalgia for the land, it is important to bear in mind the critical role the acquisition of land played in the entrepreneurial success not only of Mehta's own enterprises but also in a parallel way of those of the competing Madhvani firm. Because the "land question" in East Africa has historically focused on the struggles over the white exclusivity of the highlands in Kenya, these other land acquisitions by Asian entrepreneurs in Uganda and colonial Tanganyika have escaped much critical scrutiny.[25] And yet, even though the figure of the "exploitative" Asian dukawallah continues to fuel the popular imagination, especially during times of economic and political crisis, it is the question of Asian land acquisition and usage that has increasingly entered current discourse. It is no small irony that the anti-Asian protests and violence in Uganda in April 2007 were prompted by the Mehta Group's plans to acquire land in the protected Mabira forest reserve in order to expand the production of sugar in the Lugazi sugar factory first set up by N. K. Mehta.[26]

The cotton crop fails in 1922, and added to this loss of two lakhs of rupees, Mehta encounters business difficulties with his Indian partners. The Bombay textile firm is liquidated, and, after settling his accounts with the now defunct firm, Mehta seeks capital and partnerships in a new market—Japan. Other Indian traders in Uganda join the trade with the Japanese as well and "one third of the season's cotton crop was purchased by [Tokyo Menka Kaisha Cotton Company] from Japan" (167). Mehta's position on the entry of the Japanese into the Ugandan market is consistent with his advocacy of free-market competition throughout the text. Now, in addition to the competition between Indians and Europeans (and internally among them), the Japanese entry further shifts the market share. But, suggests Mehta, while such increased competition may be hard on individual entrepreneurs, it is good for the development of Uganda.

The narrative outlines in great detail the growth of Mehta's sugar factory, founded in Lugazi in 1924, and his subsequent venture in Gujarat, the

Maharana Textile Mill that prompts him to visit Japan in search of techno-logical innovation. While these two factories are central to Mehta's text, as he grows older his later enterprises begin to have a lesser hold on his nar-ratorial interests. Thus we learn little about Saurashtra Cement and Chemi-cal Industries Ltd., Mehta's first public venture, which began producing cement in 1961.[27] The Uganda Tea Estate Ltd. gets barely a passing men-tion, as do the East African ventures in sisal production. While he retains a keen interest in discovering new business prospects, as is evident when he visits Burma, Mehta increasingly begins to rely on his sons and other family members to develop and grow the various enterprises. He devotes more time and energy to the pursuit of philanthropy, and his travels are more oriented toward sites of religious pilgrimage than lands of commercial opportunity.

In her persuasive reading of what she terms the "anti-conquest" nar-rative, Mary Louise Pratt has shown how in Mungo Park's travel writings "expansionist commercial aspirations idealize themselves into a drama of reciprocity."[28] "Negotiating his way across Africa," Pratt notes, "Park is the picture of the entrepreneur" (79). Recalling Marcel Mauss's disquisition on gift exchange in precapitalist societies, Pratt reminds us of the centrality of reciprocity in precapitalist social relations, a centrality that with the advent of capitalism begins to be disrupted. Merchant trade finds itself literally at the cusp of this transition and, "while doing away with reciprocity as the basis of social interaction, capitalism retains it as one of the stories it tells of itself. The difference between equal and unequal exchange is suppressed" (82). Unlike Park, who is a traveler in the image of an entrepreneur, Mehta is the entrepreneur who must travel to trade. And, as such, his narrative offers a unique perspective on the transitional moment in East Africa when barter literally gives way to monetary exchange.

Remembering his own desire to go to Africa as a young boy, Mehta tell-ingly notes that he wanted to "go abroad and seek an opportunity to do something adventurous in the country of my choice, where I would not merely seek material gain but also try to serve the land and its people, win-ning their love and co-operation, till they helped themselves to rise to their stature, consciously or unconsciously" (59). This is an image of commerce that insists on seeing it as a form of romance. If the language of helping "themselves to rise to their stature" unmistakably carries a sense of what we might call the "brown man's burden," the words "love and co-operation" invoke the language of reciprocity signaled by Pratt. In this latter regard, Mehta's descriptions of his early encounters with Africans are masterpieces of sentimental narration. On his very first voyage to Madagascar, after the ship has suffered significant damage in a storm, Mehta and his shipmates find themselves on Moyote Island, where the local inhabitants offer them hospitality. Mehta's reflections betray his own antipathies toward both ruthless politicians and ruthless businessmen: "At one end of our voyage there was India and at the other end this French island. Both of them were hundreds of miles apart from each other. But the heart of man was full of love for his fellowmen. A natural bond of affection would grow if power-mad politicians and money-making merchants did not spoil and vitiate the love of men, the love which is the echo of God's love on this unhappy earth" (48).[29] A similar sentiment is echoed later in the text when Mehta describes what for the world of commerce is a foundational scene. It is 1907, and Mehta is in the village of Kalaki, Uganda, on a trading trip. The chiefs, he writes, bring him gifts to show their "gratitude for putting their territory on the crossroads of civilization and for bringing things which they would hardly expect to see, much less receive" (94). Mehta finds not only gratitude but also love among his client-hosts: "I could see a sparkle of love in their twinkling eyes as they talked about us. Love is God's greatest gift to mankind, for no commerce can be had between men and men in whatever state of civilization until they possess it" (95). And, if love underwrites this consensual exchange of goods and commodities, such an exchange is to Mehta's mercantilist imagination the motor of history: "Crowds visited us every morning from the neighboring villages and exchanged their products for things they wanted from us. It is the law of demand and supply that moves this world and out of the workings of this law civilizations rise and fall. Life gets its momentum, society progresses and culture rises. The thirst for freedom and the hunger for well-being crop up in men's hearts. But as men's desire loses its just limit and burns like an unrestricted bonfire, woes descend on mankind, cultures and civilizations perish and there is an end to all its finest possessions and values" (94).[30] Echoing the earlier note on the material greed of "money-making merchants," Mehta despairs at what he sees as the current state of excess where, as he puts it, "the natural bond of affection between the buyer and the seller seems to have disappeared with the passage of time and self-interest has taken the place of service" (95). What he calls for, instead, is love, "the elixir of life and cementing bond of humanity . . . to be re-created and men's mind and spirit . . . to be rehabilitated with the values of a new humanistic culture" (96). Such a new humanism, Mehta writes with a Kantian proclivity, will necessitate a new form of political order: "No narrow nationalism or sheer anti-colonialism can serve the ultimate need of mankind. We require men and statesmen, who, though devoted to their soil, possess the vision of a World State, if we are ever to survive in this dangerous world of ours" (96).

This vision of a world state is not pursued at length in the narrative. But the impulse behind it, a vision of a cosmopolitanism that is open to difference as long as it is predicated on a healthy and not unequal give-and-take is one that permeates the text. For if extreme self-interest can corrupt what Mehta sees as the potentially benevolent contributions of commerce, then exchange that is predicated upon force is also corrosive. The best cross-cultural engagements, Mehta suggests, are those that are based on mutual gain, not ones based on unequal power. This is why, for Mehta, it is the Indian traders and not the Europeans who have a more ethical relation with Africans. While the Europeans did their part in modernizing Africa, they did so, claims Mehta, through force: "The Europeans did so, wherever they had gone and established their colonies but the Indian merchants have never dreamt of establishing their power anywhere; they rather chose to mix freely with the sons of the soil, sat and talked with them on the same carpet, carried their trade and remained for years to earn their livelihood. They thus indirectly contributed to the progress of the land and resided there with goodwill, co-operation and love of the inhabitants of the country they adopted" (146).

It would be easy enough to question the veracity of some of the claims being made here about the actualities of the exchange, the degree of Indian-African social intermingling "on the same carpet," as well as the allegedly unequivocal embrace of Indians by East Africans. Indeed, there are several moments in the text where Mehta himself presents evidence to the contrary when he shows Africans who maintain a "reticence towards Indians" (80) or others who resist the encroachment of the railway by removing at night the rails that Indian laborers had laid during the day. We also encounter Africans who steal from Mehta's caravans and those who threaten the security of his passage when they are slighted by his caravan's headman (91). The fact that Mehta allows these acts of resistance to enter the text but simultaneously prevents them from interrupting the narrative of commerce as romance speaks volumes about the ideological work that *Dream Half-Expressed* performs. Written in the mid 1950s and early 1960s, at a time when African independence and the corollary discourses of nationalization were causing anxiety among Asian entrepreneurs in East Africa, Mehta's text is clearly a response to the changing times, even when it chooses to downplay these concerns. The silences in the text are considerable—events that Mehta would surely have known about by the time he composed his narrative remain completely unmentioned in the text. These include the massive labor unrest and strikes of 1945 and the April 1949 protests in Buganda against the virtual monopoly of cotton processing and marketing by Asians.[31] And, as might be expected in such an autobiographical narrative, Mehta also leaves out details that are personally more damaging to his family's reputation.[32] Instead, by repeatedly calling attention to the historical contribution of Indians in East Africa, and by casting that contribution as something that the Africans of the time both welcomed and appreciated, Mehta is eager to advocate for a peaceful transition and a multiracial future.[33] Commenting upon the hard work and sacrifices, including the loss of life, of Indians building the Uganda railway, Mehta writes: "Such enormous human sacrifice at the altar of civilization bears testimony to the truth that no nation can stay alone and flourish in isolation. The great assembly of men and races which forces of history form, enables us to sacrifice for others and humanity gets richer by the mutual give and take. *It also teaches us that the debts of the past must be recognized and should bear a just relation to the future*" (73, my emphasis). While the implicit audiences of this statement are the leaders of postcolonial African states, they are also invited to overhear Mehta's speeches, occasioned by the turn of events in the Congo to his Indian colleagues at a number of meetings in East Africa in July 1961. Mehta's advice to his fellow Asians is to have faith in the East African leadership and to know that "there is no possibility that the events in the Congo [will] be repeated here where the leaders have been trained to observe and perpetuate the rule of law" (284). The inclusion of this speech in the text, as well as laudatory statements on postcolonial African leadership that follow, are in no small part performative utterances aimed at urging African leaders to stay the course and protect the interests of the Asian minority.

The commercial plot of *Dream Half-Expressed* is intertwined with a number of travel narratives that involve not only Mehta himself but also his family and business associates. Echoing the sentiment expressed earlier by Ebrahimji Adamji, Mehta notes that no education can be complete without travel (59), and like Adamji, he finds travel to be a means by which one can "make oneself free from the fetters of a humdrum life" (59). Married against his own wishes at the young age of thirteen, Mehta seeks an escape from marital obligations and travel offers him the opportunity for such an escape. His reading of literary and historical texts, which have a profound influence on his sense of self throughout his life, suggest to him that "a soft man wedded to the life of a householder cannot sail the high seas, scale the tallest mountains and take up hazards that draw the attention of the world" (29).

But if the life of domesticity is what Mehta seeks to escape, it is precisely in the context of family life that Mehta first ponders the possibilities offered by travel. Mehta's earliest encounters with travelers are the many sadhus and pilgrims on their way to Dwarika who are hosted by his father. Much influenced by the example of these pilgrims and also by the religious stories of traveling for penance that he has read, the young Mehta at one point even runs away from home along with a friend to worship at a Bhuvaneshwar temple in a neighboring village. At an early point in the narrative, when he is unsure as to what lies ahead, the young Mehta speculates, "During such moments of musing I said to myself that if I could not go to Africa, I would visit those sacred places of which I had heard from the pilgrims" (61). As his story unfolds, Mehta engages in both forms of travel—that primarily for commercial interest as well as that for religious and spiritual purposes. While in his older years Mehta seems to have developed an interest in visiting religious sites for their own intrinsic interest, in the early years the commercial travels are punctuated by religious trips made for purificatory purposes. His growing interest in religious pilgrimages, then, is not disconnected from his activities as a commercial man.[34]

In his religious travels Mehta becomes one of many fellow practitioners following long traditions of pilgrimage, but his commercial travels are more unique and exceptional. His youth is punctuated by trips to visit his family in India and commercial trips into the East African interior. As he grows older and wealthier, his travels take him further to Europe, South Africa, and Japan. In May 1929 Mehta embarks on a trip to Europe accompanied by his secretary Purushottamdas Dasani, who has prior travel experience in England. The trip is onboard an Italian liner where Mehta is first encumbered by the demands of European etiquette. The starched shirts and tight collars, Mehta complains, "fettered our free spirits. . . . A little freedom would have eased the situation, especially when we were travelling in a tropical country whose burning heat made such tight fitting clothes a torture" (185). Nevertheless, "manners are often like conventions and they are to be religiously observed, irrespective of the needs of time and place" (185), and so Mehta and his companion go on with the show. He bristles at other European conventions—the racism of the Kenyan settlers onboard in particular—and the attempts of the Italian cooks to make them a vegetarian-friendly meal leave him unsatisfied, but Mehta takes all of this in stride in anticipation of the experiences that await him. The first stop on the journey is at the Suez Canal, and Mehta and his companion visit the museum in Cairo and the pyramids. While his commercial eye remarks on the Egyptian production of the "finest species of cotton in the world" (187), his status as a colonial subject does not allow him to ignore British imperial power. The bridges over the Nile, he notes, "were guarded by British soldiers. Streets were properly watched lest excited mobs should rise in revolt against the foreign rule" (187). The next stop is Naples, where Mehta visits the volcano of Mount Vesuvius, and this begins a series of tourist-oriented excursions through Italy, Germany, France, Belgium, Holland, Czechoslovakia, Hungary, Denmark, Norway, Sweden, Poland, and England. In almost all these countries, in addition to taking in the sites, Mehta visits a number of factories and meets with industrialists.

In his reading of nineteenth-century travel accounts by Indians visiting England, Javed Majeed has noted that while many Indian travelers "visited what might be called 'tourist sites' in London, for the majority of them by far the most important sights in their itinerary of travel to Britain are scenes of technological progress. These include extended descriptions of steam power, steam railways and boats, industrial manufacturing processes, the infrastructure of London and other European cities, and electricity."[35] Mehta's narrative shares these tendencies, and, while he is impressed by Italian architecture and sculpture, it is a "technological marvel" such as the Eiffel Tower (193) or the "mechanised production" of Germany (192) or even the tube railway, "one of the wonders of the city life of London," that most impress him (195). Visiting the first modern planetarium of the twentieth century only six years after it had opened in Munich, and remembering it as a "really wonderful experience," Mehta must have been among a handful of Indians of his generation to have experienced this institution at a very early stage (191). Likewise, as someone conscious of the role of advertising in commerce, Mehta is impressed by "new and strange methods of advertising," in particular the "novel method of advertising by the smoke-jet of an aeroplane" (194).

Mehta's verdict on Europe is positive—he believes that Indians have a lot to gain by emulating the "courtesy and refinement" that to him characterize the people of Europe (184), but he cautions Indian youth against unnecessary material pursuits and indulgence in luxury in the name of a European-styled freedom. He is wary of the "exhibitionism" of European women who "are eager to look younger and use all sorts of devices to appear young" (189), but he nevertheless is impressed by their educational achievements and their natural sense of equality with men, which gives them more social freedom than their Indian counterparts. Mehta is impressed overall by the amount of money and labor that is spent on educating children in Europe, and while he doesn't himself make an explicit connection, it is clear that his later charitable contributions toward schooling and education both in East Africa and India are influenced by this experience.

While Europe's technological prowess commands Mehta's attention, it is Japan that fills him with awe. His visit is in the midst of the Sino-Japanese War of 1937, and he sees in the Japanese nationalistic fervor and a desire for military success. Unlike his wary attentiveness to British imperialism in Egypt, Mehta seems to have no reservations about Japan's imperial ambitions. On the contrary, war conditions seem to Mehta to bring out the best qualities of the Japanese. For instance, he notes that the war has further emphasized the generally thrifty nature of consumption, and Mehta contrasts this "admirable attitude" with the waste that he sees in India. Just as he classifies the various Europeans he meets according to what he perceives as their national traits, he finds the national character of Japan to be one of "neatness, restraint, humility, honesty and comeliness in personal and social life" (222). Mehta is not immune to the prevalent Orientalist characterizations of the "docility" of Japanese women, but he is even more impressed by the entry of Japanese women into the workplace. He finds that almost 80 percent of the workers in the factories he visits are female and they often participate in women's organizations that have been set up to help disabled or otherwise suffering women. As workers, both Japanese men and women seem to Mehta's managerial eyes the ideal type—they work hard and in an efficient way and seek no recourse to labor organizations. "In times of stress and consequent decrease in wages they keep quiet and work silently till better times prevail and never agitate for the sake of agitation" (228). As though the workers' passive acceptance of labor conditions were not enough to please management interests, Mehta suggests that the Japanese collaboration of labor and capital is predicated on a commonly held belief that "industrial concerns are concerns of public utility and it is upon their progress that the economic uplift of the nation depends" (228). Such patriotism extends from the workplace out into the street, where women go to tie auspicious threads around the wrists of soldiers off to war. Mehta is impressed by the cultural codes of honor that dictate public service and finds as a businessman that honesty in trade transactions on the part of his Japanese suppliers is something that he can take for granted. Thus, while finding much to praise in Europe, it is ultimately to Japan that Mehta turns for a version of modernity that is more palatable to him: "The revival of Japan, even after the disaster of World War II, is due to this sincerity and hard working capacity of this wide awake nation that is Asia's guiding star," concludes Mehta, "Japan was the first to accept western science and industrial culture without losing its national identity. India must surely look up to it and imitate its good qualities if it wants to survive and compete in this difficult world of ours" (229).

An important element in Mehta's travels is his ongoing engagement with the Indian independence struggle, and he is particularly appreciative of Japan's grant of asylum to many Indian revolutionaries. At the Indian Association Club in Tokyo, Mehta meets one such nationalist, Raja Mahendra Pratap, who has been in exile in Japan, and in his speech at the association's dinner Mehta calls for continued support on the part of the Japanese for the cause of Indian independence. Assured by a spokesperson for Japanese businessmen that he has their "heartfelt sympathy and moral support for [India's] freedom" (231), Mehta can further endorse in his narrative the ideal of an India-Japan alliance. The Indian struggle for independence is clearly on Mehta's mind even before he arrives in Japan. He has long supported the movement, providing a form of asylum earlier in East Africa to yet another Indian revolutionary in exile—N. I. Patel.[36] He has also attended the Indian National Congress session of 1921 in Calcutta as a representative of Indians in East Africa. But it is his visit to South Africa just a year before he sets off for Japan that seems to have had the most profound impact on Mehta's nationalist consciousness. Noting the humiliating conditions meted out to Indians and Africans under a rigid color bar, Mehta is outraged by the policies of the South African state, which passes laws "regardless of world opinion and the human urge for equality in these days of democracy" (200). He is hosted by Gandhi's son Manilal during his visit to the Phoenix Ashram near Durban, and Manilal accompanies him on his visit to Pretoria and Johannesburg. Mehta is inspired by the spirit of *satyagraha* and civil disobedience that Gandhi nurtured in this place, and on his return journey to Uganda he himself engages in such noncooperation by refusing to be fingerprinted in the neighboring Portuguese territory of Lourenço Marques. It is this visit, more than any other, that impresses upon Mehta the need for private support of the project of nationalism. "It was quite unexpectedly here," writes Mehta, "that the seeds of founding a Gurukul and Mahatma Gandhi's Kirti Mandir were sown" (202).

The Arya Kanya Gurukul, a residential school for girls based on Vedic principles in Porbandar, and the Kirti Mandir, a monument built near Gandhi's birthplace to celebrate his life, were central to Mehta's own philanthropic projects, and he devotes significant space to them in his autobiography. Before looking more closely at the Gurukul and what it has to say about

Mehta's developing sense of nationalism, one must note that these were only two of the many projects he funded both in India and in East Africa. Robert Gregory claims that Mehta was one of the first Indian entrepreneurs to establish racially integrated preprimary, primary, and secondary schools on a large scale in Uganda. His schools in Lugazi had an annual enrollment of twelve to thirteen hundred African and Asian children. "In addition to forming and maintaining these schools, Mehta paid for approximately one dozen scholarships granted annually by the Ministry of Education for the secondary level. Each year, he sent several African students to India, primarily to the Porbandar Girls Institution he had founded in his home city, but also, beginning in 1957, to various Indian universities for higher education. In 1964, for instance, he gave scholarships to five Uganda girls for study in the Porbandar school. After matriculation one of the five returned to Uganda, but two began midwifery training in Bombay, and the other two entered universities in Baroda and Ahmedabad, all with continuing support."[37] R. O. Preston's *Oriental Nairobi: A Record of Some of the Leading Contributors to Its Development* registers that by 1938, between India and East Africa, Mehta had already contributed over fifty thousand pounds to "various Government, Public, and Arya Samajic Funds."[38] Mehta's autobiography does not dwell on these charitable contributions in East Africa, the one exception being his central role in funding the Gandhi Memorial Academy in Nairobi.[39] Founded by a partnership between private interests, the Colonial Development and Welfare Fund, and the Gandhi Smarak Nidhi in India, the incorporation of the Gandhi Memorial Academy into the Royal Technical College in Nairobi represents to Mehta "a silver link of inter-racial sympathy, understanding and international friendship . . . in the educational, cultural and social advancement of East Africa" (260).

Thus his many charitable contributions on both sides of the Indian Ocean suggest that while Mehta, on the one hand, remained an ardent spokesperson for the merits of commerce and later industrialization, he was, on the other hand, equally mindful of the social obligations of the wealthy.[40] Having grown up in a village society where the less fortunate found support through socially established safety nets, Mehta remembers a time when "it was the bounden duty of the *Patel*, the headman of the village, to go over the village and see that nobody starved and went to bed without food at night. It was a sin to sell milk, curd or buttermilk. They considered it as sacred as the sunflower and these things could be had from anywhere for the mere asking" (15). But times had changed, and if in Africa Mehta found himself at the cusp of the transition between a system of barter and that of monetary exchange, in his Indian surroundings he had to negotiate the transition from a primarily feudal order of obligation to one that risked being compromised by a profit-driven ethic. His role model on these matters was none other than Allidina Visram, an elderly man in Jinja by the time Mehta had first arrived there as a young boy. Calling him a "noble-minded merchant whose munificence and charity knew no bounds," Mehta writes, "he became my ideal as Uganda's captain of commerce and man of charity. My youthful spirit sought inspiration from the legacy of fame and generosity that he left behind" (76–7).

Because the Gurukul in Porbandar played such a central role in Mehta's own sense of self, and because it sheds light on his evolving sense of nationalism and religious identity, it merits more attention than some of his other charitable projects. The Gurukul, Mehta informs us, was founded on Vedic principles of religious devotion, and the girls were expected to adhere to a strict disciplinary code that emphasized prayer and religious ritual balanced with more modern educational concerns. The students, "live, breathe and drink Indian culture when they are at the Gurukul but at the same time they do not close their minds to the great cultural synthesis that is in the making in the international field" (208). Nevertheless, despite this gesture toward internationalism, as Mehta elaborates on the various attributes and virtues of Indian womanhood, his vision increasingly becomes a conservative one. Thus, for instance, he claims, "I am sure, so long as women stick to our mode of life and preserve our culture, a thousand winds of change shall not affect the accumulated *samskaras* of the Indian nation and a happy synthesis of the East and the West will enliven our homes and enrich our society through these sweeter, softer, yet brave ambassadors of our culture" (208). Savita Nair, a scholar who visited the Arya Kanya Gurukul in 1996, confirms the essentially conservative result of such a vision. Quoting Mehta's belief that "it is the duty of Aryan women to preserve, defend and contribute to their rich culture," Nair astutely notes that such sentiment results in "devout religious training,"[41] based on a "very structured and disciplined life, almost militaristic in [its] marching and line-ups" (133). The strict discipline and religious underpinnings of the Gurukul lead Nair to suggest that this form of education is "as much, if not less, about creating skilled and literate women as it [is] about producing loyal and compliant citizens" (133–34). This model of female citizenship is usefully read as part of a larger historical context in which commercial families like Mehta's were negotiating the modernizing demands of social reform (including, for instance, colonial attempts to curtail the practice of child marriages) with their desire to hold on to the traditional institution of the joint family.[42]

Despite the emphasis on the Vedic aspects of the Gurukul, Mehta suggests that "it can be called a secular school in a way, for all those who abide by the rules of discipline can be its inmates without distinction of caste, creed and colour" (205). To be sure, as the enrollment of some Muslim girls and Christian girls from Uganda suggests, the Gurukul had indeed opened its doors across faiths. Nevertheless, its fundamental orientation cannot properly be considered to be a secular one. This tension between the desire to embrace difference, on the one hand, and the need to articulate a religiously inscribed identity, on the other, is symptomatic of a fundamental tension in Mehta's larger narrative. The central crisis involved here is the partition of India at independence and the painful history of Hindu-Muslim tensions. Mehta, the narrative suggests, is profoundly affected by this partition and, I would argue that there is a shift in Mehta's negotiation of nationalism from a more secular to a more religiously inscribed order.[43] We can trace this shift by first noting Mehta's early delight in Mauritius where he finds that Hindus and Muslims have "stayed like brothers and mixed with one another in a dignified and brotherly way that befitted their great culture and common national heritage" (176). The celebration of each others' religious festivals on the part of Muslims and Hindus reminds him of a visit that he has made thirty years earlier to the village of Raval in Gujarat where he encountered Hindus and Muslims both worshiping together at a local Shitala temple. At another point in the text, Mehta tells the story of the Hindu Pandit Jagannath who fell in love with a Muslim woman in the Mughal court and who was excommunicated by his coreligionists. Legend has it that when the two lovers were on the banks of the Ganga, the river rose to reach their feet thus sanctifying their union (295). He also refers to the mystic poet Kabir who preached Hindu-Muslim unity (293). Reflecting on such earlier religious tolerance and syncretism, he bemoans the partition of India "by her two warring children" and warns that "none of the two components of this divided Indian sub-continent could rest in peace, until they are made one by an alchemy of love and mutual choice, which is the only hope of this divided nation" (105). While Mehta repeatedly showcases the possibilities of Hindu-Muslim union, in an echo of the concerns over the modern failures of religious hybridities that we encountered in Ghosh (which we will revisit in Vassanji), the narrative is increasingly haunted by a sense of defeat both in terms of the possibility of a future religious compromise and that of overcoming the scars of past history. Mehta's pilgrimages lead him to religious sites that suggest Mughal desecration of particular Hindu temples, and this leads him to increasingly articulate a disturbingly muscular religious nationalism. So, for instance, in a discussion of the Babri Masjid in Ayodhya, Mehta notes, "Ayodhya, the great city of Shri Ramachandra, thus presented a sad sight to us and we were moved at the plight that it bore from [a] religious standpoint. It revealed that it was no part of religion to be meek. One must be strong enough to protect one's religion and holy places and should not merely indulge in the outward acts of religion" (302). While Hindu-Muslim conflicts have erupted at several points in the subcontinent's history, Mehta's narrative composed in the late 1950s and the 1960s chillingly foreshadows the Ayodhya conflicts of 1992 and the Gujarat massacres of the following decade.[44]

I suggested earlier that the literary poetics of *Dream Half-Expressed* are at least as important as the commercial narrative it presents. Mehta's focus on Rama and Ayodhya here allows us to return to the role of literary, historical, and religious narratives in Mehta's own sense of self. The story of the Ramayana is not only a recurrent motif in Mehta's text but a central part of Mehta's personal trajectory. The text ends with a visit to Ayodhya and reflects on the attendant tensions among Hindus and Muslims, but it is also in Ayodhya, rather than Gujarat, that the text begins. The very first sentence of Mehta's book—"Shri Ramachandra, king of Ayodhya, is the hero of the *Ramayana*, one of the sacred epics of India"—is at once a ritual invocation of the Hindu deity at the beginning of the text and a device for Mehta to insert himself into Rama's legacy: "His descendants were known as *Raghuvamshis*. This Ayodhya of Ramachandra was our place of origin" (1).[45] Readers familiar with the Ramayana will surely note that Mehta's vision of the "purity" and "chastity" of the Hindu woman is not disconnected from the central trope of Sita's chastity. Nor will they fail to note that Mehta's own prescriptions of the regulated codes of Hindu womanhood (as evident in the disciplinary codes of the Gurukul) are directly connected to the epic's vision of the "dangers" of women crossing over the thresholds laid out for them by their husbands. But perhaps what is most telling in the narrative is Mehta's emplotment of his own return to India from Japan via Ceylon. Reminding his readers that Ceylon is held to be the land of Lanka where Rama has defeated Ravana, Sita's abductor, Mehta registers his own return: "From Ceylon I went to Bombay happy, healthy and safe. The Diwali festivities were in full swing and Bombay had put on a glamorous appearance" (236). In case the reader has missed the affinity with Rama in the symbolism of Mehta's return from Ceylon in the midst of the Diwali festivities, at another moment in the text Mehta alludes to the devotion of his business associate Vallabhdas as being "like that of Lakshman to Rama" (318). One of the issues that scholars have often raised about merchant communities in Africa and elsewhere is their relative connection to their original homeland and the choices that they made of remaining sojourners or becoming permanent residents in new lands. As we know, despite his earlier plans to settle permanently in Uganda, Mehta ultimately chose to return to Gujarat in his old age. Whatever the material conditions involved in making this choice may have been, one might ask whether, on the imaginative plane, the choice had not already been made. For the story to be complete, Rama, it seems, must return home.

TIDES OF FORTUNE:
THE SECOND GENERATION AND AFTER

To turn from Mehta's narrative to the autobiographies of Madatally Manji and Manubhai Madhvani is to turn from a vision of commerce as romance to that of commerce as a site of conflict. In the case of the Kenyan-born Manji, the greatest source of conflict is the racial tyranny of the colonial state and to a lesser extent the forces of competition in the marketplace. In the case of the Ugandan Madhvani, the tension is equally divided between the persecutions rendered by the politically unstable Ugandan state (personified for the most part in the narrative by the figure of Idi Amin) and the family disputes over the control of the firm that lead the narrator to publicly litigate. Despite the various challenges, however, both are stories of triumph over adversity and of personal survival and success. And, focused though they are on the growth of family-controlled firms, each narrative in its own way is also a story of interethnic, interracial, and international dependencies and collaborations.

Published in Nairobi in 1995, only two years after he was honored with the title of the "Elder of the Order of the Burning Spear" by Kenyan President Daniel arap Moi, Manji's *Memoirs of a Biscuit Baron* is probably the best known and most widely read among the autobiographies of Asian entrepreneurs that I examine here. As such, it is all the more significant that its central motifs work against the grain of conventional wisdom on the nature of Asian enterprise in East Africa. Whereas Asian commercial and industrial development is often seen to be a handmaiden to the colonial state, receiving favorable treatment and protection, Manji's story highlights the difficulties Asian entrepreneurs often faced in the context of settler racism; while the arrival of independence and partial nationalization of private companies is conventionally seen to have jeopardized Asian business interests, in Manji's case Kenyan independence was of great advantage to his business success; unlike most Asian entrepreneurs who were, as Robert Gregory suggests, steadfast in their ideological leanings toward free-market economics and the absence of state controls, because of the particular nature of his own enterprise, Manji is a firm advocate of state protection of the market; finally, whereas Asian enterprises are often seen to be bolstered by the close-knit family networks in which they often originated, in Manji's story family relations are as much a hindrance as a help.[46]

Memoirs of a Biscuit Baron tells the story of the establishment and growth of a bread, biscuit, confectionary, and pasta company in the years during and after the Second World War. Manji, who grew up in smaller Kenyan towns such as Nyeri, Muranga, and Karatina, arrived in Nairobi in 1938 to help his employer open a new branch of his provisions store. He later decided to set up a distribution business of his own along with a young business partner, and in 1941, urged by his father, he acquired a bakery up for sale. Spurred by the arrival of Italian prisoners of war from Somalia, Manji found a rapid growth in the demand for his bread and cakes. Nonetheless, he faced production difficulties caused by wartime rationing of wheat flour, sugar, and oil, which the narrative describes in considerable detail. Both Italian tastes and the needs of his own Ismaili community prompt him to expand into the vermicelli and pasta business, and he even ventures into the production of writing slates and exercise books for the children of newly arrived refugees from Poland and to metal products such as irons and hammers in short supply during the war. Thus Manji's business growth is spurred not only by the arrival of Europeans and by the changing tastes for European food by Kenyans returning from the war but also by the difficulties in external trade that the war entails. Like other entrepreneurs in Kenya at the time, Manji made full use of the opportunities opened up by the wartime economy. "From a business point of view," he confesses at one point in his text, "I could almost wish that the war would continue forever, but this would be rather cynical" (72).[47]

In the postwar period the House of Manji concentrated not only on manufacturing for the domestic Kenyan market but also expanded its export base to other regions in Africa and the Middle East. By the 1970s the company had signed franchise agreements with several European firms to produce food products under their brand names. Manji became, for instance, the Kenyan manufacturer for Buitoni pasta and Weetabix cereal. Under threat of an import restriction by the government of Tanzania, the company brought its manufacturing operations to the neighboring country where it received generous offers of bank loans and favorable land prices.

Despite building a company that, at least until he wrote his memoir in the 1990s, had been "an unqualified success," Manji's narrative is pervaded by "bitter memories" of colonial racism and the "competitive, and often cruel, world of business" (vi). Of these, the ones that haunt the narrative most are those of settler racism. Recalling the "poor, ill-equipped schools" (28) and the differential educational opportunities for Europeans, Asians, and Africans, Manji writes of the difficult decision that he and his wife make in sending their children, at the tender age of nine, to boarding school in the more liberal institutions of England. He writes of the segregated public coffeehouses in Nairobi's town center where neither Asians nor Africans are allowed to enter (40–41) and tells of an ugly incident in the whites-only Blue Club to which he supplies buns, bread, cakes, and scones. On arriving at the club to claim a payment, he is told by the owner to come through the back entrance so as not to offend the sensibilities of the white patrons. "That incident," writes Manji, was "deeply etched in my mind as the exemplification of the kind of bigotry and racial discrimination that we were subjected to during the colonial era" (145). While personal slights such as these pervade the narrative, it is the behind-the-scenes discrimination that most affects Manji's business. Some barriers, such as the administration's false claim that the Geneva Convention forbade Italian prisoners of war to work for non-Europeans, are handled through cosmetic tactics. Thus, in this particular instance, where Manji seeks to recruit the Italians who have expertise with the macaroni plant that he has acquired, he hires a Greek man to "supervise" them (64–65). In other instances, the discriminatory treatment has more adverse effects. Attempting to secure an export license to send sweets amounting to ten tons to the Congo, Manji is allowed an export limit of only one ton. Aware of his difficulties in acquiring the adequate export license, Manji is approached by a British multinational, BEAC, which offers to serve as his distribution agent. "To our surprise BEAC was granted a full license to export large quantities of sweets to the Belgian Congo. It was painful to realise that we had been denied the same license earlier, and that the export permit they were given for one month was more than we were permitted to export for ten months" (90). After the agreement between BEAC and Manji ends in six months, he applies for the export license, and is once again given only one-tenth of the desired quota. Manji's narrative is unabashed about pointing fingers: "The difference between us and BEAC was that they were members of a 'superior' race. We were being treated badly and were underdogs in a field dominated by whites. The preferential treatment they got was a clear indication of white supremacy in Kenya at the time" (90).

While there are other instances in the text where Manji bristles against racial prejudice, perhaps the most dramatic is the unexpected visit of the chairman of the Commodity Distribution Board at the Ngara Bakery early in the narrative. Tipped off by Manji's European competitors in the bakery business, who Manji argues are shocked and surprised to see an Asian competing successfully with them in what has traditionally been a European-owned sector of the economy, the chairman of the board arrives to investigate the allegedly illegal acquisition of wheat flour on the part of the bakery. This is a time of flour shortages, and, in order to maximize flour supply, the government has introduced a new type of flour, "National Flour," that is a blend of wheat and maize. This blend is not conducive to the production of good quality bread, and all the bakers suffer because of this. Manji, however, has found a way to manufacture decent quality bread, and his competitors are convinced that he is illegally obtaining pure wheat flour. He persuades the chairman that his flour supplier is the same as everyone else's and that as it is a flour mill owned and managed by Europeans "an Asian-owned bakery like (his) had a snowball's chance in hell of receiving preferential treatment" (53). And yet, while on this occasion Manji's enterprise has done nothing illegal to acquire the flour, at a later point Manji confesses that the severe rationing of wheat flour compels him to find "a way around the problem by buying wheat flour directly from a number of wholesalers. It was a black market if one may call it that, and of course, we had to pay higher than the government controlled price" (84).

Even though he is bitter about the racism, Manji takes a certain pleasure in narrating how he has overcome the various hurdles placed before him not only by Europeans but also by his Asian competitors, the latter underselling their competing products or attempting to make competing bids on land that he desires for building a factory. There is an element of the underdog in the narrative, an element that extends to the role of subaltern knowledges and agency coming to the rescue. Departing from the convention of narratives that render African innovation and expertise in the workplace invisible,

Manji registers the critical role of "a new baker, an African named Joshua, who had considerable knowledge and experience baking bread, cakes, biscuits and other wheat products" (43) in the turnaround of an initially failing bakery. His staff is also instrumental in ascertaining why some Kenyans who were first introduced to the spaghetti manufactured by the company refuse to eat it—it resembles the tape worms from which many of them have suffered as children. Elbow-shaped macaroni, manufactured as a substitute, is an instant success (108–9). The acquisition of the pasta factory is itself connected to an act of resistance on the part of the Italian prisoners of war who refuse to operate the machines for their British captors but are willing to help Manji set them up (63). But the particular knowledge from which Manji derives not only market success but also personal pleasure is that derived from his wife's making of chapatis. Faced, like other bakers, with the challenge of making bread of good quality from the inferior National Flour blend, Manji speculates, "If our ladies could make tasty chapatis from National Flour, why could we not bake good quality loaves out of the same flour?" (50). The trick, he learns from the women, is the addition of butter or *ghee*, and he uses this insight to develop a technique for successful bread manufacture.[48]

Despite the colonial racism, as an entrepreneur who needs the goodwill of the state Manji attempts to stay in the good graces of the British. At times he indulges in ingratiating flattery, as in choosing to name a brand of his biscuits Baring biscuits, after the British governor, and naming an arcade he has developed in Nairobi Baring Arcade.[49] Nevertheless, while managing to get his ventures inaugurated by various British colonial governors, ultimately he finds that the economic policies of the colonial state do not help his enterprise. Thus he writes that after the war "we repeatedly asked the colonial government to provide us with some protection against the overseas competition, but the government not only turned down our requests but added insult to the injury by lowering the import duty on biscuits from 30 per cent to 20 per cent. It was as if government was determined to completely strangle our biscuit business. It seemed to have no interest whatsoever in promoting local industry" (86). In contrast, he writes, with Kenyan independence and the imposition of import bans on items like pasta, "things had changed dramatically for the better" (114). For a manufacturer in what is referred to in the economic literature as an "import-substitution" industry, market control of imports is integral to the domestic growth of his concern. This, of course, becomes a challenge when other countries such as Nigeria, to which the company has exported its products, also put such bans in place. With a population of nearly 100 million people, Manji notes, "the decision by its government [to ban imports] meant that we had lost the market, at least until trade liberalisation caught on in that country." (120) Ironically, such trade liberalization in East Africa which came into greatest effect since the 1990s, may ultimately have led to the financial troubles of Manji's company forcing its sale in 2002 to a larger multinational company. Manji's story dramatizes, then, the contingent nature of the interplay of free-market policies and state regulations. While the free flow of goods may be an asset to trade, it may also pose a hindrance and threat to local manufacture.

In addition to showing how business practices had to be negotiated with the colonial state, *Memoirs of a Biscuit Baron* also sheds interesting light on the role of family and community networks. Often claimed to be central to the growth of Asian entrepreneurship in East Africa, family becomes both an asset as well as a source of anxiety. With his father having parted company from his own brother even before Madatally has come of age, the notion of a joint family enterprise is already a shaky one for Manji (22). Nevertheless, he decides to build a larger and more modern bakery than the one already established in Ngara and, in the interests of pooling capital, goes into a partnership with a close relative. Ultimately, not only does the partnership fail, with Manji claiming a net loss, but the competition between this relative and Manji's own new company is intense and ugly. If the struggle with this relative is a difficult one, Manji is no less pained when at the end of 1973 his brothers all decide to opt out of the business, choosing to sell their shares in the House of Manji (162).

Community networks too are uncertain sources of support, Manji's own Ismaili community treating him with a certain reserve. When he forms the 21 Club, which meets at the Mayfair Hotel, to introduce ballroom dancing in the Asian community, he soon becomes the "talk of the town attracting withering criticism from many religious zealots" (156). While community members such as Madatally Alibhai Shariff offer him support in the form of a loan in a time of business need (41–42), he writes that his philanthropic work conducted under the auspices of the Aga Khan Provincial Council is treated with "a great deal of jealously and suspicion" by some of the top leaders and soon, "in a swift and inexplicable move, the economic development responsibility" is removed from his hands (152). Indeed, Manji's story provides an important caution to the communal emphasis often placed by scholars on merchant and trade networks. While he works to retain connections with business associates who are Ismailis, many of the individuals Manji mentions by name as being critical to his entrepreneurial success are those outside his immediate Ismaili community. Mulchandbhai Khimasia and Shankerprasad Bhatt, both of whom extend him credit facilities; V. S. Hukumchand, who provides a critical connection to a confirming house in London; Maghanbhai Mistry, who works with him to develop various machines and tools for his ventures; Joshua the baker, whose expertise is critical for the new bakery; H. V. Shah, the lawyer who helps first draft a purchase agreement of the Ngara bakery; and William George, the chairman of Weetabix with whom he sets up a franchise, are only a few such individuals.

It is tempting to read Manji's *Memoirs of a Biscuit Baron* and Madhvani's *Tide of Fortune*, to which I turn next, as part of the numerous CEO memoirs that have flooded the market over the past two decades. To varying degrees they share the genre's depiction of the CEO as the leader of a large enterprise, the latter often cast as a family with the CEO as (in the still predominantly masculine world of business) patriarch enforcing the discipline of an established code and providing the vision for future growth. Such narratives are often read for their offerings of business advice, and Madhvani certainly harbors a hope that younger members of his family, among others, will turn to his book for such wisdom (74). My own interest in reading these texts, however, is not to scour them for lessons in business management but rather to read them as narrative expressions of second-generation Indians in East Africa who, despite their travels and investments abroad, identified deeply with their East African contexts. If, as Manji writes, the story of his life is also the story of the House of Manji, it is equally a story that reflects the role of colonial rule and the narrative of Kenyan nationalism on the commercial imagination (v–vi). Likewise, the Madhvani story (along with that of Mehta and his descendants) is intricately linked to the colonial and postcolonial narrative of Ugandan nationalism.

Subtitled "A Family Tale," Madhvani's narrative spans five generations, from the arrival in East Africa of Vithaldas Haridas, his great-uncle, in 1893 to the coming of age of his own grandchildren who now live in many different countries. It is, he insists, a story of the education of a family, "not only in the laws of commerce, absorbed over a long period by several generations, but also in the unpredictable brutalities of life" (14). The narrative begins with the apprenticeship of Vithaldas Haridas to the firm of Allidina Visram, who, in keeping with established lore, is venerated as an inspiration for many succeeding generations. It is from Visram that both Vithaldas Haridas and his nephew Muljibhai Madhvani learn the importance of tending to the social, physical, and educational welfare of those who work for them.[50] When the author's father Muljibhai arrives in Uganda to join his uncle's ventures, he finds there the young Nanji Kalidas Mehta, with whom he will spend many an evening visiting their mentor Visram (86). Urging his readers to read Mehta's *Dream Half-Expressed*, Madhvani notes, "Nanji Kalidas and Muljibhai would spend their whole days trading in fierce competition, but as the sun set they would happily sit down together and socialize. They managed to be both competitors and friends. But the competition was unrelenting" (30). Over time, Vithaldas Haridas and his relatives branched out into new ventures including cotton ginning and the manufacture of sugar, but ultimately due to a number of factors the partners decided to separate. Muljibhai acquired the sugar estate and soon engaged in a process of growth and modernization through acquisition of more land and equipment and the hiring of technical experts. His sons Jayant and Manubhai (the author) joined him as partners in the 1950s, and the narrative's main focus is on the expansion and diversification of the Madhvani Group not only in terms of the products manufactured (sugar, cotton, beer, oil, steel) but also in terms of geography and finance.[51] Thus, for instance, the narrative provides a close look at the group's acquisition and development of enterprises in India in the 1950s and, most significantly, in light of Amin's later accusations of the outflow of Asian money from Uganda, the group's decision to restructure its finances by setting up offshore trusts in Bermuda. Set up at a time when there were no restrictions on foreign exchange transfers as were to later come in postcolonial Uganda, these trusts, writes Madhvani, "have protected the group during the bad years and gave it long-term international resilience" (99). They also show that unlike the less-established Asian traders, civil servants, and professionals who had little to no assets outside the country at the time of expulsion, families such as the Madhvanis and Mehtas had financial structures in place to see them through the crisis.[52]

The crisis itself is twofold, and both aspects hit almost simultaneously. The domestic crisis involves the death of the author's elder brother Jayant, who has been a key partner in running the enterprise along with the author after the death of their father. Jayant has also been the public face of the corporation, being involved in Ugandan national politics including serving on the Legislative Council from 1954 to 1960 (110) and chairing, at Idi Amin's request, the Export Import Corporation of Uganda. Jayant's death in 1971 leads to a major fissure in the family, his widow Meenaben wanting her son Nitin to head the family firm. This fissure is to pervade the entire narrative, and its eventual results are the divisions of the family's assets among the five male heirs (or their descendants) of Muljibhai.[53] Even after the split, family disputes do not disappear, resulting, for instance, in the author's litigation against his nephew Nitin for violating a family agreement surrounding the assets that have been left behind in Uganda after the expulsion and reappropriated following the Expropriated Properties Act of 1982 (181). Much of the family narrative past the 1970s is presented as a battle of epic proportions, and the numerous references to the Bhagavad Gita, the classical text concerned with the ethical and moral dilemmas of going to war with one's cousins, suggest that, if the authorial Mehta turns to the Ramayana for a model and inspiration, it is the epic of the Mahabharata (of which the Bhagavad Gita is a part) that structures Madhvani's family tale.[54]

The domestic crisis resulting from Jayant's death percolates in the context of a larger political crisis, the one that lends the narrative its greatest claim to being exceptional. Written with the help of Giles Foden, the author of the Idi Amin–centered novel *The Last King of Scotland*, Madhvani's book opens with a scene in the "Singapore Block," the nickname given to Uganda's infamous Makindye Prison. Madhvani writes of his terror at night when he hears the screams of his fellow prisoners and the thumping sounds that silence them in the prison compound: "Every few nights another prisoner would arrive, manacled and in leg irons and usually very badly beaten. Most of these prisoners were led away in the dead of night for execution. Their bodies were usually dumped in the River Nile, one of the guards told me, his face completely expressionless" (9). Noting that the imagination can be both a danger and a gift when one is a prisoner, Madhvani imagines the dead bodies disintegrate in the great river and wonders whether he will meet the same fate. While he fears for his life, he also knows that his arrest is a symbolic one. Imprisoning the "43 year old Asian head of Uganda's biggest industrial combine, employing more than 15,000 people and manufacturing 19 products from steel to sugar" (8–9) is Amin's way of showing both the Asians in Uganda as well as the British government that he is serious about the Asian expulsion order.

Written more than thirty years after the expulsion, at a time when Madhvani had returned home to Uganda under the auspices of a more receptive President Museveni, *Tide of Fortune* is marked by a more nuanced appreciation of Ugandan history than was articulated by many Ugandan exiles and their sympathizers around the time of the crisis. Even though the narrative indulges in pathologizing Amin as an unpredictable dictator, with references to him as an "ogre" (109) or a "ludicrous monster" (14) with a "malevolent scowl" (9), Madhvani recognizes that Amin had managed to garner a popular following by playing up existing anti-Asian sentiment in Uganda. Thus the narrative reads Amin as continuous with a larger political and economic crisis in Uganda that is not solely of the dictator's making.[55] In Madhvani's judgment, British colonialism is to carry the main burden "of much of the discord that was to follow, including friction between races, ethnicities, and cultures to which [his] family and many others—African as well as Asian—fell victim" (27).[56] As an example he points to the colonial policy of excluding Africans from the lucrative enterprise of cotton ginning throughout the twenties, thirties, and forties and shows how this led to African resentment of Indians. Unlike Mehta, whose narrative downplays any African resistance, Madhvani is interested in showing the evolution of such resistance and its legacy in later endorsing Amin's expulsion order.[57] He writes with some sympathy about the Bugandan riots of 1949 and the Freedom Fighters in the highlands of Kenya even as he recognizes growing signs of resentment on the part of indigenous Africans against his own family. Despite developing a sense of historicity about the expulsion, what most hurts Madhvani at the time are not Amin's accusations, which are "simply insulting" to "those families that had built up Uganda's trade and industry over several generations" (125), but rather the "unseemly joy" with which the announcement is received by a large majority of the Ugandan population (125).

While economic policy is the major factor driving the majority's resentment, Madhvani is not blind to the "cases of outright prejudice" (28) against Africans in the Asian community that have also led to the tensions. Nor is the narrative shy in exposing some of the criminal elements among the Asians: "The most shocking thing I discovered," writes Madhvani, remembering the expulsion period, "was that some Asian criminals had been helping Amin's goons to kidnap fellow Asians in order to extort ransoms from their families" (135). And, while the Asians received international attention because of their effect on British immigration, Madhvani insists that the worst fate—that of death rather than exile—was often meted out to indigenous Ugandans: "Across the country the police and death squads from other parts of the security apparatus had been butchering people. Anyone suspected of opposition to the new regime might be killed, although prime targets were people of Acholi and Langi extraction" (9). When a bold voice such as that of the Ugandan chief justice Benedicto Kiwanuka ruled that Amin's policies of arbitrary detention and the expulsion of Asians with Ugandan citizenship were illegal, such persons were disappeared by the regime without a trace (146).

In foregrounding the worse fate of many indigenous Ugandans under Amin's rule, *Tide of Fortune* negotiates the tensions between particularistic and more general accounts of historical experience, a negotiation that pervades the entire narrative. The story being told is at once about the plight of a particular ethnic community, about a larger national tragedy, and about the eruptions of political turmoil in the world at large. As Madhvani puts it, "We Asians might have been in the spotlight just then, but before we hit the headlines the military police had been hounding indigenous Ugandans for months. . . . In that sense our case was not exceptional. We were just another tribe" (9). Thus the story is not just about Asians but about all Ugandans. Likewise, to read *Tide of Fortune* as only a narrative about the political turmoil in Amin's Uganda would be to lose sight of its larger vision of ethnic and political strife in the world at large. The traumas of the Asian expulsion from Uganda are foreshadowed in the narrative by Madhvani's own witnessing of the "sadness and devastation" of the partition of India in 1947, where as a young man he learns that independence can simultaneously bring "euphoria" as well as tragedy (54). Even after the Ugandan crisis has passed and the Madhvani family, despite its disputes and divisions, has managed to return to Uganda, the closing pages of the narrative tell the story of yet another strike against the enterprise—the conflict this time is not African but Middle Eastern. A glass factory owned by the family in the Bekaa Valley of Lebanon is flattened by Israeli missiles, taking yet another turn in the family's tide of fortune. Once again, political and ethnic strife interrupt the march of commerce.

Tide of Fortune is an elderly man's remembrance of "farming, factories, family" (11), but it is an ardent love letter to the spirit of industry and the social goods that Madhvani clearly believes it delivers as well.[58] Arguing passionately for the transfer of technology into Africa and the importation of specialized technical expertise to ensure the best production practices, the narrator devotes considerable space to detailing the operations of both his sugar as well as glass production facilities. As might be expected, the vision of the factory in this text is quite different from the more somber image in Marx of the worker being a cog in the machine. For Madhvani, the sugar factory and the farm that feed it are sources not only of pride but also of aesthetic pleasure: "I do feel proud when I walk around our farm and factory. I feel proud of the fields folding like a green sari into the hills that surround the emerald lake. . . . I even feel proud of the irrigation pipes protruding into the lake and carrying the pumped water all round the estate" (15). In this narrative presentation, not only are there no social or environmental ills associated with the enterprise, but, in Madhvani's view, there are environmental gains: "In producing sugar here at Kakira," writes Madhvani, "I suppose we are doing our bit for the environment, even taking into consideration our emissions. For every one tonne of sugar made, 1.45 tonnes of carbon dioxide are removed from the atmosphere" (104–5). Later the industrial site begins to appear as a more compelling vision of community than the alternative of a potentially disruptive political state. Here, where the narrator is master, there is an explicit attempt to render industry and commerce back into the realm of romance rather than of conflict: "A sound I love to hear is the factory steam whistle or 'factory clock,' which sounds at specified times of the day. It can be heard all over the plantation relieving those who have just completed their shift and calling to the workers for the next shift to start their journey to work. The sound of this whistle make me happy—it is a connection with the past, it is also a sign that the factory is working and that thousands of people are coming together in a common enterprise" (108).[59]

Thousands of people coming together in a common enterprise—this is the dream of the entrepreneur, a dream that Madhvani shares with all his predecessors—Ebrahimji Adamji, Sorabji Darookhanawala, Nanji Kalidas Mehta, Madatally Manji, and many others. It is a dream of commerce with the universe, a romance with the workings of the marketplace, and one that insists on registering the fundamental complementarity rather than conflict between capital and labor. It is, at the same time, a dream that has, at best, an uneasy relationship with the stewards of the state, fearful that these stewards of power can easily turn a happy dream into a nightmare.

6. LIGHTING A CANDLE ON MOUNT KILIMANJARO

Partnering with Nyerere

In his discussion of the plight of Asians under both the first Obote regime and Idi Amin, D. P. S. Ahluwalia reminds us that the Asian community in Uganda, like elsewhere in East Africa, was not homogeneous, but rather composed of two main groups. "The first was made up of those individuals who were traders and clerks in the Civil Service and the second was a small group comprised of the industrial wing of local Asian capital. The existence of these two groups meant that the State was able to deal with each separately."[1] While it was expedient to scapegoat the former, both Obote and Amin understood the importance of the latter to the economic development of Uganda. Thus, ironically, even as he was chastising Asians for being inadequately loyal to Uganda and allegedly engaging in corrupt business practices, Amin took a moment to praise both the Mehta and the Madhvani families: "No one doubts the various positive contributions which you Asians have made since the arrival of your forefathers in East Africa as railway builders," he said in a speech delivered to the Asian Conference held on December 8, 1971, going on to list among other contributions the "big industrial concerns and farming activities which, for example, have all along been spearheaded by such outstanding families as the Madhvanis,

Mehtas, etc. All these activities have assisted employment opportunities, without which some people might have been forced to take up criminal activities."[2] And later, a year after Amin's expulsion order for Asians in 1972, when the Madhvani family published a book of remembrance as a tribute to Jayant, Manubhai's elder brother who had passed away in 1971, the book prominently featured a note of condolence from the Ugandan premier.[3] Perhaps these warm sentiments were a result of the fact that, as *Tide of Fortune* narrates, in his final years of life Jayant had been recruited by Obote to serve as chairman of the Export Import Corporation of Uganda, a role in which he continued to serve after Amin came to power.

Despite the strategic partnership that may have been made in those years between Jayant Madhvani and the Ugandan leadership, it was a partnership that was clearly made by Jayant under duress and a sense of uncertainty about the future of the family enterprise. By the late sixties the neighboring state of Tanzania had already passed the Arusha Declaration that envisioned a socialist society, based on the principle of *Ujamaa*, in which the means of production would be controlled by the people and their political representatives.[4] In the process, a number of private enterprises held by Asians were nationalized. One among these was the milling conglomerate of the Chande family, the scion of which was J. K. Chande, a man who had married a Madhvani—Jayli, a sister of Jayant and Manu. Well before their troubles in Uganda, then, the Madhvani brothers had already seen the project of nationalization affect their sister's family in Dar es Salaam, and, as Chande gratefully acknowledges in his own memoir to which I will soon turn, the brothers had helped bail the family out when they were strapped for cash to pay the monthly bills. Ironically, as Chande notes in his memoir, having been left without monetary property after the nationalization, and fearful of further risk, Jayli decided to send her jewelry back to her maternal home in Uganda for safekeeping. This protective measure misfired, of course, when the Madhvanis themselves had to abandon the majority of their local assets in Uganda at the time of the expulsion.

In this chapter I turn to three narratives of Asians in Tanganyika (later Tanzania) who played a central part in the project of nation building. My interest here is in emphasizing the difference in tone and perspective that these Tanzanian narratives present from the narratives that we have read so far.[5] All three narratives are of individuals who were recruited by President Nyerere to share in the task of nation building and who did so with considerable enthusiasm for his sense of ethics and leadership. This dedication to Nyerere and his leadership is all the more impressive when one notes that, at least in two of the cases, the particular policies that Nyerere forged were economically detrimental to the interests of the authors. Whatever we may make of the efficacies of Nyerere's economic policies in retrospect, it is important to note, as May Joseph has observed in her insightful reading of Tanzanian nationalism under Nyerere, that "the trauma of financial loss did not prevent Asians from hanging black-and-white photographs of Nyerere in their living rooms, a tribute to his charismatic impact as leader of the nation."[6]

Volumes have been written on the project of nation building in Tanzania and on Nyerere's role in fashioning Ujamaa.[7] My aim here is not to provide another review of that history, but rather to highlight some of the more personal elements of that national story as narrated in the memoirs of Sophia Mustafa, Al Noor Kassum, and J. K. Chande, all three Tanzanian patriots of Asian descent.[8] In broad strokes we might say that Mustafa's *The Tanganyika Way* is a narrative that charts what to most observers will seem an unlikely rise of an Asian woman in postcolonial Tanganyikan politics. Kassum's *Africa's Winds of Change: Memoirs of an International Tanzanian* is a narrative of a relatively wealthy young man finding his political voice and vocation as an advocate for universal and racially integrated education, gaining further expertise in the challenges of education through his development work at the United Nations, and then returning to serve his country through various politically appointed roles. Finally, Chande's *A Knight in Africa: Journey from Bukene* is an account of an uneasy but nevertheless willful partnership between a formerly private businessman and the postcolonial state that has relieved him of all of his assets.[9] It is ultimately a narrative not only about translating the skills of capitalist entrepreneurship to serve the needs of a managed economy and the traffic between private and state ventures but also about the nature of negotiation and compromise. What we see in all three narratives is a greater attempt at civic engagement and public service and a willingness to partner with the state than we have in the narratives read so far. This should not be seen as a shift from apathy to public service—since that would do a disservice to the many social contributions made by individuals all the way from Allidina Visram to the Mehtas and the Madhvanis. Rather, it is a shift from a model of philanthropy as charitable giving to a model of a more participatory and performative civic engagement with nation building, a move that Jayant Madhvani had arguably embarked on before his untimely death. Whatever the dynamics of such engagement may have been in Uganda, in the case of Tanzania, in many ways, this shift is directly attributable to the charismatic hold of the figure of Nyerere and his explicit project of engaging in what Kwame Anthony Appiah has called "soul making."[10]

Born in India in 1922 to parents who were on "home leave" from Nairobi, and raised in Nairobi, Sophia Mustafa moved to Arusha with her husband, Abdulla, a lawyer who was to go on to have a long and distinguished career as a judge in East Africa.[11] Mustafa's entry into national politics, which is the subject of her book *The Tanganyika Way*, was precipitated by the colonial government's decision to have tripartite elections in 1958 for membership in the Legislative Council of Tanganyika. Mustafa was supported by Nyerere's TANU party as their Asian candidate for the Northern Province, and her victory in the election was achieved with an overwhelming majority. Her narrative, first published in 1961 and recently republished with an editorial introduction by her daughter, the literary critic Fawzia Mustafa (who also makes several appearances in the narrative as an infant), is a remarkable story of her ongoing engagement with nationalism and the collective project of forging Tanzanian citizenship. Along with more recent work, such as that of Susan Geiger, Ruth Meena, and Marjorie Mbilinyi, Mustafa's text furnishes an exposé of the gendered nature of Tanzanian nationalism.[12] Unlike the other two narratives of Chande and Kassum, which were published in 2005 and 2007 respectively, Mustafa's is a narrative written in the thick of the moment—with no benefit of hindsight. While we do not know how she would have rewritten her text in her later years, her daughter and editor Fawzia Mustafa is right to note that what we get in the text is "a brand of idealism that we are hard pressed to duplicate today," noting further that one is uncertain whether one would even want to do so.[13] Nevertheless, what is significant is that, despite their recognition of some of the missteps in what Mustafa labeled the "Tanganyika Way," both Kassum and Chande speak of the project of Tanzanian nation building, and of Nyerere in particular, with great respect.

What was it about Nyerere that so appealed to even some of those whose prosperity was personally jeopardized by his economic policies? The three narratives are consistent in their answer—it was Nyerere's sense of an idealistic nationalism based on a firm doctrine of nonracialism and equal protection for all citizens. The idealism is best captured in the statement made by Nyerere in his preindependence speech to the Tanganyikan Legislative Council in October 1958, alluded to by both Chande and Kassum and quoted by Mustafa in her narrative: "We, the people of Tanganyika would like to light a candle and put it on top of Mount Kilimanjaro which would shine beyond our borders giving hope where there was despair, love where there was hate, and dignity where before there was only humiliation. . . . We cannot, unlike other countries, send rockets to the moon, but we can send rockets of love and hope to all our fellowmen where ever they may be" (109). And as Mustafa's narrative carefully delineates, this larger sense of humanism was, in Nyerere's mind, intrinsically connected to the challenge of creating a Tanganyikan sense of citizenship, based on principles of human dignity and equality, that trod carefully on the racial and ethnic tensions of Tanganyika's colonial history. It was a far cry, indeed, from the more racially exclusionary rhetoric emerging not only from leaders in the neighboring countries of Kenya and Uganda but also, as Chande meticulously documents, from other leaders within Nyerere's own party.[14]

The Tanganyika Way is as much an account of Nyerere's firm hold on the nonracialist agenda as about the micropolitics of the Tanganyikan nationalist party, TANU. Mustafa outlines both the rise of the settler-dominated United Tanganyika Party, built on the principle of racial representation of all three races, as well as the formation of the African National Congress, a party that mobilized under the agenda of black nationalism. Rejecting both these alternatives, Mustafa's narrative makes the case for Nyerere's nonracial understanding of citizenship and political representation. As such, as Marjorie Mbilinyi has persuasively noted, *The Tanganyika Way* is best read as an activist text designed to educate a still forming citizenry on the virtues of nonracial democratic citizenship.[15] Even as they are presented as the historical record, the extensive quotations from Nyerere's speeches are meant to be didactic.[16] So, for instance, Nyerere is quoted as upholding the human rights of immigrants to the new nation even as he is aware of the history of economic divisions between immigrants and indigenous Tanganyikans: "The division of any society into 'haves' and 'have nots' is dynamite. Here it is aggravated by its identification with racial division also. The 'haves' here are generally the immigrant minorities; the 'have nots' are the indigenous majorities. This is dangerous. This puts a stumbling block in our way. We must remedy this one, and we must remedy this as quickly as is humanly possible" (116–17). Nevertheless, such remedy, Nyerere insisted, must not be racially motivated: "Let not the world point a finger at us and say that we gained our freedom on a moral argument—the argument of the brotherhood of man—and then threw that argument overboard and began, ourselves, to discriminate against our brothers on the grounds of colour" (116).[17] As we will see in both Kassum and Chande's narratives, the attempt to remedy historical economic inequities did in fact result in the divestment of Asian property, but, quite unlike the case of Amin, who was fueled by and in turn further fueled popular anti-Asian resentment, Nyerere's political rhetoric was all about nation building and not about targeting racial minorities. As such, it generated a much more respectful and even sympathetic response from at least some Tanzanian Asians who took it upon themselves to serve the newly independent nation. [18] To be sure, there were also those who were less sanguine about the dispossession of properties and nationalization, and, to give voice to some of their concerns, we will, in the next chapter, pay attention to M. G. Vassanji's novel *The Gunny Sack*, which best represents their disenchantment.

Ironically, in retrospect, despite Nyerere's aversion to racially based criteria for political representation, it was the colonial government's insistence that elections to the Legislative Council be based on a tripartite structure with racial "parity" that resulted not only in a racially more integrated form of party politics but also, perhaps, in a more enlightened citizenry. Mustafa's own account makes this explicit in terms of her own process of learning about her African compatriots: "Our knowledge of the African and his ways and his ideals and beliefs was so superficial. Very few bothered to go deeply into it. Very few of us thought of the African's problems from his point of view. I used to think that, if it had not been for the tripartite voting system, perhaps I still would not have known anything, except superficially, about the Africans, although I have lived here all my life" (37). If this is a candid assessment on Mustafa's part, it also raises the question whether she would have been tapped for a position on the Legislative Council by TANU in the first place had the issue of tripartite elections never been raised. For, in the absence of a tripartite election, Mustafa would have been an unlikely candidate not only as an Asian but also as a woman. In this regard, Susan Berger has suggested that TANU may have chosen Mustafa as their Asian candidate "at least in part because she was not part of the fairly strong and often independent-minded Asian Association linked with the prominent Asian 'immigrant' business communities" and that the party was "probably also betting that as a woman with only moderate political experience, Mustafa would be a more malleable representative on the council than other potential Asian representatives."[19] Likewise, referring to her "sometimes cipher-like role" in the political process, Fawzia Mustafa points to her mother's uncanny narrative that "repeatedly signals the way in which her candidacy served as a bald pawn in TANU's machinations of the tri-partite system they were dealt" (x). The fact that Sophia, the "first elected non-white female legislator on the continent" and "then a nominated Member of Parliament since 1963," would prematurely retire in 1965 in the interests of her husband's career, writes Fawzia Mustafa, "signals the contradictions that women of her generation and location grappled with" (vi).

Regardless of what one makes of TANU's use of Mustafa's candidacy, *The Tanganyika Way* is a compelling portrayal of the negotiation of ethnic and gendered identity in the politics of nation building. It is not accidental, among the narratives of early Asian travelers, entrepreneurs, and nation builders that I have addressed in this book, that Mustafa's stands out as the only one written by a woman.[20] The fact that, as a woman, the odds are against her is revealed at a number of points in the narrative where European, Asian, and African constituents, when not skeptical of her abilities, are sometimes at a loss as to how to treat a political leader who happens to be a woman. And, while the most obvious emblem of patriarchy in the narrative is Mustafa's husband Abdulla, who has to be cajoled into accepting her entry into national politics, the narrator is at first herself tentative about her own standing in the larger historical moment. The suggestion that she stand as TANU's Asian candidate for the Northern Province, made to her by her husband's business acquaintance Robert Philip, is taken at first both by Mustafa and her husband as a joke, and it is only when Philip reminds her of her prior work on Arusha's Town Council that she even imagines the possibility of running for election.[21] Writing in retrospect—after her abilities as a leader had been well established—she nevertheless notes, "I am not an economist, nor have I any professional qualifications, and my knowledge of things and matters was very meagre. I really had no reason for offering myself for election for such an important and big job" (9).

Such hesitancy about her ability and authority frames the narrative.[22] Even as she writes what has become an important and invaluable account of the day-to-day experiences of the first election campaign, and about the proceedings of the various meetings of the Legislative Council and TANU's negotiations with the colonial government, quoting extensively from both official Hansards and speeches made by various statesmen, she is still cautious about giving her narrative the status of "history." "The account in this book is a personal one as seen by me, and is in no way a history of Tanganyika" (6), she writes, worrying that the space of domesticity that provides the backdrop for her story might somehow take away from the largely nondomestic sphere of the state. Here her concern is ironic, given that the notion of Ujamaa fostered by Nyerere as the emblem of the newly emergent state makes a direct reference to "familyhood" as its base. Furthermore, as the narrative suggests, it is precisely the very demands of the domestic sphere that have spurred Mustafa's political career. The moniker "A Housewife in

Politics" that she gives herself in the title of one of her chapters says more than is at first apparent. It is precisely her role as a mother, and her sense of helplessness and loss each time she has to send her very young children to school in England (because the local colonial setup has provided inadequate options for Asian children), that spurs her to turn to the workplace. "It was awful to have to send my children so far away at such a tender age. . . . I had taken up office work to pass the time and I also felt it would keep me from brooding and feeling sorry for myself" (14–15). The desire to find something to do so that she can get her mind off her children leads not only to the secretarial work for her husband Abdulla (which later puts her in the orbit of the TANU member) but also to her nomination to the Arusha Town Council. Similarly, if the absence of her children spawns a desire to expand her horizons beyond the domestic sphere, it is the racism she has earlier experienced at the hands of a local hospital, where an English nurse refused to handle her or her newborn baby, that has awakened in her a political consciousness.[23] Notice, again, the apologetic manner in which the narrator relates this significant event in her life: "My readers, perhaps, will be bored with these petty, personal incidents, but I recount them because perhaps they, indirectly and unconsciously, had turned me to politics. Having gone through these experiences I had great sympathy with the Africans and the way they were treated. After all, they were even worse off than we were" (17). In this moment as well as at others throughout the narrative, as Marjorie Mbilinyi has suggested, we see Mustafa's text implicitly recognizing, even if hesitantly, the feminist motto "the personal is the political" well before it was commonly articulated.[24]

At first uncertain about her entry into national politics and a little concerned about how the details of her domestic life will affect readers, Mustafa's account of how she came to write the narrative is of some interest. She attributes the book to the demands made by her son Mali, then at school in England, to keep him updated on her political activities. It is in response to one such letter detailing her activities in TANU that Mali asks her to write a book for his (future) children. "And that is how," Mustafa writes, "I really started writing this narrative" (131). Though one has no reason to doubt the verity of this account, we should also be alert to the fact that writing as a way of understanding and relating to the world was, by the time she wrote this book, not a new discovery for Mustafa. While she never mentions it in *The Tanganyika Way*, we now know that, even before she wrote this narrative, Mustafa had long been working on a novel titled *Nureen*. Revised over a number of years and published several decades later under the new title *Broken Reed,* the novel was based, writes Mustafa in her preface, "on my own experience of becoming a refugee and having to flee from India to Pakistan, first as part of a foot convoy, and then in a bus with my five-year-old daughter."[25] Rather than reading it merely as a response to a son's request, I suggest it would be more accurate to read *The Tanganyika Way* as part of Mustafa's aspirations to be a writer. Reading it in this light helps us to appreciate its rich texture, in particular the liberal use of dialogue that helps register the different relationships between the characters and their changing environments.[26]

There is, however, an additional element to this earlier biographical trajectory. Here, too, the personal becomes the political, though in a way that is only summarily presented in the text. Because Tanganyikan independence had the potential of being overshadowed by the political crisis in the Congo, Nyerere felt it necessary to publicly explain why the situation in the Congo could never be replicated in an independent Tanganyika. Mustafa's narrative gives due space to both the anxieties of immigrants and Nyerere's assurances. But, while reflecting on Tanganyika's independence day, she writes with enormous pleasure and satisfaction that "this was a day on which a dependent territory had achieved virtual self-government without a shot being fired or a drop of blood shed" (114), her personal point of reference is arguably more the bloodshed she has personally witnessed during the Indian partition than either the very proximate experiences of the Kenyan Freedom Struggle (called the Mau Mau Uprising by the British) or the reports coming from the neighboring Congo. Unlike Nanji Kalidas Mehta and Manu Madhvani, who were both troubled by the events of the Indian partition but nevertheless witnessed them at some distance, Mustafa's experience of the partition was the more abject one of being a refugee. For Mustafa the lesson of the partition was the importance of peacefully forging community across religious and other ethnic lines, and it is a lesson that was clearly on her mind a decade later as an Asian in Tanganyika. "My interest in nationalism," she writes, "began in India during the partition of India and Pakistan. I had gone on holiday and was in India on Independence Day. I had actually seen the killings and bloodshed and was myself a refugee. I came back to East Africa in 1948 a complete nervous wreck. Achieving independence was not easy. It could be horrible" (18).

Attention to the role that the partition of India played in the imagination of East African Asians such as Mehta, Madhvani, Mustafa, and many others allows us to read their anxieties at the time of East Africa's independence as at least partly rooted in a history that is larger than the dystopian and often racist narratives that were circulated (and often continue to circulate) around the possibilities of African statesmanship. In other words, if narratives such as Mustafa's betray a deep undercurrent of immigrant anxiety that is performatively overcome by a self-conscious partnership with a leader who paves the way to a nonracial society, such anxiety, I argue, is rooted not as one might quickly imagine, in a vision of a chaotic, primordial, and violent Africa, but rather in a vision that fears the eruption of violence in *any* society that is undergoing radical transformative political change. This, to return to an observation I made earlier, is also the main thrust of Madhvani's narrative, which moves between India, East Africa, and the Middle East, tracking each period of peace and prosperity punctuated by those of violence and disorder.

And, yet, while the partition of India and its attendant violence was a stark reminder to many East African Asians of what could go wrong in a period of political transition, the experience of Indian nationalism was also inspiring and often personally exhilarating. Madhvani writes in his memoirs of his attendance in Juhu (Bombay) at the speeches and rallies of the Indian National Congress and the commanding presence of Gandhi. He writes of sneaking away from his college with his friend to visit a prison where his friend's nationalist father had been imprisoned by the British. Bombay is the space for Madhvani's political awakening, and the nationalism that it inspires at first serves as a barrier between him and his father when he returns home to Uganda.[27] Likewise, both J. K. Chande and Al Noor Kassum write of the profound impact that their presence in Bombay just before Indian Independence has had on them. Kassum joins the Indian Congress Party, even though he admits that he does it mainly because it "was the thing to do for people of my age."[28] He is enthusiastic about meeting Mohammed Ali Jinnah, the future leader of Pakistan, but later expresses regret about the partition, wishing that a federation could have been negotiated. Kassum's other experiences in Bombay—including his meeting with Prince Aly Khan, the eldest son of the Aga Khan, his schooling at St. Xavier's College and Batlibhoi's Technical Institute (the latter of which is also part of Chande's educational itinerary), his evolving friendships with college students in India, and his toying with service in the British Royal Air Force—are all significant to the evolution of his public life when he returns to Tanganyika and then ventures abroad again to England to study law at Lincoln's Inn and later to various posts in UNESCO in Paris and New York. In Chande's case, it is the schooling he receives at St. Peter's Boys School in Panchgani that opens his eyes to Indian history, Indian culture, and Indian religions. Writing of the exuberance of the times, Chande notes, "Fate was to ensure that I was to be a witness to the independence of both my family's motherland and of my homeland, Tanganyika, and my formative experiences in India undoubtedly shaped my perceptions of independence in Dar es Salaam some fifteen years later. Thus the teenage boy who wrote letters to the *Times of India* seeking an early end to British rule in India became the man caught in the undertow of Britain's sudden withdrawal from East Africa in the early 1960s."[29] Despite his own enthusiasm at the time, in both cases Chande insists in retrospect that the British withdrawal was made in haste and bequeathed "a poisonous legacy" (37). In the case of India it "spawned division, discord and conflict that has persisted to this day. In Tanganyika, haste left a system that was ill prepared for the onerous responsibilities of nationhood, a country founded in a crippling dependency, reinforced by a chronic undercapacity that continues to blight the country's future" (38).

Just as the parallels between the exuberance as well as the challenges of independence in India and in Tanganyika appear in these narratives, so do the similarities between the two leaders Gandhi and Nyerere. The link is made most explicitly by Chande, who characterizes Nyerere (respectfully called "Mwalimu" or teacher) as a man "of unbending principle, and a moderate," and a man who would seek an end to colonialism throughout the world "but wherever possible without recourse to violence" (69). "I had seen something of such a man before," writes Chande, "back in India in the 1940s. Mahatma Gandhi had also been a man of great principle, and one similarly opposed to the use of violence as a political end. Like Mwalimu, he too had insisted on the creation of a society based on the rule of law, in which all men and women had equality of rights and opportunities" (69). This vision of a Gandhian Nyerere is implicit in all three narratives, and, while Chande makes the link explicit, it is in Kassum's narrative that Nyerere as *Bapu*—the father of the nation—gets the most sympathetic and extended treatment.

Indeed, it may be fair to say that in Kassum's narrative Nyerere is often treated on the hagiographic register. The book opens and closes with Nyerere, the schoolteacher who is a customer in Kassum's father's shop at the beginning of the narrative slowly transforming into a fellow student in England, becoming, by the end, the now deceased ex-president of the nation. While he was acquainted with Nyerere from an early age, it is only after Kassum delivered a speech on the importance of racially integrated education, in his capacity as a temporary member of the LEGCO, that he came to Nyerere's attention and was invited by him to run as the Asian candidate from the Dodoma region. Mustafa, we will recall, had already been elected from Arusha, and in their respective books they each acknowledge with some appreciation the other's presence and interventions at the LEGCO meeting. Kassum's entry into politics, like Mustafa's, was not without resistance from the Asian community since, like Mustafa, he was not a registered member of the Asian Association. Nevertheless, he garnered Nyerere's and the party's support and won the election, later becoming the chief whip of the TANU party, from 1959 to 1964, after Nyerere had successfully argued for opening up the party membership across racial lines. Appointed a parliamentary secretary at the Ministry of Education after independence, Kassum's narrative outlines the many different roles in which he is asked to serve by Nyerere. These include appointments at the Mwananchi Development Corporation, the Ministry of Industries and Mineral Resources, and the Williamson Diamond Corporation and culminate in higher positions such as the minister of finance and administration for the East African Federation and later Tanzania's minister for water, energy, and minerals. For a brief period, from 1965 to 1969, Kassum also serves on his own account, but with the express permission of Nyerere, in various capacities at the United Nations, and, despite the prospects of a longer UN career, he returns to Tanzania when he is recalled by Nyerere in the interests of government service. All along, while engaged in this political trajectory, Kassum is intensely engaged with serving the Ismaili community in various leadership positions offered to him by the Aga Khan. Of these, the duties that most engage his time and imagination are the various schools he establishes in his capacity as administrator of the Aga Khan schools in Tanganyika.

While the details of his various ventures are of some interest, what strikes the reader most in the narrative is Kassum's attachment to and reverence for Nyerere, who, much like the other two father figures in the narrative— Kassum's biological father and his religious leader, the Aga Khan—provides the narrator with guidance and direction. The relationship between Kassum and Nyerere comes across as a tender and protective one that is marked by trust, Kassum often being asked to be Nyerere's eye, such as in the de Beers-controlled diamond company where the president feels that the government is getting the runaround and he needs a trusted man within the corporation.

When Kassum first reads the Arusha Declaration, which is passed in 1967 while he is abroad, he is uncertain about its promise, but is "willing to give the party the benefit of the doubt" (56). In a literal act of faith, he immediately decides to write to Nyerere from abroad: "My love of and belief in Tanzania and my highest respect for you are such that I shall continue to do whatever I feel, to the extent of my ability, is in the interest of Tanzania and its people" (56). But, in the same breath, Kassum does not fail to remark to himself and his readers that "I was also glad that my family would not be affected, since we owned no industries" (56). Within a matter of a few years, however, this sense of relief is put into question as the government nationalizes all private buildings that generate income in excess of an established amount. "Our family owned many commercial properties in Dar es Salaam," writes Kassum, "including a very well-known bar and restaurant, the Cosy Café, office and residential buildings and cinemas" (69). To his own surprise and the surprise of his brothers, his father, who has bought these properties over a number of years, accepts the loss stoically. Nor, by the narrative's own account, is Kassum's faith in Nyerere shaken by the divestment.

What might account for this seemingly altruistic gesture on the family's part? Just as Nyerere's insistence on nonracial citizenship and the protection of immigrant rights had a major role in garnering Asian support, I suggest that it was his insistence on an economic justice that was not tied to racial claims that seems to have most impressed Asians such as Kassum.[30] As evidence, we may turn to his detailed discussions of the Arusha Declaration and particularly Nyerere's admonishment of politicians who might be tempted to appeal to the reversal of racial privilege as an economic policy. One of the most unpopular decisions that Nyerere made and inscribed in the Arusha Declaration was that no TANU leader could engage in profit-making through rent or other business practices that could be construed as capitalist. "The Arusha Declaration," he stated, "is a declaration of war on exploitation; it is not just a declaration of war on those exploiters who happen to be of a different colour."[31] Closing the capitalist door to politicians of all races, and setting the tone whereby nationalization of private property (which was overwhelmingly owned by Asians) did not mean a quick grab by politicians in power and their allies (as was happening in the Congo and later to happen in Uganda after the Asian expulsion), meant that the transfer would be based on principles of economic justice and not personal gain on the part of new elites.[32] What some Asians like Kassum's father seem to have appreciated was that even though it may have hurt their own economic interests, and even though they may have remained skeptical of the economic theories on which it was based, at least this project of nationalization was ideologically, if not always practically, thoroughly principled and egalitarian. And, as for Kassum himself, the Arusha Declaration would not have come as an entire surprise, since the principles on which it was based were in fact a logical outgrowth of the Articles of Association of the Mwananchi Development Corporation, the economic wing of TANU that was responsible, among other things, for the villagization program.[33] Kassum had himself drafted the Articles of Association for the Mwananchi Corporation in 1962 on instructions from Nyerere.

There is little in Kassum's book that directly critiques Nyerere's policies even though the book was published in 2007, more than two decades after Nyerere began to acknowledge some of those policy failures and stepped down, allowing others to take the economic lead. As we will see in Chande's account, the jury is still out on some of the concrete effects of the economic liberalizations of the eighties that some say were thrust upon Tanzania and others claim were willingly embraced. Kassum is, of course, alert to the changes that have taken place since the early Ujamaa years and, for instance, notes that "the private sector is very important" in the process of diversifying both Tanzanian agriculture and industry (155). But such concessions do not prompt any significant reevaluations of past policies, including the disastrously failed policies of villagization.[34] On this, for instance, he acknowledges that critics have complained that villagization failed because it was implemented even on unwilling citizens, but mildly responds that "Mwalimu's intention was that villagers should be persuaded — not forced — to participate" (68).

However tempting it is to read Kassum's account as one that risks blind loyalty to Nyerere, it is, I think, more useful to read it as one rooted in a loyalty that arose out of a deep sense of immigrant insecurity. Nyerere, in no uncertain terms, was for Kassum and many other Asians like him, a stark contrast to less Asian-friendly politicians such as Amin. In order to appreciate how much that meant, notice the transitions of thought in the following passage that presents Nyerere's trajectory in as positive a light as any. And notice how Nyerere's strong stance on Amin, almost unique among other African leaders, results in Kassum's own more generous reading of his economic policies: "When Idi Amin expelled Ugandan Asians, Mwalimu Nyerere was one of the few African leaders to condemn the action. Mwalimu wanted to contribute towards the self-fulfillment of every individual, not only in his own country but also beyond its borders. To do this, he had to take some drastic measures initially, because the economic structures that had been inherited from colonialism were too strong to allow an evolutionary approach. Later, having achieved the required changes, he introduced liberalisation policies that set the stage for the policies followed by his successors in office" (154).[35]

J. K. Chande's assessment of Nyerere is also highly respectful of his ethical positions, but less sympathetic toward the economic policy choices that he made. Full of admiration for Nyerere's principled leadership, Chande is nevertheless alert not only to the virtues of principled leadership but also to its potential pitfalls. In Gandhi's case, Chande believes, the cost of principles was a political assassination at the hands of one of his own religious compatriots, and, in Nyerere's, the cost is further economic hardships in an already economically underdeveloped state. Thus, at various points in the narrative, Chande shows how doing the right thing ethically—such as breaking Tanzania's diplomatic ties with Britain when it was clear that the *Tiger* talks with Rhodesia were not going to materialize in a fair outcome—resulted in further damage to an already fragile Tanzanian economy.[36] While matters of foreign affairs were to pose challenges, the internal economic policy—with its attempts at price controls even when the controls are not feasible or its suspicion of anything resembling a profit—try Chande's patience enormously.

But trying moments are sometimes offset by momentary victories such as his attempt to intervene in the price controls set by the government on rice that make it unfeasible to continue production. After much persuasion at the ministerial level, he finally has to take the matter all the way up to Nyerere for adjudication. Listening to his complaint that the Ministry of Agriculture is micromanaging the Milling Company and setting prices that are unfeasible, Nyerere, much to Chande's relief, agrees with him, telling him that the officials have clearly erred and that he should "generate surplus, taking into account further investment" (120). In private, Chande chuckles: "Mwalimu often used 'surplus' as a euphemism for profit" (120). Or, as he insists elsewhere, "even if one is a state socialist, protecting and managing a command economy, state-owned corporations still have to be run on capitalist lines" (119).

Perhaps it is because he has received a number of national and international accolades by the end of his career, including the Hind Ratna award from the Indian government, the Non-Resident of the Year award by the International Congress of Non-Resident Indians, the Pride of India Gold Award by the NRI Institute in London, and a knighthood bestowed by Queen Elizabeth II, that Chande feels entitled to exhibit uninhibited candor in his assessment of his life as a Tanzanian entrepreneur turned, as he dubs it, "Mister Corporation." In his memoir he is never overtly bitter over the fate of his assets but, at the same time, he is not as generously compliant as is Kassum. The abrupt nationalization of his family firm is clearly

the central crisis in the narrative. Chande, along with other private entrepreneurs, is ordered to attend a meeting with the minister of commerce,
A. M. Babu, a mere four days after the signing of the Arusha Declaration.
The moment is worth citing: "As soon as he came in and sat down, Babu
opened the meeting without much ado. He wished us all good morning,
in English, and then picked up the paper in front of him. It was a brief
prepared statement saying that all the shares in our respective milling companies would henceforth be vested in the Treasury Registrar, effective noon
that day. Existing shareholders would be given 'full and fair' compensation.
That was it. Babu finished as abruptly as he had started. All of our companies had been nationalised in under a minute" (91).[37] The weeks and
months that follow are, of course, filled with intense turmoil, since Chande
reveals that he has never bothered opening any private bank accounts, rely-
ing on the company accountant to provide him with money as needed.
Such access to his family company's coffers comes to an abrupt halt, and,
as I indicated earlier, the family is financially bailed out by the Madhvani
brothers. A critical meeting between Chande and Nyerere follows in which,
after Nyerere has tried to reason with Chande, telling him about the importance of nationalization and offering him a position in the government to
make up for his loss, Chande does not hesitate to tell the president that he
believes that the nationalization of private industry is bad economic policy.
He cannot convince Nyerere of this, and the latter is visibly irritated by this
affront, but in an important move on the part of both actors, he acquiesces
to Chande's request that he continue to manage the company in its new
parastatal form. It is this decision on Chande's part, and Nyerere's own recognition that all talent regardless of race needs to be used in the new nation,
that allows Chande to embark on a long career as a manager of state-owned
corporations. Having been dissuaded from entering politics by his father,
and himself believing that he can best offer his services to the state as a businessman rather than as a politician (even though he has briefly served on
the Tanganyika Executive Council in the preindependence days), Chande,
unlike Kassum and Mustafa, manages to become integral to the interests of
the state without directly being an elected or appointed politician. Reflecting back on his decision to stay in Tanzania rather than leave the country as
does his brother, Chande remembers the choice as a self-conscious rebirth:

> Tanzania was my home, my country, for good and for ill, and in order to be re-
> baptized as a true Tanzanian, I had to experience vicariously, if only for a few
> months, the life that had been the lot of so many of my fellow countrymen since

the first colonial incursions into East Africa. By sharing the harsh experience of so many of my countrymen, I finally came to comprehend that their reality consisted of an uncertain present and an even more uncertain future. Like them, I learned to accept my lot, whatever it might be, with patience, with dignity, without rancour, and with hope for the future.

(104)

Reminiscent of Mustafa's learning experience about her black African compatriots in her election campaign, Chande's reflection demonstrates the critical role of empathy and shared destiny across ethnic and class barriers in forging the path of a productive nationalism.

It is his standpoint as a business leader rather than as a politician that I believe gives Chande's narrative the critical edge that a narrative such as Kassum's lacks. More so than even Mustafa and Kassum, Chande spends considerable space outlining the ways in which Nyerere directly took on any racially inscribed policies that might find favor in the party and the citizenship at large. But he does so not so much to praise Nyerere as to highlight the real threats of a racialist consciousness that surrounded the nationalist agenda. Consider, here, the contrast between Chande's narration of the same event in Tanganyika's history and Kassum's. Kassum registers Nyerere's temporary move away from the office of prime minister as follows: "Mwalimu Nyerere became the first Prime Minister and then soon resigned thereafter, and Rashidi Kawawa became Prime Minister. Then, on 9 December 1962, when the country became a republic, Mwalimu became President and Rashidi Kawawa remained Prime Minister" (40). The reasons as to why Nyerere would become prime minister, resign, and then later become president are completely glossed over, but Chande's narrative fills in the excruciating details. Chande reveals that Nyerere's decision to resign from the prime minister's position is prompted by the unrest that has been precipitated in the country by the new Parliament's first significant debate on race and citizenship. Some members of Parliament and their followers have vigorously argued for a "Tanganyika for Tanganyikans" policy of citizenship that would prevent even long-term residents who were immigrants from acquiring citizenship. Battles on this issue were sparked all around the country and, writes Chande, "instead of running the country as prime minister, Mwalimu found himself forced to go back to his roots, and those of his party, travelling the length and breadth of the country to engage in a new political debate with his people" (77).[38] As the cause of this furor, Chande cites the lackluster efforts made by the British in preparing the majority of Tanzanians for a democratic sense of citizenship. This was something that was to fall on Nyerere's shoulders and he had to take his message about nonracial democracy to the people, claims Chande, against the more racially based rhetoric of grassroots leaders who had a "much more visceral approach to politics" (77). Unlike Kassum, Chande addresses the policies of Africanization that are immediately put in place by the party while Nyerere is temporarily away, resulting in a massive turnover in the workplace, placating indigenous African frustrations while raising the anxiety of immigrants.[39] He highlights the challenges to Nyerere's party by new political parties, like the People's Democratic Party, that are in formation. Even more significantly, unlike Kassum, who would sweep such unpleasant policies under the carpet, Chande is explicit about the role of political detentions (without trial) that Nyerere instituted against political opponents who threatened the direction he had mapped out for the country. Kassum's Nyerere is a benevolent father figure who is much loved, never resisted, and therefore one who does not need to discipline. Chande's Nyerere, in contrast, is a man who has high principles, but who is also politically savvy and not unwilling to use some force when necessary to mold a political sphere based on his ideals.

While Nyerere is a major force in Chande's narrative, the author is intent on casting his own memoir in a wider frame. This includes a concern with social work that is beyond the parameters of Chande's corporate world. Philanthropy, as we have seen, has often been an undertaking of many of the most established Asian traders and businessmen, but, as I suggested earlier, there is a move in Chande's narrative in particular from charitable contributions to more participatory forms of civic engagement. Chande is explicit about this move, writing that his father's philosophy of giving was a "disinterested" one in which "when you give something away, your left hand should not know what your right hand is doing" (51). While the elder Chande's generosity to both Asian and black African causes garner him admiration and respect, the younger Chande directs his social efforts to more collectively organized projects such as those supported by the Round Table Movement, the Rotary Foundation, and the Freemasons, all of which he joins in Tanzania as one of the first Asian members. The narrative includes what to many readers must come across as an unexpected chapter on Freemasonry, its global history, the allegations of its nefarious secrecy, the establishment of the movement in East Africa, its (very) gradual opening up to members of all races, and its support of a number of social projects. These included both long-term ones—such as the Kindwitwi Leprosy Center in Utete, the Mother Theresa Home for Children, the Pongwe School for the Blind, the Arusha

Orphanage, the Mnazi Mmoja Hospital in Zanzibar, and the Buguruni School for the Deaf—as well as emergency funds for disaster relief such as those related to the 1996 accident on Lake Victoria of the MV *Bukoba* or the 1998 bombings of the American Embassy in Dar es Salaam. Chande's rise to positions of leadership in these various organizations, including his service among the Freemasons as district grand master for East Africa, a position he held for nineteen years, need not detain us too much here, but, given the consistently negative resonance in popular consciousness of the "Asian as dukawallah" image, his work in these areas is certainly worthy of note.

It should be clear by now that Chande's book is as much an analysis of Tanzanian history as it is a personal narrative of a private businessman turned state employee. What, in the final analysis, are Chande's views on the history he has lived through? By his own admission, the reasons that Tanzania in 1980 was almost as poor as it was in 1961, despite receiving over $2 billion in aid, are not "susceptible to any simple diagnosis" (171). Nevertheless, of the factors that he most holds responsible is first and foremost the "half-hearted" nature of British colonialism in Tanganyika. Reminiscent of Walter Rodney's argument in his manifesto *How Europe Underdeveloped Africa*, but without its Marxist edge, and very much in keeping with the recently published *How Colonialism Pre-empted Modernity in Africa* by Olufemi Taiwo, Chande argues that the British were never fully committed to setting up the institutions and structural measures that would enable the newly independent nation to flourish.[40] In this sense, what Sorabji Darookhanawala had complained about almost ninety years earlier seems to be confirmed by Chande's analysis. In the Tanzanian case, part of its drawbacks was the natural environment, which, unlike the environment of neighboring Kenya, did not encourage significant expatriate settlers and enterprise during colonial times, thereby resulting in a comparatively less developed industrial and agricultural infrastructure. In postcolonial times, Chande lays a significant amount of blame (and this is where he becomes most heated) on "academics or retired politicians hell-bent on social re-engineering" (76) or, as he puts it later, "academically brilliant but inexperienced and sometimes perhaps misguided people . . . [who] gave a false veneer of credibility to some of the stranger experiments that were being conducted in the name of African Socialism" (98). Finally, even though foreign aid was crucial to survival and to growth, Chande writes that "money to countries like Tanzania came on a leash, and often a shortish one that all too often was tugged hard" (174). In pointing to these primarily external causes, Chande is not forgetful of the internal missteps taken by Nyerere and TANU, most particularly the villagization program, but in the final analysis he writes that "given all we know

now, it seems truly miraculous that Tanzania emerged from the early days of its foundation without having suffered from civil war, or famine, or military dictatorship, or pandemic" (175).

Chande's account closes on a hopeful but cautious note. As someone who has been an advocate of private enterprise and the free market, he is in favor of the liberalization policies that Tanzania undertook in the late eighties. The economic reforms begun under the Mwinyi government and continued under Presidents Mkapa and Kikwete have opened prospects for foreign investments in the country, investments the book argues are much needed for future economic growth. Nonetheless, the analysis is not blind to the new challenges that such liberalization have posed. Social services, in particular, have been seriously curtailed, leading to increased belt-tightening on the part of both the government and the people, and in some instances, "such as basic health and access to primary schooling," the social indexes have shown a further decline from levels that were already low (188). The challenge for the country, Chande argues, will be to strike a balance between a liberal economy and the provision of social safety nets for the poor.[41]

In the next chapter we will have occasion to revisit some of the pressing issues Chande and his Tanzanian compatriots raise through a close reading of M. G. Vassanji's *The Gunny Sack*, a novel that covers similar historical ground in fictional form. My primary goal in this chapter, as well as in chapters 4 and 5, was to help complicate and add historical nuance to the prevailing flattened stereotypes that exist of both the economic and political lives of Asians in East Africa. To do so, I have focused on the autobiographical writings of two turn-of-the-twentieth-century Asian travelers, of East African Asian men of commerce, and of two men and one woman who were intricately involved in postindependence politics in Tanzania. While alert to the silences and gaps in their texts, my overwhelming interest was not so much to fault them for their social, economic, or political lapses, but rather to unearth their own sense of self as Asians in East Africa. Along the way, I have highlighted their oftentimes conflicted negotiations with the black Africans they encountered, particularly in the first half of the twentieth century, and their increasing sense over time of the need as a community to undergo what Chande called a "re-birth" in their African environments. Such a rebirth would mean a shift in the role that Asians had mythologically cast for themselves—from being the external deliverers of a commercial modernity to learning to become equal partners in a common and shared postcolonial enterprise.

To choose to focus on written autobiographies (or even texts like Mehta's that were dictated and published in translation) is already, in the contexts that we are concerned with, to limit our purview to elites. I am aware that my focus has been for the most part on individuals who, having come from a variety of socioeconomic and religious backgrounds, did relatively well for themselves in the eyes of their peers. Ebrahimji Adamji and Sorabji Darookhanawala may not have reached the pinnacles of financial success as did Nanji Kalidas Mehta, Manubhai Madhvani, or Madatally Nanji, but as early Indian travelers to the interior, one of whom successfully pursued his family's commercial interests, the other having served as the community's commercial prospector and returned to write about his travels, they both earned the esteem of their communities. Sophia Mustafa may not have gone on to receive as many awards or lead a life in the public limelight as did the two men, Al Noor Kassum or J. K. Chande, but she along with contemporaries like Bibi Titi Mohammed will continue to be remembered as significant women politicians of the era of Tanganyikan independence.

If I highlight the lives of these particular individuals, it is because despite their elite status and their standing in their communities, their life work has not yet made any significant mark on our understanding of either East African or South Asian history and the ways in which we go about narrating those histories. They have remained invisible in both imperial as well as nationalist histories of East Africa because as Asians they have seemed to be oddities, alien, not quite fitting comfortably in the Manichaeanisms that structure colonial and nationalist historiographies. Likewise, as I suggested earlier, in South Asian historiography, it is only of late that the significance of the Indian diaspora as both appeal and agent in the project of Indian nationalism has begun to be registered. And, finally, if neither imperial nor nationalist histories could easily accommodate these narratives, given their bourgeois provenance, they have not been of much interest to Marxist historians or to those interested in subaltern histories.

Having argued for the importance of their narratives to our understanding both of East African and South Asian histories, I move in the next chapter to a text that focuses on Asians in Africa who were less empowered and less fortunate. Predictably, such individuals left fewer written texts like autobiographies. To imagine their lives, we turn to a work of fiction that, by recasting the history of the East African Asian presence in a larger temporal frame, invites us to hear the resonances of the twelfth-century world of Ashu, Bomma, and Ben Yiju in a time closer to our own.

7. ANTI ANTI-ASIANISM AND THE POLITICS OF DISSENT

M. G. Vassanji's *The Gunny Sack*

Asians in East Africa have always engaged in imaginative projects, participating in plays drawing on historical figures, performing in religiously derived drama such as the stagings of the Ramayana, writing poetry and sharing it in community readings, engaging in essay competitions, and writing short fiction and play scripts for newspapers. Literature, performance, and associated cultural forms have, as I argued in the case of Mehta, Madhvani, and Mustafa, also played a significant role in the shaping of modern Indian Ocean lives much like poetry did in the twelfth-century world of Ben Yiju. Most of this Asian creativity has been invisible outside the community because, even when it was in written form—like Ebrahimji Adamji's book— it remained unpublished until very recently, or, like Sorabji Darookhanawala's book, it was written and published for limited circulation in Indian languages (in this case Gujarati). Beginning in the late sixties and early seventies, a new generation of East African Asian writers increasingly began to write plays, poems, and some fiction in English. Despite this long tradition of creative writing and performance among East African Asians, it is, I argue, the 1989 publication of M. G. Vassanji's *The Gunny Sack* that heralds a new era of Asian writing in East Africa and its diaspora.[1] In many ways,

Simon Gikandi's claim about the inaugural role of Chinua Achebe's *Things Fall Apart* in the tradition of the African novel finds a parallel in my reading of Vassanji's text within the East African Asian imagination.[2] Much like Achebe's use of Ibo traditions and folklore in *Things Fall Apart*, it is Vassanji's creative use of myth, storytelling, and folklore in *The Gunny Sack* that first gave historical depth to the Asian community's sense of identity as a community of immigrants in East Africa.

My interest in *The Gunny Sack* is in examining the ways in which it creates a genealogy of Asian presence in East Africa while providing historical density to the formation of Asian ethnic identity. What makes Vassanji different from his predecessors is not only the weight and substance that he gives to a cross-generational ethnic history, it is also his insistence that ethnic identities matter, that they must be recognized and engaged with before they can be set aside for the sake of larger, cross-ethnic national imaginaries such as those advocated by President Nyerere and his supporters. Like history, which the novel sees as both illusory and inescapable, leaving its traces on individual lives in a manner that may not always be fully comprehensible, ethnicity too affects individuals, even those who may wish to leave it behind as just so much unnecessary baggage.[3] One of the primary ways in which ethnicity works is through the deployment, circulation, internalization, and rejection of stereotypes. A central project of *The Gunny Sack* is to investigate the nature of ethnic stereotypes of both Asians and black Africans in East Africa and to challenge their veracity. By doing so, I will argue that Vassanji's novel eventually gestures toward a postethnic form of writing where political engagement with the nation-state by citizens goes through the boundaries of ethnic identification before going beyond them.

While Vassanji has gone on to write other compelling novels set in East Africa such as *The Book of Secrets* and *The In-Between World of Vikram Lall*, both of which have garnered him prestigious awards, I focus on *The Gunny Sack* because it remains his most complex novel and provides his most sustained reflections on Asian ethnic identity in East Africa.[4] Furthermore, while several important critical discussions of the novel have already been published, they are driven for the most part by the key interests of metropolitan postcolonial literary studies in the nineties—issues such as diaspora, migration, transnationalism, homelessness, and postmodernity.[5] These issues continue to resonate in my reading here, but I am more concerned with Vassanji's representation of race and ethnicity and with the novel's direct engagement with Tanzanian socialism.[6] Published in 1989 at the cusp of the cold war, *The Gunny Sack* is best read as a dissident novel by a writer who is skeptical of the ideological turn taken by his national leaders. While the racial and ethnic tensions between black Africans and Asians are a central theme in the novel, and while, as I will argue, one of the goals of the novel is to present what I call an anti anti-Asianism, it is the battle of ideologies between free-market capitalism and multiparty democracy, on the one hand, and a socialism inspired both by Tanzanian family traditions as well as by Chinese Communism, on the other, that drives the political motor of the novel.

ACTS OF INAUGURATION: THE LITERARY PRECURSORS OF *THE GUNNY SACK*

To argue that Vassanji's *The Gunny Sack* is an inaugural text in the tradition of recent East African Asian writing is to invite critique from a scholar such as Eleni Coundouriotis who, in *Claiming History: Colonialism, Ethnography and the Novel*, suggests that every such gesture of inauguration risks an erasure of history in the name of ethnic (or racial) authenticity. "It has become a critical commonplace," writes Coundouriotis, "to inaugurate the African novel repeatedly as a means of identifying the 'authentically' African."[7] Such moves inevitably tend not only to freeze the literary traditions in which texts emerge, they also tend to ignore the text's own historical negotiations of precisely those elements that are deemed "authentic." Thus, not only are texts written by earlier authors marginalized in favor of the new, but even texts that are explicitly historical in orientation are read as "ethnographic fictions and their authors' historical questioning obscured."[8]

Any engagement with Vassanji's novel must be wary of this risk—of erasing history in the interests of ethnicity, and it is a concern to which I will soon turn. But what of the charge that we may risk erasing a prior *literary* history in crowning *The Gunny Sack* as an inaugural text? Ironically, it is not so much the writing of *ethnicity* in *The Gunny Sack* that makes it seem so different from texts that preceded it, it is in fact its deep engagement with ethnic *history*. To note the difference, we may turn to Bahadur Tejani's novel *Day After Tomorrow*, which, published in 1971, is generally considered to be the first full-length Anglophone novel written by an East African Asian. Written in the mid sixties in the context of a newly independent Uganda, the novel dramatizes the urgent issues of multiracial integration faced by a culturally and racially diverse population. Tejani's hopeful resolution of racial divisions is in the literal mixing of the races. The novel opens with a focus on a young child of African and Asian parentage, "the mixed blood of two races proudly announcing itself" (6). If this child is meant to symbolize future hope, the novel insists that his coming into being also registers an active struggle and a coming to consciousness on the part of his parents, Samsher, the son of an Indian settler-merchant, and Nanziri, a Buganda woman who is a head nurse in a hospital in Kampala. What brings Samsher and Nanziri together is a mutual respect for the environment in which they live and a shared sense of unease with the rather imitative modernity they see in the industrialized city of Kampala.

In his role as literary critic, Tejani has noted the legacy of British Romanticism on early nationalist writing in East Africa. "In the recording of the experience of disharmony, alienation and cultural discord," writes Tejani, "African artists often found a ready friend among the British Romantics."[9] In contrast to the mountaineering trip and its associated romance with nature where Samsher and Nanziri first meet, the city becomes the site of potential rupture. Disharmony and alienation characterize Nanziri's skeptical thoughts about going to movies made elsewhere for other audiences (85–86) or about the upwardly mobile youth who emulate Western fashions in both dress and decorum (87–88). They characterize Samsher's own experiences with the seedier sides of Kampala life, with his sense of disgust with himself for having picked up from a local club a young woman who is no more than a child (133–35). But perhaps the greatest sense of alienation comes about through the classic trope of the worker as cog in a machine. Touring a brewery, Samsher and Nanziri both come face-to-face with the monotonous drudgery of the assembly line, with human bodies disciplined to accommodate the demands of the machine: "Suddenly Samsher screamed and backed, knocking himself violently against the rotating machine which quickly thrust him back with a flipping rotating motion: he had seen a hideous paw, hairy and softly fleshy, like the crushed leg of a hippopotamus coming at him through the glass. But it was only the arm of the man, entering beyond the magnifying glass, removing a bottle of impure beer from the conveyor belt" (106).

Even as this battle between machine and human is being staged, the novel urges a self-consciousness in the protagonists about their futures and the roles they seek to play. Reflecting on the patriotic pride of a victorious African American woman at the Olympics in Rome, Nanziri decides that she too will do something of which her nation will be proud. Samsher challenges the family legacy of becoming a shopkeeper and trader in order to answer to the higher calling of becoming a teacher. In what is clearly meant to be their greatest act of courage, the two decide to marry, with a child forthcoming, daring a conservative, clannish society into trying new forms of interracial relationships.

While hopeful about such a newly configured future, Tejani's novel leaves little doubt that the greater inertia against change would be found on the Asian rather than black African side. "Yet a brown figure was far more acceptable among the black figures than it would ever be the other way. Despite the colonial impact the Africans had kept their creative social life, where a man was still a man, not a colour" (118). By contrast, the Asian community is consistently presented as parochial, limited by its "instinct for bargaining" and trading (8), fearful of black peasants, (15) having no interest in the lives, customs, food habits of Africans (15), and with a troubled sense of sexuality resulting in lives that oscillate between sexual deprivation and excess (58). Indeed, it is precisely against this community of individuals as "life-less automatons (who) sat in shops, their beady eyes lighting up when a customer entered" (57), that Samsher rebels. One might want to suggest Samsher's rebellion is no more than that commonly found in the modernist hero alienated by his society, but it does seem that the intensity of his feelings against his community overextend such a scenario. "A hatred of all men of his race and civilization grew in Samsher's heart" (37), we are told at one point when he is perturbed by the badly behaved children of his neighbours. "They only showed the worst aspects of life with which Indians, especially the traders, were saturated. In public the elders stole, cheated and maneuvered a thousand ways that would fatten their treasury somehow. The children, deprived of any humanitarian ideals, learnt from their parents, swore freely, were lewd to the females since they could not talk to them, both of their own colour and especially of other colours" (37).

While the problems of equating characters with authors are manifold, one may risk suggesting that Tejani seems to have shared Samsher's despair over what they both see as Asian intransigence in a newly independent nation.[10] Just as Samsher the teacher attempts to extricate himself from the trading demands of his community, Tejani the university educator and novelist seeks in this novel to trade in ideas, to force both Asians and Africans to confront the very real material conditions of their future together. But in so doing the novel risks essentializing racial differences rather than historicizing the connections between the races. If the Indian is "instinctively" a trader in the novel, the African is almost naturally connected to nature. So, for instance, the peasants around Samsher's childhood village are consistently portrayed as "people who live life in the open, at one with the earth, the beast and the elements" (14). "They had a marvelous unconcern about them, in the freedom with which they used their bodies and were unconscious of it. . . . He wished to escape with one of them, wanting to be as free as they were" (15). The Indian village children like Samsher, we are told early in the novel, have felt "the call of the wilderness of the country and the semi-nakedness of the peasants around them. Despite their ancient heritage, which despised the body, they felt a call in the blood: of the black African to the brown Indian" (7–8). It is only by answering this earthy call, *Day After Tomorrow* suggests, that a multiracial harmony can be found.

It is no surprise, then, that given its investment in what we might call a "blood narrative" in which what is to be overcome is not history but race, Tejani's novel has little use for anything but a cursory treatment of history.[11] There are glimpses of such a history, at least for the Goan community, in the novels of Peter Nazareth, but here too the author's ultimate interests lie not in the ethnic particularities or histories of the Goan community but in the more urgent issues of contemporary nation building.[12] Indeed, in a telling interview with Bernth Lindfors, Nazareth suggests that the focus on the Goan community in his novels was more a result of societal expectations than personal desire. Reflecting on the genesis of his first novel, Nazareth remembers a conversation with Ngugi wa Thiong'o, who suggested that he write "something about the Goans because that was my background." This suggestion confirmed Nazareth's sense that his audience was expecting a particular focus on Goans in his writing. "It had never struck me as any contradiction that my plays had African characters. But the society did not think that way, as I noticed when *Brave New Cosmos* was produced at the National Theatre at Kampala for the Uganda Drama Festival. Two of us actors were Goans, acting as Africans, which destroyed the illusion for the outside audience."[13] This recognition, enhanced by Ngugi's no doubt well-intentioned advice to draw upon his own ethnic background, led Nazareth to work on *In a Brown Mantle* when he returned home from his studies at Leeds. But the Leeds experience, "full of iconoclasts with radical ideas,"[14] an enthusiastic embrace of socialism, and extensive readings of Frantz Fanon, meant that Nazareth confronted the question of "how to write a novel about Goans which was simultaneously a political novel about Africa."[15]

Nazareth's novels, then, are most fruitfully read as engagements with Fanon's theories of nationalist struggles and postcolonial traumas. While it is possible to read them as ethnohistories of Goans, framed by their own colonial legacies and struggles against the Portuguese in Goa, their subsequent arrival in Uganda primarily as civil servants under the British, and their expulsion by Amin along with other Asians, I suggest that Nazareth's narratives draw greater force from the author's bitter frustration with what, drawing on Fanon, he calls the "epidermalization" of the colonial economic system.[16] This epidermalization, this reduction to skin color, suggests Nazareth, in his own reading of the "Asian Presence in Two Decades of East African Literature," is responsible for the problematic term *Asian* in the East African context in the first place. "Yet there never was an 'Asian community' in East Africa. There were several different 'tribes,' all mutually exclusive: Patels, Ismailis, Sikhs, Bohras, Goans, etc."[17] And, further, there were class distinctions that were often ignored in the political rhetoric that invoked the Asian. "What did I, a socialist and not a businessman, have in common with the late Jayant Madhvani, an enlightened capitalist but a capitalist all the same?"[18] asks Nazareth.

In reading the works of Tejani, Nazareth, and other Asian writers of this period, we cannot forget that many of them were either students at Makerere University or had their plays produced there. And, as Carol Sicherman has shown in connection with her reading of Ngugi's experiences at Makerere in this same period, we cannot ignore the strong influence of Leavisite criticism and its modernist canon on both budding writers and critics at the university.[19] It is this legacy, with its emphasis on the alienation of the individual along with the influence of Fanon that most marks the writing of this period. Reflecting back on her studies at Makerere in the years following independence, Yasmin Alibhai-Brown writes,

> in 1970 Makerere was a distinguished and possibly utopian place, where students and lecturers felt incredibly privileged and powerful. We were going to make the future and break from the past which had kept so many down and out, and some of us were going to make amends. We were writing a new history which showed the world that Africa was neither intellectually barren nor uncivilized before the European, greedy for wealth and status, conferred that dishonest past on an entire continent. We were making a new destiny for ourselves—black, brown and white Ugandans together for the first time and able to think in a way that our parents simply could not have.[20]

In such a liberal context, race and ethnicity were at best embarrassments and at worst barriers to social progress. And yet, even while students and teachers attempted to forge a multi-racial society in places like Makerere, these attempts could not evade the ramifications of racially coded tensions and conflicts such as the Zanzibar revolution, the Amin expulsions from Uganda, and the economically and educationally motivated migration of East African Asians from the neighboring countries of Kenya and Tanzania to Europe, the United States, and Canada. It would take nearly two decades after these events for the literary world to receive an epic treatment of the history of East African Asians in Vassanji's *The Gunny Sack*.

HISTORY, MEMORY, AND THE WRITING OF ETHNICITY

"Ethnicity," most scholars would agree, is a particularly elusive concept. "Pertaining to nations not Christian or Jewish; Gentile, heathen, pagan" is the first definition offered by the *OED*, with a second usage described as "pertaining to race; peculiar to a race or nation; ethnological." The term seems to have gathered currency after the Holocaust as a way of avoiding race talk and the terrors of eugenics. Unlike race talk that tends to foreground biological and genetic inheritances, ethnic affiliations and identities are negotiated through narrower narratives of descent that invoke such traits as religious beliefs, a shared language, an inherited folklore, and a whole range of customs, rituals, habits, and taboos that mark the quotidian experiences of daily life. Nevertheless, in the context of immigrant societies such as the Asians in Africa, as Peter Nazareth cautions us, the most immediate markers of difference have oftentimes been the phenotypic and epidermal ones, resulting in considerable slippage between the discourses of race and ethnicity. Thus in both the Asian and African imagination the "other" has often been perceived in racial and epidermal — black, brown — terms, rather than in more variegated readings of ethnicity — Gikuyu, Luo, Maasai, Ismaili, Sikh, Punjabi Hindu. The contingent interplay between these two orders of interpellation is one of the investigative projects of the literary imagination.

By virtue of its incipient entry into the practices of everyday life, ethnicity tends to allow for affiliations that transcend differences such as those of class, and it has therefore tended to be treated with skepticism by those who see it as a locus of conservative tendencies. Marxist critics have feared the elision of class analysis by those who foreground ethnicity, while feminists have had warrant to worry about the ways in which an uncritical embrace of ethnic identities may obscure the gender hierarchies that often structure ethnic affiliations. Ethnic identities, such critics point out, tend toward essentialisms and calls for authenticity that often police individual choices and behaviors, thereby replicating historical inequities. In the context of colonial and postcolonial Africa in particular, scholars have argued that many of the ethnic identities that circulate today have in fact been tainted, manipulated, and indeed even "invented" in the interests of colonial policy and rule.[21] In their ugliest postcolonial manifestations, the parade of ethnicities has resulted not only in mass ethnic deportations and civil wars but also in genocides such as those in Rwanda and Darfur. As a result, as critics such as Christopher Miller and Dan Odhiambo Ojwang have suggested, the study of ethnicity as a meaningful category of literary analysis has often seemed suspect.[22] Ojwang writes, "within the atmosphere of the self-consciously secular and 'modern' tradition of intellection in post-colonial East Africa, there has been a reluctance to discuss ethnicity in any sustained manner. In fact, when ethnicity is raised as a topic for formal scholarly discussion, more often than not it is viewed as something to be condemned rather than understood or explained."[23]

How then is one to read a text such as *The Gunny Sack*, which explicitly seeks to stage an ethnic history? And how, furthermore is one to ascertain its political entry onto the literary stage? Is this a form of ethnic writing that risks a "substitution of the 'contents' of history but leaves untouched the very forms and structures in and through which historical and empirical contents are legitimated" or is it instead a form of double writing that is, as R. Radhakrishnan has put it, as disruptive as it is inaugural?[24] How, for instance, do differences such as those of gender and class mediate the ethnic frame? Can we see in Vassanji's text an attempt at naming an ethnic identity that also gestures toward the postethnic?

The Gunny Sack announces its ethnic difference at the very outset. The novel opens on a cold November afternoon in the North American continent at a funeral that proceeds "with clockwork precision in the hands of a Westernised funeral committee" (3). The funeral marks not only the death of the elderly Ji Bai but also that of an ethnicized temporality. "Once when time was plenty and the hourglass slow" (4), the funeral would have seen each member of the community come up to the body to kneel, pray, and pay its respects—today a procession of community members, most of whom have not even known the deceased, file past in collective homage. This move from "once" to "now," a move from the ethnic time of a remembered past to the empty time of clockworked modernity, is accompanied as well by a spatial dislocation to a "cold earth that would soon freeze" (4). The narrative sets itself up for a somewhat nostalgic remembering of this past, a past that takes the reader in a matter of a few paragraphs from North America to East Africa to India, from the empty time of modernity to the ethnic time of the past century to the mythic time of an even more remote religious past.

What such a move reminds us is that, ironically, part of the condition that enables the writing of a text such as *The Gunny Sack* is the spatial and temporal *distance* from the world that is being evoked, remembered, and, as Vassanji suggests, mythologized.[25] The creation of fiction, much like the Freudian game of *fort/da* attempts to recapture an experience that threatens to fade away, to make real that which is increasingly felt to be lost. Both *The Gunny Sack* as well as Vassanji's later novel, *The Book of Secrets*, make collective memory and history the central focus of narration, alerting the reader to always be attentive to the possibilities of mimetic excess and misrecognition, much like the disclaimer at the beginning of *The Gunny Sack*: "This is a work of fiction, with some historical events and characters as background. The Shamsi community is fictitious, as are the towns of Kaboya and Matamu and much else" (vi).

In foregrounding the *fictitiousness* of the Shamsis, Vassanji insists on the role of mythologies in the underwriting of communal histories. The ethnographic impulse is thus put in check by a mythological register, even as the compelling residues of history attempt to contain the possibilities of excessive poetic license. Thus, as the narrative answers to the European call for a chronological, linear history—"Begin at the beginning" (6), says Miss Penny, Mrs. Gaunt—it finds itself explicitly attempting to distinguish between the two registers of mythology and history. The story of the origin of the Shamsis, with their conversion to a syncretic form of Islam that considers "Allah as simply a form of reposing Vishnu" (7), is interrupted rather abruptly. "And so much for mythology, says Shehru. Now for some history" (7). While the narrative proceeds to tell the "history" of Dhanji Govindji's own migration to Zanzibar and Matamu, it is clear right from the outset of the novel that such "history" is also susceptible to the vicissitudes of memory. Furthermore, while memory in this novel is quite literally reified in the objects of the gunny sack, such objectification does not preclude the possibilities of alternative histories that circulate beyond its immediate frame. So, for instance, the politics of historical construction are not lost on the villagers of Matamu who, in the context of encroaching German rule, make much of their previous hospitality toward the German Karl Peters (13).

While the gunny sack is the primary vehicle of personal and communal memory, it is the model of a ship in a showcase that provides the narrator Salim with a symbolic epiphany on the nature of history. At one point in the narrative, Salim and his cousins try in vain to find in Dar es Salaam's harbor the original ship on which the model in their showcase, the SS *Nairobi*, is based. What they find instead is "a white passenger liner, like a plastic toy ship with holes punched in the windows" (126). There are two lessons to be learned here, the first of which Salim explicitly learns. In this simulacral world of models without originals the "past is just this much beyond reach, you can reconstruct it only through the paraphernalia it leaves behind . . . and what you manufacture is only a model" (127). But the other lesson, one that Salim fails to elaborate, which I suggest is symptomatic of Salim's own perceptions of the world around him, is that the *present too*—in the form of the white passenger liner that the children see in the harbor—is often experienced as no more than a model, "a plastic toy ship with holes punched in the windows." Furthermore, if history is, as Salim suggests, like the model ship in the Kariakoo showcase, there is at least some irony in the fact that "for want of a better name" the children have named it after the landlocked city of Nairobi.

The ultimate capsizing of this ship in the showcase meant to allegorize history is significant in a narrative that insists on holding on to both personal and collective memories in the space of diaspora. A capsized ship or, for that matter, a landlocked one is the sign of closure, a state of rest, a cessation of travel and circulation. It is, in a sense, the antithesis of the long history of the community's travel across the Indian Ocean with its often restless travelers like Nanji Kalidas Mehta or Salim's own father Juma, who at one point escapes the strictures of his family by crossing the Indian Ocean, if only to see the city of Bombay from the ship's porthole (65).

Unlike Vassanji's later novel *The Book of Secrets*, which depends on the written word and is receptive to an archival approach to history, *The Gunny Sack* privileges oral traditions and local knowledges. Baffled by the padlocks on Dhanji Govindji's books of which he, once again tellingly, only has copies, Sona's varied scholarly efforts to decipher the meaning and significance of these texts amount to little. His theory that his ancestor may have locked up the books to prevent some "djinn" from reading them gives his rhetoric a discernible Orientalist edge. Significantly, it is the nonacademic brother, Salim, or Kala, the one who, ever since childhood, has sought to listen to the stories of the elderly Ji Bai, that is best positioned to decipher the significance of the padlock. The books are locked, we learn, not to keep out the djinns, but rather because they are the records of community funds held in trust by Dhanji Govindji — funds that he has pilfered in search of his alienated son Huseni.

In thus privileging folk knowledge over academic book knowledge, much like Chinua Achebe before him, Vassanji is explicitly attempting to reintroduce into the genre of the novel forms and structures of knowledge that the European novel was historically seen to have transcended. *The Gunny Sack* is Vassanji's homage to the storyteller whose prototype, Walter Benjamin tells us, is the traveler and the trader. What distinguishes the modern novel from storytelling, suggests Benjamin, is that it "neither comes from oral tradition nor goes into it. The storyteller takes what he tells from experience — his own or that reported by others. And he in turn makes it the experience of those who are listening to his tale. The novelist has isolated himself. The birthplace of the novel is the solitary individual, who is no longer able to express himself by giving examples of his most important concerns, is himself uncounseled, and cannot counsel others."[26] *The Gunny Sack*, with its insistence on portraying an elaborate oral culture, replete with a range of speech genres — proverbs, riddles, songs, wordplays, nicknames — in the expert hands of a constellation of storytellers — Ji Bai, Kulsum, Edward bin Hadith, Shamim and Salim himself among others — is Vassanji's performative tribute to a culture now increasingly found only in its residues.[27]

Yet Vassanji's tribute is not an uncritical one. *The Gunny Sack* is at once a chronicle of the anchor offered by ethnic ties *and* the dangers of excessive ethnic zeal in the form of puritanical policing. If the Shamsi community has at its origins a willful hybridity embracing aspects of both Hinduism as well as Islam, over time the community in India sees the rise of purists who tear it apart. Such divisions lead to murders not only in the original homeland but also in the diaspora of Zanzibar and East Africa at large. Even when the new space provides for the possibilities of further mixings so that a Dhanji Govindji can have a child with the African Bibi Taratibu, or can go to the African seer Bwana Khalfaan for help in tracking his son, or so that his descendants, albeit as a form of escape, can take on the new family name Hasham that is distinctly Arab, such possibilities are put in check in the novel by strictures associated with the homeland. "In Junapur and other towns in Cutch, Kathiawad and Gujarat a cry went up. Our sons are keeping golis, black slaves in Africa. And there are *children*, half-castes littering the coast from Mozambique to Karachi. Do something! It was claimed that a group of young preachers, called 'missionaries,' had set out from Bombay to help keep the community in line. They never made it past the allures of Zanzibar, for no one saw them in the coastal towns" (11).

Vassanji wryly hints here at the hypocrisy of the missionaries who, by succumbing to the pleasures that Zanzibar has to offer, participate in the same violations they have professed to help curtail. But ideologies of purity exceed these particular missionaries and not only do other proselytizers follow, but they, in time, are joined by those who have never been to the homeland. Thus we learn that Ji Bai's husband Gulam joins a group of missionaries who have arrived from Bombay in the 1930s. Their mission is to "keep their brethren in line and to teach the faith to the African" (137). While they are unsuccessful in the latter endeavor, having nothing but punishment and fear to offer—no hospitals, no shoes, no clothes—they are "phenomenally successful" in their efforts at policing the community: "few intermarriages, fewer concubines or multiple wives, mosques and schools going up everywhere" (137).[28] The missionaries die collectively in a car accident and become instant martyrs in the eyes of the community. Vassanji's readers, however, are invited to be more circumspect in their judgment.

Although newly taken family names such as Hasham offer to erase ethnic particularities, it is through a reading of names that Salim learns about continued intersect rivalries. Thus, as he is being hosted by a man named Jaffer Meghji in Kaboya, Salim is struck by an oddity in his granddaughter's name. "Zainab! What young, pretty Shamsi girl has an ancient name like that? . . . The names should have told me (and the beards, yes!) but blindly I walked in, into a nest of—not Shamsis but rivals" (219). What Salim discovers, through his Dawoodi interlocutor Yusufali Adamjee, is that Meghji, who is in fact a Sadiqi, has tried to "pass" as a Shamsi with the ulterior motive of finding in Salim a suitor for his granddaughter. The fracturing of the Shamsis into "Hindus and Muslims, progressives, fundamentalists and mystics" has resulted in a number of splinter groups, one of the sects being the "fundamentalist Sadiqi, with its dress code and the Prophet's beard, its imposed modesty for women" (220). Old rivalries across the Indian ocean have often, as in the case of Kaboya, intensified, so that members from one community have refused to eat with those of another, until by the time of Salim's arrival in the town the Shamsis have all either left or converted.

This depiction of the historical trajectory of religious identities from the homeland of India to the mainland of Tanzania conveys Vassanji's distaste for the modern rise of religious fundamentalisms, a distaste he shares with the Amitav Ghosh of *In an Antique Land.*[29] When Salim notes that the old photograph of Jena—Jaffer Meghji's now deceased wife—"did not show her in a veil" (220), not only is the implication being made that "tradition" is in fact a product of modernity but also, as feminists have long argued, that such appeals to tradition often invest themselves in a regulation of women and their sexuality. Oftentimes such regulation is enforced by women themselves, as is the case with Awal, who, in the interests of preserving the *khandaanity* of the family, rails against the younger women, "If your pachedis keep slipping off your heads, use a nail" (68). But, at others, male hypocrisy rears its ugly head, as with the negative gossip surrounding the character of Roshan Mattress, who is deemed to be both sexually licentious yet not licentious enough to satisfy all the lustful desires of those around her.

Vassanji's characterization of Roshan Mattress highlights one of the ways in which, as I suggested earlier, not only perceptions of the past but even those of the present are affected by a set of judgments and values—stereotypes, to be precise—that preexist the act of interpretation. Since Vassanji's handling of stereotypes will become even more significant in our later discussion of interracial relations, it is worth looking at here in some detail. The occasion is a Friday on which, as usual, Pipa's chauffeur Idi has taken, on his employer's behalf, two plates of food to the mosque. One plate, of rich and fresh food, is for God, "and the other stale and hard, for Mzee Pipa's sister, a pauper who sat outside the mosque with a white enamel plate and a begging bowl" (122). Idi, we are told, "had a joke at the expense of God and switched the two plates" (122). An important passage follows: "If you wanted to point out the meanness of the Pipas, you would point a finger to the old man's sister, a pauper to whom her brother sent charity in the form of stale chappatis and a fifty-cent coin every Friday. . . . Yet Idi's act was considered generally not as charity towards the sister but as a crime against God. The only person who lauded his act was the Pipas' old enemy Roshan Mattress. But this woman was carrying on an affair in broad daylight with a Punjabi policeman, what could she have to say about good and evil?" (122). The passage works on several registers. First there is a very obvious critique here of the financially comfortable Pipa's disawoval of a sister in need. In this Pipa's sister shares the fate of relative disposability with other female characters, such as the narrator's Aunt Gula (who, on discovering her husband's extramarital affair, douses herself with kerosene and sets herself aflame; 75) or the unclaimed body of an anonymous woman found in the back ditches of Kariakoo (110), "unclaimed, not missed . . . an unknown woman, a woman with her own memories and her own world" (110). Such female characters are typically introduced and dropped out of the narrative in a matter of a few sentences, their brief appearance dramatically becoming a stylistic correlative of their seemingly inconsequential lives. And yet it is precisely such a cursory treatment that jars the reader into recognizing that these women too must have a story to tell — a story not of communal belonging but of disillusion and despair.

If Idi's act of switching the plates is considered by most members of the community not as charity toward the sister but as a crime against God, this invites a reading of religious piety as being at odds with family loyalties. Such a tension pervades the novel, and it is in fact the primary locus of the conflict between both Dhanji Govindji and his half-African son Huseni and, in the next generation, between Huseni's son Juma and his extended family. Thus readers will recall that Govindji's racist expletive against his son's choice to visit his black African friends is made in anger over Huseni's absence from the mosque. And, again, while as a person with part-African ancestry Juma is always on the margins of his family, his specific departure from home is occasioned by what is considered a crime against God — his drunken arrival at the mosque. The fact that the physical punishment for his crime, meted out by his religion teacher Raju Master, is so severe that even a police car appears to ask about the howls suggests the excessive demands of religious piety. When Juma returns to the family after disappearing for several years, his next break away from the extended household will also be occasioned by defiance against religious decorum. This time, along with his wife Kulsum, Juma will walk arm in arm "in the best European fashion" (69) to the Odeon movie theater when the "sinful couple" should instead be at the mosque.

Despite being written off as Idi's "joke at the expense of God" then, the suggestion remains that Idi could well have meant the switching of the plates as a form of corrective charity and social justice. While Salim the narrator draws authority from the communal disdain toward Roshan Mattress, depicting her approval of Idi's act as one coming from a morally compromised source, it is important to note that Vassanji, the author, leaves open the possibility of reading in this gesture Roshan's incipient feminism and sense of solidarity with a fellow woman. Thus it is Roshan who, later, with the arrival of independence, becomes a leader in the women's movement. Unlike the university activists, who are cast in a rather negative light, Roshan Mattress's organizational skills in bringing together "nuns, teachers, prostitutes, shopkeepers and politicians" (183) are portrayed on a distinctly positive note. Vassanji's handling of the stereotype of the sexually licentious woman thus allows both an intimate look at the community's structures of interpretation *and* at the same time calls for the disruption of those structures as problematic stereotypes. Such a move, I will later argue, also characterizes the way in which Vassanji interrogates Asian stereotypes of black Africans.

TOWARD A POLITICS OF DISSENT: THE CHANGING FUTURES OF ETHNIC IDENTITY

In narratives like Bahadur Tejani's *Day After Tomorrow*, which are narrowly circumscribed temporally and spatially, ethnic difference appears reified and essentialized. In the historical framework of an epic novel such as *The Gunny Sack*, ethnic difference becomes more complicated as the borders being drawn and redrawn between communities change over time and across space. Even as "Asian" becomes an increasingly important if contentious marker in the novel's postindependence period, the novel ultimately places more emphasis on a postethnic politics of dissent.

A convenient way of historicizing the changing fates of ethnicity is to examine it within the three generational markers through which the novel is structured. While identifying these periods can itself be tricky in a novel whose narrative structure attempts to experiment with temporal linearity, it is nevertheless possible to suggest a general historical movement in *The Gunny Sack* that is indeed relatively linear. The first period, presented in the section entitled "Ji Bai," dates from Dhanji Govindji's arrival in Zanzibar in 1884 and his move to Matamu the next year and takes the readers through the Maji Maji rebellion in Tanganyika to after the end of the First World War. The second period, the longest section in the novel named after Kulsum, picks up in the 1930s, includes the Kenyan Mau Mau war and emergency rule in the 1950s and shifts with Salim's family to the Dar es Salaam of the fifties and early sixties. This period sees the formation of the Tanganyika African National Union (TANU) under Julius Nyerere's leadership in 1954, Tanganyikan independence in 1961, and the Zanzibar revolution and union with Tanganyika to form Tanzania in 1964. The final section, "Amina," focuses on the mandatory National Service instituted in 1963, the Ujamaa Declaration of 1967, which led to the nationalization of much of the property held by Asians, Idi Amin's expulsions of 1972, and his attack on Tanzania in 1978.

The overwhelming tone of the first period is one of fear and loathing of the Germans. German justice is seen to be "harsh, swift and arbitrary" (14), and the punishment of the *khamsa ishrin*, or twenty lashes, is legendary. Work on German farms is hated, and Mzee Guaro, an agent for the Germans who is responsible for collecting forced labor to work the farms is loathed "like the angel of death." German atrocities against Africans soon engender resistance in the form of the Maji Maji movement, led by an African seer. In retaliation, the seer Bwana Khalfaan is caught and hanged to death by the German Bwana Wasi. While the narrative point of view clearly sympathizes with the African resistance, we also learn that Wasi himself has been a long-time customer at Dhanji Govindji's shop, that his wife has been the teacher of Govindji's children, and that when the war begins it is he who warns Govindji's heirs to leave before an impending attack by the British. The Indian community is seen, then, to be caught between competing interests and seems to prefer keeping a distance from both. Thus, while he gives shelter to three black men who are hiding from the Germans, thereby engendering the solidarity and respect of Matamu's Africans, Govindji prefers that this deed be forgotten "lest inquisitive German ears come to know about it and destroy all he had built up" (21).

Dhanji Govindji's travels in search of his son provide the occasion for a glimpse at the conditions of Indians in other parts of Eastern Africa. It is through his travel narratives that we learn of the growth of Dar es Salaam, its racialized geography and architecture, of the old trade routes in which the "likes of Jairam Shivji and Amarsi Makan made their crores" (29). We learn of the city of Mombasa, the Indian-built and run railroad and the various Indian settlements along the rail line into the interior. While he himself has an unpleasant encounter with an Englishman in Mombasa who interrogates him for no apparent reason, Govindji's estimation of the British remains a positive one. The advent of the war leaves the Indians in a state of uncertainty and confusion. Their initial departure from Matamu and later dispersal from Rukanga only lead to further separations both communally as well as within families. Vassanji is keen to focus here on the physical hardships that the community faces in the midst of the war, and, at least in the context of Ji Bai's family, he recounts the complete loss of assets as the German currency in their possession is deemed valueless in a British territory. "We had to start from scratch," recollects Ji Bai, "and we opened a small duka in the African section, selling kerosene by the jigger and packets of spice, and our fortunes never rose again" (53).

The second section of the novel, entitled "Kulsum," is more character based than plot driven and it thus gives Vassanji an opportunity to introduce great diversity in his depiction of the community. Readers will recall that Dhanji Govindji's disavowal of Bibi Taratibu and their son Huseni is echoed by his grandson Juma who, in the midst of the Mau Mau struggle, first takes in but then exposes to the police the son of his "adopted" Gikuyu mother Mary. This betrayal, which Salim later reads as his "loss of compassion for those of whom he was also a part—if only a quarter" (66), marks Juma's performative attempt at assimilating into an Indian identity with which he has had considerable friction. It is no small irony, then, that even as the narrative presents this betrayal as a "bad memory . . . a pang of conscience that's been eating away at the insides" (78), it is accompanied by yet another memory that "we would all like to forget" (77). This memory, of two European military policemen interrogating Juma on the streets of Nairobi and Kulsum's subsequent denial of its implications—"Don't be silly . . . did your father look like a Kikuyu?" (78)—speaks volumes both for the possibilities of epidermal misrecognition as well as for the hierarchies of racialized power in a colonial world.

Unlike the Maji Maji of the previous generation, which, as I have suggested, is treated with a certain degree of narratorial sympathy, the Mau Mau is presented in *The Gunny Sack* almost entirely from the point of view of the Europeans and the middle-class Indians of Nairobi. Juma's family members read the Mau Mau with a paranoia verging on the irrational: Ali Chacha's abusive strike at the servant Abdullah, calling him a "Blaady Kikuyu Mau Mau—" (77), despite the fact that, as Kulsum is quick to note, Abdullah is a coastal Muslim and not a Gikuyu, suggests that the middle-class Indian households of Nairobi care little about the distinctions between black Africans. This depiction of the arrogance of the Indian elite in Nairobi is, I argue, crucial to *The Gunny Sack*'s project of representing ethnicity through the lens of class, thereby interrupting the generic stereotype of the "Asian." In his later novel, *The In-Between World of Vikram Lall*, Vassanji will return to the depiction of the Mau Mau and further complicate the notion of a monolithic class ideology pitting the politics of Lall's pro-British father against that of his pro-Gikuyu Uncle Mahesh. But in the early novel that is *The Gunny Sack* it is the class differences among East African Asians that are highlighted, the cast of Asian characters in the urban setting of Dar es Salaam explicitly staging such differences with the extremes marked on the lower end of the class spectrum by Abunawas (alias Fateh the Coalseller) and on the upper end by his two political opponents in the elections for the Tanganyika Legislative Council, Mrs. Radha Patel and Dr. Habib Kara. Fateh predictably loses the elections, but Vassanji loses no opportunity to educate his readers about class differences in the Asian community:

> She (Mrs. Patel) has a mpishi at home, and a gardener, and a houseboy, he would tell the Africans, you think she will abandon them? And this Daktari. His children are studying in England. What will he do for you? Fateh threw his challenges in Swahili, he was answered in English. Whatever Swahili Dr. Kara had spoken in Mombasa now eluded him. Mrs. Patel, it was said, was acquiring the language and could read her speeches in it. But Fateh did not know English. In other words, he was not educated. He had been to school only to take other people's children there. He was scruffy-looking, often unshaven, and in not the cleanest clothes as befitted his profession.
>
> (147)

Fateh's clear camaradarie with the Africans of Kariakoo, his fluency in Swahili, and his general "underdog" status make him the choice of "drifters and dreamers" and idealists, the likes of Salim's uncle Bahadur and the tailor Edward bin Hadith. Within the narrative structure, Fateh is Vassanji's symbol for the possibilities of interracial community and political mobilization, which are woefully fractured by the power of money and class interests. Dr. Kara and Mrs. Patel can garner support through extensive communal networks and the dispensation of funds for an effective political campaign, but Fateh has neither the monetary means and the community networks nor the cultural capital of an English medium education that all work in his opponents' favor. Despite their alienation from the vast majority of the poorer Asians and black Africans, Patel and Kara, by virtue of their class positions, are better poised to win the elections. The idealistic character of Fateh serves, then, as a symbolic vehicle in Vassanji's exposition of the ways in which class structures ethnicity.

Just as the urban spaces of Dar es Salaam are divided racially into European, Asian, and African quarters, there are, as well, class distinctions that map themselves onto the cityscape. Thus neither Mrs. Patel nor Dr. Kara are residents of the poorer areas of Kariakoo, and we occasionally see, as in the case of Nurdin Samji, the educated young bachelor or Jenny Auntie, the independent typist, the arrival into Kariakoo of marriageable individuals who promise instant upward mobility. While such characters are important in the novel, *The Gunny Sack* is more concerned with depicting the lives of the less prosperous of Kariakoo, of widows such as Kulsum whose own efforts to raise a number of children against the odds require inordinate discipline and strength. There is much pain and sorrow in the lives of those who live in Kariakoo, as in the case of the Bubus, the mutes of Habib Mansion, or the "unbearable gloom" (123) of the building's Goan household. Even the relatively prosperous Pipa is seen to suffer from the tragic and mysterious death of his son Amin, while his daughter, Roshan, married to an alcoholic and physically abusive husband, commits suicide. But there is also much pleasure, much humor, and a well-knit sense of neighborhood and community that, despite the racial divisions that sometimes manifest themselves, is nevertheless more racially integrated than any of the other settings in Vassanji's work.[30] Kariakoo, unlike the Asian suburbs of Nairobi or the Upanga area of Dar es Salaam, or even arguably the town of Kikono in *The Book of Secrets*, is a space where African and Asian necessarily (if not always harmoniously) meet. Foregrounding the pain and sorrow but also oftentimes the humor that accompanies and underwrites his Kariakoo characters, Vassanji succeeds in humanizing them, and, more importantly, distinguishing them from the likes of Mrs. Patel and Dr. Kara who emerge in the narrative as flat and rather soulless characters chauffeured into the neighborhood by their drivers only to woo the requisite election votes.

It is in this second, long section of the novel that the term *Asian* first begins to resonate with meaning for the community, and it is important to note that it does so in the context of the partition of India. The sentiment that "we are one . . . we Asians must stay together" is articulated in an attempt to resolve a fight that erupts between the opposing Hindu and Muslim cricket teams (with, appropriately, a supposedly neutral Goan as umpire). The notion that Asians "must stay together" is a direct response to the increasing demands by black Africans of rights and opportunities that have historically been foreclosed to them by the racial hierarchies of colonialism.[31] But despite such public displays of Asian togetherness, as the forthcoming elections to the legislative council will show, votes are cast according to communal loyalties, and "Asian" identity is thus seen to be one that is more compulsively reactive to political urgencies than an organic effort to reimagine the boundaries of ethnic affiliation.

It is tempting, in the last section of the book that deals with the National Service, to read Asian identity—or at least the identity of Asian men—as one fraught with a form of castration anxiety. There is, of course, the oft-cited passage where a group of Asian men who have completed their National Service compare notes on the allegedly small size of their penises relative to those of their fellow black comrades. These insights into sexual anatomy and about what pleases women most might serve to build mutual confidence about Asian virility, but here, too, the internal differences within the community are potentially encoded, to take up Sona's pun, on their members: "'Indian boys studiously avoiding each other at the showers, but (I swear!) all the while throwing casual glances at each other's members as if to ask: Hindu or Muslim, Muslim or Hindu?'" (210).[32] While the masculine anxieties in this conversation revolve around physical endowments, in the case of at least one major character we meet in the National Service, Afande Shivji of Shivji Shame fame, the violent and aggressive masculinity he exhibits is seen to arise from a lifelong struggle against being bullied, often in a sexualized way: "People would pat my arse. Why, even when I was older, when I had left school and was ferrying oil—little Arab boys ran after me" (215). After years of being victimized as poor and coded as effeminate by his own community and neighbors, the proximate cause of Shivji's turn to a violent hypermasculinity is his physical and sexual humiliation by a Maasai NSP guard. The novel's suggestion that Shivji may be involved in a coup attempt against the state is, in this context, in keeping with the character's newfound determination to challenge any authority that by his lights is seen as emasculating.

Castration anxieties are, in large part, anxieties about the father. The father in this case is Nyerere, the father of the nation, and the overwhelming sense of the Asian community in Kariakoo is that the father has failed them. Rather than seeing *The Gunny Sack* as a novel primarily about diaspora, displacement, and homelessness, readings that are, of course, all sanctioned by the novel, I want to suggest the novel is best read as a dissident novel, one that is critical of the particular path of socialism taken by Nyerere. As such, readings that echo the larger social claim that the Asian community was in general nervous about independence because it had lost the privileged position that colonialism provided are only partially true. In the case of *The Gunny Sack*, for most of the Asians depicted in the novel, independence is indeed painless, but *socialism* and the associated political structures that are put in place by the socialist state cause much pain.[33]

In calling for a reading of *The Gunny Sack* as a dissident novel, I am compelled to note that critics have, all too often, missed the codes that Vassanji, through Salim, introduces at several points in the narrative to signal such dissent. Even though an entity such as the "United Democratic Party" is a fictional construct for the time (similar parties have formed since the state allowed for multiple parties in the early 1990s), the reference to Chief Abdalla resonates with the historical figure of Chief Abdallah Said Fundikira, who, along with other critics of Nyerere's one-party state, was detained by Nyerere under the Preventive Detention Act.[34] There are several references to Oscar Kambona in the novel, the secretary-general of TANU and a close adviser and friend of Nyerere, but one who fell out sharply with him on his chosen path of Ujamaa socialism with the Arusha Declaration. Kambona appears in the novel with considerable historical accuracy as the reassuring voice of the state after the 1964 army mutiny. But he is also seen by some in the community as a possible check on, if not an actual threat to, Nyerere: "Who would be the Brutus to our Julius? Kambona, some whispered" (177). Having made a break with Nyerere and having left the country under considerable political duress and fear, Kambona became in his new home in England a vocal critic of Nyerere's socialist policies and the one-party Tanzanian state. His reach into the world of political activism and dissent within the borders of Tanzania are depicted in the novel at two moments. First, in the reference to one of Amina's activist friends, Geoffrey Umbulla, who several years later "was detained for seditious activity, distributing Kambona leaflets at the university" (227), and later in the immediate aftermath of Abeid Karume's assassination in Zanzibar: "A twin-engine plane flew low over Dar one day, scattering pamphlets calling for the President's overthrow. . . . Kambona, people said" (246).

In addition to the references to Chief Fundikira and Oscar Kambona, which are meant to signal protests and resistance to Nyerere from fellow politicians, the novel also dramatizes student resistance to the new national demands. The National Service, in particular, is abhorred by the students, both black and Asian alike. After having worked hard all their lives to find through education a means of upward mobility, the students are not thrilled to be told that they have to enter National Service: "having taken three exams every year for fourteen years, all to be successful in life, and now to be subjected to the ignominy of tilling the fields and chanting slogans and marching for six months, and after that to go to work in uniform and give sixty percent of your salary to the government for eighteen months!" (196). The student outrage is not shared by the larger public who see them as privileged, but the novel is keen to show Nyerere's use of force in the handling of the student protest: "The University was closed, the unions banned . . . the students, in the State House grounds, saw themselves surrounded by the army" (196).

It is the National Service that becomes a catalyst for the growing sense of unease among Asians, particularly the younger students among them. While the older Nuru Poni has "progressed and departed from traditional beliefs, becoming more rational and more political, so that he admired Mao and Tito, Nkrumah and Nehru" (225), and while he has become a "progressive man in a progressive country" (225), he is sadly a lonely man "out of step with his community" (225). His son Alu Poni returns from the National Service an avowed anti-Communist and is set to go to America, "thinking that the CIA were God's emissaries" (225). The narrator Salim may not share Alu's estimate of the angelic benevolence of the CIA, but he certainly admits to being envious of Alu, who has managed to escape to a society that promises more opportunities than his own.[35]

Not all students who depart for the U.S. do so enamored by its political ideology: Amina, for one, leaves and returns as a committed Marxist-Leninist. But, as in the case of Alu Poni, it is with a mixture of envy and pride that Salim remembers Amina in New York: "How proud we were then, our own Amina raising hell in New York. 'Free Amina!' we said exultantly, closing our own fists, but ours was a call not to free Amina but in praise of a free Amina" (195). Here the novel does three things at once. First, it stages the opposition between what it sees as a suffocating socialism and a more liberatory space of a liberal market democracy. Second, it significantly codes this as a preference and choice made not only by Asians but also by Africans like Amina. And, third, by representing Amina as an avowed Marxist-Leninist who returns from the U.S. reconfirmed in her faith in the doctrine, the novel indulges in some mockery of radical intellectuals even while showing Salim to be enamored of Amina.[36] Hence, for instance, the comments on Alex, the Caribbean poet, whose use of the word *ujamaa* in a poem seven times brings him plenty of opportunities for readings, or the particularly harsh indictment of Brother Zahir (meant clearly to represent Marxist intellectuals), whose "cold-blooded theoretical Marxism" throws "every historical event to the cogs of a class struggle machinery, letting it churn out" the same conclusion in a predictable way (251). But the fact that this group of activists ends up being under the surveillance of the state suggests that dissent to the state comes not only from the supporters of a free market but also from those who would want it to move further left.

That this group of activists is presented as international and cosmopolitan in nature (in addition to Amina, Alex, and Zahir are Rashid, who is born in Durban and raised in Glasgow, Layla, his English wife, Mark, Amina's American boyfriend, and Beverley St. George, a Canadian, to name only a few) also suggests that the state's interest in controlling political opinion reaches beyond ethnic affiliation. This, I argue, makes the novel in its postindependence stage more a dissident novel about an ideological position taken by the state than merely a novel about the plight of a particular ethnic community. Indeed, it is rarely noted in the critical commentary on the novel that Salim's departure from Tanzania to the United States via Lisbon is occasioned *not* by his ethnically Asian identity, but rather because of the state's suspicion that he may be involved in a radical insurrection against the regime. Salim's departure is not of his own volition (as is the case with Sona, Alu, and Amina), but forced upon him instead by political circumstance. He leaves as a political refugee, not as an ethnic one.

BROWN MYTHOLOGIES:
THE ASIAN ENCOUNTER WITH AFRICA(NS)

To argue, as I have, that *The Gunny Sack* is best read as a dissident novel against the Tanzanian socialist state is not, of course, to evacuate it of its interest in race and ethnicity. On the contrary, unlike Tejani and Nazareth before him, for whom ethnic identity is a hurdle to overcome, Vassanji's project is to account for ethnic identities and the roles they play in the task of nation building.[37] Ethnic affiliations can be both empowering and restrictive, liberating and confining, and, rather than wishing them away in the interests of a larger notion of citizenship, Vassanji seeks to examine the manner in which ethnically identified citizens negotiate the larger public space of nation-state citizenship. Unlike the political theorist invested in an abstract sense of ideal citizenship, Vassanji the fiction writer is interested in how particular individuals negotiate the demands that their societies make on them. Thus, in the very act of presenting a fictionalized communal history, Vassanji ensures that it is the individual characters and their quotidian interests, pleasures, fears, and concerns that strike the reader as the most memorable. Rather than presenting a history of the community through a focus on its leaders, the novel tells the stories from below. And, instead of focusing an inordinate amount of space to male voices and characters, the novel, despite its male protagonist Salim and his quest to come to terms with his dead father, tells its stories structured not only around the looming presence of Ji Bai, Kulsum, and Amina but also around other female characters such as Begum, Jenny Auntie, Roshan Mattress, Ms. Penny, and even the much feared Timbi Ayah. If one didn't already know some of the biographical details of the author's life, one would, on reading this novel, find it hard not to speculate that he had grown up in a female-centered household.[38]

This attention to the traditionally neglected aspects of a community's history, its women, its poor, and its disabled, means, as I suggested earlier, that Vassanji can give voice to the history of Asian presence in East Africa, but also look to its seams for the stories that seep out and are swept away. Domestic abuse against women, child abuse, and mental illness all make appearances in the narrative, if only in passing. Despite the real horrors of the Zanzibar revolution and the anxieties over forced marriages that reverberate in the hearts and minds of the Asian community in Dar es Salaam, the most palpable act of physical violence against Asian women depicted in the novel is by a gang of four leering Indian men in Nairobi who lure middle-class Indian women into an empty godown under false pretexts, only to rape them, photograph the rapes, and subsequently blackmail them. Here the threat to the *khaandanity* of Indian womanhood, much talked about by the community ("They have their eyes on our daughters" Uncle Hassan claims of black Africans [162]), comes not from black Africans but from within the Asian community. Indeed, in contrast, the novel suggests that the relationship between the Indian Kulsum and the African Edward bin Hadith is, despite being employer/employee, a tender, loving one. While the feelings are never acted upon, because social norms would not sanction such a relationship ("I have known love but I have controlled it" (229), Edward tellingly says to Amina), Edward is, in effect, a surrogate father to Salim. It is Edward who is Kulsum's envoy to Salim on a mission to detract him from his relationship with Amina. It is Edward who entreats Amina to give up the relationship, because it will, he tells her, kill Kulsum. And, to further underscore his bond with Kulsum, we remember that it is he who acts as intermediary when Kulsum runs into demands for additional compensation from Omari.

Salim and Amina find themselves working out their ethnically different histories and falling in love at Camp Uhuru, only to find that on their return to the city they are made to carry, as Salim puts it, "the burden of our races" (228). Dar es Salaam, the city that, at least according to the story told by Edward, is founded as a result of an illicit affair between Badula, the son of an Indian merchant, and Mwatatu, the daughter of an African elder in town (83), is still not prepared to sanction such a relationship.[39] For Salim the barriers are Asian racism and malicious gossip; for Amina, likewise, the social stigma is that of being seen as a young, educated African girl with a lot of promise settling for an "oily, slimy, cowardly" Asian, a member of an "exploiter class" (228). The relationship, deferred in the interests of Amina pursuing a scholarship in New York, and with the hope that such relationships will have become more acceptable on her return, is ultimately derailed, Amina returning home with a new American partner. Salim and Amina remain friends to the end, much to the consternation of Salim's wife Zuleikha, but in this failed relationship, which could have been so much more, *The Gunny Sack* meditates mournfully on the difficulties of interracial and interethnic bonding.[40]

Readers will recall that this failed relationship between Salim and Amina is set against the historical backdrop of an earlier relationship in the novel. In an early interview with Chelva Kanaganayaka, Vassanji stated that he had given his character Salim partial African ancestry to give him "deeper roots in Africa. . . . I felt like an African and I gave my narrator a more tangible Africanness by making one of his ancestors an African."[41] Vassanji is referring, of course, to the liaison between Dhanji Govindji, Salim's great-grandfather, and the African slave Bibi Taratibu, with whom he has a son. This relationship and its allegorical signification has generated a fair amount of critique among commentators of the novel, and it may be worthwhile for our understanding of Vassanji's project to parse out some of the arguments being made.

In a powerful reading of the gendering of Africa in *The Gunny Sack*, Dan Odhiambo Ojwang argues that Vassanji's rhetoric of Zanzibar as the "isle of enchantment" (8) and Africa opening "its womb to India" (39) suggests a reading of African compliance and consent in "its own conquest."[42] The feminized space of Africa is often presented in the text as an empty space, a void that has to be filled by a superior Indian seed. "In this scheme," writes Ojwang, "the influence of India is seen as one of insemination and civilisation, while the role of the East African landscape in the encounter is one of passive acceptance."[43] Ojwang reads such passivity not only in Vassanji's depiction of the landscape but most significantly in the relationship between Dhanji Govindji and Bibi Taratibu. Taratibu, Ojwang argues "is restricted to the status of an empty womb that provides the 'pioneer' with a terrain for cultivation, whilst remaining herself agency-less and without desire." [44] Nevertheless, Ojwang concludes, Salim's later attempt to reimagine her history "threatens to render unstuck the myths through which the (post)colonial Indian-African diaspora fashions an impeccable genealogy for itself."[45]

Ojwang's reading foregrounds two key rhetorical tropes, both highly problematic, often associated with the arrival of Asians in East Africa—those of civilization and seduction. The first points to the notion of civilizational superiority that accompanied many of the Indian migrants who made their way to Africa in the late nineteenth and early twentieth centuries. While Europeans and Indians may have disagreed about which kind of civilization (Western or Eastern) would best suit Africans, or even the means by which it was to be delivered (colonialism or commerce), the record suggests that there was very little doubt on the part of either Europeans or Indians at the time that some sort of intervention was necessary to include Africans in the orbit of modernity. Africa and Africans were indeed, as Ojwang notes, blank spaces in *both* the European and Asian imaginaries.[46]

The second trope, that of seduction, is centrally concerned with the degree to which a specific cultural contact or sexual relation is based on the notion of consent. In a parallel discussion in the context of the American plantation South, Saidiya Hartman has pointed to the ways in which the trope of seduction rather than that of rape gets mobilized in the construction of master-slave sexual relations. Hartman writes, "Seduction erects a family romance, in this case, the elaboration of a racial and sexual fantasy in which domination is transposed into the bonds of mutual affection, subjection idealized as the pathway to equality, and perfect subordination declared the means of ensuring great happiness and harmony."[47] Such a family romance, based on an erasure of violence, suggests Ojwang, underwrites the relationship between Dhanji Govindji and Taratibu. Whatever we ultimately make of the specific relationship between these two characters, it should be clear from our earlier discussion of Nanji Kalidas Mehta, among others, that the trope of seduction (and romance) is entirely in keeping with the mythological charter that the East African Asian trading community has often created for itself—as traders rather than rulers, so the charter holds, Asian arrival was meant to foster mutual exchanges rather than engage in acts of coercion.

A dilemma that critics often face when reading literary representations is to ascertain the extent to which a text furthers an ideological position and the extent to which it instead interrogates it. Ojwang notes in this regard that Vassanji operates in "an ironical mode" enabling him to be both an 'insider' and 'outsider' in relation to the diasporic South Asian community that he represents.[48] As such, we need to be alert to the ways in which a text like *The Gunny Sack* simultaneously attempts to construct an "impeccable genealogy" for the Indian community *and* recognizes the limitations of such an imagining. It is not, I think, incidental that the entire family saga of *The Gunny Sack* is seen to be a direct result of two primal sins committed by Dhanji Govindji—the first is an act of racism, the second is an act of theft. If these two sins lead to Dhanji's insanity and ultimate death, they are also tellingly the two primary accusations made against the Asian community in later times. In centering the novel around the sins of Govindji, Vassanji points, I would argue, not to an "impeccable" history, but rather to a compromised one.

In objective, historical terms the relationship between Govindji (the trader) and Taratibu (a female slave) cannot be read as anything but an exploitative one.[49] The text nevertheless puts greater blame on Dhanji Govindji for his act of *abandoning* Taratibu than his original act of having a child with her.[50] This is, of course, entirely in keeping with the problematic rhetoric of seduction that Ojwang has pointed to. But, in juxtaposing the story of Taratibu with those of Ji Bai and Moti, the text invites a broader consideration of female agency in the period. So, for instance, readers will remember that, despite her protests, Ji Bai has been married off and sent to Africa at the tender age of thirteen, and Moti, a local girl who is married off by her guardians to Huseni, is an orphan of fifteen. Despite their lack of agency in marriage, the narrative explicitly stages Ji Bai and Moti as having completely internalized the ideologies of patriarchy. They are seen to pamper their father-in-law, who, we are told, "was like a god to them, whom they daily propitiated, whose attributes they sang to each other, whose idiosyncracies gave them joy to recall" (20). While such an indulgence in the biopolitics of patriarchy on the part of these women—or more precisely girls—may be troubling to us, the point to note here is that the text urges the reader to ask similar questions about Taratibu. "A slave woman kept by an Indian trader in a small town. Think about it, about her. Perhaps she always hated his guts, hated it when he touched her, undraped her, screwed her . . . or perhaps she liked him a little, or even a lot . . . her name was Taratibu, she was not incapable of love . . . and he risked damnation for their son" (150). Here the narrative explicitly stages the relationship as tenuously caught between the extremes of rape and affection, rendering seduction as a complex dynamic.

Ojwang's claim that the text evacuates Taratibu's agency perhaps underestimates the narrative strategy being employed here. For, as in the case of the other subaltern women I discussed earlier, Salim's speculations about Taratibu serve precisely to call attention to the fact that we do not hear her story, that she indeed remains, within the framing of the narrative, a subaltern. And, by the same token, the intentionally incomplete portrayal also cautions us *not* to presume that we can fully know her story.[51] So, for instance, many critics rightly fault Govindji for abandoning Taratibu in the wake of his marriage to Fatima. She is, as Salim suggests at one point, "used and discarded" (40). But the implication that often accompanies this assessment itself curiously prejudges Taratibu's ultimate fate. "She is pushed to the margins," writes Rosemary Marongoly George, "the location of Bibi Taratibu's house at the border of the forest throws her back in the African section of the village." Although George is right that, in so doing, the "immigrant community constructs its own marginal places and persons," [52] it is important to recognize that such marginality is itself perspectival. What is marginal from the point of view of the Indian community may in fact be experienced as central within the black African community. While such an experience does not find representational space in a novel centered around the Asian community, surely it is not beyond our critical speculation? We know that Taratibu sets herself up as a provider of tea and sweets to people who come from the interior (13). We know there is a deep bond between her and her son Huseni, who keeps "seeing her against his father's wishes" (24). Might this not suggest the existence of alternative ethnic communities that have their own affective bonds and their own appeal?[53]

If I seem to be belaboring this point, it is because I want to insist that rather than closing off alternative narratives and histories, *The Gunny Sack* demands that its readers recognize the limits of its own narrative authority. The novel's own insights and critiques are limited to the experiences, memories, and points of view of its principal characters. At times this can be deeply disorienting and demanding for the reader, particularly when the experiences narrated revolve around sensitive issues such as race. Much of the narration in the section titled "Kulsum" takes place from the point of view of Salim as a child growing up in Kariakoo, and it is easy to mistake the child's point of view with that of the older narrator. But no careful reader would take at face value a claim such as "Jenny Auntie was a witch" (95), more appropriately reading it instead as coming from the point of view of a child. Similarly, though it is more difficult to decipher, the childrens' fear of Timbi Ayah, the African Pombe Shop owner, and their belief that she takes away bad children is textually undermined by what actually happens in the narrative. To the child Salim's eyes, Jenny Auntie is taking revenge on his family by turning him over to Timbi Ayah. A careful reading of the text suggests, however, that what is actually taking place is that Salim is being drawn into a dance by a friendly Timbi Ayah in the midst of the "squeals and laughter" of "dancing drunken people" in the pombe shop (95).

This disconnect between Salim's fears and the actual events transpiring around him take on exaggerated force at two other moments in the text that are structurally similar. The first is a vision Salim has in the immediate aftermath of the Zanzibar revolution and comes in the wake of the Karia-koo Indian community's fear that they will suffer a similar fate. Salim imag-ines a "mob rushing up the stairs, led by Omari the tailor, eyes red with rage, seething with revenge" (179). The second is a similar vision of "strange black men chasing (him) through a thick, palpable darkness, carrying raised flaming torches and uttering strange oaths" (202). This second vision is pre-sented in the context of Salim's arrival at the National Service camp "in the interior of Africa" (201). Both visions share a tropology of primitivism, with black men appearing irrational and subject to excessive passion. In the case of the first vision, as Ojwang notes, "the objective fear of class dispossession is displaced by an exorbitant attention to the corporeality of the African,"[54] and, in the case of the second, a similar focus on black corporeality insists on recasting the interior of Africa in the familiar trope of the heart of dark-ness. But the text is careful to show that Salim's fears in both these instances are themselves irrational. In the first instance, in contrast to the vision of a black mob rushing upstairs, we are told that "none of the runners on the street had thought of climbing the stairs to the flats above" (180). Indeed, the extent of the damage to the community is registered as some minor looting of the shops and nothing more. In the case of the second vision, what Salim actually finds in the interior of Africa is not the darkness that he fears, but rather love. It is at Camp Uhuru (where, we remember, he has been sent because of his African name) that he meets and falls in love with Amina. Again, it is important to underscore that the violence Salim actu-ally faces in the interior comes not from black Africans but from the Indian Faruq and his gang of supporters.

I suggested earlier that the model of the ship in *The Gunny Sack* is meant to signify not only one's approach to history but also one's approach to the present. Just as Salim can only experience the real ship that sails out of the harbor as "a plastic toy ship with holes punched in the windows," so, too, at moments that he perceives to be crisis-ridden, does he experience black Africans based on a preconceived set of (racist) assumptions about them. Or, to put it differently, at moments of perceived crisis the discourses of black hypermasculinity, irrationality, and primitivism, so easily available to him through both the Euro-colonial as well as Asian archives, take hold of Salim. That the text shows Salim's fears to be ultimately groundless suggests repudiation of such racist discourse on Vassanji's part. But, by representing a character such as Salim, who is at least part African and quite invested in his black African heritage, as nevertheless being vulnerable to a racist ideology that has been handed down to him, the text redramatizes in him a tension that has haunted his father—a loss of "compassion for those of whom he was also a part" (66).

ANTI ANTI-ASIANISM

In an astute reading of the work of M. G. Vassanji, Stephanie Jones has suggested that "in both his novels and his more directly personal commentary, Vassanji's writing is stretched between a wariness of communalism and a valuing of community."[55] While Vassanji has claimed on several occasions that he does not consider himself to be a political writer, a significant contribution of *The Gunny Sack* is a politics of what we might, rephrasing Clifford Geertz, call "Anti Anti-Asianism." When Geertz invoked the notion of "Anti Anti-Relativism," he specifically did so not to align himself with relativists but to critique those antirelativists who had, in the process of their dispute with the alleged horrors of relativism, made it into an unrecognizable ogre. Geertz suggested that, unlike a mathematical equation, his use of the double negative did not result in a positive stance toward relativism, but rather a more circumspect look at the critiques being offered against it. As he explains, with the use of an analogy, when someone is an anti anti-abortionist, one is not thereby proclaiming that the world would be a better place if there were more abortions—rather, what is being registered is the danger of the anti-abortionist claim to dictate over the lives and bodies of women.[56]

In suggesting that Vassanji's position is an anti anti-Asian one, then, I am making a similar claim. Vassanji's project is to write against the grain of an uncritical and all too easily available anti-Asian sentiment that has often circulated at times of crisis in East Africa, from colonial times to the present. With remarkable analytic precision, by representing communities and families such as Ji Bai's that were not on the elite side of history (families, for instance, that were left penniless by the twists and turns of European rivalries as they played themselves out in East Africa), *The Gunny Sack* deconstructs the image of the always rich, always exploitative Asian. Yet, even as Vassanji engages in the project of critiquing and challenging the rhetoric of anti-Asianism, in part by representing a fuller range of Asian experience in East Africa than was available in the fictional (and ideological) register before his writing, his is not an uncritical praise song of the community. Indeed, as I have tried to show in my reading of *The Gunny Sack*, Vassanji's harshest critiques are toward members of the Asian community: the Indian patriarch Dhanji Govindji, who not only abandons his African partner Bibi Taratibu but further commits the double sins of racism and theft; Salim's father Juma, who betrays his Gikuyu "mother"; the shopkeeper Pipa, who abandons his sister; Pipa's alcoholic son-in-law, who prompts his daughter's suicide; the lecherous Indian men who gossip viciously about Roshan Mattress; the Indian men in Nairobi who callously rape Indian women; Faruq and his gang, who beat up Salim because of interreligious rivalries; the richer Asian politicians, who have little in common with their mass of supporters (and who make no effort to learn the national language Swahili); and the community at large, which ignores the plight of its poor and downtrodden.

Furthermore, despite the novel's invocation of the racist stereotypes of African darkness, primitivism, and black male aggression, I have argued that, in fact, the text invokes these stereotypes in order to ultimately derail them. Omari's threat of a labor lawsuit against Kulsum turns out not to materialize not because of any Asian intervention but because the labor bureau itself supports Kulsum on the matter; Salim's two visions of black male aggression turn out to be utterly baseless; the much feared threats to the *khandaanity* of Indian women by African men never occur (with Indian men instead being the aggressors); and the much feared Timbi Ayah turns out to be no more than a friendly and gregarious pombe shop owner. If, by showcasing a cast of Asian characters who are not rich or elite, *The Gunny Sack* asks black Africans to be a little more circumspect in accepting prevalent anti-Asian rhetoric, by the same token, by showcasing the racist stereotypes of Africans among the Asian community and by demonstrating the baseless nature of those stereotypes, the novel asks its Asian readers to also be more critical of the ways in which they go about imagining their black African neighbors. It is in this double gesture, characteristic not only of *The Gunny Sack* but arguably of Vassanji's larger oeuvre that I locate his ethics of ethnicity as one that is ultimately nonpartisan, insisting on sharing stories across communities and asking us to read the lives of others so that we might better our own.

Vassanji's writings suggest that working through the often tense registers of ethnic histories in the interest of ultimately coming together as a national community is a more productive approach than one that seeks to efface or ignore difference in the nation's name. The fundamental principle at work here is the principle of charity and mutual love, both of which Vassanji develops further in his novels *The Book of Secrets* and *The In-Between World of Vikram Lall*. Each of them extends the community beyond those of the Asian and the African to also include the European. These later novels are radical departures from a conventional anticolonial or postcolonial politics, since they insist on humanizing many of the European characters to the point where they gain the reader's sympathy.[57] Even as they are critical of the violent excesses of British colonialism in East Africa, both *The Book of Secrets* and *The In-Between World of Vikram Lall* tend toward an anti anti-Europeanism that is structurally analagous to the anti anti-Asianism that I have charted here. To many readers schooled in anticolonial thought, such an anti anti-Europeanism will surely risk coming across as colonial apology. But, to others, Vassanji's insistence on the principle of charity and the possibilities of mutual love across communities—including communities that have historically been antagonists—will seem at once a turn away from the Manichaean inheritance of anticolonial thought as well as a return to an earlier, Gandhian model of engaging with empire on intimate terms.[58] It is to such intimacies and entanglements that I finally turn.

CODA

Entangled Lives

But the ninety days had not been just a tragic event, they taught me a
political lesson, a very simple lesson, but a lesson I would learn again in
my next ninety days in Britain: unless you belong to the class that rules, a
good argument will never be enough to safeguard your interests. Unless
you are willing to sacrifice some of your immediate interests, and thus
form a community with others, your future can never be secured.
　　　　　　　　—*Mahmood Mamdani*, From Citizen to Refugee

Africa is for Africans—Black Africans.
　　　　　　　　—*Okello in Mira Nair, dir.*, Mississippi Masala

Writing in the midst of the Kensington refugee camp in the immediate
aftermath of Idi Amin's 1972 expulsion of Asians from Uganda, Mahmood
Mamdani recalls a particularly dramatic moment in Kampala prior to his
arrival in England. Standing in a long line of Asians at the Uganda Immigration Office waiting to have documents processed, Mamdani overhears a
fellow Asian ask a black Ugandan officer, "So you think we milked the cow
but didn't feed it?" The question is an echo of an accusation made by Amin
in his public speeches denouncing the Asian community—accusations that
included charges of social exclusivity, racial prejudice, and exploitative economic practices. As such, in the context of a queue full of frustrated and
somewhat bitter Asians standing with the "tropical sun above and the

scorched earth below," the question addressed to an officer who symbolizes Amin's regime can only be challenging. But let me allow Mamdani's scene to unfold:

> The fellow looked up and smiled.
>
> "If you think that is the whole story, you are not only wrong but in trouble," he continued.
>
> The official looked up, a question on his face.
>
> My neighbour persisted. "Do you know what an Asian would do if he were in your place?"
>
> Silence.
>
> "Do you see this queue of people?"
>
> "Yes."
>
> "And the cruel sun?"
>
> "Yes."
>
> "And how uncomfortable people are?"
>
> "Yes." But now the official was becoming a bit impatient.
>
> "If I were in your place, I'd have a stand of Coca Cola out there, pay somebody to sell the cokes and maybe some groundnuts, and make myself some money."
>
> Everybody in the queue laughed. The official smiled good naturedly.[1]

The incident and the events leading up to it encapsulate in many ways the enigmatic position of the Asian in much of twentieth-century Africa. At once suspected of economic misdeeds, but also often admired for his business acumen, the Indian, or Asian, appears here in the most prevalent role cast for him in colonial and postcolonial Africa—that of the *dukawallah*. In this particular episode in Mamdani's narrative, the Asian appears as a figure that is at once all too familiar and yet one that is susceptible to being misread. What we witness in the exchange is both the spectacular act of a self-consciously ethnicized performance *and* a warning that to believe in the plenitude of this stereotyped representation of Asian as quintessential moneymaker is to not get "the whole story" and to potentially risk "trouble." If, as Homi Bhabha has suggested, the figure of the "unhomely" is a "paradigmatic colonial and post-colonial condition" this is so quite literally to those in that immigration line in the process of being unmoored from their Ugandan homes.[2] The laughter of the crowd in the midst of such tragedy can only signal its experience of what Freud would have called the uncanny—a return, in this case, of repressed fears and doubts of postcolonial Ugandan futures that have hitherto been overshadowed by hopes and dreams of shared multiethnic and multiracial futures. Civil servants, schoolteachers, lawyers, academics (such as Mamdani himself), artisans, industrialists, and minor shopkeepers—all are at this moment, in this story of what an Asian would do under such circumstances, invited to recognize themselves in this insistent image of the Asian as moneymaker.

Even as the incident speaks to the anxiety of the Asians in line that day, it also speaks to the economic history of the emerging postcolonial state. As Mamdani meticulously shows in his account, the crisis of the Ugandan Asian was experienced in effect as a *class* conflict between, on the one hand, a community that had historically benefited from the colonial racial hierarchies that provided it with relative economic protections and, on the other, a newly emergent native Ugandan trading class that found itself at a competitive disadvantage to this more established economic entity.[3] In the context of colonial Uganda, writes Mamdani, "Laws hindered Africans from entering trade and Asians from owning land. In the economy that emerged, Africans were primarily peasants and workers; Asians primarily shopkeepers, artisans and petty bureaucrats; and Europeans bankers, wholesalers and the administrative and political elite. Race coincided with class and became politicized. Thus, in November 1971, Amin produced a list of 'Asian business malpractices,' not just 'business malpractices.'"[4] And even though it could be shown that it was actually the British rather than the Asians who controlled the greatest economic assets in Uganda through the sector of commercial banking, it was ironically (despite the realities of racial segregation), the *proximity* of the Asian to the African either in the role of employer (both domestic and industrial) or trader or office bureaucrat that resulted in the scenes of greatest tension.[5]

While he is not himself the shopkeeper but rather a regular customer, Mamdani's own encounter with such African hostility occurs in the contested space of a retail shop. A young man stares at him and asks, "Why are you still here?" (as in, "why haven't you left Uganda yet?"). Mamdani chooses to avoid a confrontation and a crowd gathers. "For the first time I felt like a foreigner in this country, my home, and the whole weight of the events of the past few months suddenly sank into me. I looked into the faces around me. Staring into my face was the malice of class hatred. One single emotion gripped my whole being: fear."[6] And if the hostility around him evokes fear here, it is instructive to read this moment against an earlier moment in the narrative, when Mamdani relates how his friend John, a visiting British lecturer, manages to walk him right through the front doors of the British High Commission unannounced, while scores of British subjects of Asian origin seeking entry into Britain are made to wait in long lines under the scorching heat only to be slowly let in through a side door. Envious of such white racial privilege, Mamdani remembers, "As we came out, I said to John, 'How does it feel to be white?' He hadn't heard me and I decided not to press the point. But I learned something that afternoon."[7]

In the quotation that I have used as my first epigraph for this coda, Mamdani implies that the Asian community's suffering could be traced to at least two factors—first, to their lack of political power and, second, to the mistaken choices the community had made in not sufficiently reaching out to its fellow black citizens. The life narratives that I have read, particularly those from the early half of the twentieth century, give credence to this claim, but we have also seen instances of Indian-African collaboration such as that between M. A. Desai and Harry Thuku or the later partnership of Mustafa, Kassum, and Chande with Julius Nyerere. While such individuals may not have been the norm, they did provide models of social and civic engagement that were not insular or limited to their own communities. One such individual makes an appearance in Mamdani's narrative.

On one of the last days before his departure from Kampala, Mamdani goes out for a drink with two friends, Jagdish and Malik, who have jointly put money together to set up a multiracial school for the children of some farmers. Jagdish, Mamdani writes "was one of the few people I knew who was not trapped by the social conditions he was born into; who had successfully risen above his social environment to be able to see its limitations. He revolted against the perverse nature of the society around him, especially affluent Asian society, with its totally privatized experience and increasingly conspicuous consumption. His life, in contrast to that of others, knew no barriers of race or class."[8] Referring to the affluent classes of Asians, Jagdish expresses his disappointment to Mamdani: "Most of us have five senses. These people have only one—the sense of property. Come, let's have a drink and forget about it all."[9]

A little less than two decades after this incident, the scene, with a few notable revisions, made its way into the award-winning blockbuster that was for many in the United States an introduction to the Ugandan Asian experience. A Jagdish-like character, not a schoolteacher but a lawyer, is the protagonist. He too, like Jagdish, is seen to be an exceptional man, a man who risks social ostracism and rebuke because he defends the interests of his black African clients. I refer, of course, to the character of Jay, the lawyer father in Mira Nair's *Mississippi Masala*.[10] On the eve of his departure from Uganda, in a session over drinks with friends, Jay echoes the words of

Jagdish. We Asians, he tells his friends, are responsible for the creation of Amin, we Asians, he says have lost all senses other than the sense of property. Nair's *Mississippi Masala* is a text that warrants a much closer reading than I can offer here, but I want to register a few differences with the prevalent readings of this film.[11] First, I think that the very legitimate and necessary critique of Indian racism toward African Americans and toward black people in general is too easily brought to bear on a reading of Jay's resistance of his daughter's relationship with the African American Demetrius. For the film makes it painfully clear that Jay's doubts about this relationship are based not on some primordial racist element that erupts in a form of patriarchal control over his daughter's sexuality (a reading that would be justifiable were it made in the context of almost any of the other Indian men in the film), but rather from a genuine personal anxiety about the possibility of interracial friendship in a racially divided and divisive world. Indeed, it bears remembering that other than this one issue, Jay is cast in the film as a liberal and loving father. Unlike his wife Kinnu, he is in no rush to see his daughter married off into a life of domesticity, even with the likes of the eligible Harry Patel. And, in a touching scene that points to the downward mobility of the family, he confesses to Mina that he thinks he has failed her as a father since he wants her to go off to college, an option that Mina foregoes, knowing full well that he does not have the financial means to support her.

Let me not be misunderstood here. There is plenty of evidence to show that Indian communities both in Africa as well as elsewhere are insistently endogamous, with marriages and relationships tightly controlled and often proscribed within the bounds not only of a larger sense of race but also of very particular ethnic identifications such as those of common language, region, or caste. When there *is* interracial marriage, it is more likely to be with white partners than with black. There is also plenty of evidence in Nair's film to show that the Greenwood Indian community's sense of scandal over the relationship is marked by a virulent racism. Nevertheless, Jay's own response to the relationship is far more mediated through his own Ugandan past and particularly his loss of friendship with his childhood friend Okello. We are meant to put considerable weight on Jay's statement to Demetrius when, responding to what he sees as idealism in the young couple, he says: "You know, once I was like both of you. I thought I could change the world, be different. But the world is not so quick to change." As viewers of the film, we may not want to defend Jay's disavowal of the possibilities of interracial alliances here, and, indeed, by the end of the film, after he has returned to

Uganda, Jay himself acknowledges that Mina has been right all along about his questioning of Okello's love and friendship toward him. "There is so little love in the world, and yet so much," he says in a letter to Kinnu, recognizing that he was wrong to have shunned Okello on the family's departure from Uganda. We miss the layered historicity of the film if we simply dismiss Jay's resistance to the interracial relationship as predictably continuous with a demonstrable Indian racism.

Here again, a point needs to be made about the particular characterizations of Jay and Okello that have also seemed to some critics to come across as unrealistic. Equal friendships like these between black Africans and Asian Ugandans, it is alleged, just didn't exist in Uganda, and the only possible relations were those that were hierarchically marked, such as between a client and a patron or a homeowner and a servant. The historical class divisions between most black Africans and most Ugandan Asians were, as Mamdani suggested earlier, very much a part of the colonial legacy of independent Uganda. But that doesn't mean that interracial friendships on equal terms were impossible among a certain professional class of black and Asian Ugandans around the time of Ugandan independence. On the contrary, as I discussed in the last chapter, the multiracial atmosphere prevalent at Makerere University at the time suggests that such cross-racial friendships were indeed within the realm of possibility. When critics suggest that the film takes too long to let us know that Okello is not Jay's servant, they overlook the progressive changes that were taking place in Uganda as the country gained its independence. Some readings of the film have noted that Okello's mother was most likely a servant in Jay's household, a reading the film neither endorses nor denies, but one that, it should be said, is entirely within the realm of possibility. But, if this were the case, it is all the more significant that the bond between Okello and Jay as they grow up has become an egalitarian one, not based on a sense of patronage. We must recognize here that the liberal Jay is not a typical member of the larger Ugandan Asian community, but rather, as Mamdani says of his friend Jagdish, an exception. Nair's choice of such an exceptional character in the lead is a subtle reminder that in any general indictment, ethnonationalist or otherwise, there will always be those who disproportionately bear the wrath and share the blame. As individuals they may stand against the set of values and belief systems that are associated with others like them, but their reach beyond the parochialities of their communities may not be sufficient to protect them at moments when their communities as a whole are targeted.

Most readings of the film locate Jay's disillusionment in what he sees as Okello's acceptance of Amin's edict. When Okello pleads with Jay to consider the deportation as an opportunity and not as a burden — he urges him to go and be king of London or of Bombay — Jay is exasperated and claims that Uganda is his home. "Not any more, Jay. Africa is for Africans — Black Africans," retorts Okello, and it is this statement, more than Amin's edict itself, that the film structures as the critical disavowal for Jay. But, as Adeleke Adeeko rightly notes in his nuanced reading of the film, there is no reason offered as to why Okello, who has always come across as a very good friend, getting Jay released from jail, helping him with his departure arrangements with the utmost sensitivity, being a good family friend much loved by both Jay's wife and his daughter, would suddenly mouth Amin's rhetoric. Given the lack of explanation, Adeeko suggests that "Okello, one is left to speculate, probably thinks — as do many of his countrymen and women — that Amin is right."[12] I am not sure that this particular speculation is entirely correct. There are clues in the film that even Jay doesn't quite believe Okello's parroting of the slogan to be a genuinely felt belief on his part.

There is a revelation that is made late in the film, on Jay's brief return to Kampala, that I would like to turn to here. Hoping to reunite with Okello, the first place Jay visits on his way from the airport is the Norman Godinho Junior School where Okello taught at the time of the expulsion. He learns that Okello died around 1972 (soon after the Asian expulsion), and the evidence suggests that he was a victim of Amin's violence. "*I wrote him so many letters*" (my emphasis), says Jay, indicating that, rather than being so upset with Okello's disavowal that he stopped communicating with him, he has in fact, over the years, made several attempts at reconnection. Because the film so carefully presents an angry and disappointed Jay at the moment of the original expulsion from Kampala — with Jay refusing even to say a proper good-bye to Okello — this revelation at the end of the film comes as a complete surprise. Like Njoroge's attempts at reconciliation with the anonymous Indian boy who has offered him a sweet in Ngugi's *Weep Not Child*, Jay's attempts at reconciliation with Okello also fail. In retrospect, however, we can recognize his eagerness and anticipation in Greenwood for any correspondence from Uganda as at least partially a hope for a return communication from Okello and not just a wait for the documents pertaining to the official legal case surrounding his property in Uganda. And, if this is the case, then perhaps what Jay is ultimately disappointed by is neither Amin's edict nor his sense that Okello actually believes in it, but rather

Okello's (and for that matter anyone else's) inability to do anything about the situation. In actuality, however, the risks that Okello has already taken in his publicly recognized friendship with Jay are considerable, and, while we are never told what it is that leads to his untimely death, it is not out of the question to assume that a resistance to Amin's forces, real or perceived, may have something to do with it. Jay's greatest moral failure is his inability to recognize at quite an early stage that while Amin's expulsion of the Asians was undeniably a painful experience and an egregious act of injustice, his worst victims, as Madhvani acknowledges in his memoir, were the many black Ugandans who were killed during his regime.

A statement as innocuous as "I wrote him so many letters" makes us completely reconsider Jay's years in exile. Despite appearances to the contrary, he, for one, has not lost all his senses other than the sense of property. In fact his clear renunciation of all his interests in his property and his unwillingness to pursue the legal case after he has learned that Okello is no more suggest that what has really motivated his return is not his lost property, but a longing for a reunion with his childhood friend. Corny as it sounds, his statement to Kinnu, when he says that "home is where the heart is and my heart is with you," can, in fact, only be truthfully uttered after he has learned that Okello is dead. Until then his heart does not in fact belong fully to Kinnu. Seeing the film as no more than a heterosexual romance between the young lovers fails to register the equally strong interracial homosocial bond that makes Jay pine not only over a lost home but also over a part of his heart that he has left behind.

What Mamdani's friend Jagdish, Ngugi's characters Njoroge and Kamiti, and the film's characters Jay, Okello, Demetrius, and Mina all share in common are their tendencies to challenge the political, racial, or sexual orders their communities have thrust upon them. They are not always guaranteed success — as we are reminded in the tragic case of Okello or in the Ugandan imprisonment of Jay. Their forms of engagement range from the most publicly political, such as Jay's chastising of Idi Amin on the BBC, to the most intimate personal space of the bedroom. Standing up to the oftentimes restrictive mores and social codes of the societies they inhabit, they have to accept the risks of being ostracized, ridiculed, and even defeated in order to become agents of societal change. Their politics is not one that speaks the language of revolutions, but rather a biopolitics of affect, where interpersonal relationships take a significant center stage. Such a biopolitics will always seem suspect to those for whom political efficacy can only be measured in large-scale institutional and structural change. A bond such as that between Okello and Jay, or between Mina and Demetrius, can in this sense not be seen as any meaningful counterpoint to the racist legacies that surround them. But, even so, such bonds do help individuals make meaning in their lives and prepare the way for the less divisive future they hope is yet to come. As Jay feels about Okello's comment on Africa being for black Africans, when such interpersonal bonds break, they oftentimes hurt even more than the edicts coming from a repressive state.[13]

Some viewers of the film have suggested that the price of Demetrius and Mina's relationship is a radical break from their families and communities. The film leaves open, however, the possibility of reconciliation. Demetrius's father Willy Ben has already given his blessings to the two, and Jay's final epiphany in Uganda suggests that he will come to terms with the young couple as well. But perhaps there is a part of me that insists on a hopeful ending not only because of all the clues that the film itself offers, but because, in an uncanny kind of way, that fictional relationship is in a sense foreshadowed by a real-life relationship taking place off camera. Like the relationship between an Indian and an African American, this relationship too crosses over a divide—Hindu/Muslim—which, along with the specter of the Indian partition, has continued to haunt (as I have suggested in my readings of East African Asian texts) the South Asian imagination. Jay's house in Kampala is in fact the house that the Hindu Mira Nair shares with her Muslim husband Mahmood Mamdani, whom she met in the process of researching and directing the film. Here, then, the imaginative possibilities of a fictional world intersect with real-life choices, inviting us to consider new alliances and new imaginaries that may well be our biggest leaps of faith.

I'd like to end on a personal note. While it was only around 2001 that I started actively working on this book, it is in many ways informed by my years in Nairobi and Dar es Salaam as a teenager. My very first memory of arriving in Nairobi is of driving from the airport past the city center on a road called Harambee Avenue. I had already picked up by then that the word *Harambee* was coined at around the time of Kenyan independence to convey the momentum of nation building, the translation of which was "let's build together in unity." In a few days after the family had settled, we were told by an elderly Asian neighbor that the word had its origins in the praise songs sung by Indian indentured laborers who had been recruited by the British to build the railway. To my Hindu Maharashtrian ears, this explanation sounded very plausible—the word insistently ringing as *Har-Ambe,* a phrase praising the Goddess Ambabai, a diety worshipped as a family goddess by my own ancestors. As I passed by the railroad tracks in Nairobi for many months thereafter, I could visualize in my mind's eye Indian indentured laborers working in a chain gang singing "Har Ambe" in unison, in the midst of their fellow Kenyan coworkers. There was something compelling and also reassuring (remember that we had arrived after the mass exodus of Asians from East Africa) in this image to a boy who had quite unwillingly been uprooted from his well-settled life in the cosmopolitan city of Bombay.

In the three decades that have passed since my first arrival in Nairobi, I have on occasion turned to scholars and scholarly resources to learn more about the etymology of the word *Harambee*. I had no inkling one way or the other whether the story about the origins of the word in the world of indentured labor had any historical substance. A colleague who has considerable expertise in historical linguistics and in East Africa informed me that it was unlikely that the word had an Asian origin. After the development of the Internet and the world of online forums and blogs, I continued the search intermittently, googling "Harambee" to see if anyone had further insight. At one point I found a lively debate that piqued my curiosity. A commentator on the forum suggested that the word may have had an Indian origin. There was a long list of angry responses from other commentators who faulted the Indian origin theory as being racist, as being in keeping with the long tradition of ethnocentric suggestions that anything that was good had come from out of Africa, and that such claims further attempted to alienate Africans from Asians. Given the blatant racism that has shaped discourses on Africa for centuries in the past, the reaction was completely understandable. And yet the original posting did resonate with the story I had been told.[14]

A few weeks later, as I was in the final stages of revising the manuscript of this book, I once again decided to look up the word. By now, thanks to the dubious wonders of Wikipedia, I learned that a controversy had emerged of late in Kenya around the origins of the word. Wikipedia is, of course, no objective lens on history, but it can indeed play a significant role in what David William Cohen has called the "production of history." Hence, I quote:

> Some conservative Christians in Kenya have opposed the use of the word "Harambee," alleging that it is derived from an expression of praise to a Hindu deity: Ambee Mata (a reincarnation of Durga riding a Tiger). The railway lines-men carrying huge loads of iron rails and sleeper blocks would chant "har, har ambee!" (praise, praise to Ambee mother) when working. The first president, Jomo Kenyatta, has been said to have witnessed a railway line team as it worked

in cohesion and harmony. It represented the metaphor he wanted to reflect: a nation working together and communicating and sharing its load. Others dismiss such objections, arguing that this explanation of the word's origin, even if true, is irrelevant to its modern usage and meaning.[15]

Were he to provide a reading of this, Amitav Ghosh would no doubt suggest that much as in the case of Abu-Hasira and Bobbariya, the story of Ambee Mata was an instance of a spirit of the past "reveng(ing)" itself on the contemporary "enforcers of history." More prosaically and tragically, however, we might note that if *Harambee* had now become a part of a recognizably ethnicized lexicon in a way in which it had not in the past, such a recognition ironically worked counter to the very proposition *Harambee* had meant to offer. Rather than coming together to work in unison, the ethnic particularity of the term, and especially its association with a historically immigrant community, threatened, at least in the minds of the few Christian objectors, to disrupt efforts to forge a society that was best fashioned in a (Christian) religious mode. Such are the dangers of ethnicity (and religion), and they have often encouraged ethnic communities, especially when they have felt themselves to be vulnerable, to willingly go under the radar, to not call controversial attention to their ethnic difference, to hope that their difference will not be meaningful in any socially significant way. As the historian Cynthia Salvadori noted when she conducted oral histories and interviews with a wide range of Asians in Kenya in the eighties and early nineties, oftentimes her interlocutors were circumspect, asking her to edit their comments for fear of being misread. And yet such a choice to remain relatively silent has often made the community appear isolated, insular, not engaged with the nation at large, and, as at least the Naipaul brothers suggested, uninterested in the life of the imagination. If this book has shed light on some of the imaginative projects undertaken by East African Asians in the twentieth century, it has done so, ultimately, not in the interests of advocating Asian difference, but rather in the hopes, along with Paul Gilroy, of "imagining political culture beyond the color line."[16]

NOTES

1. OCEAN AND NARRATION

1. Narrator, in Téno, *Afrique, je te plumerai*.
2. My reading here resonates with the observations of scholars who have written on the cultures of consumption, in particular the cultures of Hindi movie consumption, in Africa. Thus, for instance, reading together the form of romance offered by Hindi films along with the Hausa genre of *littatafan soyayya* (love stories), Brian Larkin has traced the common structures of feeling in these two genres. Hindi films, suggests Larkin, "offer Hausa viewers a way of imaginatively engaging with forms of tradition different from their own at the same time as conceiving of modernity that comes without the political and ideological significance of that of the West." Larkin, "Indian Films and Nigerian Lovers," 407. See Brian Larkin, "Itineraries of Indian Cinema: African Videos, Bollywood and Global Media," in Ella Shohat and Robert Stam, eds., *Multiculturalism, Postcoloniality and Transnational Media* (New Brunswick, NJ: Rutgers University Press, 2003), 170–92, for a further discussion of the intertextual relation between Hindi films and Hausa video production. See Heike Behrend, "Love à la Hollywood and Bombay in Kenyan Studio Photography," *Paideuma* 44 (1998): 139–53, for an account of how images of Hindi film actresses were incorporated in studio photos in Lamu; See also Laura Fair, "Making Love in the Indian Ocean: Hindi Films, Zanzibari

Audiences, and the Construction of Romance in the 1950s and 1960s" in Jennifer Cole and Lynn M. Thomas, eds., *Love in Africa* (Chicago: University of Chicago Press, 2009), 58–82, for an account of the reception of the 1951 film *Awara* by Zanzibari audiences across generations. Fair makes an astute case for the film's role in gendered identification among Zanzibari women and proceeds to show how the space of the cinema hall also figured as a clandestine space for romantic encounters. See Haseenah Ebrahim, "From 'Ghetto' to Mainstream: Bollywood in South Africa," *Scrutiny2* (2008): 63–76, for a discussion of the historical consumption of Bollywood films in South Africa. Ebrahim shows that increasingly Bollywood films are reaching audiences beyond those of the South African Indian diaspora, and she also shows the recent growth of partnerships between South African production companies and Bollywood studios so that an increasing number of contemporary Bollywood films are being shot in South Africa. For the influence of Indian iconography on West African Vodun art, see Dana Rush, "The Idea of 'India' in West African Vodun Art and Thought," in John C. Hawley, ed., *India in Africa, Africa in India: Indian Ocean Cosmopolitanisms* (Bloomington: Indiana University Press, 2008): 149–80; For an account of Senegalese dance groups that embrace Indian identities, see Gwenda Vander Steene, "'Hindu' Dance Groups and Indophilie in Senegal: The Imagination of the Exotic Other," in Hawley, *India in Africa, Africa in India*, 117–47.

3. Gatheru, *Child of Two Worlds*.
4. After his studies in India, Gatheru did indeed receive a U.S. visa and pursued further studies in both the U.S. as well as Britain.
5. The Zanzibari writer Abdulrazak Gurnah is also exceptional here. His works are populated with Arab, African, Indian, and mixed-race characters. While I do not engage with his work in this book, Gurnah's interest in older forms of cultural hybridities and cosmopolitanisms along with their more modern ruptures shares much in common with the work of M. G. Vassanji and Amitav Ghosh.
6. E. M. Forster, *Aspects of the Novel* (New York: Houghton Mifflin, 1985), 65–82.
7. All the novels listed here with the exception of David Maillu's *The Untouchable* were published in the Heinemann African Writers Series. Maillu's novel was published by Maillu Publishing House. While the figure of the Indian may only get a passing reference in the greater majority of African literature, Indian commodities—film and magic in particular—do appear in various literary texts. For references to Indian cinema, see, for instance, Kole Omotoso's *The Edifice* (1971), Cyprian Ekwensi's *Beautiful Feathers* (1971), Obinkaram Echewa's *The Crippled Dancer* (1986), Biyi Bandele Thomas's *The Man Who Came in from the Back of Beyond* (1992) and *The Sympathetic Undertaker and Other Dreams* (1993), and Benjamin Kwakye's *The Clothes of Nakedness* (1998); for references to Indian magic, see T. M. Aluko's *One Man, One Matchet* (1966), Nkem Nwankwo's *Danda* (1970) and *My Mercedes Is Bigger Than Yours* (1975).
8. Ngugi's novel does not entirely escape the negative stereotypes of Indians in East Africa. Nevertheless, Ngugi is as interested in the circulation of those stereotypes and what they may have to say about the legacy of race relations in colonial Kenya

as he is in the stereotypes themselves. Consider the stereotype of the exploitative trader. We are told at an early point in the narrative that "some people said that black people should stick together and take trade only to their black brethen" (8). Though he does not criticize this view directly, the narrator proceeds to report the sentiment of an elderly Gikuyu woman who takes issue with those advocating such economic nationalism by pointing out that the African traders do not currently provide the marketplace with the low-cost pricing as do the Indians: "Why grudge a poor woman the chance to buy from someone, be he white or red, who charges less money for his things?" (9). If what is being subtly expressed here are the strains of a Gikuyu economic nationalism in the marketplace and the logic of an economic rationality which has no regard for ethnicity or race, a later episode suggests that race can indeed play a role that defies logic in marketplace behavior. I refer here to the plight of Njoroge, toward the end of the novel, when he finds himself working in the shop of an Indian "out of sheer necessity" (143). A customer who has tried to bargain hard with him over the price of cloth accuses him of treating her like an Indian would, a statement that Njoroge rightly reads as the insult that it is meant to be. But, though he retains his cool, what irks him most is the fact that the Indian owner eventually persuades the woman into buying a different piece of cloth of the exact same quality for even more than what Njoroge had himself quoted for the original one (143). There are two ways of reading this episode. One, of course, is in keeping with the image of the cunning Indian who can sweet-talk a customer into making a purchase, even if the purchase may not make the best economic sense. The other, and perhaps equally important to Ngugi's narrative, is the fragility of ethnic solidarity—intent on striking the best bargain, the African woman ends up being more suspicious of the African employee than the Indian owner (143). My reading of the novel differs from a compelling critique of the novel's representation of Indians in general, and Gandhi in particular, offered by Robert Muponde. Both our readings are marked by similar political sympathies, but while Muponde faults Ngugi's narrative for engaging in a form of Orientalism and for not fully dismantling negative stereotypes of Indians, I emphasize the ways in which the narrative might be seen to gesture toward such dismantling. See Robert Muponde, "Ngugi's Gandhi: Resisting India," *Scrutiny2* 13, no. 2 (2008): 36–46.

9. Tajirika, Kamiti's potential employer, is not convinced of this positive take on India and Indians. But it is Kamiti's and not Tajirika's position that the narrative sanctions, and there are other references to historical and cultural events and artifacts from India offered on a positive note. For instance, there are complimentary references by the character Nyawira to Indian women's writing such as that of Arundhati Roy, Meena Alexander, and Susie Tharu (83) and there is the didactic telling of the story of the Mahabharata by Kamiti, the Wizard of the Crow, to Tajirika in his prison cell (382–83). Of biographical interest is the fact that Susie Tharu and Ngugi were students together at Makerere, and she acted in the staging of Ngugi's play *The Black Hermit* when it was first performed.

10. Mbembe, "African Modes of Self-Writing," 256.

11. Ibid., 264. An unfortunate display of such essentializing rhetoric in which

Africanness is reduced to blackness is evident in the argument made by Wole Soyinka against Ali Mazrui when he suggested that Mazrui, a descendant of Omani Arabs, was not an authentic black African. So while my primary focus in this book is on South Asians in Africa, the Swahili-Arab community of which Mazrui is a part is also one that has from time to time been seen as a "foreign" element in Africa. The most violent ramifications of such thought were manifested in the Zanzibar revolution of 1964. For the Soyinka-Mazrui exchange, see Wole Soyinka, "Triple Tropes of Trickery," *Transition* 54 (1991): 178–83; Ali Mazrui, "Wole Soyinka as a Television Critic: A Parable of Deception," *Transition* 57 (1992): 134–46; Wole Soyinka, "Footnote to a Satanic Trilogy," *Transition* 57 (1992): 148–49.

12. See Mamdani, *When Victims Become Killers*. While Mamdani's discussion of the ways in which colonial authorities manufactured and utilized ethnic and racial identities is relevant to our discussions here, one should not assume that such identities were solely the product of colonial intervention. For a compelling argument about the nature of racialized identities both within and beyond the colonial frame in Zanzibar, see Glassman, *War of Words, War of Stones*.

13. Mbembe, "African Modes of Self-Writing," 258.

14. Here, too, the work of Achille Mbembe is useful in rethinking the ways in which African space and borders have been conceptualized in African studies. See Mbembe, "At the Edge of the World." See also Gilroy, *Against Race*, for an argument for a more expansive reading of African identities not based on "the sedentary poetics of either soil or blood" (111). A recent article by Moradewun Adejunmobi argues that the politics of autochtony should be thought of as a battle over territories and not as a reversion to nativism. As such, Adejunmobi writes, "The challenge for African intellectuals and policy makers today is to propose productive ways of engaging with territoriality that do not involve embracing xenophobia, ethnic cleansing, and racism, etc. There must be a concerted effort to reclaim current practices of territoriality from diverse demagogues, and this effort I propose as a new *ethics of locality*." Adejunmobi, "Urgent Tasks for African Scholars in the Humanities," 86.

15. This question was poignantly asked by Francoise Verges in her article, "Looking East, Heading South." While I do not follow her lead by looking at Africa from the specific location of the islands in the Indian Ocean, my project shares the appeal of the cognitive map that Verges offers.

16. John Hanning Speke, *Journal of the Discovery of the Source of the Nile* (London: Blackwood, 1863), 13.

17. For an account of the rise of an Africa-centered paradigm in writing about African history and the corollary search for what Terence Ranger dubbed "a usable past," see Vansina, *Living With Africa*. See, in particular, chapter 6, "The Roaring Sixties," 111–36. One of the trickiest challenges for Africanist researchers in opening up new arenas in Indian Ocean studies has been to differentiate this scholarship from earlier diffusionist models that sought to "explain" African cultural innovations in terms of non-African arrivals and imports. What seems clear in retrospect is that, while rejecting the racism that underwrote such work, nationalist

histories tended in turn to inadvertently foreclosing any discussion of hybridities, exchanges, and movements that might shift the focus from discussions of African agency. Abdul Sheriff puts it more bluntly: "Africa's exclusion may have been inspired by the myopic nationalist Africanist historiography in the immediate post-independence period in the 1960s, which was preoccupied with 'discovering African initiative' in African history, and deliberately turned its back on the ocean, which was seen as a source of distraction." Sheriff, *Dhow Cultures of the Indian Ocean*. See also Michael Pearson, who offers a highly readable and thoughtful account of how political concerns have underwritten the writing of history in both East Africa and India and how these have shifted over time. Pearson, *Port Cities and Intruders*, 1–29.

18. D. R. Banaji, *Bombay and the Siddis* (Bombay, 1933); Harris, *The African Presence in Asia*; Shanti Sadiq Ali, *The African Dispersal in the Deccan: From Medieval to Modern Times* (Bombay: Orient Longman, 1995); See also Shihan de Silva Jayasuriya and Richard Pankhurst, eds., *The African Diaspora in the Indian Ocean* (Trenton, NJ: Africa World, 2003); Amy Caitlin-Jairazbhoy and Edward A. Alpers, eds., *Sidis and Scholars: Essays on African Indians* (Noida: Rainbow, 2003); Kenneth X. Robbins and John McLeod, eds., *African Elites in India: Habshi Amarat* (Ahmedabad: Mapin, 2006); Pashington Obeng, *Shaping Membership, Defining Nation: The Cultural Politics of African Indians in South Asia* (Lanham, MD: Lexington, 2007). See also the recently produced Web site on the African Diaspora in the Indian Ocean World at the Schomburg Center for Research in Black Culture (http://exhibitions.nypl.org/africansindianocean/index2.php; accessed June 29, 2012).

19. Senghor wrote two important pieces on the relationship between Negritude and Dravidian India. See Leopold Sedar Senghor, "Why Create a Department of Indo-African Studies at Dakar," *Journal of Tamil Studies* 5 (1974): 1–11; "Negritude and Dravidian Culture," *Journal of Tamil Studies* 10 (1974): 4; See also Ka Aravanam, *Dravidians and Africans* (Madras: Tamil Koottam, 1977). For a treatment of the commonalities between various African culinary cultures and those of Dravidian India, see Diane Spivey, *The Peppers, Cracklings, and Knots of Wool Cookbook: The Global Migration of African Cuisine* (New York: State University of New York Press, 1999). Note here that in both cases—linguistic and culinary—the claim being made is of an outward dispersal from the African continent and not, as in the case of Hindi cinema, a movement from India to Africa.

20. These themes are outlined on the center's Web site: http://www.cisa-wits.org.za/ (accessed August 1, 2011).

21. I cite much of this literature in other notes in this chapter and throughout the book. However, two recently published edited volumes are good examples of such scholarship. See Ghosh and Muecke, *Cultures of Trade*; Moorthy and Jamal, *Indian Ocean Studies*.

22. See, for instance, Piot, "Atlantic Aporias." See also the special issue of *Research in African Literatures* guest-edited by Simon Gikandi. Gikandi's introduction to the issue and the essay by Ntongela Masilela in particular speak to the absence

of Africa in Gilroy's framework. See Gikandi, "Introduction"; Ntongela Masilela, "The 'Black Atlantic' and African Modernity in South Africa," *Research in African Literatures* 27, no. 4 (1996): 88–96.

23. K. N. Chaudhuri, *Asia Before Europe: Economy and Civilisation of the Indian Ocean from the Rise of Islam to 1750* (Cambridge: Cambridge University Press, 1991), 36.

24. See Pearson, *Port Cities and Intruders*.

25. Mahmood Mamdani notes, "The trans-Atlantic slave trade racialized notions of Africa. It fueled the conceptual tendency to divide Africa in two: that above the Sahara and that below it. From a bridge that had for centuries facilitated a regular flow of trading camel caravans between civilizations to its north and south, the Sahara was now seen as the opposite: a great civilizational barrier below which lay a land perpetually quarantined, 'Negro Africa.'" Mamdani, *When Victims Become Killers*, 78.

26. As has now become conventional in academic writing on the subject, I use the terms *Asian* and *Indian* relatively interchangeably in this book, the choice often based on the historical time period being discussed. For the most part, in East Africa *Asian* as a term began to be substituted for the earlier term *Indian* at around the time of the partition of India. Nonetheless, I should note that the term *Asian* is by no means universally embraced by the different communities in Africa that trace their origins to the subcontinent. In the South African context, for instance, the favored term is *South African Indian*, but *Indian South African* also makes an occasional appearance, and, more recently, Pallavi Rastogi has argued for the term *Afrindian* to mark the fact that "Indianness exists in South Africa in an Africanized state." Rastogi, *Afrindian Fictions*, 18. In the long and varied history of Indian presence in Africa, a number of different terms, some pejorative and others not, have been associated with them: *coolie*, *Arab* (for Muslim traders), *passenger Indian*, *Sammy* and *Mary* (in South Africa), and *baniani*, *muhindi*, *mugoa* (for Goans), *kalasinga* (for Sikhs), *chotara* (for mixed-race children in East Africa) are all part of the historical record. The connotation of the term *Asian* in East Africa as referring mainly to immigrants from the Indian subcontinent cannot be easily transported to the South African context, where Asian immigration included, in addition to Indians, Chinese indentured laborers recruited in the nineteenth century and Asian slaves brought to the Cape Colony by the Dutch East India Company in the seventeenth century from various Asian locales. Separated by a colonial and apartheid ideology, the categorization of individuals under markers such as *Chinese*, *Coloreds*, *Indians*, and *Malays* has meant that the term *Asian* in this context has had less purchase. And yet, even in postapartheid times, such separations continue to belie the often syncretic traditions and historical trajectories between communities. So, for instance, Loren Kruger has argued, in a seminal essay on reading the continuities between Cape Colored and South African Indian identities, that for too long the narrative of the Indian presence in South Africa has begun with the arrival of the indentured laborers in 1860, thereby erasing an earlier history of Indian arrival in the context of slavery in the Cape. There is, she writes, "almost a

willful ignorance of the fact that the majority of the first-generation slaves brought by the Dutch to the seventeenth-century Cape Colony were from Bengal and Madras rather than from Malaya as is still commonly supposed." Kruger, "Black Atlantics, White Indians and Jews," 112. See also Nigel Worden, "VOC Cape Town as an Indian Ocean Port," in Himanshu Prabha Ray and Edward Alpers, eds., *Cross Currents and Community Networks: The History of the Indian Ocean World* (New Delhi: Oxford University Press, 2007), 142–62. Recent South African scholarship has increasingly begun to engage with mixed inheritances. See, for instance, Mohamed Adhikari, *Not Black Enough, Not White Enough: Racial Identity in the South African Coloured Community* (Athens: Ohio University Press, 2005); Zimitri Erasmus, ed., *Coloured by History: Shaped by Place* (Roggebai: Kwela, 2001).

27. While the term *Afrasian* echoes the term *Afrindian* offered by Pallavi Rastogi, my usage is meant to reflect not the naming of a particular ethnic community—such as Indians in South Africa—but rather the entire nexus of individuals who have historically crossed (and continue to cross) the Afrasian sea. Thus, in my usage of the term, the Tunisian Jew Ben Yiju is as much an Afrasian as the twentieth-century merchant Nanji Kalidas Mehta. Pearson's interest, incidentally, is in carving out a geographical zone out of the much larger space of the Indian Ocean for the purposes of his particular study. This zone "at least heuristically, has some unity, beginning at Sofala and extending right around the coast down to the southern tip of India, Kanya Kumari, Once the Portuguese arrive, the African southern limit goes right down to what they called the Cape of Good Hope. Both the Gulf and the Red Sea are included, and of course this area has intricate links with much further areas" (36–37). In search of a name for this area, Pearson discards the term *Indian Ocean* as a "little ethnocentric" and finds that the concept of an "'Asian' sea excludes East Africa" (36). He offers instead the term *Afrasian Sea*, which I adapt for the subtitle of my book. I am also indebted to Barbara Herrnstein Smith who first introduced me to the phrase "Commerce with the Universe," which I have adopted as the title of this book.

28. See Bose, *A Hundred Horizons*; Metcalf, *Imperial Connections*; Hofmeyr, "The Idea of 'Africa' in Indian Nationalism"; Tejaswini Niranjana, *Mobilizing India: Women, Music and Migration between India and Trinidad* (Durham: Duke University Press, 2006); John Kelly, *A Politics of Virtue: Hinduism, Sexuality, and Countercolonial Discourse in Fiji* (Chicago: University of Chicago Press, 1992). An excellent recent volume on these connections is Bose and Manjapra, *Cosmopolitan Thought Zones*. See also Mark Ravinder Frost, "'That Great Ocean of Idealism': Calcutta, the Tagore Circle, and the Idea of Asia, 1900–1920," in Moorthy and Jamal, *Indian Ocean Studies*, 251–79.

29. Here it is useful to track the ways in which Indians abroad mediated between a sense of imperial citizenship and increasingly over time, towards a more national orientation. See Sukanya Banerjee, *Becoming Imperial Citizens: Indians in the Late-Victorian Empire* (Durham, NC: Duke University Press, 2010).

30. McGregor Ross reports, for instance, that in 1908 the Nairobi Indian Association sent a "cablegram to the Secretary of State in London in support of the grievances

of the Indians in the Transvaal, and another to Mr. Gandhi in Johannesburg supporting his action in challenging the legality of the Registration act there." They reported these acts in the local press, thus annoying the local white settlers. Ross, *Kenya From Within*, 310. Zarina Patel notes that there were ties between Marxist groups in India and South Africa in the forties: "Y. Dadoo and G. M. Naicker of the South African Communist Party would stop over in Kenya and meet with the group. Their visits were always shrouded in secrecy and on one occasion when Piyo, Rawak, Sharda, Sheth and Indu Desai met Dadoo, Piyo remembers Makhan Singh asking Dadoo a lot of detailed questions and following up on news of several individuals." Patel, *Unquiet*, 143.

31. This book was written in 1914 and published in 1916 in India. For a biography of Bhawani Dayal, see Prem Narain Agrawal, *Bhawani Dayal Sannyasi: A Public Worker of South Africa* (Ajitmal: Indian Colonial Association, 1939). Agrawal notes that Dayal was a prolific writer in Hindi and lists among his books titles such as *History of Passive Resistance in South Africa*; *My Experiences of South Africa*; *Story of My Prison Life*; *Biography of Mahatma Gandhi*; *Indians in Transvaal*; *Natalian Hindu*; *Vedic Religion and Aryan Culture*; *Educator and Cultivator*; *The Vedic Prayer*; and several other booklets in Hindi and English (ibid., app. 1:i). Dayal also served as editor of the Hindi section of the *Indian Opinion* for a short period (ibid., 37–38).

32. The April 6th, 1912, edition of the *Indian Opinion* listed among its subscriptions readers in "India, Rangoon, London, Zanzibar, Mozambique, Mombasa, Delagoa Bay, Tamakan, Naivasha, Chinde, Chaichai, Blantyre and Local, including the whole of South Africa." Reprinted in Fatima Meer, *The South African Gandhi: An Abstract of the Speeches and Writings of M. K. Gandhi, 1893–1914* (Durban: Madiba, 1996), 895. For a recent account of Indian politics and nationalism in Indian newspapers in colonial Tanganyika, see James Brennan, "Politics and Business in the Indian Newspapers of Colonial Tanganyika," *Africa* 81, no. 1 (2011): 42–67.

33. In his survey of Indian newspapers, Robert Gregory notes that all the papers published in India around the turn of the century were sympathetic and supportive of the predicament of Indians in Africa. However, there was a divide when it came to discussions of black African rights and interests—Anglo-Indian newspapers such as the *Pioneer* showed little interest in the rights of Africans, whereas newspapers edited by Indians such as *Native Opinion* were often more sympathetic to African interests and "tended to equate the problems of Africans under imperialist domination with those of Indians in India." See Gregory, *India and East Africa*, 137–38. See also Hofmeyr, "The Idea of 'Africa' in Indian Nationalism."

34. Addressing his fellow settlers in Nakuru, Kenya, on January 30, 1923, Lord Delamere welcomed in their midst the South African Trade Commission, noting that it "will bring us into closer touch with the Union of South Africa, the only unit in Africa, which is consolidating a civilization on Western lines." In Waiz, *Indians Abroad*, 58.

35. Quoted ibid., 509.

36. Quoted in Andrews, *The Indian Question in East Africa*, 61.

37. Waiz, *Indians Abroad*, 258.

38. Ibid., 259.

39. In the interests of having a manageable project, I have left out of this book some of my own current writing on Gandhi in South Africa. However, there is an extensive literature that examines Gandhi's South African career and its implications for both South Africa as well as for the struggle for Indian nationalism. See, for instance, Maureen Swan, *Gandhi: The South African Experience* (Johannesburg: Ravan, 1985); Surendra Bhana, *Gandhi's Legacy: The Natal Indian Congress, 1894–1994* (Pietermaritzburg: University of Natal Press, 1997); Surendra Bhana and Goolam Vahed, *The Making of a Political Reformer: Gandhi in South Africa, 1893–1914* (New Delhi: Manohar, 2005); Judith Brown and Martin Prozesky, eds., *Gandhi and South Africa: Principles and Politics* (Pietermaritzburg: University of Natal Press, 1996); David Hardiman, *Gandhi in His Time and Ours: The Global Legacy of His Ideas* (Pietermaritzburg: University of Natal Press, 2003); James Hunt, *Gandhi and the Non-Conformists: Encounters in South Africa* (New Delhi: Promolla, 1986); J. N. Uppal, *Gandhi: Ordained in South Africa* (New Delhi: Ministry of Information, Government of India, 1996); E. S. Reddy, *Gandhiji's Vision of a Free South Africa* (New Delhi: Sanchar, 1995); T. G. Ramamurthi, *Nonviolence and Nationalism: A Study of Gandhian Mass Resistance in South Africa* (New Delhi: Amar Prakashan, 1992); Nagindas Sanghavi, *The Agony of Arrival: Gandhi, The South Africa Years* (New Delhi: Rupa, 2006). An excellent sourcebook and collection of contemporary tributes to Gandhi in South Africa may be found in Meer, *The South African Gandhi*.

40. See Padmini Sengupta, *Sarojini Naidu: A Biography* (Bombay: Asia, 1966), 174–78; 249–52.

41. "Letter from Sarojini Naidu to Gandhiji, February 29, 1924" in Mrinalini Sarabhai, ed., *The Mahatma and the Poetess: Being a Selection of Letters Exchanged Between Gandhiji and Sarojini Naidu* (Bombay: Bharatiya Vidya Bhavan, 1998), 37 (37–39).

42. Sarojini Naidu to Gandhiji, February 13, 1924, ibid., 35 (34–36).

43. Extract printed ibid., 169. Along with the case of Sarojini Naidu, the later history of Indian women who joined the struggle against colonialism—leaders such as Urmilaben Ramabhai Patel, and Saraswati Manubhai Patel in Kenya and Dr. Goonam, Amina Chachalia, Zainab Asvat, P. K. Naidoo, and Suriakala Patel, among others, in South Africa—suggests that Indian women were not merely passive observers in a male political game. In some cases, as Aili Mari Trip has shown in the context of Uganda, they actively sought to form multiracial coalitions with African and European women in the interests of resisting colonial patriarchy. See Aili Mari Tripp, "Women's Mobilization in Uganda: Non-racial Ideologies in European-Asian-African Encounters, 1945–1962," *International Journal of African Historical Studies* 34, no. 3 (2001): 543–64. On the Kenyan women, see Ambu H. Patel, comp., N. S. Thakur and Vanshi Dhar, eds., *Struggle for Release: Jomo and His Colleagues* (Nairobi: New Kenya, 1963). U. R. Patel is quoted as saying, "The man who kindled the Fire of Independence in Africa, as Mahatma Gandhi did

in India, is Mzee Jomo Kenyatta. The Asians and Africans alike as well as many great leaders of other nations have full faith in him" (170); S. M. Patel is quoted as saying, "Asian women have full trust in Kenyatta's leadership. They believe that Kenyatta's long years in Europe will make him understand women's role in nation's affairs and expect of him that he will afford full protection to all women as is done in all the civilized countries of the world" (170). Both women were active in getting other Asian women to sign petitions asking for the release of Kenyatta and were involved in gathering donations from the Asian community for poor and unemployed Africans. On activism by Indian women in South Africa, see Cheryl Walker, *Women and Resistance in South Africa* (London: Onyx, 1982), 105–12; See also Dr. [Kasavello] Goonam, *Coolie Doctor: An Autobiography* (Durban: Madiba, 1991).

44. On this, Stephen Muecke writes,

The fascinating "conceptual space" that is constituted by Indian Ocean Studies today is a historically formed image where we see European enlightenment thought (reflected back in the waves of the seventeenth century) meeting the transcontinental mercantile-religious complex that was the pre-colonial Indian Ocean. That particular conjunction gives us the potential to see postcolonial thought, which, after all, developed out of the meshing of European theory and empirical analysis of the colonial situation, further localized in the Indian Ocean, instead of developed only elsewhere, in the northern diaspora for instance.

Stephen Muecke, "Fabulation: Flying Carpets, and Artful Politics in the Indian Ocean," in Moorthy and Jamal, *Indian Ocean Studies*, 35 (32–44).

45. See Mudimbe, *The Invention of Africa*; Chakrabarty, *Provincializing Europe*; see also the exchange between Ghosh and Chakrabarty, "A Correspondence on Provincializing Europe."

46. Naipaul, *A Bend in the River*, 11.

47. Ghosh's book allows us to imagine a dialogue between Africa and Asia, that, as Ashis Nandy once put it sarcastically, has become hard to imagine:

Such a conversation [between Africa and Asia] has become doubly dangerous. Because, during the last two hundred years, we have obediently learnt to converse with our neighbours under the auspices of—and with the help of "correct" categories popularized by—our distant, benevolent, wise mentors, usually located in the respectable universities and think tanks of North America and West Europe. These mentors are obviously the partisans of sane, rational, transparent exchanges in the global market place of ideas. As a result, these conversations do not have to be translated for the global cosmopolis; they have to be merely translated for the benefit of the hoi polloi of Africa and Asia."

Nandy, "Who Wants an Afro-Asian Dialogue?" 2.

48. Mbembe, "African Modes of Self-Writing," 258.

49. See Scott, *Refashioning Futures*.

50. I have attempted a brief answer to this particular question in a recent essay. See

Gaurav Desai, "Between Indigeneity and Diaspora: Questions from a Scholar Tourist," *Interventions* 13, no. 1 (2011): 53–66.

51. This last question is, of course, an echo of the question raised by Mahmood Mamdani in his inaugural lecture, "When Does a Settler Become a Native? Reflections of the Colonial Roots of Citizenship in Equatorial and South Africa," University of Cape Town, Department of Communication, 1998.

52. See Simon Gikandi, "Chinua Achebe and the Invention of African Culture," *Research in African Literatures* 32, no. 3 (2001): 3–8. See also Simon Gikandi, *Reading Chinua Achebe: Language and Ideology in Fiction* (London: James Currey, 1991).

53. See Gilroy, *The Black Atlantic*, 1–40.

54. Sheriff, *Dhow Cultures of the Indian Ocean*.

55. See Frank, *ReOrient*; Bose, *A Hundred Horizons*, 73. David Washbrook reminds us that "the world system and world capitalism were not simply imposed from the outside on an innocent and unsuspecting non-European world." Rather, he argues that the experience of South Asia (and by extension that of the Indian Ocean), "calls for a serious reappraisal of what 'capitalism' and 'Modernity' might mean. Some start in demystifying them may be made by turning to history and, first, by seeking to abandon, or at least to modify, purely Euro-centred theories of them." David Washbrook, "South Asia, the World System and World Capitalism," in Sugata Bose, ed., *South Asia and World Capitalism* (New York: Oxford University Press, 1990), 78, 77 (40–84).

56. Julius Nyerere, quoted in Annar Cassam, "Nyerere talks to El Pais" in Chachage and Cassam, *Africa's Liberation*, 72–76.

57. Francis Fukuyama, "U.S. Democracy Has Little to Teach China," *Financial Times*, January 17, 2011 (http://www.ft.com/cms/s/0/cb6af6e8-2272-11e0-b6a2-00144feab49a .html#axzz2DSD1kONy; accessed June 29, 2012). This new assessment is a departure from his earlier position articulated in Francis Fukuyama, *The End of History and the Last Man* (New York: Free Press, 1992).

58. Kaplan, "Center Stage for the Twenty-first Century." On the commercial potential of Africa, see Vijay Mahajan, *Africa Rising: How 900 Million African Consumers Offer More than You Think* (Upper Saddle River, NJ: Wharton, 2009). There is a growing amount of literature on the role of China and India in Africa. See, for instance, Deborah Brautigam, *The Dragon's Gift: The Real Story of China in Africa* (New York: Oxford University Press, 2009); Chris Alden, *China in Africa* (London: Zed, 2007); Axel Harneit-Sievers, Stephen Marks, and Sanusha Naidu, eds., *Chinese and African Perspectives on China in India* (Cape Town: Pambazuka, 2010); Emma Mawdsley and Gerald McCann, eds., *India in Africa: Changing Geographies of Power* (Cape Town: Pambazuka, 2011); V. S. Sheth, ed., *India-Africa Relations: Emerging Policy and Development Perspective* (Delhi: Academic Excellence, 2008); Elizabeth Sidiropoulos, "India and South Africa as Partners for Development in Africa?" (London: Chatham House, 2011), www.chatham house.org.uk (accessed August 1, 2011); Renu Modi, "India and South Sudan: Potential Areas of Co-operation," Gateway House, Indian Council on Global

Relations, August 23, 2011, http://www.gatewayhouse.in/publication/analysis-amp -background/articles/india-and-south-sudan-potential-areas-cooperation (accessed August 27, 2011).

59. I refer here to the anti-Asian rhetoric circulated at the time not only in South Africa and Kenya but also in other white settler colonies such as the United States. I discuss some of this rhetoric in chapter 3. A good book to read on this is Neame, *The Asiatic Danger in the Colonies*. The book garnered a review in the *New York Times* when it was first published. The byline of the review reads "Student of Oriental Character Points Out How Insidiously the Patient East Is Undermining Western Supremacy," June 29, 1907 (http:// query.nytimes.com/mem/archive-free/pdf?res= FA0B17F9385A15738DDDA00A94DE405B878CF1D3; accessed June 29, 2012). I am not suggesting that Africanists remain silent about any unequal or exploitative relations between Africa and the East. I am only cautioning against the echoes of that earlier discourse that I increasingly hear in the U.S. national media in discussions of the alleged rise of China or that of India.

60. Rorty, *Contingency, Irony, and Solidarity*, xvi.

61. Appiah, *The Ethics of Identity*, 257.

62. Scott, *Refashioning Futures*, 201.

2. OLD WORLD ORDERS

1. Ghosh, *In an Antique Land*. All citations in this chapter are from the Vintage paperback edition. Page references to this edition are provided parenthetically.

2. Clifford Geertz, "A Passage to India," *New Republic*, August 23–30, 1993, 38 (38, 40–41); Ahdaf Soueif, "Intimately Egyptian," *Times Literary Supplement*, January 15, 1993, 7; Anton Shammas, "The Once and Future Egypt," *New York Times Book Review*, August 1, 1993, 26; Jonathan M. Elukin, "Cairene Treasures," *American Scholar* 63 (1994): 137–40.

3. Amitav Ghosh, "The Imam and the Indian," *Granta* 20 (1986): 135–46. This piece was reprinted in a volume of critical essays in cultural studies, Angelika Bammer, ed., *Displacements: Cultural Identities in Question* (Madison: University of Wisconsin Press, 1994), 47–55; Ghosh, "The Slave of MS. H.6." In addition to these two previews of what was to come in *In An Antique Land*, we should also note that, although it was not disseminated to a large public readership, Ghosh's dissertation was produced in 1982. Written in the formal style of an ethnography, the dissertation is of great interest to those pursuing a comparative study of the scholarly and popular modalities of "writing culture." See Ghosh, "Kinship in Relation to Economic and Social Organization."

4. James Clifford, "Traveling Cultures," in Lawrence Grossberg, Cary Nelson, and Paula Treichler, eds., *Cultural Studies*, 96–116 (New York: Routledge, 1992); See also Clifford, *Routes*, 1–15.

5. There are, of course, a number of scholars of Asian descent in Africa — Mahmood Mamdani, Abdul Sheriff, and Issa Shivji to name only three from the East African context. The point I make, recalling Kamiti (in Ngugi's *Wizard of the Crow*) is

that one often has to be reminded that "An Indian is not all dukawallah and noth-ing else" (54). If this is a point about popular representations of Indians in Africa, a related point also needs to be made about the academic standing of Eastern scholarship on Africa. There has been a long tradition of South Asian academic engagement with Africa and African studies, including the important journal *Africa Quarterly* published by the Indian Council on Cultural Relations. Very little of this work has reached scholars in the West, who have had a regrettably parochial sense of the paradigms of area studies. A case in point is the work of Ramkrishna Mukherjee, whose study *Uganda: An Historical Accident? Class, Nation and State Formation* was first published under a different title in 1956. This book, republished in 1985 by Africa World Press, anticipated in significant detail many of the discus-sions of the "invention of ethnicity" and "tribalism" that later became common par-lance in African studies. Yet, if citations are to be a measure, there seems to be little to no historical memory of this particular book. See Mukherjee, *The Problem of Uganda*; Ramkrishna Mukherjee, *Uganda: An Historical Accident? Class, Nation and State Formation* (Trenton, NJ: Africa World, 1985).

6. The Vintage paperback edition subtitles the book "History in the Guise of a Traveler's Tale."

7. Behdad, *Belated Travelers*, 1–17.

8. The name *Ifriqiya*, from which the word *Africa* is derived, refers to the area in North Africa that roughly corresponds to present-day Tunisia.

9. See Goitein, *Letters of Medieval Jewish Traders*, 185–206, for biographical details on Ben Yiju and for letters addressed to and sent by him to business colleagues and relatives.

10. S. D. Goitein explains that, while the majority of documents in the Geniza were written in the Hebrew script, the languages used were various forms of Arabic ver-naculars used in Spain, Sicily, and different parts of Northern Africa and Western Asia. A few documents written in the Arabic script are also present in the Geniza material, indicating the close connections between the Jewish and Islamic public spheres. See Goitein, *A Mediterranean Society*, 1:14–17.

11. The latest document Goitein records noting is a 1879 divorce bill from Bombay (*A Mediterranean Society*, 1:9).

12. Goitein takes pains to distinguish the materials in the Geniza from a proper his-torical archive. Archival materials are usually those that are consciously preserved for later referral, and care is taken to protect them from deterioration. Such documents are usually also of social, economic, or political import to the people concerned and not, as in the case of the documents discarded in the Geniza, those that have outlived their intended purpose. Compared to a proper archive, the doc-uments found in the Geniza retain a decisively chaotic element about them. But it is precisely this chaos that allows one to reconstruct scenes of everyday life and to get an unadulterated flavor of a bygone society. See Goitein, *A Mediterranean Society*, 1:7–28.

13. This brief biography is drawn from Abraham Udovitch's foreword to volume 5 of *A Mediterranean Society* (ix–xviii).

14. On the notion of the "production of history," see Cohen, *The Combing of History*.

15. Paul Rabinow, "Representations Are Social Facts: Modernity and Post-Modernity in Anthropology," in Clifford and Marcus *Writing Culture*, 234–61.

16. See Clifford and Marcus, *Writing Culture*; James Clifford, *The Predicament of Culture: Twentieth Century Ethnography, Literature, and Art* (Cambridge: Harvard University Press, 1988); George Marcus and Michael M. J. Fischer, *Anthropology as Cultural Critique: An Experimental Moment in the Human Sciences* (Chicago: University of Chicago Press, 1986); Hayden White, *The Content of the Form: Narrative Discourse and Historical Representation* (Baltimore: Johns Hopkins University Press, 1987); Michel de Certeau, *The Writing of History*, trans. Tom Conley (New York: Columbia University Press, 1988).

17. Fieldwork has always been the major initiation ritual in the discipline of anthropology. It is the fact that the anthropologist has "been there" and lived among the "natives" that is presumed to give the scholar the necessary scientific authority. For a critique of the presuppositions of this tradition, see the essays in Clifford and Marcus, *Writing Culture*, in particular, Mary Louise Pratt, "Fieldwork in Common Places," 27–50.

18. Ghosh, "Slave of MS. H.6," 176–77.

19. See, for instance, Samir Dayal, "The Emergence of the Fragile Subject: Amitav Ghosh's *In an Antique Land*," in Monika Fludernik, ed., *Hybridity and Postcolonialism: Twentieth Century Indian Literature* (Germany: Stauffenburg, 1998), 103–33; Hind Wassef, "Beyond the Divide: History and National Boundaries in the Work of Amitav Ghosh," *Journal of Comparative Poetics* 18 (1998): 75–95; Javed Majeed, "Amitav Ghosh's *In an Antique Land*: The Ethnographer-Historian and the Limits of Irony," *Journal of Commonwealth Literature* 30, no. 2 (1995): 45–55; and Indira Bhatt and Indira Nityanandam, eds., *The Fiction of Amitav Ghosh* (New Delhi: Creative, 2001).

20. It should be noted that such amusement signals an implicit primitivism rather like the humor created around the Coca Cola bottle in the popular movie *The Gods Must Be Crazy*.

21. Thus, for instance, when he proposes joining the villagers in their fast for Ramadan, he is told not to do so since he is not a Muslim. The villagers, despite their ridicule of his religious background, respect the boundaries of religious difference itself, while at the same time, as Nabeel's comment implies, putting less of a premium on the following of custom by those outside the fold. It is this that allows them to take Ghosh in even though he professes a religion other than their own.

22. The Milch Cow in Ancient Egypt, worshiped in the form of the Goddess Hathor, was said to be both the mother and the wife of the Sun. Likewise, in the Hindu pantheon, Brahma is said to have had two wives, Savitri and Gayatri. Savitri is said to be the mother of the Sun, while her co-wife Gayatri is often worshiped in the incarnation of a cow.

23. The relevance of the Pharaonic past to contemporary Egyptian identities has been the subject of much debate over the twentieth century. In this sense the invocation of *Antique* in the title of the book appears odd—Egyptian antiquity is almost completely absent in Ghosh's frame. For a concise account of the debates on Egyptian

identity and its pan-Arab, Islamist, and Pharaonic dimensions, see Ahmed Abdalla, "The Egyptian National Identity and Pan-Arabism: Variations and Generations," in Roel Meijer, ed., *Cosmopolitanism, Identity and Authenticity in the Middle East* (Surrey: Curzon), 171–81.

24. Ghosh's vision of the tolerance of Jews on the Malabar Coast during this period is confirmed by most of the scholarship. See Salo Wittmayer Baron, *A Social and Religious History of the Jews* (New York: Columbia University Press, 1983), 389–415, and Nathan Katz, *Who Are the Jews of India?* (Berkeley: University of California Press, 2000). However, the nature of the relations between Hindus and Muslims is open to debate. The fourteenth-century traveler Ibn Battuta notes the following about the Malabar Coast: "at every half-mile there is a wooden shed with benches on which all travellers, whether Muslims or infidels (read Hindu), may sit. At each shed there is a well for drinking and an infidel who is in charge of it. If the traveller is an infidel he gives him water in vessels; if he is a Muslim he pours water into his hands, continuing to do so until he signs him to stop. It is the custom of the infidels in the Mulaybar lands that no Muslim may enter their houses or eat from their vessels; if he does so they break the vessels or give them to the Muslims." Ibn Battuta, *Travels in Asia and Africa*, 231. Citing other scholars who have written on the period, Aditya Bhattacharjea argues that Ghosh's evocation of a "culture of accommodation and compromise" is a sanitized view of India's past. See Aditya Bhattacharjea, "Privileged Fiction: The Stephanian Novelists and (Their) Others," in Aditya Bhattacharjea and Lola Chatterjee, eds., *The Fiction of St. Stephen's* (Delhi: Ravi Dayal, 2000), 184–85 and n13 (167–206).

25. It is somewhat curious that the Imam does not bring up circumcision, especially since the imam, who in this community is also a barber, would by common practice also be the one who helped with the circumcision of young boys.

26. Ghosh, "The Imam and the Indian," 145.

27. In a volume of essays on the fiction of Indian writers such as Ghosh who were products of St. Stephen's College in Delhi, several contributors note that the representation of women and gender issues is often stilted in these narratives. An all-male college until 1975, these critics claim that St. Stephen's seems to have produced writers who were most comfortable in depicting scenarios of male bonding. There is much truth to this claim vis-à-vis *In an Antique Land*. The majority of the text revolves around male society, and no female character, with the possible exception of Busiana, gets sustained narrative space. Yet what is important is that we do learn about the Egyptian women who resist patriarchy even if we do not fully enter their point of view. The depiction of Ashu in the historical narrative is considerably more complicated, and we will turn to it later in the chapter. On the gendered aspects of the fiction of St. Stephen's writers, see the essays by Salim Yusufji and Brinda Bose in Bhattacharjea and Chatterjee, *The Fiction of St. Stephen's*: Salim Yusufji, "On Reading the Entrails," 71–78; Brinda Bose, "Of Voids and Speculums; Or, Where Is the Woman in This Text?" 135–50.

28. The Eurocentrism of the term *medieval* and the *Middle Ages* is evident when one remembers that, in its normative formulation, the period so designated is that

between the Classical world of Greek/Roman antiquity and the early modern and Renaissance world of Christian Europe. What were allegedly the "Dark Ages" for Europe were in fact the Glorious or Golden Age of Islam. For an articulation of how Eurocentric scholarship on the so-called medieval period might benefit from a recognition of this aporia and a consequent, alternative contrapuntal analysis of the Islamic world, see Cohen, "Introduction: Midcolonial." In a similar vein, for a consideration of the "middleness" of the Middle Ages, see Paul Freedman and Gabrielle M. Spiegel, "Medievalisms Old and New: The Rediscovery of Alterity in North American Medieval Studies," *American Historical Review* 103 (June 1998): 677–704; and Kathleen Biddick, *The Shock of Medievalism* (Durham: Duke University Press, 1998). For a discussion of how Christians in the Middle Ages themselves "read" Islam, see, R. W. Southern, *Western Views of Islam in the Middle Ages* (Cambridge: Harvard University Press, 1962).

29. On the rapid changes in the countryside resulting from the forces of globalization, see Galal Amin, *Whatever Happened to the Egyptians: Changes in Egyptian Society from 1950 to the Present* (Cairo: American University in Cairo Press, 2000).

30. Nicholas Dames, *Amnesiac Selves: Nostalgia, Forgetting and the British Nation, 1810–1870* (Oxford: Oxford University Press, 2001), 6.

31. Ibid, 7.

32. In the modern frame, the "cosmopolitanism" of Nabeel and his compatriots who travel to Iraq in search of employment is characterized by a similar melancholy.

33. For the anthropological literature on cultural "survivals," see Melville Herskovits, *The American Negro: A Study in Racial Crossing* (New York: Knopf, 1928); William Bascom and Melville Herskovits, eds., *Continuity and Change in African Cultures* (Chicago: University of Chicago Press, 1959).

34. For an excellent account of how different religious communities may participate in the "same" ritual, see Peter van der Veer, "Syncretism, Multiculturalism, and the Discourse of Tolerance," in Stewart and Shaw, *Syncretism/Anti-Syncretism*, 196–211. I am much indebted to this article and to this collection as a whole in my thinking through of the issues presented here. Van der Veer's article is also cited by Gauri Viswanathan in an important essay that advances a critique of Ghosh along lines similar to my own. However, in her case, the argument is drawn primarily on a theoretical register concerned with the "place of syncretism in the Post-Orientalist" project. Viswanathan's essay works best when it interrogates what she sees as the homologous nature of syncretism and "culture" in the sense given to it by Matthew Arnold. Discourses of "syncretism," Viswanathan rightly reminds us, are themselves inventions of the colonial imaginary and thus need to be used with caution in a postcolonial project. While I share her unease with the category, I have nonetheless found it to be indispensable in reading Ghosh's text on its own terms. The "syncretic" refers here to the cultural mixing and exchange that become for Ghosh a defining condition of the precolonial era. In my own reading of Ghosh, I point to the limits of such mixings and exchanges, but I do not wish to disregard entirely their presence either. How we read these syncretisms is, I suggest, key to understanding Ghosh's construction of history as nostalgia. As will become clearer

later, Viswanathan and I part company on our evaluation of the use of nostalgia in Ghosh. She sees this as a failure ("mere nostalgia"), whereas I find it redeeming. Readers who are interested in pursuing these issues further should benefit, as have I, from her analysis. See Viswanathan, "Beyond Orientalism."

35. An account of this episode is found in Goitein, *Jews and Arabs*, 182–84. The verdict, incidentally, was in favor of the worshipers.

36. Goitein dates the letter as having been written sometime between 1355 and 1367, thus at a later date than during Ben Yiju's own lifetime. Yet, given the fact that for Ghosh the division between the world of Ben Yiju and our own really only takes place in the late fifteenth century with the arrival of the Portuguese in the Indian Ocean, the letter still speaks to a time that he includes in his utopian frame. See Goitein, *A Mediterranean Society*, 5:471–74.

37. Ibid., 5:473–74. For ease of reading, I have omitted the internal notations that Goitein uses in his transcriptions of the letter.

38. Goitein, *Mediterranean Society*, 5:472.

39. There are other examples of the limits of the syncretic in the Geniza world. Thus, for instance, Goitein's work suggests that while the influence of Islamic Sufism on Judaism was definitely a reality, the form of that borrowing was very much in keeping with the fundamental tenets of Judaism. Goitein writes, "Despite the great dependence of medieval Jewish piety on Sufism, there was one point on which it parted company. Judaism never consented to blur the distinction between the Creator and the created. Love of God, emulation of God, nearness to him, longing for Him—yes; but union or identification with Him, this idea meant to Jews—at least to Jews living inside the Muslim civilization—nothing but blasphemy and self-deification." Goitein, *Jews and Arabs*, 153. In his notes, Ghosh cites Paul Fenton's translation of Obadyah Maimonides' text "The Treatise of the Pool." "Fenton's introduction," writes Ghosh, "provides an outline of Sufi influences on Jewish mysticism." Ghosh, *In an Antique Land*, 379. The introduction is indeed very good, however, it demonstrates not only the influences of Islam but also the antisyncretic and purist reactions to it on the part of some members of the Jewish community. See 'Obadyah Maimonides, *The Treatise of the Pool*, trans. Paul Fenton (London: Octagon, 1981), 1–71.

40. "Egypt Cancels Jewish Festival After Protests (Reuters)," *Jerusalem Post*, December 26, 2000, 5.

41. In other words, the rule of the Almohads in North Africa or the Egyptian Mamluks, who ruled subsequently, would present a different picture—a rather negative one—of interfaith relations between Jews and Muslims in the medieval world. The most readable and concise account of such variations is found in S. D. Goitein, "Interfaith Relations in Medieval Islam," Yaacov Herzog Memorial Lecture, delivered at Columbia University, New York, October 1973.

42. Cohen, "Islam and the Jews." The book in which this essay is included contains other essays in addition to Cohen's that would be of interest to Ghosh's readers.

43. By "performative" specificity I mean the ways in which religious beliefs are actually practiced, enforced, or, alternatively, ignored.

44. Goitein, A *Mediterranean Society*, 7:273–311.
45. Goitein, *Letters of Medieval Jewish Traders*, 214.
46. In his writings on his travels throughout the Mediterranean world, Benjamin of Tudela noted the cosmopolitan nature of the city of Alexandria. It was a point of convergence for merchants from all corners of the Indian and Mediterranean regions. In the notes to this section of his text, A. Asher discusses the fact that the trade was so important that religious warfare was, in its context, irrelevant:

> The enterprises of the Crusaders were directed against the powers of the sovereigns of this country, who consequently might be said to be at war with the whole of Europe; and it might have been reasonably supposed that all commercial and other intercourse should have ceased, but mutual interests and political considerations produced different results. The importation of asiatic goods had become a source of so much profit to the inhabitants and of revenue to the government, that the Sultans never contemplated the idea of closing their ports to the Europeans, who not only purchased, but also imported and paid duty upon those articles, which were made available objects of exchange in Arabia and India. Thus do we see religious prejudices waived in consideration of pecuniary profit, by the most inveterate enemies, by two sects, who took up arms in defence of the religions they professed!

> A. Asher, ed. and trans., *The Itinerary of Rabbi Benjamin of Tudela* (New York: Hakesheth, 1900), 2:217. The argument for the relationship between commerce and toleration is also made by M. G .S. Narayanan for the Kerala coast. Noting the fact that foreign traders were made welcome by the indigenous rulers of Kerala, Narayanan writes, "charity began at the marketplace." M. G. S. Narayanan, *Cultural Symbiosis in Kerala* (Trivandrum: Kerala Historical Society, 1972), 5.

47. Goitein, A *Mediterranean Society*, 2:ix (my emphasis).
48. Indeed, Goitein reads the intrusion of the state in trade as a prime cause of the breakdown of the Islamic Golden Age in the thirteenth century. "The conquest of Southwest Asia by the central-Asian Seldjuks ushered in a new period in Islamic history which was characterized by the oppressive rule of foreign mercenaries, propped up by closest cooperation with a well paid orthodox clergy and replacing free enterprise by a government-controlled state economy. In Egypt this state was reached by the middle of the thirteenth century, which was, according to the definition given before, the end of the classical period of Islam." Goitein, "Interfaith Relations in Medieval Islam," 27–28.
49. And it is carried over in much of the subsequent research undertaken by other scholars. Stefan C. Reif, for instance, echoes the sentiment in his book, A *Jewish Archive from Old Cairo*. He writes,

> On the domestic front, Fatimid achievements had their roots not so much in how the rulers directed their subjects but rather in the degree to which they permitted them to exercise their own initiatives. The energy, administrative ability and economic enterprise of Tunisians, Christians and Jews were given their head and major advantage thereby accrued to the state. At the same time, by their relatively liberal approach to the people and their skillful use of propaganda, the administra-

tion ensured that it remained internally tolerable and that no pretexts were given for outbursts of popular dissatisfaction.

Reif, *A Jewish Archive from Old Cairo,* 5.

50. Goitein, *A Mediterranean Society,* 2:66.

51. Thus, for instance, the early history of the "Commerce clause," which barred any disruption of interstate commerce, resulted in a desegregation of hotels and other facilities.

52. Usually transcribed as Qais, the island is in the Persian Gulf.

53. See Wink, *Al-Hind,* 1:56. See, also, S. D. Goitein, "Two Eyewitness Reports on an Expedition of the King of Kish (Qais) against Aden," *Bulletin of the School of Oriental and African Studies* 16, no. 2 (1954): 247–57.

54. Goitein, "Two Eyewitness Reports," 247 (my emphasis). At a later point in the article, Goitein refers to the Persian Gulf as "the sea *controlled* by the King of Kish" (252, my emphasis).

55. Unfortunately, the research on Indian Ocean pirates in this period is still minimal, but comparative studies of piracy and privateering (that alliance established between a state and pirates) in later periods and other contexts are informative. For the Indian Ocean, I have found most useful Charles Davies, *The Blood-Red Arab Flag: An Investigation into Qasimi Piracy, 1797–1820* (Exeter: University of Exeter Press, 1997). I cannot claim sufficient expertise in the area to judge the merits of its rebuttals of earlier scholarship on the Qasimi, but the book is an excellent staging ground for precisely the kinds of definitional and indeed conceptual differences that arise in discussions surrounding "piracy." Thus we can see that, depending on their ideological or historical orientations, one commentator's "pirate" is another commentator's "privateer" who is yet another commentator's "warrior." For scholarship on piracy in other contexts, see, in particular, Marcus Rediker, *Between the Devil and the Deep Blue Sea: Merchant Seamen, Pirates and the Anglo-American Maritime World, 1700–1750* (Cambridge: Cambridge University Press, 1987); David Starkey, Jap de Moor, and E. S. van Eyck van Heslinga, *Pirates and Privateers: New Perspectives on the War on Trade in the Eighteenth and Nineteenth Centuries* (Exeter: University of Exeter Press, 1997); C. R. Pennell, ed., *Bandits at Sea: A Pirates Reader* (New York: New York University Press, 2001).

56. Chaudhuri, *Trade and Civilisation in the Indian Ocean,* 60.

57. On the *cartazes,* see Curtin, *Cross-Cultural Trade in World History,* 139–40.

58. Wink, *Al-Hind,* 1:92.

59. Goitein's article on the subject, "Two Eyewitness Accounts," suggests that one of the other reasons for the attack on Aden by the ruler of Qais "may have been the fact that owing to the rapacious character of his rule, much of the Indian Ocean trade had been diverted from the sea of Oman to Aden." Goitein, "Two Eyewitness Accounts," 248. I quote this because it once again points to Goitein's implicit understanding of the mutual dependence of trade and state power. Let all future rulers beware—this sentence at one level says—if the character of your rule is "rapacious," you too will lose your commerce to other rulers.

60. Subject to some debate has been the role of Sudanese gold in the prosperity of

North African rulers. While he himself takes the position that the role of gold—and particularly of the disruption of its northwards flow in the eleventh century—has been overplayed, Michael Brett's article on Ifriqiya and its Saharan trade is a useful reminder that the Indian Ocean trade was integrated not only with a Mediterranean economy looking toward Europe but also with an African economy looking to the south. See Michael Brett, "Ifriqiya as a Market for Saharan Trade from the Tenth to the Twelfth Century, a.d.," *Journal of African History* 10, no. 3 (1969): 347–64.

61. A. Paul, *A History of the Beja Tribes of the Sudan* (London: Frank Cass, 1971 [1954]), 71. For a discussion of the importance of Sudanese slaves to the Egyptian rulers, see Bernard Lewis, *Race and Slavery in the Middle East* (New York: Oxford University Press, 1990), 9, 14, 66–69.

62. For a visual documentary on the Zar ritual, see Hani Fakhouri, dir. and prod., *The Zar* (1988, videocassette).

63. Goitein, *Jews and Arabs*, 100–6.

64. The phrase "structures of feeling" is from Raymond Williams. See Raymond Williams, *Marxism and Literature* (Oxford: Oxford University Press, 1977), 128–35.

65. An early comprehensive study of the institution as well as a critique of prevalent modes of discussing it is found in Gordon, *Slavery in the Arab World*. In recent years, the subject has received careful treatment by scholars interested in Indian Ocean studies. See in particular, Campbell, *The Structure of Slavery* and *Abolition and Its Aftermath*.

66. Goitein notes at one point that, in Ben Yiju's time, the word "'abd,' or slave, was increasingly considered improper and was often replaced with euphemisms such as 'boy' or 'young man.' Since these terms could be equally applied to free persons as well as slaves, it is often difficult to establish the legal status of a given individual." See Goitein, *A Mediterranean Society*, 1:131.

67. Rosenthal, *The Muslim Concept of Freedom*, 92, 30n71.

68. Patterson, *Slavery and Social Death*.

69. Popovic, *The Revolt of African Slaves in Iraq*; see also Ronald Segal, *Islam's Black Slaves* (New York: Farrar, Straus and Giroux, 2001).

70. Isaac Klein, ed. and trans., *The Code of Maimonides, Book Twelve: The Book of Acquisition* (New Haven: Yale University Press, 1951), 266.

71. Goitein, *A Mediterranean Society*, 1:133. See also Goitein's transcription of a letter detailing the event in *Letters of Medieval Jewish Traders*, 335–38.

72. I use the masculine pronoun here because the slaves who did acquire some social status were business agents who were male. Female slaves were primarily domestic servants or concubines.

73. In his presentation of the relationship between Ben Yiju and Ashu, Ghosh seems to be aware that his reading it as a sign of an interracial romance is probably a stretch of the imagination. Referring to the union, he writes, "If I hesitate to call it love, it is only because the documents offer no certain proof." Ghosh, *In an Antique Land*, 230.

74. In other words, despite their subaltern status, both the fictional Taratibu and the

historical Ashu enter the pages of Vassanji and Ghosh's texts respectively. In so doing the texts at least set up a number of possible scenarios for readers to contemplate in terms of their lives. In contrast, the twelfth-century slave woman (and perhaps her child) abandoned on the coast of Somalia by Ibn Jumahir receives no mention in Ghosh's text, thus remaining absent to modern readers.

3. POST-MANICHAEAN AESTHETICS

1. See Edmund Burke, "Speech in the Impeachment of Warren Hastings," in Gaurav Desai and Supriya Nair, eds., *Postcolonialisms: An Anthology of Cultural Theory and Criticism* (New Brunswick: Rutgers University Press, 2005), 34 (25–34).

2. Bartle Frere, "Memorandum Regarding Banians or Natives of India in East Africa," March 31, 1873, quoted in Metcalf, *Imperial Connections*, 166. Metcalf's book is an excellent companion piece to this chapter. There are numerous historical studies and surveys of Asians in East Africa. I list some of the more useful ones. For a history of Indian presence over the centuries, the most comprehensive is "Introduction: Historical Perspective" in S. A. I. Tirmizi, *Indian Sources for African History, vol. 1.* (New Delhi: UNESCO and Indian Writers Emporium, 1988), 1–42. For Indians in East Africa, see Gregory, *India and East Africa*; Dharam P. Ghai and Yash P. Ghai, eds., *Portrait of a Minority: Asians in East Africa* (Oxford: Oxford University Press, 1965); Gregory, *Quest for Equality*; Mangat, *A History of the Asians in East Africa*; Seidenberg, *Mercantile Adventurers*; R. Nagar, "The South Asian Diaspora in Tanzania: A History Retold," *Comparative Studies of South Asia, Africa and the Middle East: A Journal of Politics, Culture, Economy* 16, no. 2 (1996): 1–19; Savita Nair, "Shops and Stations: Rethinking Power and Privilege in British/Indian East Africa," in Hawley, *India in Africa, Africa in India*, 77–93.

3. Burton, *Zanzibar*, 1:316.

4. Ibid., 1:327–39.

5. W. Cope Devereux, *A Cruise in the "Gorgon," or Eighteen Months on H.M.S. "Gorgon" Engaged in the Suppression of the Slave Trade on the East Coast of Africa* (London: Bell and Daldy, 1869), 97.

6. Ibid., 101.

7. Johnston, "The Asiatic Colonization of East Africa," 170.

8. Lugard, *The Rise of Our East African Empire*, 1:489.

9. Lugard was yet to write his best-known work, *The Dual Mandate in British Tropical Africa* (Edinburgh: Blackwood, 1922).

10. Lugard, *The Rise of Our East African Empire*, 1:488.

11. See Morison, "A Colony for India"; see also Sydenham of Combe, "The Future of India: India as a Colonising Power," *Nineteenth Century* 84 (1918): 762–70; Lepper, "An America for the Hindu"; Aga Khan, *India in Transition* (London: Bennett, Coleman, 1918), 128. Claims for Indian colonization were to appear yet again in 1946 and 1951 when Tanganyika was proposed as a place to resettle South African Indians. On this see James Brennan, "South Asian Nationalism in an East African

Context: The Case of Tanganyika, 1914–1956," *Comparative Studies of South Asia, Africa and the Middle East* 19, no. 2 (1999): 30–31 (24–38).

12. Churchill, *My African Journey*, 32.

13. However, when Churchill later became secretary of state in 1921, he was less friendly to Indian interests and proclaimed that he intended Kenya to become a "characteristically and distinctively British colony" (quoted in Gregory, *India and East Africa*, 213). For a discussion of what Robert Gregory calls "Churchill's Vacillation," see *India and East Africa*, 198–222.

14. Churchill, *My African Journey*, 36.

15. Ibid., 37.

16. Ibid.

17. Traveller, "'Muddling Through' in British Tropical Africa," *Empire Review* 18 (1910): 266 (258–268).

18. Ibid., 267.

19. Hyde Clark, untitled response, *Journal of the Society of Arts* 37 (February 1, 1889): 173.

20. General Smuts noted,

> I think that every thinking man is South Africa takes the attitude that an Indian is not inferior to us because of his colour or any other ground. He may be our superior. It is the case of a small [European] civilization, a small community finding itself in danger of being overwhelmed by a much older and more powerful civilization. . . . You cannot blame these pioneers, these very small communities in South Africa and Central Africa, if they put up every possible fight for the civilization which they started, their own European civilization. They are not there to foster Indian civilization. They are there to foster Western civilization and they regard as a very serious matter anything that menaces their position which is already endangered by the many difficulties which surround them in Africa.

Quoted in Waiz, *Indians Abroad*, 510.

21. Mangal Dass, "Defense to Allegation," on behalf of the Indian Association, Nairobi, April 18, 1921, reprinted in East African Standard, *The Indian Problem in Kenya*, 15 (15–16).

22. Dass, "Defense to Allegation," 16;

23. Letter from M. A. Desai to the editor of the *East African Standard*; Reprinted in East African Standard, *The Indian Problem in Kenya*, 21 (21–22).

24. Andrews, *The Indian Question in East Africa*.

25. Here Andrews quotes from the Kenyan settler Major Grogan who once wrote, "We have stolen the African's lands. Now we must steal his limbs." Ibid., 75–76.

26. Andrews, not surprisingly, was not received quite as warmly by the white settlers as he was by the Bugandans. McGregor Ross notes, "One brawny European fellow-passenger assaulted him at several successive stations on a journey on the Uganda railway when he was going up the line, and only the miscarriage of a telegram interfered with a concerted assault upon him by a troupe of patriots on his return journey." Ross, *Kenya from Within*, 351.

27. Lord Delamere and Kenneth Archer, *Memorandum on the Case Against the Claim of Indians in Kenya*, in East African Standard, *The Indian Problem in Kenya*, 11 (5–13).

28. M. A. Desai to Prime Minister et al., telegram, July 21, 1921; quoted in Gregory, *India and East Africa*, 203.

29. "Resolutions of the East African Association" July 10, 1921, reprinted in Thuku, *An Autobiography*, 82.

30. See Gregory, *India and East Africa*, 205, 294.

31. Kyle, "Gandhi, Harry Thuku." For a short biography of Desai, see Chanan Singh, "Manilal Ambalal Desai," in Kenneth King and Ahmed Salim, eds., *Kenya Historical Biographies* (Nairobi: East African, 1971), 139–41.

32. So, for instance, the degrading system of the *kipande* (passes) for Africans is presented by Thuku right after he describes the racial insult suffered by M. A. Desai when his white employer castigates him for smoking in a European area (Thuku, *An Autobiography*, 18–19). The letters between Thuku and Desai included as appendixes in Thuku's published autobiography suggest a warmth between them.

33. See Desai's letter to Thuku dated May 7, 1922: "I told your mother that Abdullah and myself were to be regarded as just like her own son Harry (you) and she can come to us for news about you or for anything she wants and she was very pleased to hear that. I also told her that I will do my best to get you released at the earliest possible date. I gave her Florins 6 to meet her present requirements. She did not want more just now. She said she may require some help to pay Hut Tax and if so she would come when she wants it." Thuku, *An Autobiography*, 94. See also Thuku's own account of his jail experience:

> But it was a difficult time for my Indian friends; the police raided the offices of Mr. Desai, and also of his paper, *The East African Chronicle*. You see, they wanted to arrest people like Desai, Shams-ud-deen, and Mangal Dass, but they could not find any proof against them unless they used me. That is why the first night in prison in Nairobi, I got word that if I said that those three men had really engineered my whole protest and my Association, then they would let me off. I saw that this was a bluff to put them in along with me. I told them, "If you want to arrest my 'guilty' friends, then start earlier with the Europeans—especially the dangerous ones who taught me English!'"

In Thuku, *An Autobiography*, 38.

34. Both letters are reprinted in Waiz, *Indians Abroad*, 147–48.

35. Quoted in Kyle, "Gandhi, Harry Thuku," 18.

36. Twaddle, "Z. K. Sentongo and the Indian Question." For a contextualization of *Sekanyolya*, see James F. Scotton, "The First African Press in East Africa: Protest and Nationalism in Uganda in the 1920s," *International Journal of African Historical Studies* 6, no. 2 (1973): 211–28. See also Sana Aiyar, "Empire, Race and the Indians in Colonial Kenya's Contested Public Political Sphere, 1919–1923," *Africa* 81, no. 1 (2011): 132–54. In her discussion of Thuku, Aiyar further contextualizes Sentogo's position as well as that of other Africans who resisted such an alliance with Indians.

37. I should note that even this formulation does not entirely capture the complexities, since it sidelines the often tense negotiations of identity surrounding the Arab community in Zanzibar and much of the coastal areas of East Africa. The Zanzibar revolution was cast in terms of the politics of race and indigeneity with the Afro-Shirazi party calling for the ouster of Arabs and South Asians who were both seen as privileged immigrant communities. For a compelling recent account of the production and circulation of racial identities in Zanzibar, see Glassman, *War of Words, War of Stones*.

38. This claim will be familiar to readers of the important collection edited by Cooper and Stoler, *Tensions of Empire*.

39. Fanon, *The Wretched of the Earth*, 41.

40. Naipaul, *A Bend in the River*, 124.

41. Joseph, *Nomadic Identities*, 2.

42. There has been increasing interest in this history among Asians in East Africa as well Asian Africans in the diaspora, not least because of the work of Salvadori who is often cited as an inspiration. In terms of official recognition, one might note the special exhibit devoted to the "Asian African Heritage" by the National Museums of Kenya in 2000. See Nowrojee, *The Asian African Heritage*.

43. Salvadori writes, "(I tried very hard to get stories of con-men and crooks, but . . .)." Salvadori, *We Came in Dhows*, 3:193.

44. *Transition* 34 (1968): 6.

45. Theroux, "Hating the Asians."

46. Naipaul, *North of South*, 108.

47. In an important essay published in the wake of Idi Amin's expulsion of Asians from Uganda, "Black Attitudes to the Brown and White Colonizers of East Africa," the Ugandan political scientist Dent Ocaya-Lakidi asked, how did the Asians in East Africa end up getting the worst of black African ire when in fact it was the white British who were the true colonizers of East Africa? How did the whites, who were "culturally arrogant, politically dominating as well as patronizing and economically exploitative," end up being more highly regarded than the Asians? (81). Ocaya-Lakidi suggested three factors to explain this historical development—first, he noted, "the so-called African attitudes to Asians are in fact European attitudes that were assimilated and internalized by the Africans" (82), second, the Asians "were manipulated to serve the colonizer's economic interests by acting as middlemen between the white colonizers and the black Africans" (82) and third, the Asians' own "social customs and ways of life" (82) which were exclusionary and insular led to African resentment. Ocaya-Lakidi goes on in the article to document how the relatively superior material culture of the West was backed by an explicit ideology of a "civilizing mission," a mission to which Asians had little to no claim. The role of missionaries in this imperial project was by no means uncertain-Christianity provided not only the promise of a better life in the world to come, but also access to European style literacy and education that offered a better life in more immediate terms. Even if Asians had chosen to engage in a conscious civilizing mission, they would not have been likely to have many takers. The moral puritanism of the East,

suggested Ocaya-Lakidi, would have repelled Africans. See Ocaya-Lakidi, "Black Attitudes to the Brown and White Colonizers of East Africa."

48. Or, as Salim was to put it in *A Bend in the River*, "The Europeans wanted gold and slaves, like everybody else; but at the same time they wanted statues put up to themselves as people who had done good things for the slaves. Being an intelligent and energetic people, and at the peak of their powers, they could express both sides of their civilization; and they got both the slaves and the statues." Naipaul, *A Bend in the River*, 17.

49. Taban Lo Liyong, *The Last Word*, 34.

50. Simon Gikandi, "The Growth of the East African Novel," in G. D. Killam, ed., *The Writing of East and Central Africa* (Nairobi: East African, 1984), 231 (231–46); Gregory, "Literary Development in East Africa."

51. Gregory, "Literary Development in East Africa," 442.

52. Kuldip Sondhi, *Undesignated and Other Plays* (New Delhi: Orient Longman, 1973); Kuldip Sondhi, *With Strings* in Cosmo Pieterse, ed., *Ten One-Act Plays* (London: Heinemann, 1968), 135–66; Jagjit Singh, *Sweet Scum of Freedom* in Gwyneth Henderson, ed., *African Theatre: Eight Prize-Winning Plays for Radio* (London: Heinemann, 1973), 156–59; Jagjit Singh, "Portrait of an Asian as an East African," in David Cook and David Rudabiri, ed., *Poems from East Africa* (London: Heinemann, 1971), 156–59; Amin Kassam, "Metamorphosis," in Wole Soyinka, ed., *Poems from Black Africa* (New York: Hill and Wang, 1975), 117; Bahadur Tejani, "Leaving the Country," ibid., 190–91; Tejani, *Day After Tomorrow*; Nazareth, *In a Brown Mantle*; Kuldip Sondhi, *Sunil's Dilemma*, in Gwyneth Henderson and Cosmo Pieterse, eds., *Nine African Plays for Radio* (London: Heinemann, 1973), 1–23. A more comprehensive bibliography of Asian writing in both East as well as South Africa can be found in the appendix to Gaurav Desai, "Asian African Literatures: Genealogies in the Making," *Research in African Literatures* 42, no. 3 (2011), v–xxx.

53. "A Literary Organ," *Indian Voice* (Nairobi, Kenya), May 15, 1912, n.p.

54. "Municipal Committee," *East African Standard*, July 24, 1915, 22.

55. "Indian Drama: Monday Night's Entertainment," *East African Standard*, January 18, 1918, 8.

56. "Standard Notes," *East African Standard*, March 7, 1914, 15.

57. "Indian Drama," *East African Standard*, December 19, 1914, 19.

58. "Hindu Theatricals at Mombasa," *East African Standard*, January 6, 1914, 4.

59. J. H. Patterson, *The Man-Eaters of Tsavo* (New York: Pocket Books, 1996), 185–90. This poem is the only document that I have come across that was definitely penned by Indian indentured laborers in East Africa. There may be others, but I don't know of their existence. One of the regrets in framing this study has been the paucity of first-person narratives of indentured laborers in this region. For a comparative context, see the excellent study by Marina Carter, *Voices from Indenture: Experiences of Indian Migrants in the British Empire* (New York: Leicester University Press, 1996); and Marina Carter and Khal Torabully, *Coolitude: An Anthology of the Indian Labor Diaspora* (London: Anthem, 2002).

60. A similar story can be told about the literary activities of Indians in South Africa. A brief discussion can be found in Desai, "Asian African Literatures."

61. "Message from the Prince," *Supplement to the Indian Voice*, 1912 (sometime after September 20), n.p.

62. "To Africa," *Indian Voice*, April 19, 1911, 6.

63. "An Appreciation," *Indian Voice*, April 26, 1911, n.p.

64. P. S. Joshi, "Literature of South African Indians," in Ellen Hellman, ed., *Handbook of Race Relations in South Africa* (New York: Oxford, 1949), 614 (612–14).

65. For some of this history, see Peter Benson, *Black Orpheus, Transition, and the Modern Cultural Awakening in Africa* (Berkeley: University of California Press, 1986).

66. While Asian writing in East Africa has been on the literary radar since the sixties, it was the 1989 publication of M. G. Vassanji's *The Gunny Sack*, which received the Commonwealth Writers Prize for the Africa region, that prompted a renewed interest on the part of Asian writers of East African origin to narrate facets of that experience in both fictional as well as semi-autobiographical form. Many (though not all) of the newer authors write, as does Vassanji himself, from a base in the West, and their writings are informed by the politics of multiculturalism and citizenship they encounter in their new homes. There is also a noticeable gender shift with more women writers entering the scene, writers such as Yasmin Alibhai-Brown, Jameela Siddiqi, Sikeena Karmali, Parita Mukta, Zarina Patel, Rasna Warah, and Neera Kapur-Dromson. The richly textured narratives that they each offer greatly enhance the palimpsest that is the Asian experience in East Africa and its diaspora. Likewise, writing by South African Indian writers has also mushroomed over the past few decades. The rapidly growing interest in South African Indian literature among critics is perhaps best marked by the publication of three monographs on the subject (Govinden, Rastogi, Frenkel) published within a span of two years. These books, along with works such as Rajendra Chetty's *South African Indian Writings in English* (Durban: Madiba, 2002), which collects a number of literary works as well as interviews with authors, are significant contributions not only to our understanding of South African Indian literary production but also to the production of social identities in apartheid and postapartheid South Africa. See Devarakshnam Govinden, *'Sister, Outsider': The Representation of Identity and Difference in Selected Writings by South African Indian Women* (Pretoria: UNISA, 2008); Rastogi, *Afrindian Fictions*; Ronit Frenkel, *Reconsiderations: South African Indian Fiction and the Making of Race in Postcolonial Culture* (Pretoria: UNISA, 2010).

67. Alidina Somjee Lilani, *A Guide to the Swahili Language in Gujarati Characters* (Bombay: Education Society, 1890), 7.

68. Sadru Kassam, *Bones*, in David Cook and Miles Lee, eds., *Short East African Plays in English* (London: Heinemann, 1968), 125–31.

69. Abdulaziz Lodhi, *Oriental Influences in Swahili: A Study in Language and Culture Contacts* (Goteburg: Acta Universitatis Gothoburgensis, 2000), 78.

70. Vanoo Jivraj Somia, *A History of the Indians of East Africa* (Derbyshire: Country, 2001), 159–60.

71. Cynthia Salvadori, *Through Open Doors: A View of Asian Cultures in Kenya*, ed. Andrew Fedders (Nairobi: Kenway, 1989 [1983]), 335.
72. Kapur-Dromson, *From Jhelum to Tana*, 292–94.
73. Patel, *Unquiet*, 32.

4. THROUGH INDIAN EYES

1. Taylor, *Sources of the Self*, 35.
2. The term *relational selves* appears as a chapter title in Moore-Gilbert's recent study, *Postcolonial Life-Writing*, 17–33. In addition to Moore-Gilbert, I have also found useful Smith and Watson, *Reading Autobiography*.
3. Here I adapt Judith Butler's notion of gender as performative to consider the performance of ethnicity. Butler writes that gender performance is an act "which has been rehearsed, much as a script survives the particular actors who make use of it, but which requires individual actors in order to be actualized and reproduced as reality once again . . . just as the play requires both text and interpretation, so the gendered body acts its part in a culturally restricted corporeal space and enacts interpretations within the confines of already existing directives." Judith Butler, "Performative Acts and Gender Constitutions: An Essay in Phenomenology and Gender Constitution," in Sue Ellen Case, ed., *Performing Feminisms: Feminist Critical Theory and Theatre* (Baltimore: Johns Hopkins Univ. Press, 1990), 277 (270–82).
4. See Bhabha, *The Location of Culture*, 85–92.
5. The only exception that I have come across is a brief paragraph on Adamji in an essay by Stephanie Jones. Jones finds the text to be a "monotonous and precise account of every transaction, meal and travel arrangement, with particular attention paid on the just-completed railway." I hope to show that behind the tedious details one can read a fascinating performance of ethnic identity. See Stephanie Jones, "Merchant-Kings and Everymen: Narratives of the South Asian Diaspora of East Africa," *Journal of East African Studies* 1, no.1 (2007): 22 (16–33).
6. The fact that Adamji's family played a supporting role in British colonial atrocities is noteworthy here, since it validates the claims of critics who point to Indian complicity with British colonialism. But having noted such complicity, we should not remain inattentive to other aspects of Adamji's life story. If we are to have a nuanced sense of history, we need to read all kinds of lives, even those marked by political choices that are, in retrospect, appalling. In addition to the editorial material in this edition, see the account of the Adamjee family entitled "150 Years of Trading in Mombasa," by J. Aldrick (with Gulamali and Abdulhassan E. Noorbhai Adamjee), in Salvadori, *We Came in Dhows*, 1:56–57.
7. Baluchis (or Balochs, as the text names them) were men from the Persian side of the Gulf of Oman, many of whom had first come to East Africa as soldiers employed by the sultan of Zanzibar.
8. In his early years in South Africa, Gandhi writes that he encouraged his wife and children to wear Parsi-style clothing: "The Parsis used then to be regarded as the

most civilized people amongst Indians, and so, when the complete European style seemed to be unsuited, we adopted the Parsi style. Accordingly my wife wore the Parsi *sari* and the boys the Parsi coat and trousers." Gandhi, *Autobiography*, 162.

9. Salvadori and Aldrick, *Two Indian Travellers*, 185–86.

10. Ebrahimji's father, Noorbhai Alibhai, and his eldest brother Jivanji died in 1887 while on a pilgrimage to Mecca, leaving the eldest surviving son Alibhai as the head of the household. Salvadori and Aldrick, *Two Indian Travellers*, 76.

11. At one point, we learn, for instance, that Adamji's porters carry him and his belongings from Kampala to Entebbe, a distance of approximately twenty miles, in eleven hours on one day. Even with breaks, given the fact that each man is carrying a heavy load of ivory, other equipment, or Adamji himself, that is a physically demanding day! For a nuanced history of caravan porterage in East Africa, see Stephen J. Rockel, *Carriers of Culture: Labor on the Road in Nineteenth-Century East Africa* (Portsmouth, NH: Heinemann, 2006).

12. Pratt, *Imperial Eyes*, 69.

13. On the Indian trade in clothing in Kavirondo, Daniel Hall reported in 1930, "Ten years ago most of the Kavirondo natives went mother naked; now they are all clothed in cotton-prints bought from the Indian traders and made on Bombay looms. Manchester seems to be too much interested in the politics of the African native to care to clothe him." Daniel Hall, "The Native Question in Kenya," *Nineteenth Century* 107 (1930): 70–80 (75).

14. The term *Kavirondo* was used at the time to refer to ethnic groups in Kenya around Lake Victoria.

15. Steve Clark notes, "Travel writing . . . is founded upon an almost irresistible imperative to abandon home, wife and children." Steve Clark, "Introduction," in Clark, *Travel Writing and Empire*, 20 (1–28). We will see this again in the case of Nanji Kalidas Mehta's narrative in the next chapter.

16. Gregory, *India and East Africa*, 68–69.

17. Sorabji takes a certain amount of pleasure in narrating the way in which he has led the German on: "I had never let him guess how much I was worth and he assumed I was a very wealthy man, and every time he talked about his great plans I used to encourage him . . . When he came back he again begged me to join him. At that time I told him that it was not possible for me to join him because I could not leave my family." Salvadori and Aldrick, *Two Indian Travellers*, 124.

18. I use the term *African* in the pages that follow to refer to indigenous black Africans, just as I use the terms *Indian* and *Asian* in their colloquial usage. The larger point of my project is, of course, to rethink all of these terms—to think both of Africa as a multiracial space and to recognize that the Indian or Asian in Africa is best thought in Afrasian terms.

19. While Sorabji is a Parsi and not Goan, it is useful to compare his self-fashioning as a European with a note by Cynthia Salvadori on the reading of Goans in colonial Kenyan society. She writes: "Because Goans, who were mostly educated clerks, could not be called 'coolies,' they were sometimes classified as 'white men'—even in the caption of a photograph of seven people who were the 'first white men to settle in and around Nairobi' in which one of the two Goans, da Silva, is con-

spicuously dark and the other, his cousin Elvira, a woman!" Cynthia Salvadori, "Introduction," in Salvadori, *We Came in Dhows*, 1:x.

20. James Scott, *Weapons of the Weak: Everyday forms of Peasant Resistance* (New Haven: Yale University Press, 1985).

21. Hammond and Jablow, *The Africa That Never Was*, 11.

22. The book referred to is Sir Harry Johnston, *The Uganda Protectorate*.

23. Sorabji writes, "When I looked at the coffee he was growing, it was inferior to 'Mocha,' 'Berbera' and 'Hodeida' coffee but superior to the coffee of Hindustan. If you have not experienced the taste of the other three coffees I have mentioned, then you would find the 'Uganda' coffee to be a very good drink." Salvadori and Aldrick, *Two Indian Travellers*, 128.

24. "They are humble and liberal to the strong armed Arab, savage and murderous and cannibalistic to small bands, and every slain man provides a banquet of meat for the forest natives of Manyema." Henry Morton Stanley, *Through the Dark Continent*, vol. 2 (London: Sampson Low, Marston, Searle and Rivington, 1978), 86. Hammond and Jablow write, "A new fillip was added to the beastly savage conventions by many sensational tales of cannibalism. There had been, earlier, minimal interest in the subject, though it had been occasionally reported. . . . Exploitation of the theme began in the mid-nineteenth century. Stanley was carried away in his zealous horror of anthropophagy and repeated every tale of cannibal tribes that he heard in addition to creating quite a number of his own." Hammond and Jablow, *The Africa That Never Was*, 94.

25. Hammond and Jablow, *The Africa That Never Was*, 95.

26. For different positions in this debate, see, Mangat, *A History of the Asians of East Africa*, 23–25. See also, N. Benjamin, "Trading Activities of Indians in East Africa (with Special Reference to Slavery) in the Nineteenth Century," *Indian Economic and Social History Review* 35, no. 4 (1998): 405–19; Chizuko Tominaga, "Indian Immigrants and the East African Slave Trade," *Essays in Northeast African Studies* 43 (1996): 295–317.

27. See Gregory, *India and East Africa*, 26; Seidenberg, *Mercantile Adventurers*, 63.

28. Of the many debates on the nature of cosmopolitanism that have emerged of late, I am most indebted to Bhabha, "Unsatisfied"; and Appiah, *Cosmopolitanism*.

29. Bart Moore-Gilbert notes that such linguistic heteroglossia is a relatively common feature of colonial and postcolonial life narratives. See Moore-Gilbert, *Postcolonial Life-Writing*, 91–94.

30. See Sheriff, *Dhow Cultures of the Indian Ocean*. See also Bose and Manjapra, *Cosmopolitan Thought Zones*.

31. See Chakrabarty, *Provincializing Europe*.

5. COMMERCE AS ROMANCE

1. Mangat, "Was Allidina Visram a Robber Baron?"

2. Salvadori suggests an age of fifteen. For a slightly revised and updated biography of Visram see Seidenberg, *Mercantile Adventures*, 66 (65–69).

3. The list of charitable contributions is in Mangat, "Was Allidina Visram a Robber Baron?" 35; The estimated amount is from Gregory, *The Rise and Fall of Philanthropy in East Africa*, 51–52.

4. The Madhvani Group does not list total international assets on its corporate Web site. In addition to the Uganda enterprises, the group has business interests in several African countries, Europe, Asia, the Middle East, and North America.

5. Seidenberg, *Mercantile Adventures*, 69.

6. See Weber, *The Protestant Ethic and the Spirit of Capitalism* (New York: Penguin, 2002). For a brief rebuttal of Weber's position as well as informative essays on Indian entrepreneurship from the seventeenth century, see Makrand Mehta, *Indian Merchants and Entrepreneurs in Historical Perspective* (Delhi: Academic Foundation, 1991).

7. Subrahmanyam, "Foreword," vii (vi–ix).

8. And other Kenyans as well. I was told by a Kenyan friend that the inaugural issue of the in-flight magazine of Kenya Airways had a lead article on Allidina Visram as an inveterate traveler. I have not been able to verify this myself. Visram has also been memorialized in a biographical novel: M. G. Visram, *Allidina Visram: The Trailblazer* (Nairobi: Visram, 1990).

9. In the article, Oonk draws on the Zanzibar archives to relate stories of Asian bankruptcies and other business failures. Gijsbert Oonk, "South Asians in East Africa (1880–1920) with a Particular Focus on Zanzibar: Toward a Historical Explanation of Economic Success of a Middlemen Minority," *African and Asian Studies* 5, no. 1 (2006): 57–89.

10. So, for instance, in V. S. Naipaul's novel *A Bend in the River*, the character Nazruddin finds himself explaining to a Canadian businessman who has cheated him: "My family have been traders and merchants in the Indian Ocean for centuries, under every kind of government. There is a reason why we have lasted so long. We bargain hard, but we stick to our bargain. All our contracts are oral, but we deliver what we promise. It isn't because we are saints. It is because the whole thing breaks down otherwise." Naipaul, *A Bend in the River*, 236.

11. As in Weber's discussion of the Protestant ethic, one form of the "culturalist" explanation focuses on alleged religious proclivities. An early warning against such readings in the East African context was made by Frederick Cooper in his seminal work, *Plantation Slavery on the East Coast of Africa*. Addressing the relative success of Indians over the Omanis in mercantile matters, Cooper writes, "A full explanation for Indian predominance as merchants and money-lenders must await further study of the Indian Ocean Commercial system and the Indian communities." To this he adds a footnote: "One explanation that is clearly incorrect is that the Islamic religion was the cause of the Omanis' lack of entrepreneurial vigor. Many of the Indians in Zanzibar, Tharia Topan included, were Muslim, and Islamic jurists have developed numerous ways of avoiding the Koranic restrictions on usury" (143). Again, while emphasizing the "culturalist" traits of a group's economic success can be inherently questionable, we must note that the identity of the group can also be an issue. While most discussions in the East African context focus on "Asian" commercial success, economic historians such as Claude Markovits remind us of

further distinctions among Asian communities. So, for instance, noting the comparative success of merchant communities from Kutch as opposed to other regions, Markovits writes, "However, it remains to be understood why the different merchant communities from Kutch were so uniformly successful in their commercial and financial ventures abroad. . . . Further inquiries into the 'Kutchi miracle' are obviously needed." Claude Markovits, "Indian Merchant Networks Outside India in the Nineteenth and Twentieth Centuries: A Preliminary Survey," *Modern Asian Studies* 33 no. 4 (1999): 899 (883–911).

12. Chege, "Paradigms of Doom" and "Introducing Race as a Variable." In addition to Chege's essays, see Paul Vandenberg, *The Asian-African Divide: Analyzing Institutions and Accumulation in Kenya* (New York: Routledge, 2006), for a further analysis of this issue. See also, on Himbara's book, Dickson Eyoh, "Review," *Canadian Journal of African Studies* 28, no.3 (1994): 538–40.

13. Robert Gregory writes about this tension in colonial times: "Most Asians thrived in circumstances in which there was a maximum of free enterprise. The British colonial governments, in contrast, pursued policies that involved, at least for the Africans, a strict regulation of the economy. As a result, the Africans throughout the colonial period were subjected to two powerful stimuli of social and economic change. One was the contact with the Asians, which from the outset drew them into a capitalistic form of economic endeavour. The other was their association with the government, which ultimately channelled much of their production and distribution into a socialistic system based on public agencies, parastatal companies, and co-operative societies. The Asians and the government were thus almost perpetually in conflict." Gregory, *South Asians in East Africa*, 2. On the effects of market legislation in colonial East Africa, J. S. Mangat notes, "Much of the restrictive marketing legislation introduced in the East African countries during the 1930s, apart from its immediate impact on Indian enterprise, in the long run prevented the rise of an African commercial class, and had in fact aroused considerable African opposition also, although the main justification for it, paradoxically enough, was the need to protect African interests." Mangat, *A History of the Asians in East Africa*, 167. See also Vali Jamal, "Asians in Uganda, 1880–1972: Inequality and Expulsion," *Economic History Review* 29, no. 4 (1976): 602–16.

14. Kitching suggests that even those academics who may have believed that capitalist development would have a positive role to play in Kenya nevertheless recognized that such a belief would be unpalatable to progressive Kenyans at the time, and so they did not articulate such positions. See Gavin Kitching, "Politics, Method, and Evidence in the Kenya Debate," in H. Bernstein and B. Campbell, eds., *Contradictions of Accumulation in Africa: Studies in Economy and State* (Beverley Hills: Sage, 1985), 115–51. See also Colin Leys, "Learning from the Kenya Debate," in David E. Apter and Carl G. Rosberg, eds., *Political Development and the New Realism in Sub-Saharan Africa* (Charlottesville: University Press of Virginia, 1994), 220–43.

15. Yash Tandon, "The Pragmatic Industrialist," in Robert Becker and Nitin Jayant Madhvani, eds., *Jayant Madhvani* (London: Privately Printed, 1973), 10 (10–21).

16. Mehta, *Dream Half-Expressed*.

17. Nanji Kalidas Mehta, *Mara Jivanani Anubhavakatha* (Porbander: Snehimandala, 1955).
18. The unsigned acknowledgment to the English translation suggests that it is penned by Mehta's children. The acknowledgment contains the following statement: "However, there was a little time gap between the publication of the original book in Gujarati and the present one in English. Therefore, the text had to be re-edited, revised and brought up-to-date under our personal guidance at Porbander, without however changing the basic pattern." Mehta, *Dream Half-Expressed*, vii.
19. Mehta claims, "Money was not to be an end but a means to a better and kinder life. Commerce was the field where I could seek the means for this end and be charitable and helpful to my brethren whose love had blessed me so much" (ibid., 142).
20. In particular, Birla's project aims to study the ways in which British colonial laws map the divide of the public/private in terms of a divide between economy/culture. Thus, for instance, she is concerned with the ways in which the "family firm" is read by such law in a culturalist frame (since the assumption is that capital accumulated remains under the private control of the family), while a publicly held firm is seen to be properly within the domain of economic development. See Birla, *Stages of Capital*, 6.
21. The vernacular aspect of his literacy is important. While the book includes quotations from the English literary and historiographic tradition, as is the case with the book's epigraph from a poem by Kipling, it is most likely that these embellishments were added by the translators of the Gujarati original than by Mehta himself. The original epigraph of the book appears to be the one that is placed not before the preface and foreword to the English translation (Kipling's poem), but before the opening chapter of the original text. This epigraph, derived from the *Upanishads*, and testifying to the importance of youths who are "firm in character, diligent, optimistic, determined and strong in body," sets the tone for Mehta's autobiographical narrative. Mehta, *Dream Half-Expressed*.
22. For Mehta in his old age, the commercial journey is now over and the emphasis is on the spiritual one. As Sudhir Kakar notes in his study of Hindu childhood and society in India, "The measure of a man's work lies not only in what it enables him to achieve and maintain in the outside world, but also in how far it helps him towards the realization of his *svadharma*: how far it prepares him 'inside' and brings him nearer to that feeling of inner calm which is the dawning of wisdom and the prerequisite for *moksha*." Sudhir Kakar, *The Inner World: A Psycho-Analytic Study of Childhood and Society in India*, 2d ed. (Delhi: Oxford University Press, 1981), 39.
23. Mehta's life and career has been studied by the historian Savita Nair in her dissertation, which I cite in note 34 this chapter. Nair's interest, however, is primarily historical and not on the text as a narrative. For brief discussions of Mehta's text, see Mala Pandurang, "The East African *Dukawallah* and Narratives of Self-Discovery," in Zbigniew Bialas and Krzysztof Kowalczyk-Twarowski, eds., *Ebony, Ivory and Tea* (Katowice: Wydawnictwo Uniwersytetu Slaskiego, 2004), 180–93; and Bose, *A Hundred Horizons*, 97–100. See also Dan Ojwang, "In a Restless State: Mercantile

Adventure and Citizenship in the Autobiography of Nanji Kalidas Mehta (1888–1969)," *Africa Today* 57 no. 3 (2011): 57–75.

24. Robert Gregory notes that the entry of such Indian capital in Uganda was not unique to Mehta's enterprise: "A large number of ginning companies had financial backing from India." Gregory, *South Asians in East Africa*, 277.

25. Mehta's keen sense of land speculation is most explicit a little later in the text when he writes, "I had bought this land at twenty rupees per acre in those days. It would now be considered fifty times costlier. When land in Africa was thus cheaply available, I wrote to several wealthy Princes and merchant-magnates of India to invest Indian capital in East Africa and earn more and at the same time contribute their share indirectly to build up the economic life of this vast continent." Mehta, *Dream Half-Expressed*, 169. Idi Amin was to have a different reading of Mehta's acquisition of Ugandan land and British colonial complicity with such acquisitions. In a speech delivered on December 17, 1972, in the aftermath of his expulsion of Ugandan Asians, he stated: "Instead of promoting a policy of social and economic collaboration between the British Asians in Uganda and the indigenous Africans, the British preferred to cultivate and manure multi-nationalists like the Madhvanis and the Mehtas who exploited the Africans day-in and day-out and were hoping to do so to the end of the world. The two tycoons, for example, holding 99 year leases of thousands of acres of land on which they grew their sugar estates, were paying the African owners of the land a minimal two shillings per acre per year." Amin, "Midnight Address to the Nation by His Excellency," 24. See also Gregory's discussion of Asian agriculture in East Africa in chapter 8 of *South Asians in East Africa*, 237–70. Concluding his discussion of Asian agricultural activities, he notes, "Whether the Asians' agricultural involvement should be regarded more as a contribution to the economic development of East Africa or as an instance of colonial exploitation will always be a debatable subject, but the evidence seems to fall heavily on the side of contribution" (ibid., 264).

26. See "Uganda Forest Sparks Racial Violence," *Guardian*, April 13, 2007 (accessed online at www.guardian.co.uk). Faced with anti-Indian riots and protestors carrying placards asking Asians to leave, many commentators were reminded of the 1972 expulsion. What no one seemed to note was the historical continuity of the pressures on land use from colonial times to the present. Environmental concerns over deforestation that circulated in 2007 around the encroachment on the Mabira forest were similar to the concerns of the colonial conservator of the forests. D .P. S. Ahluwalia has presented the most comprehensive account of the politics of land acquisition and sugarcane production in Uganda in general and Mehta's factory in particular. Writing about a 1936 application by Mehta for a lease of land surrounding his sugar factory, Ahluwalia notes, "The application was referred to the Conservator of Forests who objected to the granting of the lease on three grounds; first, the statistical position of forests in the Protectorate generally and in Buganda in particular where all but some 480 square miles of forest had been destroyed, second, the wastage of the existing or potential supply of timber, and finally, the adverse effects on local rainfall by the removal of forest cover from this

block of land. The sugar company, however, indicated a willingness to cooperate with the Conservator of Forests by undertaking certain conservation measures which would minimise the ill-effects feared by the latter." The application was approved on the urging of the land officer and the director of agriculture. See Ahluwalia, *Plantations and the Politics of Sugar in Uganda*, 65–66; Ahluwalia also discusses tensions surrounding the rights of tenants on land leased to the sugar corporations (ibid., 70).

27. This may in part be explained by the fact that the original Gujarati version of the autobiography was published in 1955. While the English translation is no doubt "updated" to include the establishment of this factory and to include Mehta's speeches to the Indian community in East Africa in 1961, such updating remains selective and not comprehensive.

28. Pratt, *Imperial Eyes*, 76.

29. It should go without saying that Mehta's aversion is not to profit making in itself, but rather to an excessive pursuit of profit. Ritu Birla reminds us that, unlike biblical traditions that condemn usury or equate money with sin, the rituals surrounding the worship of Lakshmi, the goddess of wealth, around the time of Diwali suggest that Hinduism does not eschew the pursuit of wealth. Birla, *Stages of Capital*, 87. Yasmin Alibhai-Brown notes in a more tongue-in-cheek manner about the Diwali festivities: "There was a wonderful, if incomprehensible, marrying at this time of worldly and otherworldly interests, and I think the rich genuinely began to believe not only that God had ordained it that they should get even more prosperous but that they were actually sitting closer to the lap of the gods by having become richer than they were the year before. None of this guilt inducing or placating stuff about the poor entering the kingdom of heaven first." Alibhai-Brown, *No Place Like Home*, 63.

30. Mehta reads the growth of commerce in East Africa as an integral part of Africa's entry into modernity: "Slowly and wonderfully life in Africa has been changing since then and a great network of asphalt roads has once more accelerated the speed. A new vitality and vision have brought [Africans] their freedom earlier than expected. Such are the forces released with the advent of the modern age and if the resources of this newly awakened continent are utilized with wisdom and foresight by her astute statesmen, the continent has a bright future." Mehta, *Dream Half-Expressed*, 85.

31. On the 1945 strikes, which incidentally included among other episodes looting and rioting at the Kakira Sugar Factory, owned and operated by the Vithaldas Haridas Company, see Ahluwalia, *Plantations and the Politics of Sugar in Uganda*, 122–24. On the 1949 protests, see Ramchandani, *Uganda Asians*, 139. The fourth chapter of Ramchandani's book provides useful context on the development of the cotton industry in Uganda (ibid., 118–47).

32. Dana Seidenberg reveals, for instance, that at one point Mehta's son Khimji, who was managing his Ugandan holdings, had to leave East Africa and go to Switzerland due to exchange control violations. Seidenberg, *Mercantile Adventures*, 85.

33. In his foreword to the English translation, S. K. Patil recognizes this commend-

able endeavor as a major political goal of the book: "No one but the writer of this book will be more happy to see if this book helps to build understanding, eliminate fears and disarm prejudices which are born of a long lasting struggle for freedom which the people of the country have rightly earned. May it help to build a new and united Africa, nationally strong, racially accommodating and internationally inclined towards a goal of one world which is the genuine desire and aspiration of all the common people of this planet." S. K. Patil, foreword, in Mehta, *Dream Half-Expressed*, xiii.

34. The purificatory rites are related to a Hindu taboo of crossing the sea, sometimes referred to as *Kala Pani*. Savita Nair notes, "Mehta's son Dhirendra told me that his paternal grandfather disliked overseas travel as a general principle. In fact, whenever Nanji Kalidas returned from Africa, his father would demand that he first go to Dwaraka to perform purification ceremonies before re-entering the family home." Nair, "Moving Life Histories," 128–29. Nair's reading of Mehta rightly places him in the lineage of a long line of Gujarati merchants, and her discussion of the role of a Gujarati transregional identity in the makings of Indian nationalism is exemplary. See, in particular, ibid., 125–40.

35. Javed Majeed, *Autobiography, Travel, and Postnational Identity: Gandhi, Nehru and Iqbal* (New York: Palgrave Macmillan, 2007), 78.

36. Narsimbhai Ishwarbhai Patel (1874–1945) was a Baroda-based revolutionary who published literature on bomb making under the surreptitious guise of providing recipes for making herbal medicines. He was under the surveillance of the colonial Indian government and sought refuge in exile in East Africa. See Mehta, *Dream Half-Expressed*, 125–26, for more on Patel and Mehta's involvement with Indian nationalism.

37. Gregory, *The Rise and Fall of Philanthropy in East Africa*, 192.

38. Preston, *Oriental Nairobi*, n.p.

39. Gregory notes that Mehta provided the largest single private contribution (of 20,000 pounds) to the fund. Gregory, *The Rise and Fall of Philanthropy in East Africa*, 137.

40. See, in addition to Gregory's book on Asian philanthropy in East Africa, Ritu Birla's discussion of the relationship between gifting, dharma, and the establishment of family trusts. Birla, *Stages of Capital*, chapters 2 and 3. Birla suggests that while the impact of charitable contributions on social welfare is undeniable, one should also understand the role such charity played in establishing the social standing of the philanthropists themselves. Her remarks on the Marwari community are applicable to other communities such as Mehta's as well: "For mobile commercial groups like the Marwaris, making a gift for dharma, whether it be a local temple, a *dharamsala* or other form of social welfare, was a way to negotiate their entry as immigrants to a new social world, performing both ritual purity and material conquest" (ibid., 74). As Birla herself carefully points out in the introduction to her book, despite the invocation of the notion of dharma here, philanthropy was not limited to Hindu entrepreneurs alone. As the examples of Allidina Visram and Sewa Haji Paroo, among others, suggest, Muslims also engaged in considerable charitable work.

Indeed what is remarkable is that both Visram and Paroo gave not only to Muslim causes but also to Christians. Paroo, Gregory tells us, "bequeathed all his property to a Catholic mission for benefit of the indigenous people." Gregory, *The Rise and Fall of Philanthropy in East Africa*, 64. Matson notes that Sewa Haji also endowed a multiracial government school in Bagamoyo. See A. T. Matson, "Sewa Haji: A Note," *Tanzania Notes and Records*, no.65 (1966): 93 (91–94).

41. Nair, "Moving Life Histories," 134.

42. The joint family is the locus of the commercial "family concern." For a nuanced discussion of the role of colonial governmentality on indigenous social reform projects involving women, see Birla, *Stages of Capital*, chapter 5. One should note here that Mehta's position seems divided on the issues of social reform—he applauds the efforts of the Arya Samaj to curtail child marriages, but he remains in awe of the practice of sati (widow burning), noting at one point, "I paid a silent tribute to those brave and self-sacrificing women who held chastity and freedom more valuable than all earthly possessions and I realized that loyalty and character were the dominant notes of Hindu womanhood" (63).

43. While Mehta argues that ideally Hindus and Muslims should live peacefully together in an undivided India, his sense of India as a nation is a profoundly Hindu one.

44. More work remains to be done on the links between the rise of a right-wing Hindu nationalism in India and its diasporic networks in Africa. On this, see Agehananda Bharati, who provides a rare glimpse at the ideology and workings of the East African Bharat Seva Sangh, a religious organization modeled on the India Rashtriya Seva Sangh: Bharati, *The Asians in East Africa*, 231–41.

45. The ritual invocation of one or more gods is a common feature among Hindu believers when embarking on a new venture or project. Here the project is the narration of one's own life history.

46. As a companion piece to this account of Manji's commercial enterprise, see Zarwan, "Indian Businessmen in Kenya During the Twentieth Century." See also Nicola Swainson, *The Development of Corporate Capitalism in Kenya, 1918–77* (Berkeley: University of California Press, 1980), 124–30.

47. For a parallel history of a different family firm that was involved in manufacturing spurred by the war, see Murray, "The Chandarias."

48. Since women rarely get mentioned or credited for the role they have played in the entrepreneurial successes of their male kin, particularly important is Manji's revelation that when he started the House of Manji in 1954, his wife "Fatima provided lunch for 20 members of the staff every day. She continued to provide meals to factory staff for more than 20 years afterwards." Manji, *Memoirs of a Biscuit Baron*, ix.

49. Sir Evelyn Baring was the British colonial governor at the time. Perhaps it is to make up for such blatant flattery that Manji devotes a passage in his memoir to the more radical stance taken by his brother Hassanally: "During the Mau Mau struggle for Kenya's independence in the 1950s, Hassanally was in the front line. He played an important role as a courier between people from Karatina who lived

and worked in Nairobi and their rural folk. . . . His involvement in the Mau Mau struggle was in fact deeper than the colonial government knew or suspected. He frequently supplied foodstuffs and other requirements to Mau Mau fighters in the forests around Karatina." Manji, *Memoirs of a Biscuit Baron*, 24–25.

50. Writing of his father's early practices as a small trader, Madhvani notes, "Indeed, he very soon started taking an Allidina Visram-inflected approach to his life and work, running an open kitchen at the back of the Vithaldas Haridas office in Jinja." Madhvani, *Tide of Fortune*, 31. At the height of its operations in the fifties and sixties, Madhvani's industrial complex at Kakira had "12,000 employees; and 100 miles of internal railway system with steam-operated locomotives. There were also schools providing free primary, secondary and technical education, a 100-bed hospital offering free healthcare, and finally a welfare shop selling at cost to employees, who also had the benefit of sports facilities" (ibid., 67). The importance placed on the workers' social welfare by the Madhvani Group in these years is confirmed by nonfamily observers such as Yash Tandon, in his essay "The Pragmatic Industrialist," in Becker and Madhvani, *Jayant Madhvani*, 10–21, and Mathias Ngobi, "Nascent Uganda," in Becker and Madhvani, *Jayant Madhvani*, 64–70. Tandon draws attention as well to the Madhvani family's 1967 decision to open up shares in the company to workers so that they would have a greater sense of ownership in the enterprise ("The Pragmatic Industrialist," 14). Ngobi focuses on Jayant Madhvani's efforts at enabling the Africanization of the enterprise: "Jayant Madhvani was sincerely concerned about the training of Africans in various fields, especially in the fields of commerce and farming, as this would be the sure way of enabling them to develop" ("Nascent Uganda," 64).

51. Ahluwalia's *Plantations and the Politics of Sugar in Uganda* provides a useful context for the commercial narrative of *Tide of Fortune*. See especially 165–77. See also Seidenberg, *Mercantile Adventurers*, 79–83.

52. So, for instance, Seidenberg writes, "Despite their loyalty to East Africa, at the elder Madhvani's insistence, for security, the Madhvanis began investing in properties abroad. They bought a tea estate from European farmers at Nilgiris in South India and in 1952 they started a sugar factory at Shimoga near Barg while two years later when Manu Madhvani returned to Uganda his first assignment was to buy a textile mill on auction in Bombay." Seidenberg, *Mercantile Adventurers*, 81.

53. What Muljibhai's daughters receive, if anything, we are not told.

54. As is often the case with such disputes, the reader is left with no real sense of Meenaben's or her children's perspectives on the matter, and their appearance in the narrative ultimately casts them in a negative light. That gender may have something to do with it is acknowledged even by the author: "Dealing with non-blood relations such as Jayantbhai's widow Meenaben was another challenge. I must admit that I had not dealt with women in business and I wasn't very good at it. In any case, we had developed quite an aggressive relationship." Madhvani, *Tide of Fortune*, 162.

55. Mahmood Mamdani was among the first intellectuals to caution against readings of Amin that saw him as simply irrational or unpredictable. In his memoir *From*

Citizen to Refugee, Mamdani offers a portrait of Amin as a savvy politician who knew how to play to the fears and desires of his followers. Mamdani's book, *Politics and Class Formation in Uganda* attempts to understand the political and economic crisis that led to the predicaments of the Obote and Amin eras.

56. Citing the 1967 Labour Government Act of Parliament that restricted the migration of former British colonial subjects into Britain, Madhvani also highlights the British role in precipitating the citizenship crisis in Uganda. The act, he writes, "sparked an overnight exodus of Indians from Tanzania, Kenya and Uganda before the Act came into effect. This action by the British government of barring its own nationals from entering the country, unprecedented in modern legal history, had the effect of marooning thousands of Indians with British nationality in East Africa. The seeds had been sown for a humanitarian disaster." Madhvani, *Tide of Fortune*, 111–12.

57. Sometimes such resistance is only subtly noted, as in this sentence about Muljibhai's acquisition of land for his sugar estate: "Others [African landowners] were reluctant to part with their property, but eventually Muljibhai succeeded in forming one unified block of land." Madhvani, *Tide of Fortune*, 34.

58. Among these social goods, Madhvani certainly counts as important the training of local citizens. Curiously, the narrative does not describe the efforts made by the Madhvanis in the field of education. In addition to opening schools for the children of the workers of the sugar factory, the Madhvanis also founded a technical school and a commercial college. Robert Gregory notes, "The [commercial college] which opened in Kampala in 1950 as the Muljibhai College of Commerce, became eventually the Uganda College of Commerce. Jayant brought many of the graduates of this college and the technical school into high-level positions in the Madhvani companies. After his father's death in 1958 he founded the Muljibhai Madhvani Foundation Trust, the income of which was distributed annually in scholarships and other educational grants. In 1971, following Jayant's early death, the family, as explained, established the Jayant Madhvani Foundation. The new trust supported students in agriculture, commerce, economics, and science at the secondary and university levels, and Africans were the main beneficiaries." Gregory, *The Rise and Fall of Philanthropy in East Africa*, 192–93.

59. Needless to say, this harmonious vision is not necessarily shared by the workers on the sugar plantations and factory. See Okot p'Bitek's *White Teeth* (Nairobi: East African Educational, 1989) for a more dystopian vision of African labor on Asian plantations.

6. LIGHTING A CANDLE ON MOUNT KILIMANJARO

1. Ahluwalia, *Plantations and the Politics of Sugar in Uganda*, 172–73.
2. Idi Amin, "Document: Speech by His Excellency the President of Uganda, General Amin, to the Asian Conference held on the 8th of December, 1971, in the Uganda International Conference Centre," *East Africa Journal* (1972): 2 (2–5).

3. "Letter of Condolence Received from the President of Uganda, General Idi Amin Dada," in Becker and Madhvani, *Jayant Madhvani*, frontmatter.

4. See "The Arusha Declaration: Socialism and Self-Reliance," in Nyerere, *Freedom and Socialism*, 230–50.

5. The primary difference being a willful engagement with the state and an optimistic sense of the possibilities of partnership. As yet another contrast, see the bitter memoir by J. M. Nazareth in the context of postcolonial Kenya in which he claims that leaders like Kenyatta and Tom Mboya prevented Asians from aspiring to political office. J. M. Nazareth, *Brown Man, Black Country: A Peep into Kenya's Freedom Struggle* (New Delhi: Tidings, 1981).

6. Joseph, *Nomadic Identities*, 36.

7. See, for instance, Lionel Cliffe and John Saul, eds. *Socialism in Tanzania: An Interdisciplinary Reader* (Dar es Salaam: East African, 1972–73); Pratt, *The Critical Phase in Tanzania*; William Redman Duggan and John R. Civille, *Tanzania and Nyerere: A Study of Ujamaa and Nationhood* (Maryknoll, NY: Orbis, 1976); Goran Hyden, *Beyond Ujamaa in Tanzania: Underdevelopment and an Uncaptured Peasantry* (Berkeley: University of California Press, 1980); Idrian Resnick, *The Long Transition: Building Socialism in Tanzania* (New York: Monthly Review Press, 1981); Susan C. Crouch, *Western Responses to Tanzanian Socialism, 1967–83* (Brookfield, VT: Gower, 1987); William Michael Jennings, *Surrogates of the State: NGOs, Development and Ujamaa in Tanzania* (Bloomfield, CT: Kumarian, 2008). Nyerere's own speeches and writings on Ujamaa are collected in two important volumes. See Nyerere, *Freedom and Socialism* and *Freedom and Development*.

8. A useful companion text to this chapter as well as the next on Vassanji is the PhD dissertation of Richa Nagar. See Nagar, "Making and Breaking Boundaries." See also Brennan, "Nation, Race and Urbanization in Dar es Salaam."

9. Mustafa, *The Tanganyika Way*; Kassum, *Africa's Winds of Change*; Chande, *A Knight in Africa*.

10. "By 'soul making' I mean," writes Appiah, "the project of intervening in the process of interpretation through which each citizen develops an identity—and doing so with the aim of increasing her chances of living an ethically successful life." Appiah's interest in the discussion from which this quote is taken is "on soul making as a *political* project, something done by the state." Appiah, *The Ethics of Identity*, 164. Likewise, my interest in this chapter is to foreground Nyerere's engagement in soul making, in which the state attempted to create in the Tanzanian citizenry exemplary ethical selves.

11. After independence, Abdulla was called to the bench to serve on Tanzania's High Court. From 1970 to 1977 he served on the East African Court of Appeal and later served on the Court of Appeal in Tanzania. He also served as president of the Court of Appeal of the Seychelles. Biographical details are in Fawzia Mustafa's introduction to Mustafa, *The Tanganyika Way*, vi. See also the biographical tribute to Sophia Mustafa by the editors of the magazine *Awaaz*: "Sophia Mustafa, 1922–2005: Against the Shadows," *Awaaz: Voices from the South Asian Diaspora*, no. 3 (2005): 14–25. I thank Fawzia Mustafa for bringing this article to my attention.

12. Geiger, *TANU Women*; Meena, "Crisis and Structural Adjustment"; Ruth Meena and Marjorie Mbilinyi, "Women's Research and Documentation Project (Tanzania)," *Signs* 16, no. 4 (1991), 852–59; Mbilinyi, "Sophia Mustafa"; Susan Geiger, "Engendering and Gendering African Nationalism: Rethinking the Case of Tanganyika (Tanzania)," in Gregory H. Maddox and James L. Giblin, eds., *In Search of a Nation: Histories of Authority and Dissidence in Tanzania* (Athens: Ohio University Press, 2005), 278–89.

13. Fawzia Mustafa, "Re-Issuing *The Tanganyika Way*: 1961–2009," in Mustafa, *The Tanganyika Way*, v (v–x).

14. And just as many Asians were willing to partner with Nyerere because of his firmly nonracialist ethic, so, suggests Susan Geiger's research, did many women find TANU's charter to be explicitly nonsexist. On this, see Susan Geiger, *TANU Women*, 126.

15. Mbilinyi, "Sophia Mustafa," 157. K. L. Jhaveri also underscores the importance of nonracialism to Mustafa and points to her efforts in carrying this message to various members of the Asian community. See Jhaveri, *Marching with Nyerere*, 102–3.

16. For a recent discussion of the importance of the pedagogical role of postindependence leaders such as Nehru and Nyerere, see Dipesh Chakrabarty, "The Legacies of Bandung: Decolonization and the Politics of Culture," in Lee, *Making a World After Empire*, 45–68.

17. See also Julius K. Nyerere, "Socialism Is Not Racialism," in Nyerere, *Freedom and Socialism*, 257–61. For a memoir of life under Nyerere and particularly for an account of how Nyerere attempted to fashion a nonracial public consciousness, see Mwakikagile, *Life Under Nyerere*. For a slightly different take on the legacies of Nyerere's insistence on nonracialism, see Salma Maoulidi, "Racial and Religious Tolerance in Nyerere's Political Thought and Practice," in Chachage and Cassam, *Africa's Liberation*, 134–48.

18. Another Asian text that I do not discuss here also supports this claim. See Jhaveri, *Marching with Nyerere*. Jhaveri's book is an important window onto the internal politics of the Asian Association and its ongoing negotiations with TANU politics. What seems clear in the account is that rather than being removed or disinterested in civic or political affairs (as is often suggested in popular accounts of East African Asians), many Asians in the period of national transition were involved in political and public life. In her life history Bibi Titi Mohamed recollects the partnership between the Indian Association and Nyerere: "But the Rattensey people met and said 'We of the Indian Association'—they used the name Asian Association at the time—'we are ready and we want our independence. We have children, we have property, and this is where we belong. We don't know anything about India. We want independence with these people. We have faith in independence.'" Bibi Titi Mohamed, quoted in Geiger, *TANU Women*, 56; While he did not publish an autobiography, Amir Jamal's service to Tanzania and to Nyerere are also worth mentioning. In his eulogy at Jamal's memorial service on June 22, 1995, in Dar es Salaam, Nyerere is quoted as saying: "I almost exploited Amir. You'll find that at every point, I gave him the ministry I thought the most difficult, but not too dif-

ficult for him." Quoted in Lois Lobo, *They Came to Africa: 200 Years of the Asian Presence in Tanzania* (Dar es Salaam: Sustainable Village, 2000), 87. Jamal was elected as a TANU representative from Morogoro and went on to hold several cabinet posts under Nyerere.

19. Berger, "States of the (Tanzanian) Nation," 149.

20. Which is not to say that she was the only Asian woman of prominence in East African politics. In Uganda, Sugra Visram, married to a descendant of the legendary Allidina Visram, was elected to the Ugandan Parliament. But to my knowledge she left no memoir or other narrative of her experience. Yasmin Alibhai-Brown, in her own memoir, notes about her: "When Sugra Visram, an outstanding Asian woman, who, with the approval of her husband, stood in the first post-independence election and was elected by a huge majority of black women to parliament, my people could only question her motives and disapprove of her unconventional rise to prominence. They gossiped endlessly and mercilessly about how she might have got there, how her mixing with Africans and her friendship with the Bagandan king, the Kabaka was somehow improper, how this sort of thing was corrupting the purity which all Asian women were presumed to have." See Alibhai-Brown, *No Place Like Home*, 115–16. See also Seidenberg, *Mercantile Adventurers*, 95–123.

21. A very useful point of comparison is the life history of Bibi Titi Mohamed, who also relates her unconventional entry into TANU politics spurred by the visit of John Hatch, a member of the British Labour Party inquiring about the lack of women's participation in TANU. Bibi Titi's narrative shares some of Mustafa's initial anxieties about public speaking and about her role as a woman in politics. See Geiger, *TANU Women*, 45–63.

22. In this Mustafa's narrative is in keeping with a long tradition of women's autobiographies and life narratives. For a theoretical treatment of authority and women's voice in life narratives, see the Personal Narratives Group, eds., *Interpreting Women's Lives: Feminist Theory and Personal Narratives* (Bloomington: Indiana University Press, 1989). See also Sidonie Smith and Julia Watson, eds., *Women, Autobiography, Theory: A Reader* (Madison: University of Wisconsin Press, 1998).

23. One is reminded, here, as a point of comparison, of the experience in Nairobi of the British Joan Karmali married to an Indian. She remembers that when she was seeking admission to the European Hospital in Nairobi during her pregnancy two European nurses attempted to prevent her since her child would be half Indian. Salvadori, *We Came in Dhows*, 3:178–79.

24. Mbilinyi, "Sophia Mustafa," 157–58.

25. Sophia Mustafa, "Preface," in Mustafa, *Broken Reed*, vii (vi–ix). See also Tina Steiner, "Translating Between India and Tanzania: Sophia Mustafa's Partial Cosmopolitanism," *Research in African Literatures* 42 no. 3 (2011): 132–46.

26. As an aside, we might note that Nyerere too was engaged with imaginative literature around this time. He prepared a Kiswahili translation of Shakespeare's *Julius Caesar* in 1963 and later, in 1969, a translation of *The Merchant of Venice*. Faisal Devji presents a fascinating reading of the historical context of these translations, including a brief discussion of the use of the Gujarati-origin word *mabepari* to

translate the English word "merchants." Devji shows how the image of the Asian trader and the Jewish Shylock get conflated in the text. See Faisal Devji, "Subject to Translation: Shakespeare, Swahili, Socialism," *Postcolonial Studies* 3, no. 2 (2000): 181–89. See also Paulina Aroch Fugellie, "Migratory Cliches: Recognizing Nyerere's *The Capitalists of Venice*," in Murat Aydemir and Alex Rotas, eds., *Migratory Settings* (Amsterdam: Rodopi, 2008), 101–18.

27. Madhvani, *Tide of Fortune*, 51, 56.

28. Kassum, *Africa's Winds of Change*, 12; further citations appear in the text.

29. Chande, *A Knight in Africa*, 37; further citations appear in the text. In his book *Marching with Nyerere*, K. L. Jhaveri, who was at one point mayor of Dar es Salaam and a member of the Tanzanian judiciary, likewise reflects on his student days in India during the Indian freedom struggle and notes his own arrest in Rajkot for participating in anticolonial protests. See Jhaveri, *Marching with Nyerere*, 78–9.

30. This distinction was also felt in an early article penned by Mahmood Mamdani, who wrote of the distinction between Nyerere's economic policies and the policies followed at the same time in Kenya: "The difference is that in Tanzania it is 'economic privilege' that is considered as being undermined, whereas in Kenya it is 'Asian economic privilege' that is seen as being attacked. The emphasis in the first case is on 'privilege,' in the second on 'Asian.'" Mahmood Mamdani, "Asians in East Africa: Their Origin and Sociological Composition," *Pan-African Journal* 2, no. 4 (1969): 391 (375–95).

31. Julius Nyerere, quoted in Kassum, *Africa's Winds of Change*, 59.

32. On this, Godfrey Mwakikagile notes, as a point of contrast, President Mobuto, who "'indigenized' the economy by raiding national coffers for himself and giving property—seized from foreigners—to his cronies and family members who had also amassed great wealth by stealing from the masses." See Mwakikagile, *Life Under Nyerere*, 88.

33. Much has been written on the villagization program in Tanzania. For a critique and overview, see David Scott, "Compulsory Villagization in Tanzania: Aesthetics and Miniaturization," in *Seeing Like a State: How Certain Schemes to Improve the Human Condition Have Failed* (New Haven: Yale University Press, 1998), 223–61. See also Issa G. Shivji, "The Village in Mwalimu's Thought and Political Practice," in Chachage and Cassam, *Africa's Liberation*, 120–33.

34. To note that villagization was a failure is not to cast doubt on other social aspects of state policies that did indeed succeed. Godfrey Mwakikagile points out, for instance, that even though the villagizations may have failed, they brought "the people together and closer to each other in order to provide them with vital social services." Among these he lists medical services and free education, the latter being a high point of Nyerere's government. "Tanzania, on a scale unprecedented anywhere else in the world, launched a massive adult education campaign to teach millions of people how to read and write. Within only a few years, almost the entire adult population of Tanzania—rural peasants, urban workers and others became literate." Mwakikagile, *Life Under Nyerere*, 64. For another recent retro-

spective account of the relative successes and failures of Tanzanian socialism under Nyerere, see Chachage and Cassam, *Africa's Liberation*.

35. The significance of the Amin overthrow on the Asian community is also highlighted by Chande: "In 1979, following the takeover of a part of the Kagera region of Tanzania by Idi Amin's forces, the under-equipped Tanzanian army fought back like lions and pushed the Ugandans out of Tanzania. But Mwalimu did not stop there. Persuaded by the need for regime change in Uganda, he ordered his forces to press on all the way into Kampala, and they toppled Amin. There was great relief and joy when the news came of the overthrow of Amin. A small number of those Asians who had been expelled returned to repossess the properties that had been confiscated." Chande, *A Knight in Africa*, 145.

36. The *Tiger* talks refer to the meeting in 1966 between British Prime Minister Harold Wilson and the Rhodesian Ian Smith, who had unilaterally declared Rhodesian independence. Nyerere was a vehement critic of the racism of the Smith regime both before and after these talks. See Julius Nyerere, "The Honour of Africa," in Nyerere, *Freedom and Socialism*, 115–33; see also Julius Nyerere, "Rhodesia in the Context of Southern Africa," ibid., 143–56.

37. For a recent discussion of A. M. Babu and particularly his interest in Chinese Communism, see G. Thomas Burgess, "Mao in Zanzibar: Nationalism, Discipline, and the (De)Construction of Afro-Asian Solidarities," in Lee, *Making a World After Empire*, 196–234. For an account of the role of China in the building of the TAZARA railway and the manner in which both Tanzanian and Chinese workers remember the project, see Jamie Monson, "Working Ahead of Time: Labor and Modernization During the Construction of the TAZARA Railway, 1968–86," ibid., 235–65. See also Abdul Rahman Mohamed Babu, *The Future That Works: The Selected Writings of A. M. Babu*, ed. Salma Babu and Amrit Wilson (Trenton, NJ: Africa World, 2002).

38. For a detailed account of the politics of race, citizenship, and the policies of Africanization in this period, see Ronald Aminzade, "The Politics of Race and Nation: Citizenship and Africanization in Tanganyika," *Political Power and Social Theory* 14 (2000): 53–90.

39. Even though it was popular with the public, the Africanization policy went against the grain of Nyerere's nonracialist agenda. At much cost to him, including a military coup that had to be thwarted with the help of British troops, Nyerere decided to put an end to it. Chande, *A Knight in Africa*, 79.

40. See Walter Rodney, *How Europe Underdeveloped Africa* (Washington, DC: Howard University Press, 1982); Taiwo, *How Colonialism Pre-Empted Modernity in Africa*.

41. There is by now a considerable literature on both the promises as well as ills of market liberalization in Tanzania as well as in other African countries. A good overview of the impact of the structural adjustment programs in Tanzania is offered in Paul J. Kaiser, "Structural Adjustment and the Fragile Nation: The Demise of Social Unity in Tanzania," *Journal of Modern African Studies* 32, no. 2 (1996): 227–37.

For a strong critique of the structural adjustment measures in the continent, see Mkandawire and Soludo, *Our Continent, Our Future*. See also Horace Campbell and Howard Stein, eds., *Tanzania and the IMF: The Dynamics of Liberalization* (Boulder: Westview, 1992); Shivji, *Let the People Speak*. Perhaps the most philosophically engaged treatment of this issue is Achille Mbembe's discussion of what he calls "Private Indirect Government." See Mbembe, *On the Postcolony*, 66–101.

7. ANTI ANTI-ASIANISM AND THE POLITICS OF DISSENT

1. Originally from Dar es Salaam, Vassanji now lives in Toronto, to which he migrated several years ago. *The Gunny Sack*, published in Heinemann's African Writers Series and winning the Commonwealth Prize for the Africa region, was, in fact, written by Vassanji in Canada.

2. See Simon Gikandi, "Chinua Achebe and the Invention of African Culture," *Research in African Literatures* 32, no.3 (2001): 3–8; see also *Reading Chinua Achebe: Language and Ideology in Fiction* (London: James Currey, 1991).

3. The character Salim comes up with the metaphor of excess baggage in the novel: "We Indians have barged into Africa with our big black trunk, and every time it comes in our way. Do we need it? I should have come with a small bag, a rucksack." Vassanji, *The Gunny Sack*, 204.

4. See Vassanji, *The Book of Secrets*. Vassanji received the Giller Prize for this novel in 1994. See also his *The In-Between World of Vikram Lall*. Vassanji received the Giller for this novel in 2003.

5. My reading of *The Gunny Sack* is informed by much of the previous scholarship on it, although I also depart from these readings. This includes, in addition to the scholars whose work I engage with directly in the text (and who are cited later), Brenda Cooper, "A Gunny Sack, Chants and Jingles, a Fan and a Black Trunk: The Coded Language of the Everyday in a Post-colonial African Novel," *Africa Quarterly* 44, no. 3 (2004): 12–31; Tuomas Huttunen, "M. G. Vassanji's *The Gunny Sack*: Narrating the Migrant Identity," in John Skinner, ed., *Tales of Two Cities: Essays on New Anglophone Literature* (Turku: Anglicana Turkuensia, 2000), 3–20; Tuomas Huttunen, "M. G. Vassanji's *The Gunny Sack*: Emplotting British, Asian and African Realities," *Atlantic Review* 3, no. 2 (2002): 56–76; Charles Ponnuthurai Sarvan, "M. G. Vassanji's *The Gunny Sack*: A Reflection on History and the Novel," *Modern Fiction Studies* 37, no. 3 (1991): 511–18; Ashok Mohapatra, "The Paradox of Return: Origins, Home, and Identity in M. G. Vassanji's *The Gunny Sack*," *Postcolonial Text* 2, no. 4 (2006): 1–21; Peter Kalliney, "East African Fiction and Globalization," in Gaurav Desai, ed., *Teaching the African Novel* (New York: Modern Language Association, 2009), 259–73.

6. Here I am in agreement with Simatei, who has recently argued for a critical refocus on the ways in which East African Asian diasporic writers remain tied to a national project. See Peter Simatei, "Diasporic Memories and National Histories in East African Asian Writing," *Research in African Literatures* 42, no. 3 (2011): 56–67.

7. Eleni Coundouriotis, *Claiming History: Colonialism, Ethnography, and the Novel* (New York: Columbia University Press, 1999), 1.

8. Ibid., 5.

9. Bahadur Tejani, "Modern African Literature and the Legacy of Cultural Colonialism," *World Literature Written in English* 18, no. 1 (1979): 46 (37–54).

10. For an insight into Tejani the writer, see Annie Koshi, "An Interview with Bahadur Tejani," *Ufahamu* 21, no. 3 (1993): 43–54. For Koshi's reading of Tejani's novel, see Annie Koshi, "The Afro-Asian and American Dreams of Race Relations in Bahadur Tejani's *Day After Tomorrow*," *Wasafiri* 13 (1991): 11–13.

11. I owe the term *blood narrative* to Chadwick Allen, although his use of it in *Blood Narrative: Indigenous Identity in American Indian and Maori Literary and Activist Texts* (Durham: Duke University Press, 2002) is considerably more nuanced than mine.

12. Charles Sarvan pays attention to Nazareth as a "historical witness" in his essay "The Writer as Historian." See Charles Sarvan, "The Writer as Historian: With Reference to the Novels of Peter Nazareth," *Toronto South Asian Review* 10, no. 1 (1991): 15–24. See also Simatei, *The Novel and the Politics of Nation Building in East Africa*, 105–20.

13. Bernth Lindfors, "Interview with Peter Nazareth," in Bernth Lindfors, *Mazungumzo: Interviews with East African Writers, Publishers, Editors and Scholars* (Athens: University Center for African Studies, 1980), 90 (80–97).

14. Ibid., 89.

15. Ibid., 90.

16. Peter Nazareth, "The Asian Presence in Two Decades of East African Literature," *Toronto Review* 13, no. 1 (1994): 18 (17–32).

17. Ibid., 17.

18. Ibid., 18.

19. See Carol Sicherman, "Ngugi's Colonial Education: The Subversion . . . of the African Mind," *African Studies Review* 38, no. 3 (1995): 11–41. See also Simon Gikandi, "Globalization and the Claims of Postcoloniality," in Gaurav Desai and Supriya Nair, eds., *Postcolonialisms: An Anthology of Cultural Theory and Criticism* (New Brunswick, NJ: Rutgers University Press, 2005), 608–34.

20. Yasmin Alibhai-Brown, *No Place Like Home* (London: Virago, 1995), 156.

21. See Gikandi, "Theory, Literature and Moral Considerations." See also Kenneth Harrow, "Ethics and Difference: A Response to Simon Gikandi's 'Theory, Literature and Moral Considerations,'" *Research in African Literatures* 33, no. 4 (2002): 154–60.

22. Ojwang, "The Pleasures of Knowing." See also Christopher Miller, "Ethnicity and Ethics," in *Theories of Africans: Francophone Literature and Anthropology in Africa* (Chicago: University of Chicago Press, 1990), 31–67.

23. Ojwang, "The Pleasures of Knowing," 43.

24. R. Radhakrishnan, "Ethnic Identity and Poststructuralist Difference," in *Diasporic Mediations: Between Home and Location* (Minneapolis: University of Minnesota Press, 1996), 62 (62–79).

25. In his essay "The Postcolonial Writer," Vassanji claims that the postcolonial writer is "a preserver of the collective tradition, a folk historian and myth maker. He gives himself a history; he recreates the past, which exists only in memory and is otherwise obliterated, so fast has his world transformed. He emerges from the oral, preliterate, and unrecorded, to the literate." M. G. Vassanji, "The Postcolonial Writer: Myth Maker and Folk Historian," in M. G. Vassanji, ed., *A Meeting of Streams: South Asian Canadian Literature* (Toronto: TSAR, 1985), 63 (63–68).

26. Walter Benjamin, *Illuminations*, ed. Hannah Arendt, trans. Harry Zohn (London: Jonathan Cape, 1970), 87.

27. A relation to film techniques and cinema would be appropriate as well. See, in this regard, Keith Cohen, *Film and Fiction: The Dynamics of Exchange* (Yale University Press, 1979), which traces the influence of cinematic techniques on the modern novel. While Cohen discusses primarily European novels and cinema, his discussion of such techniques as montage, achronological narration and flashbacks, simultaneity, perspective mobility in point of view, and narrative discontinuities is very suggestive in a reading of Vassanji's text. *The Book of Secrets* specifically invokes Hindi films as an important narrative element.

28. Dent Ocaya-Lakidi claims that East Africans did not necessarily associate Islam with India and hence Indian efforts at conversion would not have been successful. "And, although prominent Asian Muslims emerged on the Ugandan scene in later years, they were unable to secure for India the kind of allegiance the Christian religion had generated for England. . . . But even had the Asians sent Hindu teachers among the natives of East Africa, where was the impressive material culture in India or Pakistan to back up their teaching? Was the black man to abandon his native religion for a new one when those who preached this new religion could not even promise a better material life in this world?" Ocaya-Lakidi, "Black Attitudes," 86.

29. See Shane Rhodes, "M. G. Vassanji: An Interview," *Studies in Canadian Literature* 22, no. 2 (1997): 116 (105–17).

30. The collection of short stories *Uhuru Street* excepted, of course, since the stories are set in the same locale of Kariakoo and in many ways overlap or extend the portrayals in *The Gunny Sack*. See M. G. Vassanji, *Uhuru Street* (London: Heinemann, 1991).

31. It is at this historical moment that the likes of Kulsum, whose bowel troubles are legendary, "in an exact literal translation, (is) scared shitless" (153), when her head tailor, Omari, decides to challenge her on matters of back pay. The novel is quick to note that Kulsum's fear is ultimately immaterial since the Labor Office sides with her in the dispute.

32. In other words, circumcised or not? Recall that this issue of male circumcision as a site of difference between Hindus and Muslims reappears in Ghosh's conversations with the Egyptian villagers during his fieldwork.

33. This, of course, is not the case with *all* the Asians. Uncle Goa's family decision to go to Lourenço Marques after independence because they cannot watch their "servants turning and throwing insults" at them (165) has often been read by critics

as a metaphor for the Asian community's response as a whole. But such a reading ignores the fact that this family, despite their own troubles, tends to think of themselves as different from, if not better than, the rest of the Asians. Why else would their son, the one with the "blue-green eyes," not be allowed to play with the other Asian children like Salim? When Kulsum reminds Mrs. Goa that she can't think of leaving because her family was born in East Africa, Uncle Goa is quick to acquiesce: "Yes, yes . . . for you it is different" (165). Vassanji, I suggest, is pointing to yet another difference within the Asian community here—not only one of Goan and Shamshi, but, further, one of new immigrant Asian and African-born Asian.

34. See George B. N. Ayittey and Ludovik Shirima, "Julius Nyerere: A Saint or a Knave?" http://www.freeafrica.org/articles/failedleadership/juliusnyere.html. For an overview of preventive detentions in Tanzania, see Chris Maina Peter, "Incarcerating the Innocent: Preventive Detention in Tanzania," *Human Rights Quarterly* 19, no. 1 (1997): 113–35. See also Helen Kijo-Bisimba and Chris Maina Peter, "Mwalimu Nyerere and the Challenge of Human Rights," in Chambi Chachage and Annar Cassam, eds., *Africa's Liberation: The Legacy of Nyerere* (Nairobi: Pambazuka, 2010), 149–59; James Brennan, "The Short History of Political Opposition and Multi-Party Democracy in Tanganyika, 1958–64," in Gregory H. Maddox and James L. Giblin, eds., *In Search of a Nation: Histories of Authority and Dissidence in Tanzania* (Athens: Ohio University Press, 2005), 250–76. While he is supportive of Nyerere's presidency in general, K. L. Jhaveri, once mayor of Dar es Salaam and former member of the Tanzanian judiciary, expresses serious reservations about the preventive detentions. See Jhaveri, *Marching with Nyerere*, 186–91.

35. In this, Salim embodies some of Vassanji's own frustrations as a youth. In an interview with Mark David Young, Vassanji remarks, "I remember when I was seventeen or eighteen what I resented was not being able to get away. When I was growing up, the government there basically put a restriction on who could leave. You felt like you were being held in. . . . When I was growing up, we always knew that there was a bigger world out there and we wanted to go and see it." Mark David Young, "Delivering the Past: An Interview with M. G. Vassanji," *Blood and Aphorisms* 27 (1997): 47 (46–50).

36. Vassanji's lack of patience with academics is most explicit when he writes elsewhere about the "Calcutta Intellectuals." Granting their brilliance and their ability to seamlessly shift from quoting Derrida and Foucault to engaging in deep conversations in Bengali, he notes, "And there is a genuine sympathy for the oppressed: after all, there exists a caste system, and the multitudes are poor beyond imagination. But with them there are no two ways. The world is divided neatly between the oppressed and the oppressors. There is right and there is wrong. They are on the side of the right." M. G. Vassanji, *A Place Within: Rediscovering India* (Toronto: Anchor Canada, 2009), 32.

37. Here Vassanji's position would resonate with Stuart Hall's observation that "we all speak from a particular place, out of a particular history, out of a particular experience, a particular culture, without being contained by that position as 'ethnic

artists' or filmmakers. We are all, in that sense *ethnically* located and our ethnic identities are crucial to our subjective sense of who we are." Stuart Hall, "New Ethnicities," in Houston Baker Jr., Manthia Diawara, and Ruth Lindeborg, eds., *Black British Cultural Studies: A Reader* (Chicago: University of Chicago Press, 1996), 169–70 (163–72).

38. Vassanji has often spoken on the loss of his father when he was a young boy, and his growing up in a female-headed household. See his interview with Chelva Kanaganayaka, "'Broadening the Substrata': An Interview with M. G. Vassanji," *World Literature Written in English* 31, no. 2 (1991): 19–35. See also Gaurav Desai, "Ambiguity Is the Driving Force or the Nuclear Reaction Behind My Creativity: An E-Conversation with M. G. Vassanji," *Research in African Literatures* 42, no. 3 (Fall 2011): 187–197.

39. Likewise, Salim's sister Begum has to elope to London with her English lover Mr. Harris since the city is not prepared for such a relationship.

40. Dent Ocaya-Lakidi suggests that, despite the general targeting of Asians for their reluctance to intermarry with Africans, such reluctance was in fact often registered on both sides. "Yet should (an African woman) go with an Asian, she can still create considerable revulsion among black African males. By going with an Asian she is seen to be sinking even lower than the lowest African can go. It follows that for a 'clean' or good African girl to want to marry an Asian is just unimaginable. As for the black males themselves, no doubt the idea of 'testing' a 'brown skin' is attractive but none would stoop to marry an Asian." Ocaya-Lakidi, "Black Attitudes," 96–97. Ocaya-Lakidi's piece was published in 1975, but, regrettably, despite some notable exceptions, the dominant societal views on interracial marriages between Africans and Asians have not significantly changed in either community. However, as both historical records as well as *The Gunny Sack* suggest, interracial relationships between Indians and Africans were not uncommon in earlier periods, until at least the first few decades of the twentieth century.

41. Kanaganayaka, "'Broadening the Substrata,'" 20.

42. Ojwang, "The Pleasures of Knowing," 48.

43. Ibid., 47.

44. Ibid., 49.

45. Ibid., 51.

46. Furthermore, one must concur with Ojwang's claim that it is too simple to suggest that Indian estimates of African capability were merely derivative of European racism. Rather, they were likely as much the result of "longstanding attitudes to colour within the Indian subcontinent" (ibid., 46, and, we might add, caste) as they were responses to European formulations. On this, see also Robert E. Washington, "Brown Racism and the Formation of a World System of Racial Stratification," *International Journal of Politics, Culture, and Society* 4, no. 2 (1990): 209–27.

47. Saidiya Hartman, "Seduction and the Ruses of Power," in Caren Kaplan, Norma Alarcon, and Minoo Moallem, eds., *Between Woman and Nation: Nationalisms, Transnational Feminisms, and the State* (Durham: Duke University Press, 1999), 125 (111–41).

48. Ojwang, "The Pleasures of Knowing," 44.
49. Ironically, one of the strategies that President Karume embarked on in the context of the Zanzibari revolution was forced marriages between Asian and Arab women and African men. He is quoted as saying: "In the colonial times Arabs took African concubines without bothering to marry them. Now that we are in power, the shoe is on the other foot." Quoted in Richa Nagar, "The South Asian Diaspora in Tanzania: A History Retold," *Comparative Studies of South Asia, Africa, and the Middle East* 16, no. 2 (1996): 62–80 (68). To further complicate our understanding of the politics of gender, race, and concubinage in the era, we might also remember that slavery in the Indian Ocean context, even as late as the nineteenth century, was not a unidirectional trade. That female concubinage worked in multiple directions is evident in the Zanzibar archives where Cynthia Salvadori reports a court document dated June 18, 1890, that refers to an emancipated slave woman, Zafarani, who had married Mohamed bin Isa, a British Indian resident in Lamu. According to a witness in the case, Zafarani was "brought years ago to Lamu and sold, she then being a child and a native of Pathan in India." Salvadori, *We Came in Dhows*, 1:33.
50. Here I have to register a slight disagreement with Peter Simatei's otherwise powerful reading of the text. Simatei argues that, because the liaison with Taratibu is what ultimately leads to Dhanji Govindji's madness and death, "Govindji's flirtations with Bibi Taratibu, and hence Africa is interpreted as having been the workings of a curse." It is not the relationship with Taratibu, however problematic it may seem to us, that the text derides—it is clearly Dhanji's abandonment of her and his racism toward his mixed-race son that is the subject of critique. See Simatei, *The Novel and the Politics of Nation Building in East Africa*, 90.
51. At another point in the narrative Salim wonders, "From what ravaged tribe, gutted village, was she brought to the coast, and did she not also think of her home, her slaughtered father and uncles, her brother and sisters also taken away" (23).
52. Rosemary Marongoly George, "'Traveling Light': Home and the Immigrant Genre," in *The Politics of Home* (New York: Cambridge University Press, 1996), 180 (171–97).
53. For a parallel reading of the possibilities of agency even in the midst of the most oppressive and brutal conditions, see Sara Salih, "Introduction," in Mary Prince, *The History of Mary Prince*, ed. Sara Salih (New York: Penguin, 2000), vii–xxxiv.
54. Ojwang, "The Pleasures of Knowing," 56.
55. Stephanie Jones, "Within and Without History: *The Book of Secrets*," in Debjani Ganguly and Kavita Nandan, eds., *Unfinished Journeys: India File from Canberra* (Adelaide: Flinders University of South Australia, 1998), 75 (71–89).
56. Clifford Geertz, "Distinguished Lecture: Anti Anti-Relativism," *American Anthropologist* 82, no. 2 (1984): 263–64 (263–78).
57. On this, Vassanji says, "I was of course very conscious of how ludicrous it was for Indians and Africans to be fighting a European war. That was a comment on the contradictions of colonial rule. But the fact is that the British administrators too were human and I don't know if it is politically incorrect to say that." "M. G.

Vassanji," in Chelva Kanaganayalam, *Configurations of Exile: South Asian Writers and Their World* (Toronto: TSAR), 134 (127–37).

58. It is also a turn that is in keeping with a preference for what Mahmood Mamdani has lately called survivor's justice as opposed to the alternative form of victor's justice based on a notion of revenge. See Mamdani, *When Victims Become Killers*, 270–82. On Gandhi and the intimacy of empire, see Ashis Nandy, *The Intimate Enemy: Loss and Recovery of Self Under Colonialism* (Delhi: Oxford University Press, 1983). See also Leela Gandhi, *Affective Communities: Anti-Colonial Thought, Fin-de-Siecle Radicalism, and the Politics of Friendship* (Durham: Duke University Press, 2005).

CODA

1. Mamdani, *From Citizen to Refugee*, 45–46.
2. Bhabha, *The Location of Culture*, 9.
3. Mamdani, *From Citizen to Refugee*, 46–49. See also Mamdani, *Politics and Class Formation in Uganda*.
4. Mamdani, *From Citizen to Refugee*, 15.
5. Mamdani notes,

> The overwhelming majority of Asian businessmen were merchants, operating in the commercial sector, heavily indebted to the banks. A study conducted in 1968 showed that approximately eighty percent of the total commercial bank assets in Uganda were controlled by three banks, Barclays Bank D.C.O., The National and Grindlays Bank and the Standard Bank Ltd.—all British. The other foreign banks, the Netherlands Bank, Ottoman Bank, Habib Bank, Bank of Baroda and Bank of India, controlled another ten percent. The remaining ten percent was controlled by the Bank of Uganda and the Uganda Commercial Bank. In October, when Asian businesses started closing down *en masse*, one could walk down the main streets of Kampala and see signs such as "Property of Barclays Bank D.C.O." or "Property of the Standard Bank" on locked up Asian businesses.

Mamdani, *From Citizen to Refugee*, 40–41.
6. Ibid., 49.
7. Ibid., 29. While Mamdani received a firsthand education in the hierarchies of racial privilege and the ways in which class divisions can take racial overtones, one could plausibly argue that he also learned other important lessons that have continued to mark his subsequent work in political theory. Mamdani's insights on the nature of colonial subjects and citizens, on the politics of indigeneity and its dangerous manifestations in the Rwandan genocide, and his more recent reflections on survivor's justice are all, I would argue, marked by the memory of the Asian expulsion. But tracing those connections will have to remain a subject for a different occasion.
8. Ibid., 42.

9. Ibid., *From Citizen to Refugee*, 41.

10. Nair, *Mississippi Masala*.

11. Many of the claims that I critique here are articulated in bell hooks and Anuradha Dingwaney, "Mississippi Masala," *Z Magazine* (July-August 1992): 41–43. See also, for a variety of positions on the film, Brinda Mehta, "Emigrants Twice Displaced: Race, Color, and Identity in Mira Nair's *Mississippi Masala*," in Deepika Bahri and Mary Vasudeva, eds., *Between the Lines: South Asians and Postcoloniality* (Philadelphia: Temple University Press, 1996), 185–203; Purnima Bose and Linta Varghese, "*Mississippi Masala*, South Asian Activism and Agency," in Wendy S. Hesford and Wendy Kozol, eds., *Haunting Violations: Feminist Criticism and the Crisis of the "Real"* (Champaign: University of Illinois Press, 2001), 137–68; Jigna Desai, "When Indians Play Cowboys: Diaspora and Postcoloniality in Mira Nair's *Mississippi Masala*," in *Beyond Bollywood: The Cultural Politics of South Asian Diasporic Film* (New York: Routledge, 2004), 71–100; Gwendolyn Audrey Foster, "Mira Nair: To Be Mixed Is the New World Order," in *Women Filmmakers of the African and Asian Diaspora* (Carbondale: Southern Illinois University Press, 1997), 111–27; Adeleke Adeeko, "*Mississippi Masala*: Crossing Desire and Interest," in Jun Xing and Lane Ryo Hirabayashi, eds., *Reversing the Lens: Ethnicity, Race, Gender and Sexuality Through Film* (Boulder: University of Colorado, 2003), 127–42; Susan Stanford Friedman, "'Beyond' White and Other: Narratives of Race in Feminist Discourse," in *Mappings: Feminism and the Cultural Geographies of Encounter* (Princeton: Princeton University Press, 1998), 36–66.

12. Adeeko, "*Mississippi Masala*," 130.

13. One of the most painful memories in Mamdani's *From Citizen to Refugee* is precisely such a moment: "In those days, for an African to be seen with an Asian was to risk both lives. It was sufficient evidence of intended sabotage. Even two months earlier, when I had gone to see Maria, a friend at the University, she had pleaded: 'Please Mahmood, we can't go out together. Don't you know how things have changed? It's not me, it's the times. I'm sorry'" Mamdani, *From Citizen to Refugee*, 66–67.

14. Subsequently the indentured origins of the word has been re-asserted by Neera Kapur-Dromson in an interview with the journal *Africa Quarterly*. See Neera Kapur-Dromson, "In Conversation: Indian Individuality Lost in Kenyan History," *Africa Quarterly* 47, no. 2 (2007): 65 (62–65).

15. "Harambee," in Wikipedia (accessed May 23, 2011).

16. Gilroy, *Against Race*.

SELECTED REFERENCES

Adejunmobi, Moradewun. "Urgent Tasks for African Scholars in the Humanities." *Transition* 101 (2009): 80–93.

Ahluwalia, D. P. S. *Plantations and the Politics of Sugar in Uganda.* Kampala: Fountain, 1995.

Ali, Shanti Sadiq. *The African Dispersal in the Deccan: From Medieval to Modern Times.* Bombay: Orient Longman, 1995.

Alibhai-Brown, Yasmin. *No Place Like Home.* London: Virago, 1995.

Amin, Idi. "Midnight Address to the Nation by His Excellency the President on 17th December, 1972." In Ministry of Information and Broadcasting, *Uganda's Economic War,* 23–29. Kampala: Ministry of Information and Broadcasting, January 1975.

Andrews, C. F. *The Indian Question in East Africa.* Nairobi: Swift, 1921.

Appiah, Kwame Anthony. *Cosmopolitanism: Ethics in a World of Strangers.* New York: Norton, 2006.

——. *The Ethics of Identity.* Princeton: Princeton University Press, 2005.

Becker, Robert, and Nitin Jayant Madhvani, eds. *Jayant Madhvani.* London: Private printing, 1973.

Behdad, Ali. *Belated Travelers: Orientalism in the Age of Colonial Dissolution.* Durham: Duke University Press, 1994.

Berger, Susan A. "States of the (Tanzanian) Nation." In Sophia Mustafa, *The Tanganyika Way,* 147–55. Ed. Fawzia Mustafa. Toronto: TSAR, 2009.

Bhabha, Homi. *The Location of Culture.* New York: Routledge, 1994.

——. "Unsatisfied: Notes on Vernacular Cosmopolitanism." In Gregory Castle, ed., *Postcolonial Discourses: An Anthology*, 38–52. London: Wiley-Blackwell, 2001.

Bharati, Agehananda. *The Asians in East Africa: Jayhind and Uhuru.* Chicago: Nelson-Hall, 1972.

Birla, Ritu. *Stages of Capital: Law, Culture and Market Governance in Late Colonial India.* Durham: Duke University Press, 2009.

Bose, Sugata. *A Hundred Horizons: The Indian Ocean and the Age of Global Empire.* Cambridge: Harvard University Press, 2006.

Bose, Sugata, and Kris Manjapra, eds. *Cosmopolitan Thought Zones: South Asia and the Global Circulation of Ideas.* New York: Palgrave, 2010.

Brennan, James. "Nation, Race, and Urbanization in Dar es Salaam, 1916–1976." PhD diss., Northwestern University, 2002.

Burton, Richard. *Zanzibar: City, Island and Coast.* Vol. 1. London: Tinsley, 1872.

Campbell, Gwyn, ed. *Abolition and Its Aftermath in Indian Ocean Africa and Asia.* New York: Routledge, 2005.

——. *The Structure of Slavery in Indian Ocean Africa and Asia.* Portland: Frank Cass, 2004.

Chachage, Chambi, and Annar Cassam, eds. *Africa's Liberation: The Legacy of Nyerere.* Nairobi: Pambazuka, 2010.

Chakrabarty, Dipesh. *Provincializing Europe: Postcolonial Thought and Historical Difference.* Princeton: Princeton University Press, 2000.

Chande, J. K. *A Knight in Africa: Journey from Bukene.* Manotick, ON: Penumbra, 2005.

Chaudhuri, K. N. *Trade and Civilisation in the Indian Ocean: An Economic History from the Rise of Islam to 1750.* Cambridge: Cambridge University Press, 1985.

Chege, Michael. "Introducing Race as a Variable Into the Political Economy of Kenya Debate: An Incendiary Idea." *African Affairs* 97 no. 387 (1998): 209–30.

——. "Paradigms of Doom and the Development Management Crisis in Kenya." *Journal of Development Studies* 33, no. 4 (1997): 552–67.

Churchill, Winston. *My African Journey.* London: Holland, 1962 [1908].

Clark, Steve, ed. *Travel Writing and Empire: Postcolonial Theory in Transit.* London: Zed, 1999.

Clifford, James. *Routes: Travel and Translation in the Late Twentieth Century.* Cambridge: Harvard University Press, 1997.

Clifford, James, and George E. Marcus, eds. *Writing Culture: The Poetics and Politics of Ethnography.* Berkeley: University of California Press, 1986.

Cohen, David William. *The Combing of History.* Chicago: University of Chicago Press, 1994.

Cohen, Jeffrey Jerome. "Introduction: Midcolonial." In Jeffrey Jerome Cohen, ed., *The Postcolonial Middle Ages*, 1–17. New York: St. Martin's, 2000.

Cohen, Mark. "Islam and the Jews: Myth, Counter-Myth, History." In Shlomo Deshen and Walter P. Zenner, eds., *Jews Among Muslims*, 50–63. New York: New York University Press, 1996.

Cooper, Fredrick. *Plantation Slavery on the East Coast of Africa.* New Haven: Yale University Press, 1977.

Cooper, Fredrick, and Ann Laura Stoler, eds. *Tensions of Empire: Colonial Cultures in a Bourgeois World.* Berkeley: University of California Press, 1997.

Curtin, Philip D. *Cross-Cultural Trade in World History.* Cambridge: Cambridge University Press, 1984.

Desai, Gaurav, ed., *Asian African Literatures.* Special issue. *Research in African Literatures* 42, no. 3 (2011).

East African Standard. *The Indian Problem in Kenya: Selections of Speeches, Articles and Correspondence.* Nairobi: East African Standard, 1922.

Fanon, Frantz. *The Wretched of the Earth.* Trans. Constance Farrington. New York: Grove, 1963.

Frank, Andre Gunder. *ReOrient: Global Economy in the Asian Age.* Berkeley: University of California Press, 1998.

Gandhi, Mohandas Karamchand. *Autobiography: The Story of My Experiments with Truth.* Washington, DC: Dover, 1983.

——. *Satyagraha in South Africa.* Ahmedabad: Navajivan Trust, 1928.

Gatheru, Mugo. *Child of Two Worlds.* London: Routledge and Kegan Paul, 1964.

Geiger, Susan. *TANU Women: Gender and the Making of Tanganyikan Nationalism, 1955–1965.* Portsmouth, NH: Heinemann, 1997.

Ghosh, Amitav. *In an Antique Land.* New Delhi: Ravi Dayal, 1992; repr., New York: Vintage, 1994.

——. "Kinship in Relation to Economic and Social Organization in an Egyptian Village Community." D.Phil. diss., Oxford University, 1982.

——. "The Slave of MS. H.6." In Partha Chatterjee and Gyanendra Pandey, eds., *Subaltern Studies VII,* 159–220. New Delhi: Oxford University Press, 1992.

Ghosh, Amitav, and Dipesh Chakrabarty, "A Correspondence on *Provincializing Europe,*" *Radical History Review* 83 (Spring 2002): 146–72.

Ghosh, Devleena, and Stephen Muecke, eds. *Cultures of Trade: Indian Ocean Exchanges.* Newcastle: Cambridge Scholars, 2007.

Gikandi, Simon. "Introduction: Africa, Diaspora, and the Discourse of Modernity." *Research in African Literatures* 27, no. 4 (1996): 1–6.

——. "Theory, Literature and Moral Considerations." *Research in African Literatures* 32, no.4 (2001): 1–18.

Gilroy, Paul. *Against Race: Imagining Political Culture Beyond the Color Line.* Cambridge: Harvard University Press, 2000.

——. *The Black Atlantic: Modernity and Double Consciousness.* Cambridge: Harvard University Press, 1993.

Glassman, Jonathan. *War of Words, War of Stones: Racial Thought and Violence in Colonial Zanzibar.* Bloomington: Indiana University Press, 2011.

Goitein, S. D. *A Mediterranean Society: The Jewish Communities of the Arab World as Portrayed in the Documents of the Cairo Geniza.* 6 vols. Berkeley: University of California Press, 1967–93.

——. *Jews and Arabs: Their Contacts Through the Ages.* New York: Schocken, 1955.

——. *Letters of Medieval Jewish Traders*. Princeton: Princeton University Press, 1973.

Gordon, Murray. *Slavery in the Arab World*. New York: New Amsterdam, 1987.

Gregory, Robert G. *India and East Africa: A History of Race Relations within the British Empire, 1890–1939*. Oxford: Clarendon, 1971.

——. "Literary Development in East Africa: The Asian Contribution, 1955–1975." *Research in African Literatures* 12, no. 4 (1981): 440–59.

——. *Quest for Equality: Asian Politics in East Africa, 1900–1967*. Delhi: Orient Longman, 1993.

——. *South Asians in East Africa: An Economic and Social History, 1890–1980*. Boulder: Westview, 1993.

——. *The Rise and Fall of Philanthropy in East Africa: The Asian Contribution*. New Brunswick, NJ: Transaction, 1992.

Hammond, Dorothy, and Alta Jablow. *The Africa That Never Was: Four Centuries of British Writing About Africa*. 2d. ed. Prospect Heights, IL: Waveland, 1992.

Harris, Joseph E. *The African Presence in Asia: Consequences of the East African Slave Trade*. Evanston: Northwestern University Press, 1971.

Hawley, John, ed. *India in Africa, Africa in India: Indian Ocean Cosmopolitanisms*. Bloomington: Indiana University Press, 2008.

Himbara, David. *Kenyan Capitalists, the State and Development*. Boulder: Lynne Rienner, 1994.

Hofmeyr, Isabel. "The Idea of 'Africa' in Indian Nationalism: Reporting the Diaspora in *The Modern Review*, 1907–1929." *South African Historical Review* 57 (2007): 60–81.

Hollingsworth, L. W. *The Asians of East Africa*. London: Macmillan, 1960.

Ibn Battuta. *Travels in Asia and Africa, 1325–1354*. Ed. and trans. H. A. R. Gibb. New York: Augustus M. Kelley, 1969.

JanMohamed, Abdul. *Manichean Aesthetics: The Politics of Literature in Colonial Africa*. Amherst: University of Massachusetts Press, 1983.

——. "The Economy of Manichean Allegory: The Function of Racial Difference in Colonialist Literature." In Henry Louis Gates Jr., ed., *"Race," Writing and Difference*, 78–106. Chicago: University of Chicago Press, 1986.

Jhaveri, K. J. *Marching with Nyerere: Africanisation of Asians*. New Delhi: BRPC, 1999.

Johnston, H. H. "The Asiatic Colonization of East Africa." *Journal of the Society of Arts* 37 (February 1, 1889): 161–70.

Joseph, May. *Nomadic Identities: The Performance of Citizenship*. Minneapolis: University of Minnesota Press, 1999.

Kaplan, Robert D. "Center Stage for the Twenty-first Century: Power Plays in the Indian Ocean." *Foreign Affairs* 17 (March/April 2009): 16–32.

Kapur-Dromson, Neera. *From Jhelum to Tana*. New Delhi: Penguin, 2007.

Kassum, Al Noor. *Africa's Winds of Change: Memoirs of an International Tanzanian*. London: I. B. Tauris, 2007.

Kruger, Loren. "Black Atlantics, White Indians and Jews: Locations, Locutions and Syncretic Identities in the Fiction of Achmat Dangor and Others," *South Atlantic Quarterly* 100, no. 1 (2001): 111–43.

Kyle, Keith. "Gandhi, Harry Thuku, and Early Kenya Nationalism." *Transition* 27 (1966): 16–22.

Larkin, Brian. "Indian Films and Nigerian Lovers: Media and the Creation of Parallel Modernities." *Africa* 67, no. 3 (1997): 406–39.

Lee, Christopher, ed. *Making a World After Empire: The Bandung Moment and Its Political Afterlives*. Athens: Ohio University Press, 2010.

Lepper, G. H. "An America for the Hindu." *Empire Review* 28 (1914): 108–16.

Lugard, Frederick. *The Rise of Our East African Empire: Early Efforts in Nyasaland and Uganda*. Vol. 1. Edinburgh: Blackwood, 1893.

Madhvani, Manubhai, with Giles Foden. *Tide of Fortune: A Family Tale*. Bermuda: Manubhai Madhvani Bermuda Trusts, 2008.

Mamdani, Mahmood. *From Citizen to Refugee: Uganda Asians Come to Britain*. London: Francis Pinter, 1973.

——. *Politics and Class Formation in Uganda*. London: Monthly Review Press, 1976.

——. *When Victims Become Killers: Colonialism, Nativism, and the Genocide in Rwanda*. Princeton: Princeton University Press, 2001.

Mangat, J. S. *A History of the Asians of East Africa, c. 1886–1945*. Oxford: Oxford University Press, 1969.

——. "Was Allidina Visram a Robber Baron or a Skillful and Benevolent Commercial Pioneer?" *East Africa Journal* (1968): 33–35.

Manji, Madatally. *Memoirs of a Biscuit Baron*. Nairobi: Kenway, 1995.

Mbembe, Achille. "African Modes of Self-Writing," *Public Culture* 14, no.1 (2002): 239–73.

——. "At the Edge of the World: Boundaries, Territoriality, and Sovereignty in Africa," *Public Culture* 12, no. 1 (2000): 259–84.

——. *On the Postcolony*. Berkeley: University of California Press, 2001.

Mbilinyi, Marjorie. "Sophia Mustafa: Nation Builder and Emancipator of Women." In Fawzia Mustafa, ed., Sophia Mustafa, *The Tanganyika Way*, 156–68. Toronto: TSAR, 2009.

Meena, Ruth. "Crisis and Structural Adjustment: Tanzanian Women's Politics." *Issue: A Journal of Public Opinion* 17, no. 2 (1989): 29–31.

Meena, Ruth, and Marjorie Mbilinyi. "Women, Family, State, and Economy in Africa." *Signs* 16, no. 4 (1991): 852–59.

Mehta, Nanji Kalidas. *Dream Half-Expressed: An Autobiography*. Ed. Ratilal Chhaya. Bombay: Vakils, Feffer, and Simons, 1966.

Metcalf, Thomas. *Imperial Connections: India in the Indian Ocean Arena, 1860–1920*. Berkeley: University of California Press, 2007.

Mkandawire, Thandika, and Charles Soludo, eds. *Our Continent, Our Future: African Perspectives on Structural Adjustment*. Dakar: CODESRIA, 1998.

Moore-Gilbert, Bart. *Postcolonial Life-Writing: Culture, Politics, and Self-Representation*. New York: Routledge, 2009.

Moorthy, Shanti, and Ashraf Jamal, eds., *Indian Ocean Studies: Cultural, Social and Political Perspectives*. New York: Routledge, 2010.

Morison, Theodore. "A Colony for India." *Nineteenth Century* 84 (September 1918): 430–41.

———. "An Indian Colony in East Africa." *Hindustan Review* 38 (October–November 1918): 221–27.

Mudimbe, V. Y. *The Invention of Africa: Gnosis, Philosophy, and the Order of Knowledge.* Bloomington: Indiana University Press, 1988.

Mukherjee, Ramkrishna. *The Problem of Uganda: A Study of Acculturation.* Berlin: Akademie, 1956.

Murray, Robin. "The Chandarias: The Development of a Kenyan Multinational." In Rachel Kaplinsky, ed., *Readings on the Multinational Corporation in Kenya*, 284–307. Nairobi: Oxford University Press, 1978.

Mustafa, Sophia. *Broken Reed.* Dar es Salaam: E and D, 2005.

———. *The Tanganyika Way.* Ed. Fawzia Mustafa. Toronto: TSAR, 2009.

Mwakikagile, Godfrey. *Life Under Nyerere.* Dar es Salaam: New Africa, 2006.

Nagar, Richa. "Making and Breaking Boundaries: Identity Politics Among South Asians in Postcolonial Dar es Salaam." PhD diss., University of Minnesota, 1995.

Naipaul, Shiva. *North of South: An African Journey.* New York: Simon and Schuster, 1979.

Naipaul, V. S. *A Bend in the River.* New York: Vintage, 1989 [1979].

Nair, Mira, dir. *Mississippi Masala.* Sony Pictures Home Entertainment, 2003 [DVD 1991].

Nair, Savita. "Moving Life Histories: Gujarat, East Africa and the Indian Diaspora, 1880–2000." PhD diss., University of Pennsylvania, 2001.

Nandy, Ashis. "Who Wants an Afro-Asian Dialogue?" *Identity, Culture, Politics* 1, no.1 (2000): 1–4.

Nazareth, Peter. *In a Brown Mantle.* Nairobi: East African Literature Bureau, 1972.

Neame, L. E. *The Asiatic Danger in the Colonies.* London: Routledge, 1907.

New, Charles. *Life, Wanderings and Labours in Eastern Africa.* London: Hodder and Stoughton, 1874.

Ngobi, Mathias. "Nascent Uganda." In Becker and Madhvani, *Jayant Madhvani*, 64–70.

Ngugi wa Thiong'o. *Weep Not Child.* London: Heinemann, 1964.

———. *The Wizard of the Crow.* Pantheon: New York, 2006.

Nowrojee, Pheroze. *The Asian African Heritage: Identity and History.* Nairobi: National Museums of Kenya and the Asian African Heritage Trust, 2000.

Nyerere, Julius. *Freedom and Development: A Selection from Writings and Speeches, 1968–1973.* London: Oxford University Press, 1973.

———. *Freedom and Socialism: A Selection from Writings and Speeches, 1965–1967.* London: Oxford University Press, 1968.

Ocaya-Lakidi, Dent. "Black Attitudes to the Brown and White Colonizers of East Africa." In Michael Twaddle, ed., *Expulsion of a Minority: Essays on Ugandan Asians*, 81–97. London: Athlone, 1975.

Ojwang, Dan Odhiambo. "The Pleasures of Knowing: Images of 'Africans' in East African Asian Literature." *English Studies in Africa* 43, no.1 (2000): 43–64.

Patel, Zarina. *Unquiet: The Life and Times of Makhan Singh*. Nairobi: Zand, 2006.

Patterson, Orlando. *Slavery and Social Death: A Comparative Study*. Cambridge: Harvard University Press, 1982.

Pearson, Michael. *Port Cities and Intruders: The Swahili Coast, India, and Portugal in the Early Modern Era*. Baltimore: Johns Hopkins University Press, 1998.

Piot, Charles "Atlantic Aporias: Africa and Gilroy's Black Atlantic." *South Atlantic Quarterly* 100, no.1 (2001): 155–70.

Pratt, Cranford. *The Critical Phase in Tanzania, 1945–1968: Nyerere and the Emergence of a Socialist Strategy*. New York: Cambridge University Press, 1976.

Pratt, Mary Louise. *Imperial Eyes: Travel Writing and Transculturation*. 2d ed. New York: Routledge, 2008 [1992].

Preston, R. O., ed. *Oriental Nairobi: A Record of Some of the Leading Contributors to Its Development*. Nairobi: Private printing, 1938.

Ramchandani, R. R. *Uganda Asians: The End of an Enterprise*. Bombay: United Asia, 1976.

Rastogi, Pallavi. *Afrindian Fictions: Diaspora, Race, and National Desire in South Africa*. Athens: Ohio State University Press, 2008.

Reif, Stefan C. *A Jewish Archive from Old Cairo: The History of Cambridge University's Genizah Collection*. Richmond: Curzon, 2000.

Rorty, Richard. *Contingency, Irony, and Solidarity*. Cambridge: Cambridge University Press, 1989.

Rosenthal, Franz. *The Muslim Concept of Freedom Prior to the Nineteenth Century*. Leiden: Brill, 1960.

Ross, W. McGregor. *Kenya from Within: A Short Political History*. London: Allen and Unwin, 1927.

Salvadori, Cynthia. *We Came in Dhows*. 3 vols. Nairobi: Paperchase Kenya, 1996.

Salvadori, Cynthia, and Judy Aldrick. eds. *Two Indian Travellers, East Africa, 1902–1905*. Trans. Vimla Chavda and Shariffa Keshavjee. Mombasa: Friends of Fort Jesus, 1997.

Scott, David. *Refashioning Futures: Criticism After Postcoloniality*. Princeton: Princeton University Press, 1999.

Seidenberg, Dana April. *Mercantile Adventurers: The World of East African Asians, 1750–1985*. New Delhi: New Age International, 1996.

Sheriff, Abdul. *Dhow Cultures of the Indian Ocean: Cosmopolitanism, Commerce, and Islam*. New York: Columbia University Press, 2010.

Shivji, Issa. *Let the People Speak: Tanzania Down the Road to Neo-Liberalism*. Dakar: CODESRIA, 2006.

Simatei, Peter. *The Novel and the Politics of Nation Building in East Africa*. Bayreuth: Bayreuth University Press, 2001.

Smith, Sidonie, and Julia Watson, *Reading Autobiography: A Guide for Interpreting Life Narratives*. Minneapolis: University of Minnesota Press, 2002.

Stewart, Charles, and Rosalind Shaw, eds. *Syncretism/Anti-Syncretism: The Politics of Religious Synthesis*. New York: Routledge, 1994.

Subrahmanyam, Sanjay. "Foreword." In Denys Lombard and Jean Aubin, eds., *Asian*

Merchants and Businessmen in the Indian Ocean and the China Sea, vi–ix. New Delhi: Oxford, 2000.

Taban Lo Liyong, *The Last Word: Cultural Synthesism.* Nairobi: East African, 1969.

Taiwo, Olufemi. *How Colonialism Pre-Empted Modernity in Africa.* Bloomington: Indiana University Press, 2010.

Taylor, Charles. *Sources of the Self: The Making of Modern Identity.* Cambridge: Harvard University Press, 1989.

Tejani, Bahadur. *Day After Tomorrow.* Nairobi: East African, 1971.

Téno, Jean-Marie, dir. *Afrique, je te plumerai.* Cameroon, Les Film du Raphia, 1993.

Thakur, N. S., and Vanshi Dhar, eds. *Struggle for "Release Jomo and His Colleagues."* Ed. Ambu H. Patel. Nairobi: New Kenya, 1963.

Theroux, Paul. "Hating the Asians." *Transition* 33 (1967): 46–51.

Thuku, Harry. *An Autobiography.* Nairobi: Oxford, 1970.

Twaddle, Michael. "Z. K. Sentongo and the Indian Question in East Africa." *History in Africa* 24 (1997): 309–36.

Vansina, Jan. *Living with Africa.* Madison: University of Wisconsin Press, 1994.

Vassanji, M. G. *The Book of Secrets.* New York: Picador, 1996.

——. *The Gunny Sack.* London: Heinemann, 1989.

——. *The In-Between World of Vikram Lall.* New York: Knopf, 2004 [2003].

Verges, Francoise. "Looking East, Heading South," *African Studies Review* 44, no.2 (2001): 141–49.

Viswanathan, Gauri. "Beyond Orientalism: Syncretism and the Politics of Knowledge." *Stanford Humanities Review* 5, no. 1 (1995): 19–32.

Waiz, S. A., ed. *Indians Abroad.* 2d ed. Bombay: Imperial Indian Citizenship Association, 1927.

Wink, André. *Al-Hind: The Making of the Indo-Islamic World.* Vol. 1. New York: Brill, 1991.

Woolfson, Marion. *Prophets in Babylon: Jews in the Arab World.* Boston: Faber and Faber, 1980.

Zarwan, John Irving. "Indian Businessmen in Kenya During the Twentieth Century: A Case Study." PhD diss., Yale University, 1977.

INDEX

CPSIA information can be obtained
at www.ICGtesting.com
Printed in the USA
JSHW031042140321
12527JS00004B/9